LONG ROAD TO
LIBERATION

To Chris
will warm regards

[signature]
10.5.16.

DEDICATION

Alongside the members of my family in Namibia and in Norway, without whose love and care I shouldn't have survived, I dedicate this book to all – to those yet alive and the late – who have given me a helping hand and a shove along the way. None more so than Professor Leonard M Thompson of UCT, and Allard Lowenstein from New York. Their shoves made me take roads I might otherwise not have taken: 'And that has made all the difference.'

The diaries of my wife, Edel Havin Beukes – which she helpfully put at my disposal – were indispensable for my account of our experiences in Zambia. Edel's optimism and fortitude were what sustained us through the years.

As to the book, I'd like to thank Netta Kornberg from Toronto, who had served as an intern at Omar Badsha's history workshop in Cape Town. Netta put a rambling manuscript into shape. Which yet needed to be completed.

Without the interest with which David and Gail Robbins of Porcupine Press, Johannesburg, responded to the story I'm telling here, it might have remained a private family chronicle.

The exacting care that David subsequently spent on the editing was most inspiring, and the dedication with which Gail took charge of the production, more than I could have hoped for.

Finally, I should like to acknowledge with gratitude a grant from the Norwegian foundation *Fritt Ord* (Free Speech) that enabled me to consult the National Archives in Pretoria.

HANS BEUKES
LONG ROAD TO LIBERATION
AN EXILED NAMIBIAN ACTIVIST'S PERSPECTIVE

PORCUPINE PRESS

Johannesburg, South Africa

First published in 2014 by Porcupine Press
PO Box 2756
Pinegowrie, 2123
South Africa
info@porcupinepress.co.za
www.porcupinepress.co.za

ISBN-13: 978-1505359022
ISBN-10: 1505359023

Produced by Porcupine Press
Cover design and text layout by Wim Rheeder: wim@wimrheeder.co.za
Set in 10.5 point on 14 point, Minion Pro
Printed and bound by CreateSpace

TABLE OF CONTENTS

MAP OF NAMIBIA WITH TRIBAL RESERVATIONS

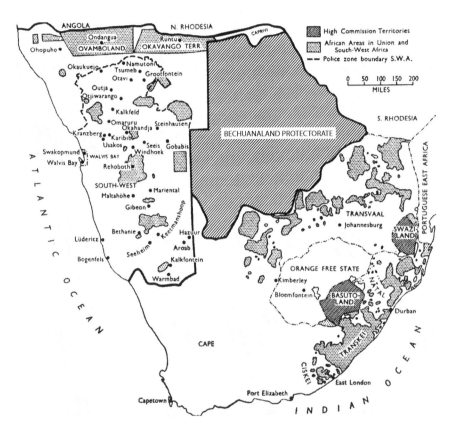

This map shows the proportions of land reserved for Africans in South and South West Africa, also the High Commission Territories administered by the British Commonwealth Relations Department.

NOTE ON TRANSLATIONS

Unless otherwise indicated, all translations are by the author.

ABBREVIATIONS

AAM	Anti-Apartheid Movement
ACLU	American Civil Liberties Union
ACOA	American Committee on Africa
ANC	African National Congress
ARM	Armed Resistance Movement
BDAF	British Defence and Aid Fund
BOSS	Bureau of State Security
CAF	Central African Republic
CID	Criminal Investigation Department
COSEC	Coordinating Secretariat of National Unions of Students
DN	*Dagens Nyheter* Stockholm
DTA	Democratic Turnhalle Alliance
Exco	Executive Committee
FNLA	National Liberation Front of Angola
FRELIMO	Liberation Front of Mozambique
GA	General Assembly
GHST	*Gothenburg's Handels- och Sjöfartstidning*
ICJ	International Court of Justice
ILHR	International League for Human Rights
IUEF	International University Exchange Fund
IUS	International Union of Students
LO	Norwegian Confederation of Trade Unions
LWF	Lutheran World Federation
MP	Member of Parliament
MPLA	People's Movement for the Liberation of Angola
NATO	North Atlantic Treaty Organization
NGO	Non-Government Organization
NNC	Namibian National Convention
NNF	Namibian National Front
NORAD	Norwegian Agency for Development Cooperation
NRK	Norwegian Broadcasting Corporation
NSA	National Student Association (American)
NSU	National Union of Students in Norway (Norsk Student Samband)
NUPI	Norwegian Foreign Policy Institute
NUSAS	National Union of South African Students

NUSWAS	National Union of South West Africa Students
OAU	Organization of African Unity
OPO	Ovamboland People's Organization
PAC	Pan Africanist Congress
PLAN	People's Liberation Army of Namibia
PRIO	International Peace Research Institute in Oslo
SABC	South African Broadcasting Corporation
SADF	South African Defence Force
SCR	Security Council Resolution
SPYL	South West Africa People's Organization Party Youth League
SRC	Students Representative Council
SWA	South West Africa
SWANU	South West Africa National Union
SWAPO	South West Africa People's Organization
SWAPO-D	South West Africa People's Organization Democrats
UiO	University of Oslo
UCT	University of Cape Town
UN	United Nations
UNIN	United Nations Institute for Namibia
UNCTAD	United Nations Conference on Trade and Development
UNECA	United Nations Economic Commission for Africa
UNHCR	United Nations High Commissioner for Refugees
UNITA	National Union for the Total Independence of Angola
UNTAG	United Nations Transition Assistance Group
US	United States
WAY	World Assembly of Youth
WCC	World Council of Churches
WFLRY	World Federation of Liberal and Radical Youth
Wits	University of Witwatersrand
ZANU	Zimbabwe African National Union
ZANU-PF	Zimbabwe African National Union – Patriotic Front
ZAPU	Zimbabwe African People's Union

INTRODUCTION

Professor Mburumba Kerina

The book of Hans Beukes could perhaps best be describe as a literary historical narrative.

It is clearly a *literary* work in technique, method and arrangement; it spans a vitally important stretch of the *history* of the genesis of a Namibian State, and; it is a *narrative* of a personal journey through the jigsaw of underlying international relations and politics which shaped the destiny of the colony South West Africa under South Africa rule.

The narrative is unpresumptuous leaving the reader to make up his own mind as to the full political and moral implications of the incidents and historical events traversed by the author. Nevertheless, Hans relates his experiences so directly and unambivalently that little doubt can remain to what extent the Namibian Nation was done in by international economic and political interests, which would lead to a poisonous independence.

The story begins with Hans's childhood years. This part of this story comprises an elucidating prelude to the main story. We are introduced through his childhood experiences to the earlier struggles of the Namibian people which preceded the full-blown nationalism which took root in urban South West Africa during the 1950's of whom I was the leader. Hans takes us on a trip with him from the rural onigmas of development and stagnation of the political heart of apartheid, South Africa, with such consummation that even the most uninitiated should get a feeling for the socio-political dichotomies of Southern Africa society.

But, the true historical drama start to unfold with his escape to Norway in 1959 where he was accepted to study as Oslo University. His political journeys took him in the initial years to the United Nations Organisation and around Europe during a period in which he linked up with Fanuel Kozonguizi and me on promoting the Namibian cause. Fanuel at the time was the leader of SWANU, the first nationalist organisation of Namibia.

In 1976 he left with his Norwegian wife Edel (Nee Havin) for Zambia with the aim to contributing to the independence struggle through SWAPO in exile. His disillusionment with the SWAPO leadership and the European supporters of Namibian independence in exile came swiftly and brutally. He landed in Zambia in the midst of an unfolding dispute between PLAN and the SWAPO Youth League on the one hand and the SAWPO leaders on the other. The Youth were demanding accountability, a political line and an investigation into corruption in the leadership. Hans inevitably joined up with the Youth.

International forces including the regimes of Zambia and Tanzania combined to suppress the discontent violently and Hans had to flee Zambia for the relative safety of Europe. There he was forced to commute between Europe and America and between Oslo and London in an effort to affect intervention in the plight of his comrades in Zambia and Tanzania where they were being incarcerated and liquidated.

Hans collided with a brick wall. The forces including the Anti-Apartheid movement who claimed support for the Namibian cause and people outright refused to use their power and influence to alleviate the Namibian tragedy unfolding in Zambia, Tanzania and Angola. They either implicitly indicated or stated outright such as the Norwegians that they had invested in and supported the SWAPO.

Hans achieves the pathos and ethos of his work by simply telling his story of how he tried to appeal to the human and political conscience and good faith of persons, organisations and governments who could do something to avert the Namibian tragedy and how they reacted contrary to his expectations.

Hans's story found its end not in this written book, but in the post-colonial situation.

The unresolved issues in the struggles of the youth against SWAPO leadership and the overall struggle for the right of self-determination led by Kozo and I in exile found their expression in the following:

Wanton Constitutional amendments without substantial or rational reasons;

The collapse of the land question into 20 hectare land allocation of over-grazed reserves to communal residents;

The Growth of tribalism against the self-determination of nationalities;

The obstruction of the reparations demands of the nationalities under German genocide and expropriation.

Hans afforded me whom he accepted as his bigger brother in exile the opportunity to write this foreword to this work. Persons who have experienced or at least observed the tribulation of a deprived people will understand that in exile we were just that bit closer than people in ordinary circumstances. He remains my smaller brother.

But, I state not out of partiality that his book is an important milestone in the history of not only Namibia, but Africa. Hans leaves the reader with total freedom to make his own conclusions of a 'long walk to liberation'. The metaphor is clear: A long walk uncovers a lot of experiences and brings a lot of realisations.

This book is a vital addition to what is now becoming a family of publications of persons who have given according to their ability for the freedom of a nation. It is a library which will be vital for true freedom. Yet to be achieved.

The walk is not over yet.

THE INTERNATIONAL CONTEXT

At the end of World War One the victorious powers established a League of Nations to eliminate the recurrence of war. The reparations exacted from the defeated German Federation were, however, such as to render that hope illusory.[1]

With regard to the colonies ruled over by Germany and Turkey, the US president, Woodrow Wilson, opposed their distribution among the victors as spoils of war. Arguing that there was 'worldwide opposition to further annexation', he advocated the principle of accountability – new in international law – that would make the League of Nations assume responsibility for the care of the inhabitants of those territories. This duty of accountability was to be exercised by states granted mandates to govern those territories on behalf of the League.

According to the US president, '(T)he whole theory of mandates is not the theory of permanent subordination. It is the theory of development of the country under mandate, of putting upon the mandatory the duty of assisting in the development of the country under mandate, in order that it may be brought to a capacity for self-government and self-dependence which for the time being it has not reached, and that therefore the countries under mandate are candidates, so to say, for full membership in the family of nations.'[2] 'The fundamental idea was that the world was acting as trustee through a mandatory, and would be in charge of the whole administration until the day when the true wishes of the inhabitants could be ascertained. It was up to the Union of South Africa to make it so attractive that South West Africa would come into the Union of their own free will.'[3]

It was a commitment that a union of European-run colonies, formed precisely for the purpose of subordinating all natives within its boundaries to 'the white man's rule', was ideologically and constitutionally unable to honour. (See Nicholas Mansergh: *South Africa, 1960-1961: The Price of Magnanimity* – for Britain's responsibility[4]). Yet, with their minds set upon the acquisition of the territory from which they had driven the Germans, the South African generals Jan Christian Smuts and Louis Botha secured a formulation of terms

---

[1] (See John Maynard Keynes: *The Economic Consequences of the Peace*, 1919)

[2] Solomon Slonim, South West Africa and the United Nations: An International Mandate in Dispute, The Johns Hopkins University Press 1973, footnote 96 p 37.

[3] Slonim, op cit. p. 23.

[4] Mansergh, op cit, quoting R.C.K Ensor *England 1870-1914*: (With the enactment by the Westminster Parliament of the law that sanctioned the creation of the Union of South Africa – the South Africa Act of 1909) 'the harsh facts of non-European exclusion from all effective participation in the political life of the Union were glossed over with philosophical generalities or sanguine but, as it proved, ill-founded expressions of hope for future betterment.' p 76.

at the 1919 Peace Conference at Versailles that would allow annexation in all but name.

After World War Two General Smuts, having led South Africa once again into war against Germany on the side of the British Empire, made a bid for the 'incorporation' of the Territory into the Union – this time with the concurrence of the UN, the world body erected on the foundations of the defunct League of Nations. Finding their purposes frustrated a second time, the Union declared their resolve to continue governing the Territory 'in the spirit of the mandate', while blocking the UN from exercising mandatory oversight and staking out a course that turned South West Africa into a fifth province of the apartheid state in all but name.

Thus was ignited a conflict that 'the international community' would prove unable to resolve except by violating the Constitution of the UN itself.

CHAPTER ONE

Childhood and schooldays

FAMILY AND COMMUNITY

I was born on a farm in the district of Rehoboth in the then South West Africa, now Namibia. I was the first of ten siblings, eight brothers and two sisters. At the time, my father and mother, Hermanus Christoffel Beukes and Elisabeth Mathilda van Wyk, were living in a one-room cottage he had built on the farm of my grandfather, Johannes Timotheus Beukes.

Known as Narabes (Nama for 'the place where the goat rejected its kid') the farm was home to several families of diverse background: my father's family; Nama farmhands with their families; and an elderly couple, the German Herr Peyken, who married one of my grandmother's nieces. The Peykens' son, Gerhard, had attended boarding school in Germany. I remember the day when he came on a hurried visit to the cottage. He told my mother about a bomb detonated over Hiroshima that had laid this Japanese city in ashes. He spoke about uranium and oxygen, words I had not heard before.

Although Grandfather was of modest means – compared with other farmers – in time I would realise he was a respected member of the Baster community of Rehoboth.[5] He was a man of few words whose advice and intercession – in personal as well as in communal affairs – would be sought by Whites and Blacks alike.

Surrounded by these people I was exposed early to the languages they spoke: Afrikaans, Nama and German. Our Afrikaans was enriched with the Dutch of the Bible Grandfather read from at the Sunday services he conducted as an elder of the Church, and at evening prayers at home, before bedtime.

The farm-dwellers had cattle, sheep and goats with horses for drawing horse carts and riding. Ox wagons drawn by spans of sixteen oxen were still used for heavy-duty tasks. Vegetables and fruit came from gardens planted on the banks of the river that divided the farm and would flow once or twice a year after heavy rains. Water for irrigation as well as for man and beast was drawn from wells dug into the sandy riverbed.

---

[5]   A comprehensive introduction to the community occupying a centrally located space in the territory of Namibia is provided in *Rehoboth Namibia Past and Present* ed. Cornelia Limpricht , Hamburg, Germany 2012.

Wildlife – springbok, kudu, baboons – abounded on the farm. While the game provided venison, the baboons were more of a nuisance. But their humanoid features and fascinating antics allowed mothers to tell their children that it was these creatures who provided people with their babies – the local version of the stork myth. One of my earliest memories is of a row I had with my sister Martha. Mother had told me that Father had fetched me from the mountain from a baboon mother. The nuns at the hospital in Rehoboth had chopped off my tail and scrubbed away the hair on my skin. That was why all babies had red skins. I didn't quite believe the story, but when Martha began to tease me about my baboon family, a surge of family loyalty welled up in me and I went for her. My mother appeared to be embarrassed about the fib, but she got out of it somehow.

All my siblings, beginning with my two sisters Martha and Anne-Marie, followed by Ludvig, were born in the maternity home run by the Catholic Mission Church in Rehoboth. For many years the German nuns tended the sick without asking what denomination they belonged to. All couples who got married, as well as anyone who wanted to have their pictures taken, went to Father Baumgarten, the priest in charge of the Church and the town's only photographer.

My parents were members of the Methodist congregation that had been formed after Grandfather and others had broken away from the Lutheran Mission Church. His walk-out, from a church whose building he had helped to erect with his own hands in 1908, was said to have been brought about by a political conflict with the German missionary who headed the church.

The Methodist congregation's very first priest was the Reverend Frank Scheepers, who spoke with the burr of the people of Malmesbury, a 'Coloured' community located just north of Cape Town. He was still around during my early childhood. I remember him as a slightly built man, kind and always formally clad in a black pinstripe suit with polished albeit worn shoes and a reversed collar. He only occasionally came to Rehoboth from the farm where the congregation had their church and where he was the headmaster of a boarding school.

On Meneer Scheepers' departure the congregation was served by one of its own members, a Damara, whose name I have now forgotten. I remember him as an old man who was liked by all. When he died my elder niece Paulina Denk and I were taken to see him lying in state in his bedroom. It was the first time either of us would see a dead person and we had to be reassured that it was safe to go there. What I remember was the light streaming from an open window on to his blue lips and the sunken sockets of his eyes. On the way back home I began to reflect on the mystery of life and death.

In the winter of 1944 my two-year old brother, Harold Henry, died in the pneumonia epidemic that claimed many lives that year. I had anxiously followed my mother's vain efforts to save this little child who had given us all such great pleasure.

To console me, my mother one evening whispered that I could expect a new brother in November. This was Kehat, who was also given the departed Harold Henry's names – with the addition of Petrus. I remember my mother spending hours perusing the Bible before she found the name Kehat. I have not encountered it anywhere else since.

After him they came in a row: Hewat, Dirk, Tony and Leon.

CONSTANTLY ON THE MOVE

In my preschool years on the farm my playmate was Tanab who, with his elder brother Namab, was one of two Nama children. As my grandfather expected everyone regardless of age to do their fair share of work, Tanab and I had to run errands and tend the calves. During these tedious chores, we hunted geckos with our catapults, forgetting all about the calves. On one such occasion I came closer to death than I like to recall. Hurrying alongside Tanab in pursuit of the vanished calves, I put my left foot right next to a full-grown pufadder that was basking in the sun. Mercifully the snake merely gave a warning hiss as it uncurled and put its head into the hole next to which it lay.

Namab remained on the farm as a handyman after his family had moved. But in those early days, I would follow him on his herding duties where he acquainted me with the veld's edible and poisonous plants.

My father's occupation required us to move from place to place within the Rehoboth district in my early childhood. Shoemaking provided a living in a community not yet caught up in changing footwear fashions. Before competition from mass-produced shoes from South Africa saturated the market, the business that Father established in Rehoboth at times employed up to two dozen men. Eventually though, his output would be reduced to a subsistence level. Father's independence of mind made the very thought of working as an employee repugnant to him. To make ends meet we therefore often found ourselves moving for shorter or longer periods from farm to farm where he produced his trademark veld-shoes for all who were willing and able to pay.

Before the family settled in Rehoboth, where the Methodist congregation had built a school, we also spent some of my early childhood days on Tsumis

Park, a farm belonging to Oupa Piet Diergaardt, at one stage a councillor of the Baster community. I remember him as a giant of a man said to have been possessed of enormous physical strength.

Some of my happiest childhood years were spent in the compound of huts that housed my Great-grandmother Martha, her husband Oupa Tobias Platt, my grandmother's stepfather, and my Grand-mother Magriet, alongside Ouma Myriam, Oupa Tobias' always entertaining sister. As a young woman she had once made a voyage to Germany in the service of a German family and told fascinating stories about her observations of life at various seaports en route. Oupa Tobias and Ouma Myriam were Damaras while Great-grandmother Martha, was born of a Nama mother and Herero father, remembered only by his Nama name of Tieseb. Adopting a child across ethnic or tribal lines was not uncommon.

I am therefore, by matrilineal descent, related to two of the major population groups in present-day central and southern Namibia, the Hereros and Namas, while my patrilineal lines relate me to Western Europeans named Beukes, Klaazen, van Wyk, Zahl and a Scot of one of the Campbell clans.

The custom that determines that families take their names from the paternal line has resulted in people of mixed descent, spread throughout southern Africa, having mainly European names. In contrast, the names and tribal affiliations of the native mothers have very seldom been passed on.

FROM TSUMIS PARK TO REHOBOTH

The railway line from South Africa ran through Tsumis Park where trains could replenish their supplies of water and coal and pass one another at the 'siding' station. I remember the place for many reasons: the trains' whistle as they approached the station or signalled their departure, the smell of steam as the locomotives hissed and puffed coming to a stop or starting their next leg northwards or southwards; the fragrance of flowers and shrubs in the stationmaster's garden, where I visited my Grandmother Magriet, who used to work for his family.

Among the people working at the railway siding there were four or five men said to be Ovambo. They were my first encounter with people from the north of the country, and we struck it off well. On Sundays I used to make my way to the station to listen to their fascinating stories about the lions, crocodiles and elephants that abounded in Ovamboland.

One such story I wanted to hear again and again, because the sense of justice involved appealed to me – even though I found the actual story difficult to believe. It concerned an elephant that had arrived at a waterhole to drink. Having drunk its fill it was about to leave when a crocodile made the mistake of sinking its teeth into the elephant's hind leg and refusing to let go. With the crocodile dangling on its leg the elephant made its way to a tree which it split in two. Then it grabbed the crocodile with its own trunk and put it into the split where the crocodile was squeezed to death.

Near the station there was also a shop, with the words General Dealer painted over the facade by the new owner Issy Scher, said to be a Jew from Germany. He had obtained the shop from Jochum Henckert, the son of a German official in the colonial regime who afterwards had settled in Rehoboth where three of his other sons ran another shop. I had heard about generals in the war my parents were reading about in newspapers that they borrowed from Oupa Piet Diergaardt. I could not quite square the image of a general in uniform with a cap, with the unimposing figure of Scher, the father of four small girls. People spoke admiringly of his insensitivity to White customers' expectations: that they should be attended to before the locals. His response to the ire of one such customer, a farmer named van der Westhuizen, was retold with glee. Unable to reach the shop counter because of the locals crowding the space in front of him, the farmer loudly demanded that Scher 'take notice' of him. To which Scher responded, 'But I do take notice of you' – meanwhile continuing to serve those ahead of him in the queue.

The stationmaster was a well-liked Boer from South Africa. While Scher's children were kept in isolation at home, the stationmaster's daughter my age was allowed to join me and my other playmates. However, her freedom was severely curtailed after she returned home one day as soiled as the rest of us. We had been cavorting in the muddy water of a rain-filled pool.

On the first Christmas that I can remember, Great-grandfather Tobias Platt disguised himself as Father Christmas for the celebration of Christmas Eve at the home of the Diergaards. Even though I recognised his deep bass-baritone and his wire-rimmed spectacles, the shock of a great red coat and white cotton-wool beard was more than I could take. The apparition sent me fleeing from the festivities and off into the pitch dark of the night in the direction of home. The following day Oupa Tobias tried to mend our friendship by reminding me that it was Father Christmas who had brought me the toy car I was playing with.

I started school in Tsumis Park. Because of the growing number of children in the little community, a school had been established on the initiative of Oupa Piet Diergaard. He wanted to avoid sending the children from his second marriage – my playmates Elsa and Paul – all the way to the Methodists' farm boarding school near Rehoboth, as he had needed to do with the children from his first marriage.

Meester Junius was our principal and only teacher. When his wife was to deliver their first-born child, Great-grandmother Martha served as midwife. As I passed their house, I overheard her talking to the worried father while his wife was in labour inside. It would be a boy, she told him reassuringly, adding that firstborns were always difficult for their mothers, but that there was no reason to worry. Then she went on smoking her short-stemmed pipe.

At the beginning of my second school year I was sent to Rehoboth, where a new school for the children of Methodists had opened. This time it was at the initiative of my grandfather, Johannes Timotheus Beukes, for whom the education of his growing number of grandchildren on the farms, as well as the children of the other members of the congregation, had become a matter of concern. My spinster aunt, Maria, kept house for several of us who were sent to the new school.

Our first teacher there was Mr Herman from Johannesburg. He had recently returned from the war in North Africa, where he had served as a corporal in the South African Army. Meester Herman was feared for meting out punishment at the slightest lapse in order or performance. He repeated the first day's lesson for what seemed like hours, with little variation: When you meet somebody for the first time, he told us, you have to look that person straight in the eyes.

Our school followed a different regimen from the town's other two schools, the Rhenish and the Catholic. We had to meet for physical exercises at 7 am, winter and summer. Pity anyone who arrived a minute late. Latecomers had to do push-ups and double-ups, with a brick or two held high above their heads. Classes at the Methodist School ended long after the children from the other two schools were home. Although at times I felt harshly treated by Mr Hermann, he let me jump two grades in consecutive years, thus saving me two years of schooling. He also saw to it that we were served cod liver oil and nutritious meals at school, an initiative that no doubt saved many of us from malnutrition.

After the third year of running the school by himself, Meester Herman was joined by Cecil Filies, a Capetonian. Like Meester Herman, Meester Filies was another native English speaker. As a result the children of the Methodist School acquired a thorough grounding in the language that was then, and still is, spoken only by a very small percentage of the country's people.

The new teacher hired rooms in Grandfather's town house where we all lived with Aunt Maria. This gave me access to discarded issues of his favourite cartoons, and some of the books that his family used to send him from Cape Town. Only once did he hold back a book from me. It was wrapped in brown paper and had been handed over to him in conspiratorial manner by a visiting colleague. A forbidden book is of course as tantalising as any other secret. It turned out to be the novel *Nineteen Eighty-Four* by George Orwell. It had been placed on the list of banned literature by the apartheid regime – with penalties for having it in one's possession. Alas, its pages lacked anything that appealed to my curiosity.

The Methodists had been without a priest for years before they managed to secure the services of a replacement for the Reverend Scheepers. So the Reverend Martin Henry Miller duly arrived from Kimberley in South Africa with his wife Anne and three small children. Reverend Miller also doubled as principal of the school in place of Meester Herman, who had returned to Johannesburg. With the Millers in place the Methodist school experienced an upswing. At the same time, the small congregation became connected to South Africa's spiritual – and I might add political – life through Reverend Miller's participation in the annual Synods of the Church. On his return he used to brief Grandfather, the congregation's senior layman, and often spent time with our family on the farm Narabes.

Physical exercises became much more agreeable with the introduction by Meneer Miller of rugby for the boys. It was a game that Kimberley, the principal's hometown, was known for. It made us lose fear of robust physical contact and of falling. In cooperation with the teachers from the other schools, the Methodist school also secured a plot for a tennis court that could be used by all – and even for a teachers' tournament for the whole region.

Mrs Miller played their piano at the school concerts we would stage that brought an evening's pleasure to an entertainment-starved town. She also set tongues wagging by appearing on the tennis court in miniskirts.

At school Mr Miller fell into the habit of sending me during the lunch-break to collect the day's mail at the post office. On the way back I used to slow my pace to peep at the headlines about the wide world in *The Diamond Fields Advertiser*, his hometown paper. One of those headlines told of the birth in London of an heir to the throne named Charles. Another article concerned a visit to South Africa by an American politician named Adlai Stevenson. He was quoted as finding it incomprehensible that a country with South Africa's wealth of resources conducted policies designed to keep the majority of its people in poverty. Such questioning of the morality of apartheid promptly secured for Stevenson a place in my private hall of heroes. Though we did not own a radio, I was often able to listen to shortwave radio broadcasts – news bulletins, discussions and music – on the Miller family's receivers. I could also borrow books from them. This obviously expanded my horizons beyond what would otherwise have been possible.

SOCIAL AWARENESS AWAKENED

I was twelve in 1948 when parliamentary elections in South Africa brought to power a political party on a plank of apartheid. What the word implied was conveyed by a slogan that appeared in all the newspapers: 'Do you want your daughter to get married to a Kaffir?' – signifying contempt for people with black skins, and kinky hair.

Though Rehoboth's status as a reservation for Basters shielded the community from daily encounter with the rules and regulations imposed elsewhere in pursuit of 'White supremacy' in all aspects of life, a number of families were nevertheless affected by legislation coming into force. This concerned in particular families where White men were cohabiting, some even having entered into marriage, with local women.

My family had been offended by the slur cast upon Great-grandfather Tobias Platt, who was pitch black.

With the arrival of the Reverend Martin Henry Miller, doubling as pastor of the Methodist parish and as principal of our school, my understanding of what apartheid involved, expanded. With the close ties that existed between Grandfather and the Reverend Miller, we were kept informed about the debates in the annual Synods of the Methodist Church usually held in Cape Town. We learned that apartheid also challenged the faithful: how were they to serve the Lord in racially segregated churches? From those reports we learnt that while the Church officially condemned apartheid, parishes were expected to bend to the official expectation that worshippers say their prayers in racially segregated temples. To me, this was an offensive but distant prospect that in due course I would become acquainted with – in Windhoek, Cape Town and Kimberley – and it began to tax my ability to relate to matters ecclesiastical.

Nevertheless, to sustain the illusion of the Church's unity, the little Rehoboth congregation not infrequently received visitations from high officers of the Church, as when the Reverend J.B. Webb, the Church's president residing in Johannesburg, arrived to conduct a service. On such occasions they had lunch at my grandparents' house.

It was not long before my vague ideas about apartheid were sharpened by a practical reality. Arriving at the post office one morning I was surprised to see workers busy making a small hole in the cement floor in front of the four metre wide counter. The next morning a bent steel pipe separated the room into two parts with gold lettering on wooden boards indicating that the left hand section was for 'Europeans Only' and the right hand section for 'Non-Whites'.

I sped back to school to inform the principal that apartheid had arrived in town. He was visibly upset and so was my father, who charged to the post office to lodge a complaint. While this was to no avail, the matter changed when Grandfather arrived in town a few days later. He reminded the magistrate and the postmaster that the plot of ground on which the post office was built belonged to the Rehoboth community, and demanded that the pipe and the offensive notices be removed forthwith. Subsequently a cement-covered hole, seven centimetres in diameter, remained on the post office floor as a monument to a small triumph over the apartheid regime.

About the enforcement of the Group Areas Act there was no such recourse. In keeping with the regime's fanatical pursuit of apartheid, the white inhabitants of the 'Rehoboth Reservation' were served notice to move elsewhere to areas designated for Whites only. As the affected families were among the district's most well off, Rehoboth took a hard knock economically – and no doubt culturally as well.

Even more obnoxious was the threat posed to liaisons between White and Black couples – married or unmarried – when the so-called Immorality Act came into force. It criminalised sexual intercourse between Whites and Blacks. Blacks and Whites of opposite sex found together in closed quarters were automatically presumed to have committed the crime of immorality. It became one of the most efficient means of enforcing social distance between Whites and everyone else, putting a premium of risk upon, if not rendering impossible, even the notion of 'inter-racial' friendship.

SECONDARY SCHOOL

The Dr Lemmer Secondary School was opened the year before I graduated from the Methodist Primary School. I joined the second intake of entrants at the first ever middle school for the territory's 'mixed-race' population. The school was named after an inspector of schools who had evidently taken most seriously his job of raising the standard of instruction in all the territory's schools. To judge by the teachers' anxiety at the primary schools when word was received that Dr Lemmer was on his way, he was evidently also feared.

I remember his giant figure, with a v-like furrow on his forehead, from his visits to our school; and I have a hunch that he was responsible for the school-feeding scheme that saved many of us from malnutrition during the world war and in the immediate post-war years.

The Dr Lemmer Secondary School's pupils came from all over the territory and from Rehoboth's own three denominational primary schools, but we did not number more than twenty in two classrooms. The teachers were South Africans: Mr Theo Sawyer, from an Afrikaans speaking background, and his colleague Mr Freddy Erasmus, who was thoroughly bilingual. The curriculum included Biology and Physiology but lacked Mathematics, which would handicap me in the years ahead.

Our parents had no idea what to expect from sending their children to school beyond the vague expectation that they would be 'educated'. They did, however, express fear that being educated, particularly in Biology, would lead us astray from the teachings of the Bible. To me this was a mystery as, having grown up on a farm I thought I had seen all there was to see about the reproduction of life in animals and plants. I was unaware of the belief that eternal damnation was the sanction for failing to take the biblical account of Adam and Eve as truth.

Our teachers didn't depart much from the curricula and the prescribed textbooks, especially when it came to history. This began in Ancient Egypt, crossed over the Mediterranean to Ancient Greece – with Pericles and other heroes but without any mention of the Greek achievements in philosophy – and moved on to the colonisation of South Africa via a speedy passage through Rome, the Middle Ages and the discovery of sea-routes to Asia, the Americas and Africa south of the Sahara. About the history of the peoples of South West Africa there was no reading material, nor any account worth remembering. Neither could there be from teachers who didn't command Nama, next to Afrikaans the central and southern regions' lingua franca, nor of Herero or any of the northern tribal languages.

Our two teachers were in their element when it came to the languages they taught, Afrikaans and English. Grammar, paraphrasing of texts, essays, and précis writing. Their efforts laid the groundwork for what command of language I acquired.

After passing comfortably the final, nationally-set (in South Africa) examinations, I encountered the first hitch in my educational progression: As there were no institutions of higher education for natives in South West Africa at the time, those wanting to further their education necessarily had to seek admission to schools in South Africa. I wished to attend a high school in Cape Town. Grandfather, on whose support I should have to rely, thought that teacher training, for which practically all the school's first class of pupils had gone, offered the best prospects of a job and career. Given no choice in the matter, I applied to the English language Wesley Teacher Training School for 'Coloureds' in Cape Town. This was the same institution that Cecil Filies, my second primary school teacher, had attended.

CAPE TOWN: SOUTH AFRICA'S MOTHER CITY

In Cape Town I stayed with Mr Filies' family in the suburb of Athlone. There I shared a room with a homeboy, Rudolf Henckert, who the year before had made the same decision as I and enrolled in the local high school. Rudolf's presence eased my introduction into the bewildering micro-cosmos that was South Africa's Mother City, situated at the foot of the mighty Table Mountain.

Our landlady, the elderly Mrs Filies, was an inexhaustible source of anecdotes about Cape Town society, and in particular about the Coloured families that 'passed' as Whites. Ironically this applied to the wife of Dr DF Malan, the leader of the National Party that had come into power in 1948 on a platform of apartheid.

Wesley Teacher Training School's teachers were mostly White, an anomaly in a city where other schools were staffed by teachers from the population groups to which the pupils belonged. Yet it never occurred to us as a problem.

We were in fear of displeasing Miss McClean, the stern teacher of Method. For reasons unknown to us, she had been nicknamed Zorro by an earlier generation of students.

We loved Mr Walter Swanson, our music teacher who used to lace his instruction with anecdotes from a musician's life. Having served as conductor at the D'Oyly Carte Opera Company in Britain, he was credited with promoting the transmission of classical music by the publicly owned South African Broadcasting Corporation. Besides instructing us at Wesley he taught at the University of Stellenbosch – known as the cradle of the apartheid doctrine. Yet an off-hand comment he made alerted us to where he stood on the issue of apartheid: He could pick up a group of Black kids off the streets and make them sing better than the all-White Boys Choir of the St George's Cathedral.

We respected Mrs Bauman – who took us through a course in literature that enriched our perceptions of English society – as we did our art teachers, and our gym teacher. Mr Abel, an Afrikaner who was our Afrikaans teacher, maintained an impenetrable aloofness. But for us his driving into Salt River all the way from the coastal town of Strand by Somerset West, to stand in front of us, spoke well of him.

Still, even though I had passed all examinations at the end of the two year course, I didn't feel qualified or attracted to the idea of standing in front of a class, to 'teach'.

BACK TO HIGH SCHOOL

Returning home to Rehoboth from Cape Town I found that the Dr Lemmer Secondary School's status had been elevated to that of a high school and that it would open at the beginning of the year. With my parents' permission I applied for admission and spent the first year there.

However, living in Cape Town for two years must have done something to me that my old teachers found difficult to deal with. My relationships with them soon turned sour and gave me reason to fear expulsion. That would have barred me from admission to schools even in South Africa. When our next-door neighbour, Herr Benedict Hummel, heard about this, he offered to pay my board and lodging if I could find a school that would accept me in South Africa.

The Hummels had been our neighbours for as long as I can remember. He was said to have settled in Rehoboth after having been discharged from the German colonial garrison. He traversed the district in his ancient Ford truck to install and fix windmills. Eventually he hired grazing on Narabes for the flock of sheep that he had collected. My mother used to send me with messages to Frau Hummel, who was deaf and had therefore never learned to speak Afrikaans. Parroting as loud as I could what Mother had told me to say to her was how I learned to speak German. And I began to decipher the probable meaning of text in the Frankfurter Allgemeine Zeitung that Mother inherited from Frau Hummel, which laid the foundation for my ability to read the language. Somewhere I picked up that Herr Hummel had returned to Germany only once – in 1925 – to find himself a wife in Frankfurt. They had a daughter that went to boarding school and subsequently seldom returned for visits.

Reverend Miller, the principal of my primary school, secured me a place at a high school, the William Pescod, that was run by friends of his family in Kimberley. Although it was a school for 'Coloureds' I was fascinated to find several Chinese and a Japanese in my class – in addition to Indians with whom I was familiar from my sojourn in Cape Town. Classified under the rubric of Asians, their communities were subject to the same impediments as were the Coloureds.

In response to the increasing value for South Africa of trade with Japan and then China, in due course the status of those communities would be elevated to that of 'honorary Whites' – with attendant privileges. Indians would, however, continue to remain Asian.

The teachers at William Pescod had all graduated at Fort Hare University, the first ever university college in Black Africa, and one to which Africans from all over Central and East Africa converged to seek higher education. Its reputation as a cauldron of political activism had likewise spread. Although our teachers were barred from attempting to influence the political orientation of their pupils, the comments they dropped about contemporary affairs were sufficient to let us know where they stood on the burning political issues of the day. Significantly, our classes in history were occasionally accompanied by a film, with discussion afterwards. The one I remember most clearly was about the adoption by the UN of the Universal Declaration of Human Rights. That was where I first learned about the heroic role played by the remarkable Mrs Eleanor Roosevelt in the drawing up of the Declaration.

The Tomlinson Committee's Report, published in 1954, cast a feeling of doom over all reflections about our future. The government-appointed committee had drawn up a blueprint for a South Africa where Whites would remain forever in charge and the Blacks would be removed to the reservations to which their different tribal groups had been assigned. The glaring unreason of the proposition was that the Whites, who constituted some 13 percent of the population claimed title to 87 percent of the land, while the Black 87 percent were presumed to be able to 'develop' – whatever that was supposed to mean – in the remaining 13 percent.

The removal into townships (a term replacing the earlier 'locations'), of urban Blacks who resided by special permission in areas otherwise considered to be the domain of Whites, had already ignited protests that would reverberate through the country: 'Meadowlands, Meadowlands, *ons darkies ons polla hie* – The mining town pidgin *Fanagalo* for 'we Blacks we stay here', was a catchy protest song from Johannesburg that was sung even in Kimberley, where the Coloureds in particular lived in fear of a zoning process that would remove them from their homes in the city centre to somewhere on the non-economic periphery.

When I was able to revisit Kimberley a lifetime later, it was to find only the dilapidated buildings of my old high school still standing. The school itself had been removed to a mine dump on the outskirts of the city. The swimming pool for Black children nearby had disappeared, as had the houses next to the city's Big Hole, now turned into the centrepiece of a museum devoted to the diamond industry. Yet it was precisely here where family friends of the Millers had accommodated me during my year at the William Pescod school.

Anxiety about their future and their security of tenure was what the majority of Blacks lived with. While considering this reality, I ran into a man with whom I had become acquainted the year before. Now he was mourning the loss of the land on which we stood, land from which his people, the Griquas, had been driven when diamonds were discovered beneath its arid surface. Showing me his copy of the Tomlinson Commission Report, he reflected wistfully about ways and means in which they could assert their title against the likes of the De Beers Company that controlled the world's diamond market from its headquarters in Kimberley.

After matriculating from William Pescod at the top of the class, in provincially set examinations, I had to accept that I had come to a roadblock in my pursuit of higher education. My family couldn't afford the fees and cost of board and lodging to sustain me at a university. Resigning myself to the fact that the next phase of my education would have to wait until I could pay for it out of my own earnings, I returned to Rehoboth to apply for a job as a teacher.

HISTORICAL NOTE

This is a good time in my narrative to recall some of the stories I had heard as a child which now in retrospect shed an interesting contextual light upon my early life. The first story I can recall my mother telling my sisters and me concerned the close brush with death that my grandfather, Johannes Timotheus Beukes, had experienced at the hands of the South African Army. The details have remained fixed in my mind.

Together with forty-two other elders of the Baster Community in the village of Rehoboth, he was to be executed at the village corral for cattle. The order in which they were to be shot had already been hung around their necks, when the postmaster, an English dwarf named Alexander, came running along as fast as his short legs would carry him, waving aloft an orange envelope. The telegram conveyed a reply from the League of Nations to a cable my grandfather's nephew, Jacobus Beukes, known to us as Oupa Koes Samuel, had sent four days earlier. The telegram saved the men's lives.

In time I would find my way back to the corral in Rehoboth where farmers used to keep livestock overnight, before moving them onward to the railway siding for transportation to markets elsewhere. Built in stone, the corral used to strike me as huge and ominous – at the thought of what might have happened there to the Beukes paterfamilias. It has since been pulled down, I suspect by people who had no idea of its role in the history of the community.

In due course I would also examine the tombstones of German soldiers in the local cemetary for the name of the officer whom I'd heard had been buried there. I was later told my recollection of the name was wrong therefore I dare not now use the name that had stuck in my mind. The graveyard now lies grossly neglected – more eloquent testimony to the loss of pride of a people who had been deprived of the right of self-determination. In my childhood the shady trees, the impressive tombstones and the simpler graves in neat rows that were marked by crosses inscribed with names and comforting texts still testified to a sense of community that had once existed.

I would also become familiar with the gaunt figure of Oupa Koes Samuel, a patriarch with a pockmarked face and disfigured nose below kindly eyes, who could often be seen in shuffling gait between the post office and his home, reading as he went along, often with a bunch of newspapers under one arm and a loaf of bread under the other. Occasionally he would stop in his tracks, deeply sunk in thought, before moving on. Books and newspapers overflowed his working space in a small three-roomed dwelling, where a Phillips radio receiver perched on a side table. In my school days he sometimes dropped by our house for a chat with my father – busy at his work of shoemaking. Invariably, the talk concerned the debate about South West Africa currently underway at the United Nations. Not infrequently, Oupa Koes would send 'petitions' to the UN protesting aspects of the South African government's appetite for full annexure.

Even if what was at stake was not quite clear to me at the time, the underlying fear became a constant but vague presence in my mind. It was like a cloud which threatened the loss of entitlement to the country of our birth and subjugation to the whims of foreign masters. The international context of our circumstances, as inhabitants of an internationally mandated territory, was nevertheless what sustained Oupa Koes Samuel's belief that the apartheid regime's designs on our country were ultimately doomed to failure. This calls for a brief excursion into the tangled historical background of my country:

In the year 1884, Imperial Germany called a conference in Berlin, the purpose of which was to draw up rules for the carving up of the African continent between aspiring European imperial powers. Consensus having been reached, Germany laid claim to territories in West, South-west and East Africa. South West Africa occupied the space between the British Cape Colony to the south, the Portuguese colony of Angola to the north and the British 'protectorate' of Bechuanaland, now Botswana, to the east. A panhandle called the Caprivi Zipfel jutting eastward toward what is now Zimbabwe, abuts Botswana to the south and Zambia to the north.

The territory claimed was home to native groups known as the Hereros, Namas (Kgoisan), Damaras, Basters, Ovambos, San (Bushmen), Caprivians ethnically related to the people of Zambia and of Botswana, and even other groups.

In 1904 the Hereros, Damaras and Namas rose up against the confiscation of their lands and their subjugation to the dictates of strangers whom they, unsuspecting of their purposes, had admitted into their midst a mere two decades earlier. The response of Imperial Germany was to give orders for the 'total elimination' from the face of the earth of native population groups that had challenged their pretensions.

In relative terms the resultant genocide exceeded in extent the atrocities committed in Europe a generation later. In 1907, the survivors of the once dominant groups numbered a mere 15 000 Hereros, some 20 000 Namas and an unknown number of Damaras. These people were now confined to reservations, while their traditional lands were declared the property of the German state and doled out to colonists.

The native groups which had escaped the carnage, were those inhabiting the northern half of the Territory from the coast through the Caprivi Strip: the Ovahimbas, the Ovambos, the Losis and various smaller tribes. Their subjugation remained unfinished business by the time Germany lost the colony.

The Basters of Rehoboth and other settlements, the descendants of settlers and indigenous peoples in the Cape Colony, whose self-determination the German occupation regime tolerated, likewise escaped the carnage visited upon the Hereros and Namas. Some had even done paid service behind the German lines, as had the Namas, before coming to realise what was afoot. However, Baster-German amity came to an end when the recently formed (1910) Union of four colonies in South Africa, led by the Boer generals Louis Botha and Jan Christian Smuts, entered the war between the imperial powers on the side of the British Empire. The Baster community refused a German demand for assistance to withstand the South African invasion of the colony. Instead, they sent a posse of commandos to Walvis Bay to offer their assistance to General Botha, who commanded the South African invasion force. The South African prime minister told them to keep out of the White men's war.

From Windhoek the German garrison dispatched a force to deal with the recalcitrant community. Their commanding officer was said to have come riding on horseback into Rehoboth late one afternoon and made for the home of the Rhenish Lutheran Missionary, where he ostentatiously settled in for the night. His troops meanwhile remained camped out of sight some distance from the village.

At dinner that evening a Damara servant by the name of !Heitab was said to have overheard a heated exchange between Schröer, the missionary serving the Lutheran community, and the officer. The officer demanded that the church bells be rung early the next morning so as to call the town's people to the church.

Realising that something ominous was afoot !Heitab alerted the community's leaders, whereupon the inhabitants vacated the village in the dark of night, with what supplies they could take along on their lumbering ox-drawn wagons. Early the next day the German troops on horseback caught up with them on the road we used to take to Rehoboth from my grandfather's farm. Rusted strips of iron could still be seen on the white quartz pebbles that cover a ridge over which the road went. The strips had formed part of the steel rims of the wagon wheels. An obese old lady, whose legs could no longer carry her was aboard one of the wagons. Taking comfort from the belief that the Lord would guard her, she urged her children to make their escape along with all the other men and women on horseback. The German troops shot the oxen before setting fire to the wagons.

Armed at best with front-loaders used for hunting, the Basters made for the Kuibis mountain range west of Rehoboth. Along the way they staged ambushes to secure hold of the modern weapons of their pursuers. In terrain they were familiar with, they proved a match for their adversaries. In my childhood in Rehoboth there used to pass by our house an old Nama gentleman on his way into the village. Always smartly dressed, his style of walking was no less fascinating, swinging a stiff leg in a wide arc as he went along. He was said to have lain in wait with a wounded knee at the bottom of an overhanging rock, from where he brought down five unsuspecting German soldiers. They had come charging the one after the other to look for their comrades who had disappeared.

On Grandfather's farm there used to be a Mauser rifle with the factory marking *Spandau 1896*. It was said to have come into his possession during the flight to Kuibis. The following exchange was to have taken place between Grandfather and a wounded German officer, whose rifle he had secured for himself.

'*Ach Mensch, tut doch kein Dummheit!* (Please man, don't do anything silly!)' the officer pleaded as Grandfather got off his steed and approached him with a knife in hand. To which Grandfather replied, '*Nein, mein Herr, Ich werde nur die Bandolier haben*, (No, sir, I just want the bandolier)', whereupon he hurriedly cut the strap with which the bandolier was strapped to the man's uniform before making his getaway.

Grandfather's forbidding visage didn't invite any query as to his encounter with the wounded German officer. It was only in adulthood that the realisation dawned on me that, as an elder of the Church, he would have been burdened by the memory of having taken aim at another man with his front-loader. He wouldn't even make comment when one of my aunts pointed out the spot where the encounter was said to have taken place. It was on a tree-lined bank of a dry stream crossing the route along which the Basters had advanced to the Kuibis Mountains.

The bloody skirmishes at Kuibis ended when the German forces withdrew and eventually capitulated on learning that the colony was being invaded by South Africans from four directions: from Walvis Bay, from Lüderitzbucht, across the Orange River, and through the Kalahari Desert. For the Rehobothers this might well have been compared to the operation of a *Deus ex machina*. Their chances should have been slim against the German army that had come close to wiping out the Hereros and the Namas. Deneys Reitz,[6] a South African military officer passing through the railway station east of Rehoboth on his way to Windhoek, and evidently unaware of the skirmishes that had taken place west of Rehoboth, observed a sizable German force moving in a direction away from the settlement. If he had known they were in retreat, he could have gone there to find the water and other supplies that he and his companion needed.

ARRESTING THE NEW WORLD ORDER – TO ENTRENCH COLONIALISM

In Europe, the war ended with treaties entered into that laid the foundations of a new world order – even while sowing the seeds of a new war.[7] Of interest to the peoples of South West Africa – and to all foreign territories claimed as possessions by Germany and Turkey – was the creation of a League of Nations. If not yet openly committed to outlawing war as a means of settling

---

[6]   Arriving in Windhoek, Deneys Reitz, who served under the generals Louis Botha and Jan Christian Smuts, noted with amusement – and evidently unaware of the irony of his own presence – an editorial in a local German newspaper. It sought to comfort its readers with the belief that in Europe Britain was about to cave in to Germany's might and that 'it (went) without saying that the Fatherland will not conclude a peace which leaves German South-West *under foreign yoke*, and we may say with confidence that the enemy's banner will not long float over us'. (My italics). *Trekking On*, 1933

[7]   John Maynard Keynes: The Economic Consequences of the Peace, http://www.gutenberg.org/files/15776/15776-8.txt)

international conflicts, it did pave the way for the United Nations that was formed after the Second World War and gave rise to the UN's Charter and its Universal Declaration of Human Rights.

According to these developments, the colonies in question were to be treated not as spoils of war, to be taken into possession as bounty by the victors, but as 'wards of the international community'. They were to be administrated by League members under mandates issued and overseen by its Mandates Commission. The Union of South Africa was granted the mandate to administer South West Africa.

Evidence of what rights, in the opinion of its leaders, rather than obligations, the mandate had conferred upon the Union, emerged shortly afterwards. The Bondelswarts, a Nama group in the south of the country, suffered several scores of casualties from bombs delivered by aircraft on the orders of Jan Christian Smuts, South Africa's then Minister of Defence.

Under their chieftain, named Christian, the Bondelswarts had defied demands to pay head- and dog-taxes – measures designed to compel them to work for White farmers who had been settled on lands confiscated from them. This was the first time in colonial history that bomber aircraft would be used to deliver weapons of mass destruction against rebellious natives.

The Bondelswarts chieftain was charged with treason in the Supreme Court in Cape Town (*Rex v. Christian*). Delivering judgement the Court opined that: 'under the Treaty of Versailles, South Africa was the successor in title to the supreme power which Germany had secured over the Territory'.

This case and this judgement, both quite clearly at variance with the purposes of the mandate as expressed by US President Wilson – as to spoils of war and with regard to the obligation to protect the inhabitants – planted the seed of a conflict that would stunt the development of society in the colonised Territory for more than six decades and come to an end only after thousands had lost their lives in a war that they were doomed to lose.

Given their interpretation of the mandate, the South African regime's first order of business in the Territory became the completion of the German project, which was to usurp the Territory's resources of land and minerals for the benefit of 'the white man' settle colonists on land confiscated from the native inhabitants, confine the survivors of the genocide in 'reservations', which would thenceforth be regarded merely as reservoirs of labour for what industry would develop in the Territory. This reference to 'the white man' is extensively used in the *Report of the Rehoboth Commission, Presented to both Houses of Parliament in 1927*, where the following citation occurs:

'The justification for the view of the civilised Powers is thus put by

Westlake: "That civilised states should assume sovereignty over new but not uninhabited countries, on a system which they arrange themselves without reference to the natives, can only be justified by the necessity of a government where whites and natives meet, and by the inability of the latter to supply a government adequate to *the white men's* needs or to their own protection. Accordingly, the modern tendency of thought is to place the original acquisition of title to sovereignty squarely on this basis, and so to furnish the doctrine of effective occupation with a new and solid support." '

In the exercise of 'sovereignty' thus claimed on *'the white men's'* consensus, the *proto-apartheid* regime in Pretoria went one step further than their German predecessors in South West Africa. By outlawing marriage between natives and whites, they stole a march even on the Nazis who in 1933 assumed power in Germany – where the notion of 'racial hygiene' had become a centrepiece of government policy, requiring the extermination of the Jews and others – including people of mixed descent – who were regarded as 'sub-human'.

THE REHOBOTH REBELLION

On an April day in 1925 the Rehobothers came close to becoming the second group amongst the Territory's inhabitants to face massacre for rebelling against the new foreign masters of the land.

The rebellion that nearly cost Grandfather and his comrades their lives was in protest at the confiscation of land and the imposition of a contentious 'agreement', that had been entered into between the new regime and a minority of the community's leaders. The community split into two, with the majority rejecting the 'agreement' as divesting the community of its right to self-determination.

To deal with the majority's rejection of the regime's authority a military force, with airplanes circling overhead to terrorise the inhabitants, invaded the village in the early hours of an April morning in 1925 and apprehended the 43 leaders regarded as *'belhamels'* – troublemakers'. These were summarily condemned to be executed the next day. Evidently the intention was to break the back of resistance once and for all, and to leave opponents of the regime dispirited.

The South African commander, named Uys, was said to have obtained five sharpshooters from amongst his men, but still having some difficulty getting the number of volunteers required – for the shots had to be fired simultaneously – when Alexander arrived with his telegram.

Among the things that the South Africans had noted with unease was that Hereros, Namas, Damaras and Tswanas had descended on Rehoboth to support the majority in the build-up to a confrontation with the regime. Their response was to include as part of the 'agreement' draconian sentences for anyone not a resident of the Baster reservation of Rehoboth entering or passing through it without prior permission. This could be seen as another precursor of an apartheid measure that would be enacted by the South African Parliament in 1950 as the so-called Group Areas Act.

The likelihood of a South African intervention was said to have been anticipated by Oupa Koes Samuel, who went around to solicit funds wherewith to send a cablegram to the League of Nations in Geneva. The Basters being short on cash, he obtained a loan of seven pounds, for a reply-paid message, from a German settler, one Gerlach, who had married a Baster woman. Oupa Koes urged Alexander to have the reply delivered to him promptly, wherever he might be held.

Although they had escaped death Grandfather, his cousin and their comrades were not to escape the vengeance of a regime that, by the decision to execute them, had signalled its intent to break the spirit of a community that would not be cowed into submission.[8] The 'troublemakers' were next sentenced to hard labour hewing rocks. This marked the beginning of an adversarial relationship with the new (South African supported) regime, one in which my grandfather and his cousin would remain deeply involved.

On their release Grandfather and Oupa Koes made it their business to raise the spirits of their dejected followers, only to discover that they had been declared outlaws by the regime's magistrate. By this time my father was in his teens.

In our last conversation before his death, Father related to me how he and Grandfather used to come stealing into the village on horseback for

---

[8] Ruth First described an encounter with my grandfather in the following terms: Rehoboth political passion is intensified by a fire-and-brimstone religious fervour. Seventy-four-year-old Johannes (Timotheus) Beukes is the father of Hermanus and grandfather of Hans Beukes, who refused a passport, and is studying in Oslo nevertheless. He is a tiny man, pale with a pixie face, and a thin gold ring in each ear. As he relived events in 1925, when government and Rehobothers were close to arms, he rose to his feet for effect. Behind him on the wall was a painting of Christ wearing the crown of thorns. The martyr strain runs through this family*, and Hermanus Beukes rounded off the interview: 'I may not see the eventual day of freedom, because, from what I know of our Christian democratic government and its history, I've learnt that if you act for your rights, you are killed in cold blood.' (Penguin African Library, South West Africa, Ruth First, 1963).
* This from a diminutive woman herself whose fearless revelation of the collusion between prison authorities and Transvaal's potato farmers that turned hundreds of thousands of 'pass offenders' into virtual slaves, fired the ANC's call for a boycott. And whose integrity as an investigative journalist would lead to the regime committing her without trial to Pretoria's notorious Central prison for 90 days in solitary confinement – only in vengeful cruelty to rearrest her as she crossed the street on her release to confine her for another 27 days – in solitary confinement. (Penguin African Library, Ruth First, 117 days). Wreaking further vengeance on one of their most redoubtable opponents, the apartheid regime would eventually have her murdered by letter bomb.

business only to make a quick exit before the sun set. On one occasion they had stayed the night to attend a family occasion the next day. Late that evening one of Grandfather's sisters-in-law arrived to warn him that an attempt would be made on his life with poison that had been supplied by the administration. They immediately saddled up their horses and hit the trail back to the farm. With fond memory Father recalled the great speed and endurance that their horses were capable of.

Further evidence, that the 'minority' were acting in cahoots with the administration to make life difficult for the 'majority' was provided when late one night Oupa Koes was assaulted by two men and beaten to a pulp. It was only when women performed the customary ablutions on what they believed to be his corpse, that they would discover that he was still breathing.

CHAPTER TWO

University of Cape Town

SCHOOL MASTER

Whether and where I was to land my first paid job kept me in suspense through the Christmas vacation. A week before the opening of schools, a letter from the Administration's Department of Education, broke the suspense. It offered me the job of starting a new school in Karasburg, a farming community situated along the railway line in the far south-east corner of the Territory. The school would be for children of the 'Coloured' members of the local Dutch Reformed Church. Even though the only teacher, I should be the principal, the letter enticingly informed me. That the salary would barely cover my board and lodging, not to mention allow for any savings, I would discover in due time.

Catering for the needs of nineteen youngsters from five or six families, with three or four in each class from first to fifth grade, was just about the most challenging task I ever had to master. Halfway through the days during the first few weeks, I could barely move my jaws to speak. But before long I was elated when the first-graders could begin to read and write. And before the end of the year I felt rewarded for my efforts.

Throughout the year of my employment as a teacher, the matter of most concern to me was of a Bill submitted in Parliament that would close the doors of the University of Cape Town and the other so-called open universities in South Africa to the likes of me. As a sop to Blacks, separate colleges, promptly dubbed tribal colleges, would be established to cater for the educational needs of the diverse Black ethnic groups. This caused uproar at the campuses of the 'open universities' with staffs and students staging impressive protest marches. The government of Dr Hendrik Frensch Verwoerd was, however, not to be deterred.

I realised there was a window of opportunity I should not miss. It would take a year or two before the so-called Separate Universities Bill would become law. So, if I wanted to avoid the indignity of seeking admittance to a racially defined institution, I should act now. To racially define a university seemed to me to destroy the idea that it might be a place where unfettered minds sought enlightenment about issues of concern to society. By this time I had also come to the conclusion that instead of medicine, which my mother hoped I would pursue, I needed to read law, so as to be able to defend the interests of my less fortunate countrymen. To me, these also included the most exploited of the Territory's inhabitants, the so-called contract labourers from Ovamboland, employed on farms, in the fishing industry and as servants and handymen by households and businesses in the so-called Police Zone.[9]

One of the loneliest persons I have ever met was a young Ovambo shepherd, younger than I. I found him standing at a windmill of a farm adjacent to Karasburg to where I had walked one Sunday afternoon. The sheep had drunk their fill and sought the shade of some bushes to escape the heat of the blazing sun. I asked the shepherd where he was from, who he was working for, how much his employer paid him, what he ate, whether he had company and whether he ever had any days off. His replies, in a soft voice and in sentences of a few words, described a life of utter desolation. His cash wages were pitiable, instead he received food rations of maize meal and some other items that never varied, nor made allowance for the human body's nutritional needs. He could not read or write.

When I took the train home to Rehoboth at the end of the year, I happened to share a compartment with an Ovambo chieftain by the name of Elifas. He was returning from Pretoria, where he had been in talks with the Government, he said. Paying scant notice to the status I was thus made aware of, I questioned him about the conditions of work to which Ovambo 'contract labourers' were subject.

It didn't appear to bother him much. The migrant labour system, on which European, American and South African 'investors' in the southern African economy could grow fat, was based on employing and discarding 'contract labourers' – on terms literally worse than slavery – with the collusion of their tribal chiefs.

---

[9] The 'contract labour' system was a cornerstone of the apartheid system, in terms of which 80+ percent of South Africa was 'white man's land' while 80+ per cent of the population were designated 'reservations' where they could legally reside. Recruited for limited periods by specialised agencies in the tribal reservations for employment in 'white South Africa's' mines, on their farms, in their industrial enterprises and commerce – contract labourers were required to return 'home' on expiry of their contracts. It was a practice literally more exploitative of human beings than slavery. Slave-owners have an economic interest in the welfare of their slaves. They have capital tied up in the bodies of healthy slaves, capital which can be redeemed by selling their slaves on a market. The employers of contract labourers had no such interest in the health and welfare of their employees; neither were they obliged by law to assume responsibility for their sustenance after the termination of contracts. Workers debilitated by occupational disease were simply required to return 'home' – to be cared for by their communities. If they were to come to grief at their places of work through the negligence of their employers, the law protected the latter from claims for compensation by their next of kin – unless their eventual marriages had been registered in terms of the law of the land, instead of having merely been entered into according to customary tribal law.

OFF TO UNIVERSITY

My grandfather, who had always insisted that I acquire a teacher's certificate first, did not have any objections to my designs on attending the University of Cape Town (UCT). But since we lacked the means to pay for board and tuition, I was advised to make an application for a bursary at the Territorial Administration in Windhoek. There I was met with courtesy by the official with responsibility for the mandated territory's department of education. He wondered, though, why I should want to read law at UCT, when instead I could apply at one of the local solicitors for a trainee position, whereafter I could sit for qualifying examinations. In any case, he could inform me, they had no scholarships available for university studies to offer me.

It might have been wise advice, given by a kind man. My life should certainly have taken an entirely different course if I had taken it. However, even as I was sitting there listening to him, I made up my mind that it would not be. I drove back to Rehoboth and onward to Narabes, to appeal to Grandfather to support an application for a loan to the Rehoboth Community chest. With his acquiescence I next addressed a letter of application to UCT, where I was accepted. When the loan was eventually granted, it was on condition that it be secured with a third of Grandfather's farm as surety. In addition, should I happen to fail any subject at the end of the year, the loan would immediately become repayable.

Anxiety and relief took charge of me by turns when early one morning I started climbing the steps of the University of Cape Town's impressive campus. I had beaten the ban on Black students entering UCT's doors, but I was anxious about my chances in a setting where I might merely be tolerated rather than welcomed. So I thought as I followed the path that led to the statue of the greatest empire builder of them all, Cecil John Rhodes. He sat on his plinth gazing over the Cape Flats at the Hottentots Holland Mountains on the horizon.

Much of my anxiety vanished during my first day on campus. While waiting for my turn to register in a slowly advancing queue, I got into conversation, for the first time in my life, with a young white man of my own age. From behind me in the queue, Adrian Leftwich commented on the line's progression with a wit that I found engaging. By the time we had to split to register, what doubts I had about my White classmates were gone.

I enrolled for the law courses leading to the Bachelor of Arts and of Laws (BA-LLB) degrees required to practice law as an advocate.

All law students were invited to the very first lecture at which we were welcomed by the Dean of the Law Faculty, a Professor Cowen. Standing informally at a table he gave us a brief introduction to the obligations attendant upon being a student: to be open to new ideas, but always to test what one accepted as truth. His comments provided me with a 'kick-off' that made whatever I would encounter appear to be manageable.

Towards the end of that first year, a remark by a classmate from Durban, Nola Levy, would strike me. We had sat through the same lectures since the beginning but had never spoken a word to one another. As we left the university's Great Hall where we had written a term paper, I asked how she had done. 'Oh, not so bad,' she replied. And then she turned to me with an earnest look on her face and said, 'You know, for the first time I am no longer afraid to think!'

It was an odd thing to say, but I thought I knew what she meant. Our studies were, I reasoned, about reflecting dispassionately about the conflicts we were likely to encounter practising law. By extension, we were considering the affairs of society as a whole.

Among other things, we gained insight into the ways in which a threefold system of laws regulated the lives of the Black majority: their own tribal customs as well as the governing systems of statutory and common law. South African common law is a hybrid of Roman-Dutch civil law and English common law, which reflects the country's history as a Dutch outpost that became a part of the British Empire. Statutory law, which determined government policy, was the monopoly of the state's White electorate represented in Parliament. The Black majority had little say in making laws governing the greater part of their lives. In civil matters, they were subject to African customary law. Decisions made under tribal custom were, however, foreign to courts dispensing 'national' legislation. The injustice this often caused when the interests of White and Black citizens collided was simply mind boggling.

Even the shortcoming of our university stared us in the face every day: In a country where Whites made up less than 15 percent of the population the staff, appointed to inquire into the condition of the society in which we all lived, was practically all White. I knew of only two Black teachers, both at the Department of African Languages: Dr Jordan and Mr Kunene. Black students made up no more than about five percent of the student body. I had played rugby at my various schools. But I was daily reminded on passing the beautiful rugby grounds on campus that I would never wear the 'Ikey' – UCT student – jersey. The Faculty of Engineering was out of bounds for Blacks. And when White cadavers were wheeled in for anatomical dissection at the medical school, Black students were alerted to turn their backs, or to vacate the theatre. As if to press home the point, students of all races could perform post-mortems on non-White cadavers.

Years later I would ask Kehat, my younger brother who became a surgeon, whether he had ever performed an operation on a white patient.

'Yes,' he replied. 'I operated a White woman for a hernia.'

'But that would have been illegal.'

'I know. But it was in Runtu, in the far north-east of Namibia. She had gone to Pretoria the year before where they had botched the job. She didn't want to return there. Both she and her husband pleaded with me. So I asked them both as well as the local police chief to sign a declaration absolving me of all responsibility for breaking the law before I would even examine her.'

'Was the operation a success?' I asked gratuitously.

He looked at me before replying, 'My operations never fail.'

During the period of political window-dressing that followed the so-called Turnhalle deliberations, the SWA Administration got caught into letting Kehat claim a position that he was entitled to by established practice. The Territory's administration of medical services was divided into five sections, each of which headed by the most senior doctor employed in Windhoek's State hospital. The surgical section happened to be run by a doctor who, albeit most capable, had a temper few of his White juniors could tolerate. As a result none of them stayed on after having completed their year of practice. Having himself been a student of Professor Jannie Louw, the renowned doctor Chris Barnard's mentor at UCT, Kehat was capable as a surgeon in addition to being the most unflappable member of my family.

'Beukes', he recalled the old surgeon advising him, 'at your places of work you are likely to encounter any number of people who would happily put a scalpel in your back. Ignore them until you are 100 percent certain of your case. Then you can afford to be 110 percent arrogant.'

Thus my brother remained unphased by the demands of his senior colleague. And when the senior resigned his position to go into private practice, the Administration was caught off guard by the fact that Kehat stood in line to claim his position as the Territory's Chief Surgeon. 'To get out of it,' Kehat said, 'they told me to apply for the job.'

But this would have meant that spurious reasons could have been found to reject his application. When they insisted, he expressed his preparedness to apply, on condition that the practice of automatic succession be scrapped and that all candidates for advancement be required to apply for their jobs. As this would have been most contentious, they next referred to the law that made it illegal for Black doctors to treat White patients. To this Kehat responded that he would have to consult his family – who stood by him. In the end he had his status as chief surgeon confirmed.

Still, he could not personally attend to any of the White patients, for the proper treatment of whom he was formally responsible. He had to rely on the reports submitted by his White juniors about their patients' condition and about the procedures followed in treating them.

When he discovered that his ex-senior used to sit in at meetings of the other four chiefs, meetings about which he was not notified, and where a recommendation he had made for the acquisition of certain medical equipment was rejected, Kehat followed Professor Louw's advice. He promptly wrote a letter to two of South Africa's foremost specialists to ask for their opinion about the advisability of using the equipment he had motivated for – as compared to the equipment in use in Windhoek. He then found out from a nurse when the next meeting of chiefs was due and turned up, uninvited, with photostats of the replies he had received: Handing out these he simply stated that he assumed that the equipment he had motivated for would be acquired without delay. He added that in future he expected to be alerted when meetings of the council were held.

Thus challenged, the meeting reached a decision that the tools Doctor Beukes required for operations would be acquired.

On another occasion Kehat's request for leave to attend a course in neurosurgery in Cape Town, was rejected by his senior – on the grounds that it would be beyond his abilities. From Windhoek airport Kehat called his senior to inform him that he was about to board a plane to Cape Town and that on his desk the official would find three differently motivated applications for leave – with or without pay; he was free to decide whichever one he would sign. To top it all, Kehat returned from Cape Town where he had come out on top of all the participants. (My informant here is Tania Reid, Kehat's younger daughter.)

Kehat was made to pay for refusing to sign a statement of loyalty to the 'government' put in place by the 'Turnhalle Alliance'. For two years he was kept on the blatantly discriminatory pay scale for Black doctors – as compared to Whites. To my question about why he didn't leave the public service, he replied that he had to keep 'the cowboys' in check – white doctors who would gladly perform operations they weren't qualified for – on Black patients, not infrequently with disastrous results.

THE ISSUE about where I would live as a student was resolved on the day of enrolment when somebody put me in contact with a senior medical student who was looking for a new room-mate. Bala Naidoo, one of a contingent of students of Indian descent from the province of Natal, was renting a room from a Malay family, the Petersens. It was located in Walmer Estate on the slopes of Devil's Peak, in Eden Road, a short stub of a street running parallel to De Waal Drive. It offered a breath-taking panoramic view of the harbour, with Robben Island visible across Table Bay and the Hottentots Holland Mountains to the east.

We used to walk up to De Waal Drive to thumb free rides to the UCT campus from the city's generous motorists. A narrow street running down the slope took us to the Gem Bioscope. If we turned right as we came out of Eden Road 15 we were soon in Hanover Street that took us right into the heart of the city through District Six. It was a part of the city that pulsated like no other with life and the cadences of its people's distinctive dialect. But it would soon be bulldozed out of existence and its community destroyed in an act of 'ethnic cleansing' that forever blights Cape Town's reputation as the Mother City.

My two sisters Martha and Anna were enrolled as freshman students when I left the campus. One evening one of them was accosted by a 'skollie' – the term for the delinquents that roamed the streets of District Six. 'Leave her alone, she is Hans Beukes' sister', he was upbraided by one of his pals. In distant Oslo my heart swelled with pride when I read this in a letter from home.

LITERARY INFLUENCES

By the end of my first year I felt a sense of achievement. The workload had been demanding, but I had passed all the examinations comfortably; I had interacted with all manner of people without ever feeling myself inferior in any way; and I could find my way about the city with a confidence that I had previously lacked.

I remained in Cape Town for the Christmas break, as I could not afford the train ticket to go back home. During the mid-year break I had attended a winter school series of lectures that the university offered visitors from all over the country. The theme was modern art. Nobody had seemed to notice my solitary presence at the back row of the lecture hall. Among the images that stuck in my mind was *Skrik* (The Scream) by Edvard Munch – an artist with whose idiom I would soon become uncomfortably familiar.

This time, during my six weeks summer vacation, one of the students from Natal who likewise remained in town helped me secure a part-time job as wine steward in a city centre bar/lounge. It opened at noon and closed at midnight. A dozen of us, paid only in tips, would shuttle to and fro between the bar and the thirsty patrons. The pickings were slim but they tided me over until the beginning of the new term. In its way, the job provided basic training in an essential skill: engaging in the sort of banter that put drinking customers at ease. I quickly acquired the knack of getting orders from up to a dozen and more without writing anything down, parroting them to the barman and delivering them with a flourish to the customers.

Before reporting for work at the bar one morning, I visited the city's nearby music library to listen to a recording or two. While I was searching a file cabinet a tall, elderly German I had served beer to once or twice moved up to express his surprise at finding me there. The conversation that ensued didn't obey the unspoken rule governing public contact between Whites and Blacks: that it be fleeting. He appeared genuinely interested in my taste in music before mentioning his own. It turned out that he was teaching philosophy at Stellenbosch, which made me wonder what sort of contribution a German of his vintage made at a campus that I thought was dedicated to expounding racism as the organising principle of society. Earlier that year, a Stellenbosch student had visited the UCT campus to deliver a speech. He sported a Hitler moustache, had his hair cut in Der Führer's style, and delivered his opinions – in support of apartheid – in the German demagogue's strident style.

The professor must have read my mind. He suggested with a kindly smile that I read Franz Kafka, whose work he and his colleagues were currently discussing. Fascinated at the possible insight it could provide into the preoccupations of the learned at Stellenbosch I left the music library and hurried over to the National Library to borrow the book he had recommended.

That evening I began to read *The Trial*, the novel that opens with an unsettling first sentence:, 'Somebody must have been telling lies about Joseph K, for without having done anything wrong he was arrested one fine morning.' Joseph K's anguished quest to find out what was being held against him would become an obsession for me too during the week that I needed to get through the slim volume. The story assaulted my senses. I was unable to take in more than a chapter a night. The tormented tale vied with the South African reality to make me feel trapped and caged in.

Walking down Hanover Street on my way into town one day a headline caught my eye, 'Trial in a Prison'. It was practically identical to a chapter heading in *The Trial*. The difference was that while Kafka's tale was about one man's distress, the newspaper reported the trial of 16 Black workers who had gone on strike at a Jones canning factory. The magistrate had moved the trial to a prison where he could hand down draconian sentences while keeping the media off-bounds.

Another chapter dealt with Joseph K responding to a cryptic message to turn up at a Cathedral for a hearing. That story called to mind the one in the local media announcing that the Treason Trial had been moved from the courts in Pretoria to a converted Synagogue: 'Trial in a Synagogue'. In 1956 charges of high treason were laid against 156 leaders of the non-parliamentary opposition. The purpose was transparent: to paralyse the regime's real opposition until all impediments to arbitrary arrest and indefinite detention could be removed from the statute book.

After *The Trial* I scoured the National Library as well as the university's library for the remainder of Kafka's works, finding only a handful, including one in Dutch about a man who had turned into an insect. Finally, halfway into the first chapter of *The Castle* I realised that I had had what I could take of Franz Kafka's world.

In my lonely Eden Road room the conflation of the current political reality and its bizarre literary counterpoint proved an unsettling brew. I found myself reacting to the oppressive feelings of guilt that seemed to affect Kafka's characters. Showing no sign of anger or protest, he provided merely an almost clinical account of what had befallen them.

When the new term started I went in search of someone on campus with whom to discuss Kafka. Eventually Shula Marks, a history major, introduced me to a Jewish woman, a concentration camp number tattoo still visible on her arm. She was working on Kafka for her doctorate and seemed to understand my need.

Hadn't Franz Kafka ever rebelled, or shown rebelliousness in his characters, I wanted to know. Not in the published works, she agreed. But in one of his diaries she had come across a remark that he had penned down. The Jews of Europe, he wrote, were like cockroaches, they were where nobody wanted them. Even though by implication it sounded like support for Zionism, I found the observation liberating.

I cannot recall what had set me off on Ernest Hemingway, but by the beginning of term I had devoured several of his books and was able to exchange conventional opinion about his merits and demerits with my favourite classmate, Andrea Goldberg, when classes resumed in African Law and Administration. What stayed with me was the gut feeling of Hemingway's characters, as if they instinctively knew that in life, as in the bullring, survival depended on being primed to fight. Though their fates were often tragic, they were easier to live with than Kafka's characters.

There was much more spring in my stride as I made my way up the steps leading from De Waal Drive past the rugby field to campus when lectures resumed at UCT in January. Having passed the hurdles of the first year I now felt a self-confidence I had not known before. I even dropped into lectures other than for the courses I was following. Campus life had become exciting, even when the work to be done left little time for socialising.

THE TEMPTATION OF A SCOLARSHIP ABROAD

An early winter's drizzle sent me scurrying on an April day in 1959 from the library of UCT to the student cafeteria. At the door a classmate and a member of the SRC – the Student Representative Council – handed me a sheet of paper and said, 'Do you want to study in Norway, Hans?' 'Yes, of course', I answered, as if that had been on my mind.

With a cup of coffee in hand, I poured over the paper I'd been handed. Issued by the National Union of South African Students (NUSAS), it invited Black students enrolled at the country's open universities to apply for a bursary tenable for three years' study at the University of Oslo (UiO) in any field except Medicine, all costs to be carried by the National Union of Students in Norway (NSU). The initiative was clearly meant to protest the so-called Separate Universities Bill that was in the process of becoming law. That evening I consulted my room-mate, Bala Naidoo, about the advisability of making a bid for the bursary. Of Indian descent from Natal, Bala belonged to a clandestine revolutionary study group that I'd hoped to join, so I didn't want to appear to be yearning for hand-outs. Bala thought that as it wasn't guaranteed that I would get the bursary, nothing bad could come out of trying. The next day I submitted an application with testimonials from our lecturer in British Constitutional History, Mr Rodney Davenport, and the Dean of the Law Faculty, William Beinart. It seemed to have made an impression on Mr Davenport that I had grown up riding horses on my grandfather's farm and that I had played rugby. Quoting *mens sana in corpore sano*, he wrote a warm recommendation. Professor Beinart checked my first year results and expressed the opinion that I ought to have no difficulties making it at a university abroad. The testimonials submitted, I forgot all about the application.

About a month later, as I went bounding up the steps towards the refectory, the Professor of History Leonard Thompson arrested my progress by calling out, 'Congratulations, Mr Beukes.' Surprised by being called mister by a professor, I couldn't think of an achievement worthy of his attention until he explained that I had been awarded a scholarship tenable for three years at the University of Oslo. Later that morning he announced it to the class in Constitutional History.

Word about the bursary spread quickly. Men and women, with whom I might only have exchanged nods before, now stopped for a chat as we passed each other. Even in Eden Road the neighbours across the street began to nod good day; previously they hardly noticed my existence. This was all a novel experience. Yet the thrill of it didn't last long.

MARCHING ORDERS

By the terms of the scholarship I was to enroll at the University of Oslo at the beginning of the academic year in Norway, which starts in August. This meant that I had to abort my enrolment at UCT half-way through my second year so as to be able to reach Oslo with time for learning the language. This would cost me a full year on my return. In addition, the realisation dawned upon me that most of my classmates would be gone from campus by then. Moreover, given that the Separate Universities Bill was becoming law, I might not even be allowed to re-enter UCT to complete my law degree. The more I thought about the matter the less well advised accepting the Norwegian bursary began to appear to me. In the end I knocked at the door of Leonard Thompson, who had chaired the commission that had awarded me the bursary.

Standing at his desk with a sheaf of papers in his hands, sun-tanned and looking fit, Thompson assumed that I had come to say goodbye before my departure for Norway. It was a country for which he had a great regard, he said, recalling that while doing service in the British Admiralty during the Second World War, he had participated in making contingency plans for an invasion of Norway that, he added, he was pleased had never materialised.

His jovial attitude changed when I began to speak about the doubts I had developed. After listening attentively to my litany of worries he dismissed them with a curt, 'At your age, Mr Beukes, it ought to be an adventure!' To soften the finality of the reproach he reassured me of his support to have me readmitted at UCT on my return.

Ironically, the next time I would see Thompson would be in New York, three years later. He had left UCT to take up a position at the University of Berkeley in California. On a visit to New York I heard that he would be at the campus of the University of Columbia, where I went to meet with him.

TAKING LEAVE OF FAMILY – AND OF COUNTRY

Having received my marching orders, I submitted an application for a passport and then boarded a train for the two and a half days' journey home to take leave of my family. I also had to apply to the Rehoboth Community's Council for a suspension of my loan obligations for the duration of my absence abroad.

My father picked me up at the station for the drive home. Though he was not given to discussing anything that might be on his mind with his children, he expressed concern about what appeared to be the full-scale implementation of apartheid policies throughout the territory of South West Africa. Earlier that year the South African Defence Force (SADF) had sent bomber planes to terrorise a defiant Nama community for refusing to be displaced from their oasis named Rietfontein in the Kalahari Desert, to make way for its occupation by White farmers.

'It's a good thing you will be going abroad', Father remarked, 'You should be using the opportunity to make our case known.'

During the train journey home I had in fact reflected on all the questions I could face abroad and come to realise that while I was fairly well informed about South Africa, I could not say the same about my own country. Our own history hadn't been a priority in the school curricula, nor had our teachers been able to fill in the picture for us informally. I had no knowledge of books about the country and its people.

On my father's advice I drove to Windhoek where a family acquaintance, Mr Otto Schimming, made me aware of a book written by an American journalist for whom he had been an informant. The book, a travelogue, had been placed on the list of forbidden literature, and would land one in prison to be found in possession of. He had made an appointment for me to see Clemens Kapuuo, an adviser to the Herero Paramount Chief Hosea Kutako. But as it was inadvisable to be seen going there, I had to make my way to his house only after sundown.

Mr Kapuuo was in company with a colleague when I knocked at his door. Offering me a cup of tea he explained the precaution that I had had to observe. Since I was on my way abroad, the powers that be would be interested in whom I saw before my departure, he warned.

The two men listened attentively to my reasons for wanting to meet with them. I replied that with the Herero chiefs having taken a lead in petitioning the UN, I was hoping for an update of their views on the current situation. Mr Kapuuo responded with facts with which I was familiar: the land question, where Whites occupied land from which the natives had been driven; the skewed distribution of burdens and favours between Blacks and Whites by an administration that was run by Whites; the impending removal from the so-called white areas of the so-called 'black spots'. This included the (old) 'location' in which Mr Kapuuo's house was situated, and where Blacks from diverse communities were living alongside one another.

As I was about to leave, Mr Kapuuo reminded me that another student whom I knew, Jariretundu Kozonguizi, had preceded me abroad some months before. Kozo, as he was called, had made his way to the UN at Chief Kutako's request. Shaking my hand he said, 'It's up to you and Kozo, Hans, to go get us the support we need to liberate this country.'

Wistful as was such an assignment, the trust thus confided in me was as heart-warming as any send-off I'd ever experienced.

The day before my departure for Cape Town, my grandparents and my eldest cousin, Paulina Denk, alongside whom I had grown up on the farm, came into town to take their leave of me. My grandparents wanted to send their grandson off with a prayer. Bidding me goodbye, Grandmother Anna delivered a homily: '*En onthou tog, Hannes, met die hoed in die hand, kom 'n mens deur die land!* (And please remember to be courteous wherever you go!)' My mother said the same thing.

As my father was driving me back to the train station, the thought crossed my mind that three years was a long time and that this might be the last time I would set eyes on either my grandmother or my grandfather.

JAPIE BASSON MP

Back in Cape Town the days went by without any word about the passport that I had applied for. Eventually it occurred to me that my chances might be improved if I were to enlist the support of Mr Japie Basson, who represented an electoral district in South West Africa in the Union Parliament. At home, the presence of White South West Africans in the Union legislature was feared as a step towards annexation, but the situation had been defended by Mr Basson and others on the grounds that it was essential for the Territory to be represented where decisions with a bearing on the Territory's interests were made. I had also noticed statements by Mr Basson that revealed an enlightened take on the multi-racial society's future.

What reservations I might have had, dissolved when a dapper figure in a smart pinstriped blue suit rose from the chair in his office to greet me. Inviting me to sit down, he asked a few business-like questions about the scholarship, and offered me a cup of coffee while he took out pen and paper to write in his own handwriting a firm recommendation to the Minister of the Interior, that I be granted a passport. As I was about to leave he remarked with a smile that we might be meeting again later that year when he was due to attend an inter-parliamentary conference in Oslo, and that I might also be interested in a statement he was going to make in Parliament two days later.

Bala, my room-mate, expressed his surprise when two days later I made my way to the Houses of Parliament. He couldn't understand why I should want to go to a place where we could never expect to hear anything uplifting. This time, however, we were both in for a surprise.

When Mr Basson rose to speak, it was to declare that he would abstain when a Bill that had been submitted to Parliament was put to the vote. The section that he found offensive would terminate the representation in Parliament – by White members – of the Coloured and Bantu communities of the Cape Province. In contrast to the lack of such representation of the Blacks in the other three provinces, the Cape represented an anomaly that harked back to concessions the self-governing province had made to facilitate its unification with the defeated Boer Republics and Natal in 1910. Mr Basson defended the status quo in much the same terms as he had justified the presence in the South African Parliament of representatives from South West Africa.

Predictably, the governing National Party would find his waywardness impossible to forgive. Calls for his expulsion from the party caucus, with which the party he represented had formed a coalition, were voiced almost immediately he sat down. It was, as he wrote shortly before his death in 2012, the darkest moment of his political career.[10]

Walking back to Eden Road through District Six that night, I assumed that whatever political influence Mr Basson might have wielded had also evaporated – so I could forget about a passport. But Mr Basson's steadfastness on a matter of principle filled me with pride to have him as my countryman.

On the advice of Neville Rubin, president of NUSAS, I next turned to his father, who represented Blacks in the Eastern Cape as senator in Parliament, and whose seat would be removed by the Bill Basson had opposed. Senator Leslie Rubin emerged hastily from the senatorial chamber where he had been participating in the debate to reassure me that he would take care of the matter.

Four or five days later, I received an official letter stating that I should present myself at an office in town to collect my passport.

---

[10] *Meneer die Speaker* (Mister Speaker) – a selection of accounts from his Political Scrapbook – the fourth in an absorbing series of autobiographical sketches by one of the longest-serving parliamentarians in the country's history. Publisher: *Politika*, Cape Town.

JAN RABIE, AUTHOR

While waiting for a response to my application, Jan Rabie, the Afrikaans author, had turned up at the campus to deliver one of the popular lunch-hour talks by which the SRC sought to keep the student body abreast of contemporary affairs. He presented statistics to show that Afrikaans was the most widely spoken language in the country, its lingua franca and mother tongue to people of diverse ethnicities. Given that language is an essential aspect of society, he argued that Afrikaans made that much nonsense of apartheid. As Afrikaans is my own mother tongue, the argument appealed to me. At the conclusion of the debate I presented myself to him. On hearing that I was from South West Africa and on my way abroad, he promptly invited me to his home in Green Point the next afternoon.

In the company of his wife, the painter Marjorie Wallace, and another painter friend, Rabie was in an entertaining mood when I knocked at their door. Over a bottle of vintage wine (to celebrate the scholarship I'd won, he said), the three of them set out to make me feel welcome. Rabie spoke about a younger brother of his, the 'family's black sheep', who had made his home in the mountain fastness of Damaraland in northwest Namibia. Unable to get along with his family in the Cape, the younger brother would never stay for more than a fortnight on his occasional visits home. As my ancestors had similarly sought freedom from colonialist prejudices in the vast open spaces of the Territory, it was an account I found hugely enjoyable.

Rabie went on to relate how his brother had once stared down a black-maned lion he'd met on a narrow mountain path. It was the lion that eventually turned to go the way it had come. In encounters with wild beasts, the younger Rabie had made his brother understand, it was one's own fear that posed the greater danger. As human beings form part of the animal kingdom, this was a piece of advice that I took to heart.

Ironically, as years later Rabie's biographer, the late Professor JC Kannemeyer, informed me, on returning to the Cape the younger brother met his death at the hands of a murderer.

Turning the conversation to my impending departure for Norway, the two friends recalled their own experiences in various European countries, not only as passive sojourners but also as participants in the life of the societies concerned. I noted, though, that Rabie's friend remained silent when he explained how he had found painting an inadequate medium for expressing the things he had to say. When I later read the pieces in the volume of short stories he had signed for me, I was struck by the graphic quality of Rabie's writing, as in a piece about the gas chambers of the Nazi concentration camps.

His text graphically etched, as it were, the outline of a pyramid of bodies piled one upon the other in a frantic struggle to reach an air vent in the ceiling from where the lethal gas was seeping.

The two friends impressed upon me the importance of boning up on Nordic literary classics so as to be prepared to meet my hosts with some knowledge about their past. I have no more recollection of a wide-ranging conversation, frequently out of my depth, with a most engaging presence in South Africa's literary world and with his painter friend that evening. Yet, with Rabie's book as a parting gift in hand, I felt myself immensely enriched as I made my way home to Eden Road that night.

RONALD SEGAL, PUBLISHER

My next destination was the offices of Ronald Segal, the publisher of *Africa South*, a quarterly magazine of contemporary affairs that offered a forum for discussion by Africanists. Sometime earlier, Segal had arrived at the campus to exhort the university's students to lend their support to a boycott of South African goods that had been called for by the African National Congress (ANC). It was a memorable performance. Letting his sky blue eyes take in the packed audience, Segal opened his talk with a dramatic flourish. He intoned: '*There comes a time in the life of every oppressed people when out of the depths of their misery they say: so far and no further!*'

At the conclusion of the highly charged session that followed, the several hundred strong audience marched back to their classes singing from full throats The International Anthem of the Socialist movement – whether in all earnestness or jest, I couldn't tell. At the exit some activists handed out the text, the tune was catchy and by the time I reached the lecture hall for the afternoon's lecture, I was adding my own voice to the chorus that echoed from the ivy-covered walls around.

I had gone to Segal's city offices for copies of the magazine he edited that dealt with the consequences for the people of Southern Africa of the policies of apartheid. He gave me an armful of back issues of *Africa South*. '*Padkos* (provisions) for the voyage,' he said with an ironic smile.

CHIEF ALBERT JOHN LUTHULI, ANC PRESIDENT

Thanks to Thulani Gcabashe, I would next be privileged to meet with Chief Albert Luthuli, leader of the ANC and his future father-in-law. On my way to campus one morning, he stopped me with an invitation to accompany him into the city where his prospective father-in-law was to chair a press conference. Chief Luthuli had availed himself of a break in the Treason Trial,[11] in which he was one of the accused, to travel from Pretoria on a whirlwind speaking tour of the country. The day before, a huge crowd had gathered on the Parade Grounds in front of the City Hall, to hear him speak. Following on a similar event in Bloemfontein, where the ANC had been founded in 1912, some political commentators expressed the opinion that the people of South Africa, including Whites, were no longer foreign to the idea of having a Black man as the country's leader. The Verwoerd regime evidently read the same message on the wall. Before Chief Luthuli had completed his tour, they issued a banning order that confined him to house arrest in his home village near the town of Stanger in Natal.

By the time Thulani and I arrived at the City Hall for the press conference, Chief Luthuli had already made his opening remarks and the handful of local pressmen were leaving the hall. A lone American journalist stepped forward to begin an interview with the standard fare of questions, then as now: What was the ANC's attitude to the future of Whites in the country? What was the relationship between the Congress and communists?

The Chief fielded those and other questions articulately, comprehensively, patiently, and with an earnestness that left no doubt that he was delivering his personal credo. Blacks didn't hate Whites, he insisted, but the system they had created in which Blacks were forever doomed to second-class citizenship. Furthermore, the ANC was committed to achieving its goal of ending the violence done by the apartheid system to the people of the land through non-violent means.

To hear the ANC's policies expounded as thoroughly as its chief spokesman had done, and afterwards to be introduced to the great man himself, was as much as anyone could hope for. He beamed on hearing that I was on my way to Norway with a scholarship.

TO PORT ELIZABETH – AND BACK

With my passport finally in hand, I made for the Norwegian Consul General's offices in town to apply for a visa and to inquire about transportation to Oslo. A tall, elegantly dressed man emerged from a room, lit a cigarette and drew a deep draft before speaking. Expelling a cloud of smoke, he wondered

---

11 On 5 December 1956 the apartheid regime had 156 leaders of the non-parliamentary opposition – the Congress Alliance – arrested and charged for high treason. The charge related to the adoption by a Congress of the People of the Freedom Charter – a document that stated the conditions under which 'The People shall govern'. The trial ended in 1961 without the charges of violent intent being proved.

what I was, a Coloured, a Black or a White, adding, 'It's so difficult to tell in your country!'

I thought it a studiedly disingenuous way of getting me to refer to myself in racist terms. I retorted that I was called a Rehoboth Baster.

When I returned for the visa the next day, he informed me that an ore carrier under the Norwegian flag would be sailing out of Port Elizabeth in a week's time and that I would be expected to work my passage to Oslo aboard it.

Shortly before my departure I attended a show by a magician named Robby Williams and was fascinated by the sleights of hand he performed. Bala was still reading by the time I returned to our digs. To him it was no mystery how a magician could make one believe one sees him plucking eggs from a model's ears. 'He merely does something to distract the audience from what he is doing with his hands', Bala explained, adding 'it's quite simple: it's a case of mind over matter.' I dropped off to sleep still trying to figure out how Williams could have done the tricks he had fooled me with that evening.

Never having sailed anywhere before, I was uneasy at the prospect of a voyage up the Atlantic Ocean. Still, on the following Tuesday afternoon I was ready to leave when Mr Petersen, my landlord, swung up Eden Road from work to drive me to the train station. To my surprise more than a dozen students from various classes – men and women, Black and White – turned up at the platform's end outside my carriage to wave me a noisy farewell. It was a gathering as gloriously defiant of apartheid as could be imagined. All those I regarded as friends were there together with others with whom I had only exchanged brief greetings on campus. As the train wound its way eastwards towards the Hottentots Holland Mountains, my mind dwelt on their beaming faces and the implicit reassurance that they had accepted me as one of them. And I recognised that in that send-off they had expressed a yearning for a freedom that we all were denied – the freedom to be ourselves.

It was an overnight journey and the train frequently made lengthy stops at small stations dotting the tracks to Port Elizabeth. At one such stop I got off to stretch my legs. Through the open window of a compartment I heard an announcer reading the late-night news bulletin on SABC. The main item destroyed the peace of mind I had been savouring the whole evening. It stated that the Prime Minister, Dr Hendrik Frensch Verwoerd, in Parliament that afternoon had announced that the British Protectorates of Basutoland (now Lesotho), Bechuanaland (Botswana) and Swaziland ought to become part of the Union of South Africa, into which their economies were already incorporated.

Back in my compartment, I took out pen and paper and wrote a letter to a classmate at UCT. With reference to the news item I wrote, 'the bloody cynic, and after what they had done to the people of this country he's brazen enough to propose that those of the "Protectorates" join his "union". It would of course make the land/population ratios look that much better...' Planning to drop the letter into a mailbox on arrival in Port Elizabeth I put it into an outside pocket of my jacket.

At break of dawn the next morning I woke up to the reflection that I was travelling over sacred ground; land on which the natives had fought against Europeans who had arrived to reduce them to servitude. I was still trying to recall what I had read about that part of South Africa's history when the steam engine hissed its way into Port Elizabeth's railway station. With wheels shrieking to a halt against the rails, I heard a pounding of running feet on the platform outside and men's voices shouting excitedly: 'Is he there? No, here!'

Had I not still been in a reverie, I might have sensed that something was amiss when a White man poked his head through the window to ask whether I was Hans Beukes. When I replied in the affirmative, he scurried off along the platform to the door at the end of the carriage. Next I heard doors flung open and slamming shut followed by the shuffling of feet in the passage outside my compartment.

Before I could take in the meaning of all the commotion, three men barged through the open door and positioned themselves around me: one at the window on my left side, another on my right, while a third in a tweed jacket slipped a handgun into his hip holster as he placed himself directly in front of me.

Identifying himself as 'Major Heiberg of the Special Branch', he informed me that the man in a blue uniform by the door was 'a gentleman from Immigration' who had orders to confiscate my passport.

As I took the passport, along with some letters from my jacket's inner pocket, Heiberg held out his hand for the letters, saying, 'I'll take those as well', before handing the passport to the Immigration official, who looked decidedly unaccustomed to the company he was keeping that morning.

Then, indicating my bags, Heiberg asked, 'Are those yours?' When I nodded he ordered his sidekicks to examine them.

Being unaware of any cause for concern, the men barging into my compartment didn't frighten me at all. But when Heiberg took my papers I realised the danger I was in – especially if they should find the letter I had written the night before.

I immediately rejected the first thought that came into my mind, that of putting the letter into my mouth. I reminded myself that paper can't be easily swallowed. Besides, Heiberg's sidekicks would have grabbed me by the throat the moment my hand reached my mouth. I next considered dropping the letter into the well of the window but thought better of that as well. It would merely give them reason to put me in prison while taking all the time needed to unscrew the panels of the carriage.

Then the incongruity of the scene struck me: four White men busying themselves with my belongings with the rustle of their movements the only sound to be heard in the compartment: the one on my left messing up the order in which I had packed my clothes; the one in front of me reading a letter that had been addressed to me; the one on my right rifling through the papers in my satchel; and the sheepish-looking man from Immigration by the door idly turning the pages of my brand-new passport.

At that moment I recalled Bala Naidoo's explanation about mind over matter and distracting people's attention before performing a sleight of hand. Resolutely I slipped my hand into the outside pocket of my jacket, enveloped the envelope and raising it as if to cover my mouth for a little cough slipped it into my shirtfront.

As if he had sensed something Heiberg looked up and told the man on my left to search me. Abandoning the suitcase, that one duly emptied all my pockets and touched up the intimate parts of my body. When he finished I put up a little charade so as to defuse any lingering impulse to carry out a more thorough examination of my clothing. In a voice intended to sound hurt I asked what I had done wrong to justify being robbed of an opportunity to study abroad for free while I had to risk the financial ruin of my family for a chance to study at UCT. Flushing at either my insolence or the guilt I had wanted him to feel, Heiberg snapped back that they didn't have to give me any reasons. Turning to march out, he told me to follow them to their office with my belongings.

At the office a block away, the three divided my papers among themselves for examination, while allowing me to sit down and smoke. They didn't object to my lighting one cigarette after the other – as if my nerves had need of the nicotine.

POLICE INTERROGATION

'I see you're taking photos', I heard Heiberg say. Noting the handful he was sifting through I wondered how to respond to what might have been something of interest when he repeated himself, 'I see you're taking photos'. Only now picking up the ominous tone in his voice, I swore at myself when he turned the photograph towards me.

It showed the sweetly smiling Andrea Goldberg, my favourite class-mate, seductively curled up on a sofa. The situation it hinted at might have been enough to launch an inquiry into a possible breach of the Immorality Act, had not the next image shown Andrea being embraced by her boyfriend, Sonny Kaplan, on the same sofa. At this, Heiberg mumbled something about the reason that you Black guys go to UCT is to enjoy sitting next to White girls in classes.

AS I'D expected, Ronald Segal's *Africa South* drew negative reviews from the man who had been examining my satchel earlier that morning. Quoting paragraph after offending paragraph from an article he asked rhetorically, 'Is this what you intended to tell people in Norway about South Africa?' I could truthfully plead innocence by replying that I hadn't had time to have a closer look at the stuff Ronald had shoved into my hands.

An excuse for a visit to the loo enabled me to get rid of the incriminating letter in my possession. With a Black police officer with strict orders not to let me out of his sight planted two metres behind my back outside the open door of the reeking convenience for Blacks, I retrieved the letter from behind my shirt front, tore it up and flushed away the pieces. That further little performance of sleight-of-hand flooded me with a feeling of triumph, knowing that I had finally outwitted my captors.

After a break for lunch, the three resumed their examination of my reading material. Holding out a slim volume one of the men on the floor called out in triumph: 'Full of communist propaganda, full of communist propaganda!'

'Let's see', said Heiberg holding out his hand for the copy of Adlai Stevenson's *Call to Greatness*. To be in possession of literature that could be branded as communist propaganda was a serious offence. *If they want to take me in, they have me there*, I thought, desperately trying to recall who Stevenson was.

Finally I remembered why I had picked up the pamphlet at a flea market in Cape Town the previous Saturday. As a schoolboy in Rehoboth, reading the *Diamond Fields Advertiser*, I had seen a statement by the American politician on a visit to South Africa. He couldn't understand, he had said, how a country as richly endowed with natural resources as South Africa, could justify a policy designed to keep three-fourths of its population in abject poverty. It was an observation on the moral basis of a political economy that had promptly secured Adlai Stevenson my esteem.

I now raised my voice to say, 'How can a man who'd almost been elected president of the United States of America be accused of writing communist propaganda?'

Even though Major Heiberg had nodded in agreement at the passages that had alarmed his sidekick, he now sought to strike a magnanimous note. They were not going to go for minor issues, he said, but would keep all my papers for further examination. With that he ordered his men to catalogue the items and, after making me sign the list, told me I was free to go. It was 16:00 and after more than a full day's work it was clearly time to knock off.

'How do I get back to Cape Town?' I asked. The two or three pounds in my pocket were insufficient for a train ticket back to the Mother City. With malicious disinterest, Heiberg retorted that that was no concern of theirs.

I left the building and made straight for a phone booth in the railway station half a block away. I placed an order for a personal call to the Minister of the Interior in Cape Town. When the minister's personal secretary answered the phone to say that he was out of town, I pointedly told her that what I wanted from *her* minister was to be informed *precisely* why he had given orders for my passport to be confiscated. The timidity of her response made me feel a tinge of guilt at the insolence of my question. In a kindly tone of voice, she replied that she had no idea why the passport had been withdrawn.

I was at my wits' end as I emerged from that telephone booth. With no money to speak of; knowing nobody in Port Elizabeth; having had my diary with addresses and telephone numbers confiscated by Heiberg and his minions, I was wondering how to get away from Port Elizabeth and what to do next. The thought of being looked at with sympathy by anyone – as yet another victim of the apartheid regime – was more than I could stomach. A return to UCT was out of the question for that reason alone, though I also stood no chance of passing any of that year's examinations after having lost several weeks' of reading.

DENNIS BRUTUS

I was still standing irresolutely at the gates of the Railway Station when a well-spoken man approached me and introduced himself as Dennis Brutus. I was familiar with the name from the sports columns of the Black newspapers where he regularly figured as a body-builder in national competitions. That he also wrote fine poetry I would be surprised to learn that evening. Dennis informed me that the teachers' association in Cape Town, of which he was a member, had asked him to offer me what assistance I might need. This was first and foremost a meal and a bed for the night at his mother's place.

Early the next morning Dennis[12] handed me a telegram from Neville Rubin in Cape Town. It stated that a plane ticket had been booked for me with a local travel agency. That afternoon I boarded a flight that, in a surprising concession to economics, didn't observe apartheid in the seating arrangements aboard. It was also interesting to spot the presence of Major Heiberg's minions on the flight. It made me recall that, suspecting nothing at the time, I had actually seen them taking strolls past my carriage at some of the stations where the train had stopped on its way to Port Elizabeth. It provided first-hand evidence of the thoroughness with which the feared security police kept track of their quarries.

---

[12] Some five years later Dennis Brutus would pass through Oslo. His once magnificent torso carried bullet wounds inflicted by police in Johannesburg. Having been an outspoken supporter of expelling South Africa from world sports competition, he had feared for his life and decided to flee the country. He was apprehended in Swaziland and returned to Johannesburg, handcuffed, late one afternoon. Because only the police knew what had become of him, he knew he was in mortal danger in their custody. Reasoning that the police would promptly catch up with him, but that some people in the crowd would recognise him, he jumped and made a dash into the crowded street. The policemen didn't even try to give chase, but shot him down at point-blank range. It took a quarter of an hour for the first ambulance to reach the scene, only to discover that he was 'Coloured' and, as it was an ambulance for 'Whites', they were barred from transporting him. An ambulance for Blacks arrived forty minutes later. It was only the well-trained athlete's shape he was in that had enabled Dennis Brutus to survive. Allowed to leave South Africa on a one-way ticket, Dennis moved to London where he began his work to have South Africa and Rhodesia banned from participation in the Olympic Movement. When I saw him in Oslo he was on the warpath, determined to see it through. That goal achieved, he moved to the United States to pursue a distinguished academic career as a professor of English at several universities. We last saw each other in Pittsburgh from where he played an active part in the World Social Forum.

CHAPTER THREE

Into exile

CITY ANGER AT TREATMENT OF ONE OF ITS OWN

Waiting for me at the airport in Cape Town was Neville Rubin and Adrian Leftwich. During the drive back to my ex-landlord's at Eden Road, they brought me up to date on the uproar that the retraction of my passport had caused on campus. In an unprecedented show of solidarity, UCT students had travelled into the city to stage a demonstration outside the Houses of Parliament; questions had been put to the government; Jan Rabie had published an angry letter of protest in which he argued that what had happened to me had convinced him that there was no truth in the government's claims that national security was at issue when they violated peoples' rights.

Both the city's English papers had carried editorials decrying the confiscation of my passport while the Afrikaans daily, *Die Burger*, had a short notice about the Ikey whose passport had been rescinded.

It was gratifying to read the headlines of *The Cape Times* for 25 June 1959, 'City Man Was to Take up Norwegian Bursary': 'City Man' – a *Capetonian*, no less! It was good to read that, particularly after their headline of the previous week had stated: 'Norwegian Bursary for Non-White.'

The day after the news of the passport seizure broke, representatives of the Black community expressed their anger at yet another insult directed at them from the country's White rulers. Following the Cape Teachers' Association, the local branch of the ANC adopted a resolution that added the seizure of my passport to the list of complaints that justified the consumer boycott they were organising.

Even Chief Luthuli, who had not yet left the city, went to 'inspect' the students' demonstration, as a newspaper report interpreted his visit to them.

A nervous Mrs Petersen let me deposit my luggage in my old room before continuing to the downtown NUSAS offices, for a meeting with a foreign guest to which Neville had invited me.

ALLARD LOWENSTEIN

Before the arrival of his guest, Neville informed me that Allard Lowenstein was a past president of the American National Students Association (USNSA) who had worked for Adlai Stevenson, Mrs Eleanor Roosevelt and others as a Congressional assistant. Lowenstein was accompanied, Neville told me, by two students, Sherman Bull and Emory Bundy, the one a medical student, the other in media.

A few years older than the two, Lowenstein arrived some minutes later. Without wasting time Al, as he asked to be called, took me aside to inform me why they were in South Africa. It was to undertake an information-gathering mission to South West Africa under the guise of tourists – after he and his companions had attended the annual NUSAS conference on behalf of the NSA as cover. The intention was to submit a report to the UN about the economic, political and social conditions under which the native peoples lived in the mandated territory. Among the people who had requested him to undertake the mission were 'friends of South West Africa in the US,' he said. Others who had asked him to take on this project were the Anglican priest Reverend Michael Scott; Mburumba Kerina who had departed for the US some years earlier; and Fanuel Kozonguizi who had left the country some months earlier that year. To assist him he had brought along Sherman Bull, a medical student, and Emory Bundy, a media specialist.

I had been impressed by Neville's reference to Mrs Eleanor Roosevelt and Adlai Stevenson – both of whose merits I was familiar with – and by Al's mention of the Reverend Michael Scott. The Anglican chaplain had been a household name for as long as I could remember because of his role in thwarting the Union's move to annex us at the very inception of the United Nations. After his first appearance at the UN to present a petition on behalf of the Herero chiefs, he was barred from returning to see them again. A book that we had to read at secondary school dealt with a character with Scott's physical appearance, represented as an instigator of unrest among Blacks – a view that even as a teenager struck me as characteristically patronising of Whites and frankly ridiculous.

Al mentioned that he had been at the University of Stellenbosch earlier that day to deliver a speech. In it he had pointed out that preventing a student from studying abroad didn't only concern the individual affected. It was an assault on the community of which he was a member as well. He had challenged the Stellenbosch students to join UCT in protesting the rescinding of my passport. On that score he thought I myself had an obligation.

'You've got to put your case, that of your people, to the world's public,' he said. As if that didn't sound daunting enough, he pointed out that the South African government enjoyed a monopoly on the information the world received about us. Then he threw out a challenge, 'Unless some of you are prepared to leave the comfort of your homes to go and fight them on the world stage, where you can hurt them, you can forget about ever getting rid of apartheid.'

Although I was impressed with what Al was telling me, at that moment I didn't quite know how to respond to him. Nevertheless, on his advice, I joined Neville Rubin and drafted a telegram to the UN Committee on South West Africa to protest the withdrawal of my passport, while Neville sent one of his own on behalf of NUSAS to draw the attention of the UN to the affair. The two of them further advised me to say more about my background in a letter to the UN Committee on South West Africa.

Availing myself of the facilities of the SRC office, I sat down to dash off such a letter. With reference to the international mandate by which South Africa was governing South West Africa, I stated that our development had been reversed 'to suit South Africa's ruling prejudices about race and colour', and that 'South Africa has in fact shown that she was not worthy of the trust confided in her in the first instance'.

As to Al's challenge, I let it rest. I reminded myself that he was a White American, from a country where Blacks were receiving no less of a raw deal from Whites than in South Africa. Moreover, even though vaunted as the leader of the free world, the US did nothing to compel the South African regime to change its policies, occasional public condemnations of apartheid by leading citizens notwithstanding.

At the conclusion of business at the NUSAS office that evening, Shula Marks included me in an invitation to a reception at their place for the Ikeys going to attend the NUSAS conference in Johannesburg. Shula and Adrian Leftwich used the occasion to draft a public appeal for funds to enable me to return to the campus to complete my studies. They described me as the most apolitical student of their acquaintance. I supposed they emphasised this impression to show how unreasonable it was for the government to prevent me from the chance of a lifetime.

Privately, the prospect of returning to campus on the charity of my peers didn't much appeal to me. Nor did I look forward to the police surveillance that I would be subject to from then onwards. I had begun to reflect on the value, in a police state, of anonymity.

Before the party at the Marks' place broke up, Adrian Leftwich passed a hat around for contributions to put me in some sort of pocket. It would have been petty-minded of me to refuse the gesture. Moreover, the sum gathered would have enabled me to look around at what alternatives there might be for me, given that a return to UCT had become pointless.

Among the guests at the Marks' that evening were my classmate Andrea Goldberg and her boyfriend Sonny Kaplan. While driving me home, Sonny, who knew that I had matriculated in Kimberley, suggested that I spend a week's vacation there. He was going to present Andrea to his parents and even though his sister would be coming along as well, there would be space in his Volkswagen.

That night, as I reflected on the situation in which I found myself, the American's comments became a taunt. By the time sleep finally came to my relief, I had made up my mind to find out if Al Lowenstein was as good as he sounded. But this discovery would take a few days and some travelling.

Early the next morning I called on the Reverend Martin Henry Miller, who had been the principal of the Methodist Primary School in Rehoboth and a family friend. Subsequently he had been called to serve the Methodist parish in Cape Town – in the building that today houses the District Six Museum. With his assurance that I would be welcome at the Kesters, his sister's family, I boarded my friends' Volkswagen for the drive to Kimberley.

The schools' winter vacation having left the town fairly deserted, I found only Mrs Kester at home. As we arrived late in the evening, she only asked the polite questions before hospitably showing me a room for my stay. Wandering through the mining town the next day without coming across any acquaintance deepened the despondency I felt. It was, therefore, with a sense of relief that I boarded a train to Johannesburg the following day, excusing myself to Mrs Kester by having to attend the NUSAS conference.

The journey through the Orange Free State was memorable for the company with whom I shared the compartment. One of my two companions sat quietly at his window while the other spent his time working off excess nervous energy. At one point he rose to change his shirt and exhibited a torso like that of Tarzan in the comic strips I had devoured in my childhood. He satisfied my curiosity by letting on that he was a policeman on his way home from an assignment.

The encounter with his colleagues in Port Elizabeth was fresh in my mind. So I asked how he could arrest and detain his own people when they were the only law-breakers he was allowed to apprehend. Evidently flustered, he mentioned a wife and children needing to be fed. At this I regretted the rancour that had driven me to score so cheap a hit.

Years later during a conference of the Organisation of Africa Unity

(OAU) that was held in Oslo, Paul Lusaka, the Foreign Minister of Zambia, identified himself as the third traveller in that compartment. He had been on his way home for the winter break from Fort Hare University where he was a student – as had been so many future leaders from the British colonies of Central and East Africa.

The NUSAS conference was held at the campus of the University of Witwatersrand (Wits) where I was assigned a bed within walking distance in a dormitory for Black students. The dormitory was a significant advance on the situation at UCT, where only Whites enjoyed the convenience of dormitories on campus. When I could finally catch up with Al Lowenstein, it was to be much relieved by his response.

'I planted that idea in your head!' he said with a triumphant little laugh when I told him I was ready to leave the country, if I could get help to do so. However, as the tour to South West Africa would exhaust what funds he himself commanded, it was necessary that we find out what help might be obtained from the ANC, the only local source that could be approached without risk.

I knew no one I could approach for an introduction to any officer of the ANC. But I recalled that in Cape Town my hosts the Petersens had spoken warmly of Ahmed Kathrada, one of the 156 Treason Trialists. Discreet inquiries revealed that he was living within walking distance from the Wits campus.

It was a nervous visit by a frightened young man, Mr Kathrada told me when I met him again thirty-two years later. I ran into him at the ANC's offices in Johannesburg's Plein Street, engaged in planning for the impending change of regime shortly after his release from prison on Robben Island. He expressed his regrets at his inability at the time to respond positively to my request for assistance to leave the country.

AN APPROACH TO THE ANC

The next morning provided me with an opportunity to observe Al Lowenstein in action, delivering the keynote speech at the opening of the NUSAS conference. Facing an audience of some of the most privileged of South Africa's young men and women, he challenged them to be prepared to engage the regime, not only on behalf of their fellow Black citizens, but also for their own sakes. He assured them that they could depend on US students for support if they were to do so. Noting that it was the fourth of July he made a vow that he wouldn't rest before the American people had become thoroughly acquainted with the evil system that was apartheid.

With some misgiving it occurred to me that had Al wanted to attract attention to what he was doing in the country, he could hardly have done better. That the Security Police must already have been following the Americans became evident when some time later they found their Volkswagen – an old vehicle they had cheaply acquired – had been broken into, but with only the papers that had been left inside missing. Nevertheless it was good to hear him have his say, fearlessly availing himself of the right to the free speech he was exhorting his listeners to practice.

When we could briefly talk to each other again, Al told me that we had an appointment the next morning with the Secretary General of the ANC, Mr Oliver Tambo, at the law offices he ran in partnership with Mr Nelson Mandela in the city centre. To avoid drawing attention to ourselves, we had to approach the building from different directions and enter separately.

If Mr Tambo considered our request naïve, if not downright hazardous, he didn't let it show. Putting aside the papers he was working on as we entered his office, he rose to welcome us and pointed out a building on the opposite side of the street, where they suspected the Special Branch to be eavesdropping on them using new technology. During our visit Mr Mandela himself stepped briefly into the office to retrieve some papers from a filing cabinet.

Al gave Mr Tambo the same briefing that he had given me about his forthcoming mission to South West Africa – to explain why he thought it important that I reach New York and that I needed assistance to do so. Tambo replied with evident sympathy that he knew about my personal circumstances as well as those concerning South West Africa, but he regretted the ANC's inability to be of assistance. The party had not yet developed underground routes out of South Africa, he told us. Our meeting ended on that note. In the passage outside a number of clients were anxiously waiting their turns on the hard benches.

Al and I reacted differently to our meeting with the ANC. Although I was impressed with the warmth with which Advocate Tambo had received us, I was only too aware that they might have had reason to be suspicious of a person who had recently been denied a passport coming to them for assistance, towed in by an American about whom they couldn't have known much either.

Al, on the other hand, vented when we met up with each other after emerging separately from the Mandela-Tambo law offices. He found it incredible that the ANC could not yet smuggle people in and out of the country when, to him, it was as clear as daylight that a hardening of the confrontation with the regime was inevitable. He mused that as South Africa stood condemned for its abuse of an international trust in South West Africa, prying loose its grip needed to be a priority.

It was only much later that I heard that the meeting with Mr Tambo had been set up by Advocate Joe Slovo, leader of the South African Communist Party and husband of the journalist Ruth First. In due time Advocate Slovo would emerge as chief of staff of *Umkhonto we Sizwe* (The Spear of the Nation) and leader of the military confrontation with the regime that Al had anticipated.

All doubts that I might still have had about him evaporated on hearing him express a thought most South Africans would be afraid of uttering, that of armed conflict. It was also reassuring to note that Emory and Sherman, although visibly much less engaged than Al was, appeared to be ready to follow him through thick and thin.

Still, the fact remained that I had been denied cover and transportation by the only agency that could be safely approached for such assistance in Johannesburg. With this rejection, the difficulties involved in escaping from South Africa became a sobering reality.

However, Al was clearly not one to let the gauntlet lie when challenged. The same evening he announced that the three of them would accompany me to Serowe in Bechuanaland. The explanation was that Seretse Khama could be expected to make a bid for the independence of the British Protectorate in the near future. In that event, Khama would certainly like to know he had friends in New York. He could therefore be persuaded to lend me refuge until such time as Al and his friends could send me money to escape via Southern Rhodesia. Afterwards, the three of them would return to Johannesburg, to drive from there to Windhoek and return to make their exit from Jan Smuts Airport – as originally planned.

The success of the scheme hinged upon the reliability of their well-used Volkswagen, – a make Al for some reason was devoted to – even though other people had to drive and fix his model for him. I would learn later that, but for Sherman Bull's technical expertise, a trip they took into the Kalahari Desert to visit the Herero chief, Hosea Kutako, might have brought their mission to a sorry end.

After Al had informed us of his plan, there was nothing to do but await the conclusion of the NUSAS conference. In the meantime, as my departure from Johannesburg had to take place unobtrusively, I had to engage in a game of charades intended to mislead any possible observers. To advertise my intention to return to UCT at the beginning of term, I visited an educational charity run by Anglo-American, to inquire about the prospects of becoming a beneficiary of their vaunted stipend program. The toothy, newly-domiciled Dutch man who headed the program brightly went to great pains to explain that their policies made it impossible to award a bursary in cases like mine. Sitting there, I reflected on immigrants from Europe doling out alms to the needy in a country whose natural resources they had laid claim to as of by divine right.

With time on my hands I next availed myself of the opportunity to become marginally acquainted with the Golden City. Shown around by a couple of fellow students from UCT and meeting with some Wits students, Johannesburg made a much more agreeable impression on me than it was credited with elsewhere. One of the students, a psychology major, gladly shared with me the sobering insights she had gained doing research into drugs that stimulate the central nervous system.

On the final day of the conference there appeared a notice about a debating competition that was to be held that evening. The prize was the TB Davie Cup, instituted by NUSAS to honour the principal of UCT who had been most steadfast in the defence of the university's autonomy. Lowenstein urged me to enter the debate – so as to gain some experience in public speaking. There were two elimination rounds before the final – which brought me up against a fellow student from UCT. At this point I switched from English to Afrikaans – with the daft notion of demonstrating my command of both the country's two official languages. Later, one of the adjudicators, an Afrikaans-speaking actress, made a kind comment to me about the limitation of bi-linguality at any particular time.

At the conclusion of the conference, word went round that there would be a farewell party for the participants at the home of Advocate Bram Fischer, who was leading the defence at the on-going Treason Trial. When I arrived there it was to find a fellow student at UCT opening the door to me. This satisfied my curiosity about the identity of a young woman who had given me a lift from the campus into the city one afternoon. When a traffic constable put his head into the back of the convertible, to make a snide remark about my presence there, she muttered a response that should have devastated his ego – if he could have heard it. I was struck by the political awareness revealed by that retort.

The Fischers' spacious drawing room soon filled up as a representative sample of the country's people, gathered for a party that was as disdainful of apartheid legislation as could be imagined: Whites and Blacks eating, drinking and dancing together. As the evening progressed, the crowd swelled with the arrival of the likes of Oliver Tambo, Nelson Mandela, Ahmed Kathrada and other luminaries of the Congress movement and of the Johannesburg Bar. Music was provided by the cast of a stage production that had wowed audiences in Cape Town as well as in Johannesburg. Called *King Kong*, the score was composed by a Black South African, Todd Matshikiza, with the female lead sung by Miriam Makeba. That this boisterous event provided cover for confidential deliberations was also obvious.

CROSSING THE LIMPOPO

Our departure from a deserted Wits campus on a Saturday afternoon didn't lack comedy. It appeared that my rescuers and I had different ideas about where we had agreed to meet. Sherman did some nerve-racking rounds of the campus before finding me sitting where I thought we were supposed to be. We then had to stop at Al's hosts for the obligatory goodbyes. To avoid having to explain my presence in the Volkswagen, Sherman parked the Beetle out of sight of the grand mansion's front door. Al had to present an excuse to keep the hosts from coming over to the car to say good bye. From there our trip to the border of Bechuanaland took us uneventfully through Pretoria, the seat of the South African Reich.

To reduce the risk of being spotted, I was advised to shrink as deep as possible into the back seat that I occupied next to Emory. From that position the only sights visible as the Beetle sped through Pretoria were the tops of the famous jacaranda trees against a blue sky and the towers of the Union Buildings in the afternoon sun.

As we were speeding along through the Transvaal, Al returned to the ANC's apparent lack of readiness for a confrontation with the regime that he saw looming. He thought it incredulous that they didn't yet have underground routes in place to spirit people in and out of the country. None of us really knew what to expect at the border, except that we'd be crossing the Limpopo River, with a reputation for being crocodile infested. Yet the matter-of-factness with which my companions kept reviewing our options revealed a spirit that was impressive. Al was deadly serious about helping me get past eventual border guards, unseen, if that was possible, with recourse to more dramatic measures if such were unavoidable. In the back seat, Emory let me know that Al had done service in the US Army of the Rhine.

The realisation that I might become the cause of an ugly scrap with South African border guards soon bore down on me. Joining the discussion I therefore let them know that I was prepared to skirt the border point in the dark on foot and to swim the Limpopo – if there turned out to be water in it.

'In that case I'll go with him', Emory declared. Sherman explained that Emory was a candidate for the US Olympic swimming team.

It didn't take long, though, before Al squelched that idea. 'Nobody's going to swim', he said firmly, after which we drove on in silence.

'Why don't we hide him in the car?' Sherman suddenly called out from the driver's seat. To a chorus of 'Where?' he simply replied, 'behind the back seat', whereupon he stopped the car to have the luggage stowed in the space removed. With me on my back in the foetus position covered by their bags, the drive continued for the next several miles. Presently a hush descended in the car as the wheels began to roll smoothly and I realised we must be crossing a bridge. Continuing for some minutes more without a word being spoken, Sherman suddenly stopped the Volkswagen to let Al out to open a cattle-gate. As we came to a standstill on the other side, my companions shouted their relief into the night.

'Get out, Hans! You are now on British Territory', Al called out with a sanguinity that overlooked all the British territory yet to be traversed on the way to freedom. Overhead I could clearly see the Southern Cross hanging in place.

'BLOODY KAFFIR'

If our departure from Johannesburg had started somewhat untidily, bedding down for some hours of sleep in Palapye proved no less so. Palapye was a siding and connecting point for Serowe on the Cape to Rhodesia railway. The locals had long since put out the lights by the time we rolled in to find a bed for the night. A road sign directed us to a bar/hotel located at the railway station, but it was a rather morose proprietor who was eventually roused from his slumbers by Al's hammering at the front door and the frenetic barking of dogs at the back.

To beat the ban on Blacks sleeping on 'White' beds, even on British administered soil, I had to sneak into Emory's room only after my companions had been signed in. But being sure that he had spotted a *'bloody kaffir'*, the irate proprietor was damned if he would let him sleep in his hotel. As he was about to barge into our room an even more irate New York lawyer blocked his path. The man slunk back to his quarters to allow silence to return to the echoing corridor.

Serowe, the capital of the Bamangwato tribe, is situated some 50 kilometres west of Palapye. Al wanted me to be seen entering the village on foot – to keep people from wondering how I had arrived in Bechuanaland.

About ten kilometres from our destination they dropped me off while the three of them drove ahead to negotiate my stay with Seretse Khama, the premier citizen of the Protectorate.

I think the realisation of just how lonely the path was that I had chosen occurred powerfully to me as the sound of the Volkswagen died away. I knew that once I had crossed Botswana's borders, there was no turning back. A two-year sentence awaited anyone who had left the Union without a passport. Exile for me could only come to an end when I could return to a free South West Africa. As I started out in the direction the Volkswagen had gone the suitcase with the few items of clothing and one or two books I had brought along wasn't heavy, but it soon became burdensome to carry. As to passers-by who could have spread a rumour about my flight, there were few. Only an unsuspecting local teenager, with his mother aboard a sixteen-span ox-wagon loaded high with sacks of maize, raised dust on the road that day, moving in the direction I had come from. My three liberators returned from their errand as I reached the outskirts of Serowe. They were beaming. The Bamangwato chieftain had agreed to put me up until they had finished their mission to South West Africa. With the reassurance that as soon as they reached New York, they would find the means to have me join them, we waved each other goodbye.

SERETSE AND TSHEKEDI KHAMA

From a few brick-walled structures at its centre, the network of family compounds of thatched huts that formed the village of Serowe spread out in all directions. The Khama home, a new split-level villa, was situated by itself on a slight rise in the landscape a mile west, beyond the centrally located District Commissioner's[13] Offices.

The family was sitting in the balmy afternoon sun: husband, wife, three small children and a female household assistant. When I entered the yard Seretse Khama lightened the awkward moment with a welcoming, 'Hello, Hans. We have been wondering when you would be calling upon us!'

Mrs Ruth Khama rose to lead me to the room I would occupy for the next several weeks. It was certainly beyond my wildest expectations that temporary asylum would mean becoming a houseguest of the man who would be independent Botswana's first president. I felt completely out of place.

A group of locals arrived on some errand later that evening. For a magical moment the elaborate ritual of their salutation made the sandy yard

---

[13] District commissioners were the officials through which the Colonial Office in London exercised authority in the British Protectorates in Southern Africa.

take on the aspect of an ancient royal court. At a distance of several yards, they sank down on their knees in obeisance while uttering a respectful Setswana greeting: '*Dumela, Rra!*'. Their Chief stood solemnly erect and returned the greeting.

When weeks later I was about to take leave of the family, Mr Khama put a surprising request to me. Entering my bedroom to hand me a loan of thirty pounds, he said, 'If you should write anything about your experiences, Hans, please don't make any mention of what you have observed while staying with us.'

'Of course not, Mr Khama' I blurted out, somewhat fazed at the thought that he should feel the need to say so. At the same time it was the most personal thing he had said to me throughout my stay.

I thought I knew what had made him ask such a thing of me. The commotion caused by his marriage in London eleven years earlier had been something that not even a twelve-year old newspaper reader, as I was at the time, could have missed. The vengeance with which the South Africans waged war on relations between Blacks and Whites had cast a shadow on the fate of several families even in my hometown of Rehoboth. Unions that had been entered into, even before the South African ban on mixed marriages, had fallen into a legal limbo.

No sooner had the news broken of the Khama-Williams wedding than South Africa and Southern Rhodesia made highly charged representations to the British government to prevent Seretse Khama from returning to his home. Even the leader of the South African Parliamentary Opposition, Field Marshall Jan Christian Smuts, warned against recognising Seretse as the chief of his people. He declared, 'White South Africans were hardly sane on the subject of miscegenation.'

The Khama-Williams marriage had displeased even members of the young chief's own family, if for entirely different reasons. Tshekedi Khama, Seretse's uncle and Regent of the Bamangwato tribe during his minority and years of study abroad, was upset because he felt that by failing to obtain the sanction of his people to enter into the marriage, his nephew had risked the unity of the Bamangwato tribe. Tshekedi feared that feuds, and an eventual split within, could tempt South Africa to take control of the territory of Bechuanaland itself 'to restore order'.

The British government proved to be overly keen to appease White opinion in southern Africa. They exploited the schism that arose between the Regent and his nephew in a manner that would eventually enable them to remove both from fulfilling their roles as the unchallenged leaders of their people. Tshekedi was banished from Serowe and Seretse was prevented from returning home from England. It was only in September 1956, after both men, in an act of reconciliation, had renounced their claims to the chieftainship, that the British government would lift the restrictions imposed on them.

Tshekedi Khama was a name with which I had become acquainted much earlier – it must have been when I was merely ten years old and long before I could understand why my family mentioned him so often. It was only later that I learned of his energetic opposition to South Africa's efforts to gain international approval to annex South West Africa.

Tshekedi must have been among the first Black leaders in Africa to appreciate the potential of the United Nations as a tool for their own political prospects. Concerned about the consequences for Bechuanaland, should the nascent UN, with British support, grant South Africa sanction to annex South West Africa, he made several efforts in 1946 to make known the opposition of the region's African leadership to any such move. Amongst those who supported him were professor Z.K.Mathews of Fort Hare University College, Dr A.B. Xuma then heading the ANC, Professor D.D.T. Jabavu, President of the All African Convention, and Dr R.T. Bokwe, a distinguished medical personality.

As Regent of the Bamangwato people, it was to Tshekedi Khama that the Herero chiefs would turn when they were alerted about the fraudulent means[14] by which the South African regime was making ready to 'deprive them of their heritage'. Tshekedi would find them an emissary to represent them at the world body: Michael Scott, the Anglican priest who had become deeply involved in the brief post-war debate in South Africa about a future for the Territory's people.

A NEIGHBOURLY NON-VISIT

Tshekedi Khama died in London on 10 June 1959 in the presence of his nephew and of the Reverent Michael Scott, his adopted 'tribesman'.[15] He was buried in Serowe on 17 June. It was, therefore, a family in mourning to whom Al Lowenstein had turned when we arrived there just three weeks

---

[14] Mary Benson, in *Tshekedi Khama*, Faber and Faber 1960 p153, describes the South African 'assurance (given to tribesmen about the consequences of an annexation of the Territory by South Africa), (as) ambiguous to the point of dishonesty in view of the question put, and not unnaturally it served to obtain the required answer from a majority of the African population'.

[15] In her biography of Tshekedi Khama, Mary Benson, who had worked with both Khama and Scott, wrote a beautiful account of a friendship that could be credited with having prevented the 'incorporation' of South West Africa into the Union of South Africa, and hence placed the future independence of Namibia on a ratchet wheel: Mary Benson: *Tshekedi Khama*, 1960.

later, a family whose lives had been deeply affected by neighbouring South Africa's racist policies. Yet no rancour was apparent in anything said or done in my presence. The household appeared to be primarily preoccupied with the same things as all cattle farmers, though on a more impressive scale than I was acquainted with on the western side of the Kalahari.

Still, there was a ripple of excitement one forenoon when a black South African-registered limousine slowly approached the house and came to a stop at the far corner of the fence. Mr Khama was not at home at the time. With only Mrs Khama, the children and me inside the house, a maidservant went out to make inquiries. On her return, she informed us that the would-be visitor was the South African Minister of Agriculture. When he heard that Mr Khama wasn't home, he turned back.

The visit could have been historic, as it would be the first visit to the Khamas by a member of the South African Government. A few days later the Minister had a chance to clear up speculation about the purpose of his visit when Mr Khama attended an auction of cattle in the so-called Triangle where South African Whites could farm. When Mr Khama returned home that evening, he quietly recounted that the Minister, himself a cattle farmer, had attended the auction. However, even though they had been standing only yards apart, the Minister had studiously ignored him. If the snub had rankled, as it clearly did, I felt it was because courtesy was so much a part of Seretse Khama's personality. But I was also depressed by the possibility that the Minister's visit and subsequent behaviour might have had something to do with my presence in the Khama residence.

FRIENDLIER VISITORS

Among the people who made their appearance at the Khama residence on the outskirts of Serowe were Tshekedi's sons, Leapetswe and Sekgoma – destined to inherit the chieftaincy of the Bamangwato that Seretse had renounced for himself and his offspring. They were studying in Ireland at the time, but had returned to Serowe for their father's funeral. Z.K. Mathews and his wife – Khama family friends – also turned up one afternoon. After having been acquitted from the sham 'treason trial', Mathews had shortly before resigned as Principal of Fort Hare University, after losing the fight against the historic university being demoted to a tribal college.

When I withdrew to my room, Mrs Khama followed to draw me back and into the lively conversation that lasted past dinner and late into the night. In what might have been a return to normalcy after a month of mourning, the host revealed an impish sense of humour that had us all roaring with laughter: During his recent visit to London he had had himself cut a couple of bespoke dress suits by tailors in Regent Street. He now slipped into the bedroom to reappear in one after the other, striking the coquettish pose of a mannequin. Mathews was aware that my countryman, Kozonguizi, who had been one of his students at Fort Hare, had left for the UN earlier that year. Without him saying much more, I formed the impression that he approved of the path Kozo and I were on.

A Quaker couple, Myrtle and Philip Radley, to whom I had been introduced by Tulani Gcabashe in Cape Town, next passed by on their way to Nyasaland (Malawi). In Salisbury they would alert another couple of friends, Margaret and Stanley Moore, about the possibility that I might be passing through soon and asked them to put me up.

Right afterwards another couple of household friends dropped by for a visit. Like the Khamas', theirs was also a so-called mixed marriage: Dr Thuynsma was a Coloured doctor and his wife an Afrikaner nurse. To live as husband and wife they had to flee from their hometown of Kimberley to the village called Maun, located in the heart of the Kalahari Desert.

As one familiar with firearms, Dr Thuynsma was asked by Mr Khama to adjust the sights of his hunting rifle. Afterwards he handed me one round wherewith to try the gun. A few days later I was able to bring down a bush buck – after my host had missed twice. Mr Khama graciously praised me at dinner that evening for putting venison on the table.

Mrs Williams, Ruth Khama's mother, next arrived for a family visit. She invited me along with the children for tennis at the only court in the village, situated in the backyard of a shopkeeper's homestead. As an indication of the extent to which stress erases memory, I'd forgotten about those enjoyable afternoons spent in the company of a spritely elderly lady until the shopkeeper's wife reminded me about it and showed me the remains of their tennis court during a visit I was able to pay to Serowe in 1970.

I'd like to think that by allowing me privileged access to the life of their household, the Khamas had anticipated what I had let myself in for, and done what they could to help me prepare for it.

However, of more immediate concern to me was the question of my status within the Protectorate. On the Monday morning after my arrival in Serowe, Mr Khama had driven me to the District Commissioner's Office to report my presence. The Commissioner informed me that visitors from South Africa could enter any of the British protectorates of Basutoland, Bechuanaland and Swaziland and sojourn there for up to a month without applying for visas or registration.

Some twelve days after their departure from Serowe, Al called from London to announce his arrival there together with Emory and to reassure me that he was working on arrangements to finance my own onward travels. As agreed, I then sent a telegram to the UN's South West Africa Committee to request a hearing. However, as the days passed by without further hearing from Al, the pressure to move on began to tell on me. When the month drew to a close, the British District Commissioner summoned me to inquire whether I'd heard yet from my friend. I understood that beneath his smile there was the message that my presence in his territory had become a problem. Moreover, however graciously they were treating me, I felt the strain of overstaying my welcome in the Khama home.

CHAPTER FOUR

Helping hands

DALE CARNEGIE

As the days went by without further word from Al, I realised that raising money was proving more difficult than he had anticipated and that I might just as well make it overland northwards as far as I could get before pressure began to build up in South Africa to haul me back. I calculated that on a combination ticket of rail, foot and thumb, I could make it to beyond the borders of the Central African Federation (CAF), a British imperial design to unite the colonies of Southern and Northern Rhodesia and Nyasaland (now Zimbabwe, Zambia and Malawi respectively). To extend my reach I asked Mr Khama for a loan of thirty pounds, which he handed over with only the request not to divulge anything about my stay. The next evening he drove me to the train station at Palapye. There I boarded a goods train bound for the Rhodesias.

'So that's what you look like', a ruddy faced young officer in khaki shorts called out brightly when I entered his office at the border post of Plumtree the next morning. He had already received two telephone calls that morning with queries about me, one from the South African Press Association in Johannesburg and one from his superiors in Salisbury (now Harare), the capital of Southern Rhodesia.

He promptly put a call through to Salisbury whereupon he made me sign a form that declared me to be an undesirable immigrant. That done, he drove me back to the station in his Land Rover. There he entered an office to chat with his pals while waiting for a southbound train on which to put me – with orders to the conductor to see that I returned to where I had come from.

As the steam locomotive chugged through the Botswana bush that afternoon, I saw myself as having landed in stocks, for all of South Africa to deride or pity. At one point I closed a book I was trying to read when I realised that I had been turning the same page over and over again, missing the thread of thought from one page to the next. As to the immediate future, the certainty of a two-year prison sentence for the 'offence' of having left the country without a passport made me realise that indefinite sojourn in Bechuanaland had become inevitable. Ipso facto, notwithstanding its size, Bechuanaland itself had become a prison.

When the train finally reached Palapye station that evening, I sought out Paul Booys, a gentleman with whom I had become acquainted during a couple of visits to the station. Booys merely quipped that he had been expecting me back, and offered me a bed in his lounge. Together we listened to the evening news bulletin of the South African Broadcasting Corporation with a report of my attempt to cross the Rhodesian border. It ended with the gratuitous information that 'He is now believed to be on his way back to Bechuanaland'.

From the post office the next morning I sent a telegram to the UN Committee on South West Africa to request a postponement of the interview that they had granted me. Then I called Ernie Wentzel, a lawyer whom I'd met in Johannesburg, to ask for his opinion about my circumstance. Ernie's response was to advise me to report my presence to the local authorities and to remain where I was. His office was 'working on my case', he informed me to my surprise.

The District Commissioner of Serowe happened to be present at the Palapye police station when I arrived there to report my presence. He commented drily that it had been smart of me to knock at Rhodesia's door rather than to try to cross its territory without permission. 'They'd have sent you back to Pretoria,' he informed me.

Yet, when I inquired about asylum in Bechuanaland, his response was non-committal. It struck me that it was probably the first time a request for asylum had been put to the British Protectorate's authorities and that they hadn't yet worked out a policy on the matter. The Commissioner nevertheless instructed a police officer to take photographs of my head, front and in profile – for registration, I presumed, of the fugitive that I'd become.

A bookcase in Paul Booys' dining room was stocked with odds and ends of reading material. Tucked in among some cowboy pulp, my eye caught a title that, incongruously, looked as if it was addressed to me: Dale Carnegie, *How to Stop Worrying and Start Living*. I took it out to have a look at the contents but closed it after glancing at a page or two. I recall the lines: 'So you are worried! How do I know that? Well, why would you otherwise have picked up this book?' Then I opened it again.

Carnegie put his argument up front: If one could remove the cause of one's worries, why not do so and save oneself the anxiety? If there was nothing one could do to remove the cause, what was the point of worrying? Neither did I see any point in continuing to read what he had written.

Nevertheless, the book became like a magnet, drawing myself to it, only to have me put it back after reading a few cases of the inveterate worriers Carnegie had made to see the futility of their self-flagellation. And then it happened. I found myself reflecting quite dispassionately about how I was to sustain myself in the situation in which I had landed myself. Considering that I might have become somewhat better qualified to teach than when I had left Wesley, I decided to apply for a job as a teacher. I promptly made inquiries – only to learn that on a teacher's salary I should be able to pay the plane fare to New York in two years' time if, in the meantime, I could make do without any food, new clothing or having to pay for a place to stay.

And then it occurred to me that I had not seen any photographer or photo shop in Serowe, said to be the largest of the country's villages. With that I recalled the photographers who had trawled the Rehoboth district and reasoned that the locals in Bechuanaland would be no less ready to pay for images of themselves than they had been in Rehoboth. But I would have to try. Imagining that even the flora and fauna might be pressed into an income-generating scheme, I wrote to the Kodak Company in Johannesburg to inquire about photographic materials.

However, in due time I would learn that other people had begun to become concerned about my circumstances.

A few days after my return to Palapye, Mr Khama sent word that it would be inadvisable for me to remain there, and that I should move to a room in his old house in Serowe. It overlooked the Khotla (customary court cum village assembly grounds). The only other resident in the house happened to be a Swazi of the Dlamini clan who was employed in the tribal administration. This brought a welcome change. In the UCT courses in Native Administration and Law, the name Dlamini had figured in many of the cases that defined the legal framework within which Blacks had to negotiate their lives. Mr Dlamini's familiarity with those cases now provided the welcome change of subject in conversations.

From student friends in Cape Town I received three letters; one from Sonny Kaplan who advised the 'hero of the plot' to 'essay wider horizons'. The second letter was from the classmate, Nola Levy, with whom I had first spoken nearly a year after we had begun attending the same courses. I would read and re-read those letters, drawing comfort from them even though I could sense that my friends had reconciled themselves to the parting of our ways. The third letter, however, would have it otherwise. It came from a classmate at Wesley Teacher Training School. Her mother had gone to intercede on my behalf with the Deputy Minister of Internal Affairs, P W Botha. Mr Botha had given her mother his personal assurances that nothing would befall me if I should return to the Union to resume my studies at UCT. Both my erstwhile classmate and her mother therefore urged me to return.

That third letter upset me deeply. It was clear to me that Mr Botha's supplicants had not understood that I had set out to have his regime's authority abrogated in the country of my birth. In any case, the thought of returning to plead for their forgiveness was out of the question.

And then, when I had fairly reconciled myself to the prospect of settling down in Bechuanaland, Mr Khama came to see me with a letter he had received from Mburumba Kerina in New York. Referring to himself as 'Representative of South West Africa at United Nations', Mburumba stated that he had just been informed by the United Nations that I was temporarily with Khama's family in Bechuanaland, and that my application for a hearing was being considered. With reference to the UN's site agreement with the USA that entitled me to a US visa, he requested Mr Khama's assistance to secure me a visa from the Americans in either Rhodesia or Cape Town.

As Mburumba appeared to have lost sight of the situation that Mr Khama found himself in, and for me to return to Cape Town was equally out of the question, we let the matter drop.

Yet shortly afterwards, a second letter from Mburumba arrived with information about the efforts he had made on my behalf 'at Kozo's request'. He had, he wrote, 'requested the representative of the Ghana government to request Prime Minister Nkrumah to personally intervene in [my] case by requesting the Prime Minister of the Central African Federation to allow [me] to pass through their territory as soon as possible'.[16] He added that Al Lowenstein was a personal friend, and that his wife had helped Al 'very much to prepare for his trip to South West Africa'.

Not many days afterwards Mr Khama again dropped by one forenoon. It was to inform me that if I would again present myself at the Rhodesian border, they would let me through. In an apparent reference to the telegrams I'd sent from the local post office prior to my departure three weeks earlier, he only cautioned me against letting anyone else in on my plans. At dusk that evening, he sent a driver in his pick-up truck to transport me once again to the station in Palapye where for the second time I would board a goods train for Plumtree.

This time I could appreciate the feigned surprise that the ruddy-faced officer put on at my persistence, as he put it, while reaching for a ledger that

---

[16]   What neither Mburumba nor I were aware of was that the case of my passport had become a matter of contention between the United Kingdom and the Union of South Africa, where the most wide-ranging interests of both states would be cited. See appendix: **Documents pertaining to the 'Beukes case'.**

evidently dealt with my case. Very recently he had made me sign an order barring me from entering the Central African Federation. Now he made me sign a document reiterating that I was a prohibited immigrant but granting me five days' grace to make myself scarce.

As I lolled in the goods train chugging onwards towards Bulawayo that afternoon, I reflected that the only risk I faced was getting abducted and returned to Pretoria with its notorious Central Prison. However, recalling my recent introduction to Dale Carnegie's art of living, I reminded myself that it was pointless to worry about it – since there was little I could do to avoid it if the South Africans put their minds to it.

The train kept stopping for long periods at every siding along the way. When it finally screeched to a halt at nine that evening, the night train to Salisbury had just started to pull out. I made a dash for the exit to find a taxi.

With a reflex dating back to my first taxi ride in Cape Town, where suitcases were barred inside the cabin, I slung my suitcase onto the roof rack and told the driver to 'follow that train'. He knew its first stop would be at a siding a few miles outside the city and, gamely responding to my anxiety, soon exceeded 70 miles an hour along the dirt road. Within minutes we were in sight of the train, and when it slowed down at the approaching juncture, the driver swung off the main road to enter the station just as it came to a stop.

But it was with abject dismay that on reaching for the suitcase I discovered that it wasn't there. Not only would I have no change of clothes for the rest of my flight, but the only papers with my name on them were in the suitcase. With nothing to be done, I resigned myself to whatever might happen and asked the taxi driver to take me to a place where I could spend the night. Early the next morning I returned to the taxi rank to make inquiries – just in case. Incredibly, as I was talking to the proprietor, a man called. The night before, he had been overtaken by a taxi that threw up a cloud of dust. The next thing he saw was a suitcase lying in the road.

With gratitude in my heart for the integrity of an anonymous Rhodesian, I next took up a position along the main road out of town in the direction of Salisbury, to thumb a lift. I didn't have long to wait. The first driver happening by turned out to be a North American, who welcomed having a passenger for a drive of several hours. With a lot to get off his chest regarding the people among whom he had settled, I didn't have to tell much about myself before he dropped me half-way to Salisbury.

Conversation was easier with my second benefactor that day, a cattle farmer of British stock who reared Herefords in the Rhodesian Highlands. With a frame as brawny as that of his beef cattle, he was generous in his understanding of his adopted country's people and their ways. His warmth brought me close to revealing my own errand to him, but prudence prevailed. Asking no questions, he delivered me at the doorsteps of my designated hosts: the Quakers, Margaret and Stanley Moore, and their three young daughters.

The Moore's had been alerted to expect my arrival by Philip and Myrtle Radley, who had passed by the Khama home some weeks earlier. Quakers also go by the name of Friends, and the family instantly made me feel welcome in the first White home, except for that of the Khama's, to offer me a bed anywhere in southern Africa. I was particularly impressed with the easy relationship they had with the local man and woman who worked for them.

On my arrival Stanley handed me a telegram from Mr Khama informing me that he had received from Al Lowenstein in New York the sum of 750 dollars for my ticket. Mr. Khama asked for instructions as to where to send the money.

I immediately phoned him with the request to deduct the thirty pounds that he had advanced me and to send the remainder to the bank where Stanley Moore was employed. The next morning Margaret took me to the American consulate where I applied for a visa, and then to book a seat on the Saturday evening plane from Johannesburg to London, which made a stop in Salisbury to pick up passengers. For good measure, she enlisted the Quaker representative in Salisbury, the American Mr George Loft, to identify me for the purposes of my visa application.

A departmental memo dated September 1959 (see appendix) records that, according to the US Consul, Mr Loft had been 'an unwilling companion and not at all happy about being involved'. This observed unhappiness had a different source than suspected. Mr Loft informed the Consul that he had 'arranged accommodation at one of his hostels' for me – a wording that had clearly been designed to deflect attention from the Moores.

Mr Loft invited us all for dinner at his home. With Black servants in white livery called upon to serve cocktails and dinner, it turned out to be a household that was run by traditional colonial custom. Noticing that the headwaiter avoided making eye contact with me, I felt out of place that evening.

It was a time of turmoil in the would-be Central African Federation, which had been formed by the British in 1953, and where fewer than half a million European colonists were handed authority to govern eight million native peoples in a land area of half a million square miles. Native resentment had broken out in violent confrontations in both Nyasaland and Northern Rhodesia earlier in 1959. With a number of people thrown into jail throughout the Federation, the political crisis was quelled but by no means resolved. In

Salisbury the tension was palpable.

Yet the papers heralded the arrival in town that week of an uncommonly accomplished Black man, a Nigerian who had been knighted by the Queen of Great Britain for his services to medicine, and elected Vice Chancellor and Principal at one of his home country's universities. Thrilled by the first ever such visit to their city, Margaret Moore found me equally keen to attend the lecture by the Nigerian. He was to speak in a hall that had to be granted special clearance to host the 'multi-racial' event.

Resplendently attired in colourful robes, the great man played the part. Striding to the dais he delivered a talk revealing deep insight into the problems that Nigerians, and the continent as a whole, could expect on gaining independence. It was an intellectual tour de force well worth attending. Yet it struck me that the Rhodesians could not have drawn much comfort from what the visitor had had to say. Neither did their newspapers do much to let their readers know what he had tried to convey.

Margaret next drove me to the campus of the fledgling University of Rhodesia where a White man, the historian Terence Ranger, and some of his colleagues were discussing their project: the rediscovery of African history. As I understood it, it was a project which told African history as a continuous narrative from an African point of view. I was not aware of anything similar being done in South Africa.

Even though I couldn't quite shake off the feeling that I was living dangerously, I thus found my days of transit in Salisbury most stimulating. Nevertheless, the premonition that I was living dangerously was so strong that I decided not to believe that I had escaped Pretoria's grip before the plane to London had lifted off from Nairobi, its next stop, that Saturday evening. Indeed, it was only once it had landed at Khartoum at midnight that I felt relief.

CATCHING UP WITH KOZO

At sunrise the next morning I woke up to an exquisite feeling just as the plane broke clear of a bank of clouds over the Mediterranean. With the shore of the African continent receding below, I indulged in a little *schadenfreude* at the embarrassment I knew my escape must have caused the men in Pretoria. I imagined them spread out prostrate on a rugby field behind me as I dived over the goal line to score a try.

As I would learn years later, on opening the file with my name on it in the National Archives in Pretoria, my reflections aboard the plane that morning were not off the mark. Enraged by the British Government's orders to the Rhodesians to let me through – something about which I had been oblivious – the Secretary of Foreign Affairs had called in the British Ambassador late on Saturday evening, to let him know in great detail about Dr Verwoerd's displeasure. In fact, the démarche signalled recognition by the South African Government that their hopes for an integration of the British Protectorates into the Union, reiterated by Dr Verwoerd in Parliament only a few months earlier, was groundless. When push came to shove, the British could not be depended on to respect South Africa's own understanding of its interests. The extensive and at times quite virulent exchanges with the British officials can be seen to have presaged the Union's exit from the Commonwealth.

When some hours later I could alight onto English soil at a London airport shrouded in thick fog, I felt no more than slight apprehension about there not being somebody to meet me. This was in stark contrast to the constant anxiety that I could never shake off in Britain's African Protectorate and in its Crown Colony.

As I entered the arrivals barracks, a young Englishwoman stepped forward to introduce herself as Doris, the Reverend Michael Scott's secretary. Doris led me past the immigration officials who appeared quite satisfied with the only identification that I could show, the American visa attached to a sheet of paper with my picture clipped onto it.

From there Doris shunted me aboard a succession of buses and underground trains to Friends House near Euston Square. As we entered the mansion's foyer, a couple of bare legs came leisurely down the main stairs, and I instantly knew that they could belong to none other than Jariretundu Kozonguizi, 'Kozo' for short.

I had caught up with only the second of my countrymen to have escaped the reach of the apartheid regime.

I first met Kozo while he was a student at Fort Hare University and I was still attending high school. Stocky of build and sporting a pair of black pants and a spotless white shirt, he had exuded the air of a young man on the go. This time, some five years later, his movements were more measured and his laughter more readily aroused. On this first opportunity to become better acquainted there was much laughter, not least at the irony of finding ourselves in the White man's world on a quest for relief from the White man's oppression.

After lunch Kozo invited me for a walk about town that took in the spectacular orators of Hyde Park's Speakers' Corner, followed by a wide-screen film, as we were on our way back to Friends House later that evening. Along the way he made me aware of the pitiable spectacle of women standing half-hidden in dilapidated doorways, open solicitation having recently been outlawed.

Kozo's account that day of how he had managed to reach London and New York – outwitting the officers in charge of the sub-continent's colonies and saved by pure chance on several occasions – was as absorbing as the tale of the ancient Greek, Ulysses.

Many years later I found a confidential departmental memo deposited in the South African National Archives. It substantially corroborated the description of the route Kozo had described to me when we met in London:

'The South West African, Fanuel Jariretundu KOZONGUIZI, of Herero descent, first came to the official notice in August 1954, when, as a student at Fort Hare, he addressed a petition to the United Nations complaining of the 'oppression' of the non-European inhabitants of South West Africa by the Union Government and protesting against the alleged intention of the Union Government to annex or incorporate the territory. Again, in December of that year he wrote a letter to the Reverend Michael Scott at the United Nations, attacking the Union Government. This letter was read to the United Nations by Scott.

'In October, 1957, Kozonguizi applied for a passport to attend the General Assembly of the United Nations as a petitioner. Since the Union Government has consistently maintained that the Charter of the United Nations does not authorise the United Nations and its subsidiary bodies to grant oral hearings to petitioners on South West Africa, Kozonguizi was refused passport facilities to enable him to proceed to the United States.

'His departure from South West Africa in February of this year was thus entirely unauthorised. What he had in his possession was an ordinary reference-book, such as is carried by all adult male Bantu in the Union. In this book was a false and unauthorised endorsement which purported to validate it for travel by its holder to various African territories 'on a missionary tour'.

'Having entered the Federation of Rhodesia and Nyasaland illegally from the Bechuanaland Protectorate, and having during February and March also visited Kenya and Tanganyika, Kozonguizi contrived to persuade the Belgian Consul in Lusaka to give him a transit visa for the Belgian Congo in his reference-book, and on the strength of this he entered the Congo early in April, en route to Ghana. As doubt was expressed by the airline with which he proposed to travel about the validity of his 'travel document', he applied to the Union's Consulate-General in Leopoldville for a passport to enable him to complete the last stage of his tour. He was accordingly given a proper South

African passport valid until the 30th of April, 1959, and for travel to Ghana, the Belgian Congo and the Union of South Africa only: an endorsement was made to the effect that the passport 'should not be renewed or its validity extended without reference to the Department of the Interior, Pretoria.

'Having reached Ghana, Kozonguizi, it is understood, endeavoured without success to secure some sort of travel document from the Ghanaian authorities on which he would be able to continue his intended journey to New York. He had also attempted earlier, while in Dar-es-Salaam, to acquire papers which would enable him to journey to England, but had been unsuccessful.

'He then turned to the United States Embassy in Accra for assistance to enable him to get to New York. The Embassy referred to Washington for instructions, saying that Kozonguizi had a South African passport endorsed for travel in Africa only which was due to expire on the 30th April, 1959. The Department of State had previously been informed by the Secretariat of the United Nations that the Committee on South West Africa had granted a request for a hearing by Kozon[g]uizi; and the Secretary of State, acting jointly with the United States Attorney-General, waived the passport requirement, permitting the issuance by the Embassy in Accra of an appropriate visa to Kozon[g]uizi. The United States authorities claim that the action taken by them in this connection was not discretionary with the United States Government but was in compliance with its obligation under the Headquarters Agreement between the United States and the United Nations.

'Armed with an entry visa for the United States Kozon[g]uizi there-upon proceeded to the United Kingdom where he was looked after by members of the African Bureau who also assisted him in his onward passage to New York which he reached at the end of April.

'From the foregoing it will be seen that Kozon[g]uizi succeeded in reaching the United Nations Headquarters in New York by means of misrepresentation and deception. Despite these, his efforts would have been unavailing had it not been for the facilities granted him by the United States authorities. It would appear that the latter's interpretation of Section 11, coupled with Section 13, of the United Nations Headquarters Agreement is that the United States is obliged not merely <u>not to impose impediments</u> to the transit of persons to and from the United Nations Headquarters, but also <u>specifically to grant visas</u> to such persons. This is an interpretation which to our mind is debatable, but, even if it were not, the question arises whether the obligation resting on the United States could be construed as embracing assistance to a person who has left his own country illegally and pursues his way by fraud and deception.

'On the 1st May, 1959 Kozonguizi made a statement at the 102nd meeting of the Committee on South West Africa, which was a tissue of half-truths, outright distortions and gross exaggerations:

'Sovereignty over South West Africa, he claimed, rested not with the Union Government but with the indigenous (non-white) peoples. The former was pursuing a policy which envisaged 'the perpetual domination and enslavement of the coloured races by the white races,' which demanded 'the ruthless repression of all thought and movement of the coloured man except if it be in the interests of the white man,' which manifested 'no respect for humanity and in its brutal implementation loses all regard for the soul of the non-white-skinned man.' He appealed to the United Nations to save the people of South West Africa from 'the irresponsible and atrocious care of the Union Government' and warned that even if legal action were contemplated the Union would in the meantime continue to 'perpetrate atrocities in South West Africa. Finally he averred that the South African Government had 'transformed our country into a huge concentration camp and our people into slaves, in the name of its exclusive policy of white supremacy'.

'Kozonguizi will probably stay on in New York for the Fourteenth Session of the General Assembly.'
DEPARTMENT OF EXTERNAL AFFAIRS
PRETORIA
22nd July, 1959

The departmental scribe made no mention of the fact that Kozo's errand had been at the behest of the venerable Chief of the Hereros, Hosea Kutako. Having laid the groundwork for the first non-racist political party, the South West Africa National Union (SWANU), it was an assignment that he had been uncomfortable with, Kozo told me. SWANU was to be officially launched later that year and he feared that his acting on behalf of the chief might be used to question his own independence.

Yet, having been appointed by his elders to the Chiefs' Council, he felt bound to take on the assignment – not least because they had provided the funds to sustain him. The extended detours he had made to Kenya and Tanganyika alone, in search for a port of exit from the continent, would have been impossible without the means they had put at his disposal.

Kozo accompanied me to the Africa Bureau on the morning after my arrival in London. The founders of the Bureau were bound together by their interest in Africa and the desire to provide a support base for Africans from the colonies who were on political errands to the seat of Empire. The seriousness of what I let myself in for would be impressed upon me as we entered the premises of the Bureau. I felt myself weighed and appraised by Jane Symonds, the secretary in charge, just as I had been by her assistant, Doris, the day before, and as I would be by Mr Scott himself when he arrived later that day.

On the other hand, the needs to which the Bureau catered were amply demonstrated that day as well. Outside Kozo's cubicle, where stacks of newspapers from South Africa and Windhoek testified to the diligence with which he was keeping abreast of developments 'at home', there sat a White South African, Patrick van Rensburg. He had recently resigned from his country's diplomatic service. Whatever the reasons had been, his presence there suggested that he had cut his bonds with the apartheid regime and his country.

The second South African to drop by later that day was Tennyson Makiwane, like Kozo an alumnus of Fort Hare University and one of the 156 accused in the Treason Trial. As one of the ANC's most capable organisers, he had been sent out of the country in early 1959 to organise a boycott of South African goods abroad and was travelling up and down the British Isles in pursuit of that objective.

The following day two leading politicians from the Central African Federation came by: burly Joshua Nkomo from Southern Rhodesia, accompanied by the dapper Kanyama Chiume from Nyasaland. Having been abroad while the colonial authorities were cracking down on their parties, the two were on a speaking tour of protest. The anger by which Nkomo was visibly driven allowed for no small talk between us.

THE REVEREND MICHAEL SCOTT

When the Reverend Scott arrived at the Bureau, he summoned me into his office. I didn't know what to expect from the man whose name at home had been a by-word for his efforts at the UN to prevent South Africa from gaining sanction to annex South West Africa; he was one of the people who had requested Al Lowenstein to undertake the journey to South West Africa. The figure before me was gaunt and reserved. Perhaps I had expected a sign of approbation, but none was forthcoming.

Mr Scott's only comment after greeting me was to apologize for having been unable to send me a plane ticket to London, as well as being unable to pay for my ticket to New York. It was a matter about which I could put his mind at rest. He next suggested that the Bureau call a press conference the following day to enable me to say what I had to say to the press. And with that he let me go.

This brief meeting fully brought home to me what I had let myself in for. To be grilled at a press conference was not something that I had even thought of.

I felt further challenged when Kozo showed me a newspaper clipping with the allegation that both my grandfather and father were unhappy about my decision to go to the United Nations. Speaking to a group of foreign correspondents that had descended on Rehoboth after one of its sons became notorious, Grandfather reportedly said that I hadn't been authorised to attack the South African Government while abroad. They quoted my mother blaming the government for my having become a bitter young man.

It was because I was fully aware that my family would never agree to my departure from the country for an indefinite period that I had left without asking for their permission. Yet knowing what they stood for, I drafted a statement which Doris typed out. In it I claimed that I would be speaking for 'my people' and that I knew I had their support – and handed it to the half dozen or so journalists who turned up the next morning at ten.

My first press conference turned out much less terrifying than I had feared. The questions put by the London journalists revealed that they had come to hear a fresh assessment of the situation in South Africa from a presumably informed student activist. It was of course a presumption for which the government in Pretoria was entirely responsible. I was particularly interested to make the acquaintance of Colin Legum of the *London Observer*, himself with a background in South African politics and one of the Bureau's founders. I had become familiar with his columns from the Khama's subscription to the *Observer* in Serowe.

From Kozo and Tennyson Makiwane's responses after the journalists left, I felt reassured that my responses had passed muster. Two days later, however, I would be appalled to read a South African press report that at the UN I was going to speak for 'the Coloured people'.

How was I to be able to let their readers know, I wondered, that among 'my people' I counted my Oupa Tobias Platt, a respected Damara and my mother's step-grandfather, on whose knees I had sat as a child; that among my ancestors there was a Herero man; that I identified with the Ovambo farm workers on contract throughout the territory as much as I did with the wretches that were daily sentenced – in court cases that literally lasted no more than three minutes – to three months in jail for being caught without passes in the land of their birth. Stowed together with them in a court's ante-room in Windhoek, I myself had been fined twenty guineas (this curiosity inherited from Great Britain that spelled a sum of one pound and one shilling, or twenty-one shillings) or two weeks in jail for having been in possession of some .22 cartridges that I had forgotten I was carrying around in a leather jacket pocket.

When we met again some weeks later in New York, Kozo would show me new clippings with the unsettling remark, 'Your people didn't seem all too happy about what you said, Hans.'

An Afrikaans paper had published the angry reactions of anonymous 'responsible Coloured leaders in Cape Town and Johannesburg' to alleged claims that I spoke on behalf of their people. 'Ridiculous', they were quoted as having spitted out. A 'prominent Coloured from Johannesburg' one clearly ignorant of my status as a native of South West Africa, was quoted as saying 'Why should we be talking at all about a man who says that he feels no loyalty towards South Africa?'

The discomfort I felt on reading that blast was to be at all associated in anybody's mind with the likes of such men who seemed to define their own lives by using the terminology of race.

The Reverend Michael Scott left London mid-week for an engagement in Oslo. He had been invited to open the academic year's programme of Saturday evening debates in the Student Union of the University of Oslo. At the time, the Union was regarded as the most vibrant platform outside of the Storting (National Assembly) for debating foreign policy issues in Norway. On being informed about my arrival in London, the students called the Africa Bureau with the request that I reroute my ticket to New York via Oslo so as to join up with the Reverend Scott for the debate about South Africa's apartheid policies.

Next, a Norwegian correspondent in London, Richard Hermann, called at the Africa Bureau with a request to conduct an interview with me. He treated me to lunch at a restaurant frequented by Members of Parliament before getting down to the questioning. His questions, like those of his British colleagues, revealed to me European anxieties about the future of their kith and kin in southern Africa. It alerted me to the issues that needed to be taken up when addressing White audiences. The first occasion for that would present itself when I landed in Oslo later that week.

Before my departure for the Norwegian capital, Kozo warned me about what to expect. Together with Tennyson Makiwane he had been on a 'mission' to Denmark that had carried them to the west coast of the Scandinavian country. The children there had never seen a Black person before. Soon a string of them, staring in disbelief, would follow behind him and Tennyson wherever they went. Their embarrassed Danish host was eventually prevailed upon to translate the insistent query of one little boy, 'Don't they have soap in the country from where they come?'

TO A TASTE OF FREEDOM

The seat next to mine on the plane to Oslo was occupied by a fur merchant on his way home. Having grown up in a Karakul-pelt country myself, we had plenty to talk about. As the plane taxied to a standstill in front of the terminal building, my companion glanced through the porthole and remarked quietly, 'I think there is a welcoming party for you out there.'

Nothing could have prepared me for what would start at that moment – and keep rolling until my departure three days later. We were still unfastening our seat belts when an airhostess arrived to lead my way to the exit ahead of the other passengers. As I stepped out onto the ramp, a young woman came charging up with a bunch of flowers for me, her broad smile lit up by the flashes from a battery of press cameras on the tarmac. It was Mariken Vaa from the Student Representative Council. A reporter from the Norwegian Broadcasting Corporation (NRK) next stepped forward with the invitation that I use his microphone to greet the people of Norway. While I was struggling to find words adequate to this unexpected elevation, a gangling character stepped forward, indicating that time was up.

'There are people waiting for you at the University Square,' he said as the radio reporter let go of me. Engagingly nonchalant, Dag Halvorsen introduced himself as an SRC official. Leaving my suitcase tag with yet another member of the SRC, Dag, Mariken Vaa and Berge Furre, the Chairman of the SRC, led me straight past passport control into a waiting taxi for the ten-minute drive into the city centre.

'I hope you have had some practice in public speaking,' Halvorsen remarked, almost as an afterthought, as we took our seats. As the taxi picked up speed, he explained that they had drummed up a demonstration and that the people there would expect me to say something. With that he reverted to his mother tongue to converse with his companions while addressing occasional questions at me. When the taxi came to a stop I still had no idea what to say as they led me through a crowd of people gathered in front of the university's Great Hall. A dais with microphones had been raised on the first platform. A row of students, male and female, had taken up position behind the dais, holding aloft torches and banners with texts welcoming me and denouncing apartheid. After words of welcome by university officials, I was invited to make a statement. The scene facing me was one of utter incongruity: a mighty crowd of white faces looking up at me in expectation.

At that moment I wished I was back in Serowe. Inwardly I had my say about the Verwoerd regime for finding myself there. By this time I had stopped thinking about what to say and simply hoped the right words would present themselves. When I opened my mouth it was to perjure myself. I declared it to be the happiest day of my life. Mercifully, Chief Albert Luthuli's remarks, when he spoke to an American journalist in Cape Town months before, came to mind. Even though his reasoning got somewhat garbled in my delivery, I tried to convey his insistence on a peaceful resolution of the conflicts between Blacks and Whites.

From the University Square I was transported to the Student Union headquarters for an informal encounter with a number of journalists. The questions they asked were the same as the American journalist had put to Luthuli at the City Hall in Cape Town; they were not hard to parry. It would be late that evening before I would finally be accompanied to a hotel and left to reflect on what I had been through that day.

I had been a witness to a Scandinavian city's people remonstrating against the policies of their kith and kin in South Africa; Whites had demonstrated for the rights of Blacks – with me willy-nilly as a stand-in. It was a sobering thought to try to get to sleep on.

The front-page headlines in practically all the city's newspapers the next morning would confirm my perceptions. No state visit from South Africa could have earned greater attention than had been given to the 'South African student' – with summaries of the opinions that I had expressed. The reports made it sound as if I spoke for the whole of Black southern Africa.

AFTER BREAKFAST Dag Halvorsen, in company with the Reverend Scott, arrived at the hotel to take us on a round of formal visits. In turn we would be met by Hans Engen, the Deputy Foreign Minister of Norway; Gunnar Jahn, the Chairman of the Norwegian Nobel Committee; Finn Moe, the Chairman of the Storting's Foreign Affairs Committee; and Konrad Nordahl, the Chairman of the Norwegian Federation of Trade Unions – all men of considerable influence in the nation's affairs.

At the Foreign Office I felt uncomfortable about the official interest that my arrival in the country appeared to have aroused. It made me apologise to the Deputy Foreign Minister for having become an issue in Norway's relations with South Africa. Mr Engen graciously denied that this was the case.

At each meeting Rev Scott would put forward his practiced argument, quietly but insistently: if Norway and the West wanted to show their opposition to South Africa's racial policies, they had a golden opportunity to do so through action regarding the territory of South West Africa, where South Africa was abusing an international trust to which Norway was party. Norway had been one of the signatories that gave South Africa its mandate to rule over South West Africa.

In discussions with the Reverend Scott, who had arrived in Oslo two days before me, student leaders had decided to establish a South Africa Committee whose stated goal was to inform the Norwegian public about anti-apartheid measures that could be taken. Mr Jahn had been invited to chair the committee, although, as he told us, he was less happy about heading a boycott campaign. There was nevertheless no mistaking the veteran liberal politician's concern about the South Africa issue. He questioned us exhaustively about the prospects for a peaceful resolution of the looming confrontation between Blacks and Whites. It was quite clear that he had no high opinion South Africa's rulers, whom he compared to those in power in the Soviet Union. Chuckling, he recalled an official visit he had paid to the latter. A self-opinionated Communist Party Commissioner had kept lecturing him about the shortcomings of Norwegian society – with its nobility – as compared to the Soviet Union where equality reigned.

It had given him great satisfaction, Mr Jahn told us, to squelch the insult by expressing surprise at so brash a demonstration of ignorance about history by an official of the Communist Party – a group that had arrogated the correct interpretation of world history, no less. He would have expected the Commissioner to know that Norway had done away with its nobility nearly a century before the thought had even occurred to the Russians.

There was an inscrutable smile on the face of Reverend Michael Scott as we emerged from Mr Jahn's office.

A support group for Michael Scott that included university teachers as well as the prominent Quaker couple of Mr Diderik Lund and his wife Mrs Sigrid Helliesen, next had to be addressed at a lunch gathering in the Continental Hotel. In one of those striking coincidences which I would be encountering not infrequently, I would learn that Myrtle Radley, whom I had last seen in Serowe, had spent the war years as a house guest of the Lund family. From there she had kept the British Intelligence Service informed about the movements of the German occupation forces.

On the Saturday morning a journalist working for an illustrated weekly news magazine, Gunne Hammarström of *Billedbladet Nå*, called to take me on a sightseeing-cum-interview tour of the city. I gathered that the magazine catered for a conservative readership, yet in Hammarström's entertaining company I could detect nothing of the difficulties that I thought people of conservative persuasion would have relating to Blacks. As we passed a newsstand I caught sight of my name on the front page of a newspaper. Ordering the driver to stop, Hammarström secured a copy of *Arbeiderbladet*, the governing Labour Party's mouthpiece, which he wrapped in a copy of *Morgenbladet*, a Conservative daily. He couldn't let anyone see him buy that paper, he explained with an apologetic smile, adding that while we had our apartheid, they had their political differences as well.

After treating me to a fine lunch at a hillside restaurant with a spectacular view of the city and adjoining fjord, Hammarström wrote an informative piece about the policies of the apartheid regime and about my departure from South Africa. Printed over the magazine's cover the caption read '*Thank You, Freedom Tastes Fine*'

The Saturday evening debates of the Student Union took place in a location known as *Kroa* (The Inn). It was located in a basement hall where a central aisle divided the Radicals from the Conservatives. The dais was placed in front of a raised platform where an upright piano stood on one side. A bar and stalls occupied the back of the hall.

Presentations by the Rev Scott and me were followed by a debate that was interesting for what it revealed about prevailing attitudes to Africans' quest for liberation. The first question from the Conservative side was whether Blacks could govern themselves; the second revealed anxiety about our attitudes towards communism.

In my view the first question proceeded from a mystification of the process of government that in the colonial context was the justification for 'civilised' Europeans taking control of all aspects of the common society.[17] The second question held support for our liberation at ransom – with the price an assurance that Western interests would never be put at risk, if a concession were to be made on the first question. It was of course an assurance no Black

---

[17] In early 1960 when 'the Congo crisis' broke and the Western media used alarm headlines to report the death of a few Whites at the hands of advancing Black hordes, Sven Hamrell, a journalist on Dagens Nyheter, the premier Swedish newspaper, did something extraordinary. He got hold of a book published in 1906 by a Swede who had spent stolen time in the Belgian King Leopold's Congo and on his return home published a booklet with the misleading title: '*Under Palmernas Skugge*' (Under the Shade of the Palm Trees). The booklet provided a detailed account of the reign of terror to which the Congolese were subjected by Europeans. Hamrell wrote and Dagens Nyheter published a review of the book as if it had come hot off the press. Thereafter Hamrell campaigned for the establishment of a Scandinavian Institute of African Studies in Uppsala – so as to heighten his people's insight into African history and contemporary affairs.

person could give without betraying his peoples' right to choose their form of government, the exercise of which right, paradoxically, spelled the supposed dividing line between the so-called Free World and the rest. My response that evening was to emphasise that as Africans we were more concerned about regaining our worth and dignity as human beings than with joining the ideological conflicts between the East and the West. That response was given prominence in the reports of the Norwegian press, as well as the Swedish newspapers that, I was told, also attended a meeting of the Norwegian Student Union that evening.

The Saturday night gatherings always included a break for artistic entertainment. Before setting off the debate, the speaker announced to applause that the singer Ruth Reese would be the performer that evening. In strode a tall, strikingly handsome Black American woman. Looking us over, she began by making a bittersweet announcement. The first of her songs was dedicated, she said, to Michael Scott and Hans Beukes. It was the Negro Spiritual *Joshua fit de Battle of Jericho* (*an' dem walls came tumblin' down*).

Until that moment I had not reflected much about the time perspective of my commitment. Ruth Reese's song was a doleful reminder that what had begun as an act of rebellion had become a march of indeterminate duration. It struck me that I had no idea how long I'd have to be '*blowin' dat ram-horn at dose walls*'.

Among the non-students present at *Kroa* that evening was a White South African girl on a visit to family friends in Oslo. She identified herself with a gentle objection to a point I'd made. It revealed the discomfort White South Africans had to suffer abroad – having to listen to facts about their country that their press assiduously shielded from them at home, facts that might have compelled them to reconsider their own views of the society of which they were members. I sensed that many in the audience were experiencing a similar distress at the account I was giving of the dismal life of Black people in the apartheid state.

AN AUGMENTED WE

My visit to Oslo came to an end on the Sunday afternoon when I had to board a Scandinavian Airlines flight bound for New York. Alongside the Reverend Michael Scott, who was waiting for his own plane to London, there were some members of the Oslo SRC as well as friends of theirs who had taken me on a second round of sightseeing that morning. As they all wished me luck with my errand to New York I reflected that, for reasons I couldn't quite comprehend, the 'we' of my friends and allies that I had left behind in Cape Town, had expanded.

It was a beautiful autumn day. The many lakes dotting the landscape below provided a sight worth writing about to the folks living where the Kalahari Desert meets the Namib. I fished for my little pocket camera to take a snapshot. Observing this, an airhostess rushed towards my seat to inform me firmly that photography was not allowed, and would I please put the camera away.

This made me wonder whether there were military installations down below that had to be protected from prying eyes. A sobering reflection, it clouded the memory I was savouring even then about the reception that had been lavished on me in Oslo.

As to the political significance of that reception, my spirits would have been greatly lifted if I could have read a dispatch sent to his superiors in Pretoria by the South African Chargé d'Affaires in Stockholm:

GESANTSKAP VAN DIE UNIE VAN SUID-AFRIKA
LEGATION OF THE UNION OF SOUTH AFRICA
CONFIDENTIAL
17th September, 1959
The Secretary for External Affairs,
Pretoria
Hans Beukes

I wish to inform you that, according to Swedish Press reports, the student Hans Beukes arrived in Oslo by air on the evening of the 11th September and left by air again on the 13th en route for New York.

It would appear that after his proposed approach to the UN, he intends to return to Oslo in order to commence his studies there.

Translations from the Swedish Press relative to his actions in Norway are enclosed for your information. (Annexures A, B and C)

Although shortage of staff had made it impossible for the Legation to as yet complete the translation of the enormous number of newspaper clippings concerning the Beukes affair which are being received daily from Oslo, there is unfortunately no doubt that his visit and statements have triggered off an unprecedented wave of anti-South African sentiment in the press of that country.

Photographs of Beukes and Michael Scott (who was also, whether by accident or design, in Oslo at the time) were given prominence in most of the Norwegian newspapers, and front page coverage was given to statements by Beukes under such headings as 'The Spokesman of Freedom', 'Welcome to Norway, Hans Beukes', 'The proudest Day of my Life, says Hans Beukes', etc., etc.

Michael Scott of course did his best to 'cash in' by appearing together with Beukes on public platforms in Oslo. There is no doubt that these two persons, in combination, have succeeded in the space of only a few days, in doing us an unprecedented amount of harm in Norway.

As will be noted from the attached translations from the Norwegian Press (Annexures D, E and F) the possibility of an extensive boycott of South African goods in Norway has been suggested by the National Union of Students in Norway which, as already reported separately, has established a special 'South Africa Committee' one of whose tasks will be to investigate the possibilities of such action. Both Beukes and Scott have spoken in public support of the proposed trade boycott.

In the temporary absence of our Hon. Consul-General in Oslo, we were obliged to turn to the Commercial Secretary of the British Embassy in Oslo for information regarding this matter. It was understood from him that, in his opinion, there was no immediate cause for alarm and that up to now it was merely a question of 'student talk' which had been given prominence by a portion of the Norwegian Press.

He undertook to keep us au courant with any further developments that might take place.

Under the circumstances it was decided that it would be both unnecessary and unwise at the present juncture were the Commercial Secretary of the Legation to proceed to Oslo to investigate the position, as had at first been considered. Any such action on our part would undoubtedly be taken up by the anti-South African Press in Norway and used as evidence that the boycott threat had caused us concern.

I am afraid that there can now be little doubt that the prevailing anti-South African sentiment in Sweden had badly infected Norway and – as the Legation is of course not accredited to that country – there is nothing we can do directly to attempt to stop the rot.

Mr J S van Eeden, the European Manager of the South African Tourist Corporation who called at the Legation today en route from Oslo, has confirmed the bad impression that we received from Press cuttings emanating from Norway.

Denmark, as far as can be gathered from the Press-cutting service we have just started from that country, still remains relatively uninfected. We have still time, in my opinion, to prevent the spread of anti-South African sentiment taking a firm hold there, as it unfortunately already has in Sweden and Norway, provided appropriate and energetic steps to this end are taken without delay.

A copy of this minute has been sent to our Permanent Representative to the United Nations for information,
(Signed) E.M. Malone, Chargé d'Affaires a.i.

CHAPTER FIVE

New York, New York

THE LOWENSTEINS

The sun flooding through a porthole of the SAS plane woke me on the approach to New York early the following morning. The thought that dawned on me was the absurdity of crossing the Atlantic to deliver a litany of complaints to strangers from whom I could expect nothing more than a sympathetic chorus of 'Uh-Uhs'.

Yet, the moment I stepped through the entrance to hear a familiar voice calling out my name, I knew that such misgivings were to be put aside. Having spotted me from a balcony, Al Lowenstein headed for the stairs to shepherd me past two immigration officers, a tall Black one and his shorter White colleague. They showed no more than mild curiosity about the visa, attached to a sheet of paper that served as my travel document in lieu of a passport.

With friendly nods in both Al's and my direction, they collected the forms I had filled out – *inter alia* about what race I belonged to, that I didn't suffer from venereal disease and wasn't a member of a Communist Party – stamped the visa and welcomed me to the United States.

Within minutes of landing we were sitting in Al's convertible, with a personable young man from the Midwest by the name of Jim Reeves behind the wheel. A student leader at his own college campus, Reeves had been present at the annual conference of the American National Students Association in Philadelphia that Al had attended on his arrival back from South Africa.

Jim would not be the only person I'd meet in the coming days who would look at me with scarcely veiled amusement. It was as if they could hardly believe that Al had actually 'smuggled' me – the word they used – out of Africa.

From Jim I now heard about a spine-chilling account of our night time crossing of the crocodile infested Limpopo River that Al had delivered at the annual conference of the US National Students Association. Unlike the Scarlet Pimpernel of the French Revolution, who ferried nobles condemned to death across the English Channel to safety, he told his audience he regrettably had to leave his charge stranded in the Kalahari Desert.

When told that by helping me get to the United Nations they would assist the southern African revolution, the conference unanimously carried a motion to pass the hat around for a collection that brought in $750 US. A sizeable sum for any number of students in those days, it also led to standing invitations to visit a number of university campuses around America.

New York City filled me with wonder as the car sped past mysterious clouds of steam billowing from underfoot, along canyons that reverberated with the thundering traffic of men and machines. From a parking lot on Third Avenue, Al led us in characteristically hurried gait to Granson's, a family-run restaurant on the ground floor of the Lexington Towers Hotel, situated a stone's throw from Grand Central Station.

Inside Granson's the paterfamilias of the Lowenstein family, Doctor Gabriel Lowenstein, emerged from his office corner to welcome me to New York. Assuming that I must be hungry, he told a waitress to serve me some breakfast, before leaving me to digest my impressions. Jim had taken his leave and Al, in the meantime, had disappeared. According to the waitress he had gone for a session of his daily wrestling practice before hurrying off to keep other appointments. Later that morning, Al's stepmother arrived to take charge of the preparations for lunch and dinner. In due course I would become introduced to most members of the Lowenstein family – which included Dorothy, Al's sister, brother Larry and sister-in-law Marie. They would occasionally join the restaurant's regular guests for lunch or for dinner.

Until Christmas of that year, Granson's would be where seven of us – Reverend Michael Scott, Al Lowenstein, Sherman Bull, Emory Bundy, Mburumba Kerina, Jariretundu Kozonguizi and I – would meet between errands at the UN.

THE KERINAS

Mburumba Kerina turned up after office hours to accompany me to his apartment on Third Avenue. While still in Serowe I had become aware of his efforts on my behalf, 'at Kozo's request'. At the apartment, Jane, Mburumba's American-born wife – a tall good-looking woman – welcomed me with their firstborn, an infant named Mandume, on her lap.

She proudly explained that the infant had been named after the last Kwanyama king, who had died at his own hand rather than allow himself to be taken prisoner by the invading Portuguese. Jane struck me as a competent woman, one who had identified completely with and harboured intense ambitions on behalf of her husband. With her by his side, Mburumba appeared well qualified to play his self-assumed role as 'Representative of South West Africa at United Nations'.

In due course I would discover that their apartment was always open to Africans from southern Africa who might be in need of a hideaway while on laudable errands in New York. When the singer Miriam Makeba arrived in pursuit of a career, they introduced her to the actor Harry Belafonte with the request to take her in tow. We were all thrilled late one night to watch her debut performance on TV from a studio in Los Angeles as she sang *The Click Song* (with her introduction 'In my native village in South Africa …').

A South African journalist turned up one morning to seek an interview with Miriam. It turned out that he was not interested in her career plans, as might have been expected, but about her views on the political situation at home. Our hearts swelled with pride when we returned to the apartment that evening to hear Jane tell how Miriam had dealt with her pursuer: 'I am not a politician. Please go and talk to my brothers Kerina, Hans Beukes and Kozonguizi at the United Nations. They will tell you what you want to know.'

MBURUMBA KERINA – STRATEGIST OF NAMIBIA'S LIBERATION MOVEMENT

At breakfast on the morning after my arrival, Mburumba showed me letters he had been sending correspondents at home. From his vantage point at the UN he had advised them in detail about the steps they needed to take for them to be taken notice of by the international community as represented at the UN.

If I should have forgotten the details of our conversation, an extraordinary set of documents that I would come across years later, refreshed my memory. As part of memoranda submitted to the International Court of Justice in the course of the South West Africa Cases, 1960-1966, the Agents for South Africa produced copies of letters and telegrams that had been sent by Mburumba and Kozo to their correspondents at home. These had been intercepted and copied before delivery, and circulated as well among delegates at the UN. The intention was to call into question the integrity of the petitioners on whose testimony the case against South Africa was built.

To my mind the letters bear witness more eloquent than any memorial hewn in stone to the heroic efforts of two young Africans to lead their people out of bondage. Regrettably they also reveal a jockeying for leadership with predictable consequences.

The communications were addressed to among others Andimba Toivo ya Toivo and Sam Nujoma. Toivo was one of a group of Ovambo 'contract labourers' who had formed an Ovambo People's Organisation in Cape Town. He was expelled to his tribal area in 1958, after sending an appeal to the UN, the script of which he had been sent to read into a tape recorder by Mburumba. Nujoma was employed on the South African Railways; he joined Kozo to recruit Ovambo workers for the SWANU – SWA National Union that Kozo, on being expelled from UCT in 1958, had set out to build up.

With Mburumba's permission, I quote extensively from his letters.

In a letter dated 14 February 1959,[18] he exhorted Andimba Toivo ya Toivo to organise an Ovamboland People's National Congress. The letter opens with 'Toivo, Please', and comes with an entertaining suggestion for getting the tribal chieftains – who were in the regime's pay – inveigled into joining the cause: 'make them First Vice-President, Second Vice-President, Third Vice-President, etc., etc., etc., this will break the inter-tribal rivalry that may come about'. And then he proceeds to the business at hand:

'The first task of the Congress should be a petition to the Prime Minister of South Africa with copies to the Windhoek Advertiser, New Age, United Nations, Cape Times, and a copy to me, the American Committee on Africa, Africa Weekly, Rev. M. Scott, etc. This petition should ask four things. Of course a copy should be sent to the Chief Native Commissioner. These four things should be as follows: Ask for –

(a) Direct African and Coloured People representation in the Government of South West Africa.
(b) Introduction of Universal Safrage (sic) in South West Africa irrespective of Colour, Creed, Religion and National Origin.
(c) Immediate liquidation of South West Africa Representation in the Parliament of South Africa.
(d) Immediate placing of South West Africa under the United Nations Trusteeship System.'

Throughout, Mburumba shows an awareness of the thought processes of his countrymen – evident in the pains he takes to make things clear.

'Toivo, I urge you not to accept part of these demands. Tell the Prime Minister of South Africa that you want all four to be granted and no compromise whatever. Please remember Toivo, I will play this up here at the UNO. But to make it effective, the Congress should petition the President of the United States Government and the Prime Minister of Russia for immediate

---

[18] ICJ South West Africa Cases 1960-1966, Counter-Memorial of South Africa Chapter III The Petitioners p 40.

Military Action against South Africa collectively and individually to enforce the decisions and authority of the United Nations … But if you want me to draft these petitions please inform me, because they have to be legal and specific and also non-committal on our part. I can consult with some of my legal friends here … Please Toivo digest these few points. They may sound less forceful but that is just the point. They have power. I shall play the ball here at the UNO.'

Mburumba also directed himself to the lack of cohesion amongst the people of his country. So he informs Toivo:

'I shall also suggest that representatives of the African people from South West Africa be invited to the UNO. At the UNO we shall stand together. Just tell our people in Ovamboland to keep together and not to say anything … Toivo, do not worry. I will build you up if you promise to keep my name alive before our people. There are 200 000 people in Ovamboland more than the rest of the territory. Fear not my friend. Kozonguizi is also working hard in the South, together we shall have more than 300 000 African people behind us. Together we shall smash those Whites out of the government without using force but our brains. All we want is just strong men to tell the Whites in their faces what we think of them and what we want. You are one of those men and Kozonguizi is another one of our comrades.'

I expressed only two reservations to Mburumba's ideas when he showed me this letter. I thought that his choice of 'Congress' in the title of the organisation he had proposed might lead to an unfortunate conflation with the South African congress movement in our people's minds. I also queried the limitation of his organisation to the Ovamboland region only, when what we needed was a political organisation that encompassed all population groups.

Mburumba readily accepted both of my objections. In a letter dated 16 September 1959, addressed to Sam Nujoma, he wrote:

'After careful and thoughtful consideration of our situation I think it is advisable for you, Mr Nujoma and your friends to think about the possibility of turning your organization into a full fledge national organization representing everybody in the whole territory. I further suggest that it would be to our advantage if you can change the name of the Ovamboland People's Organisation to The South West African National Congress (sic). This can mean that we who are representing you at the UNO now have power behind us. It is very good to start with a regional organization but now your tactics should be geared to the achievement of something greater for South West Africans. Other African states would support us strongly if we can have such a national organization. Please do inform the UNO if you change the name of the present organization to that of S.W. African National Congress, this is very important for our position here. I am sending you under separate cover a copy of a constitution for the Congress that I have proposed and a manifesto to be distributed widely if you approve of the idea.'

Mburumba followed up this letter to Nujoma with one to Andimba Toivo ya Toivo, one in which he showed some anxiety about whether the Ovambos, who were mostly so-called contract labourers, could remain in charge of the organisation he was urging them to form. In this regard he might have been underestimating the influence of the intellectual climate of Cape Town on the founders of OPO, with the likes of Professor Jack Simons and his wife, Ray Alexander, as mentors.

'…Toivo, listen, I have been urging Mr Nujoma to change the name of Ovamboland People's Organization into the South West African National Congress. This will give the organization a national character which can be of great use to our position here. I have also drawn up a draft constitution for him for this purpose. He informed me recently that this Congress will be formed next year. Would you please get in touch with him and tell him that he should try to see that you Toivo or Him (sic) be the president. Or one of you the President and a Herero a Vice-President, etc. You see what I want to say is that do not allow the OPO when it is changed into the S.W. African National Congress to be dominated by other groups. Be very careful about this very much. But please even if other groups do not want to co-operate with the OPO to form the Congress just go ahead and change the OPO to the new Congress. Please write to Mr. Nujoma about this and keep it very secret do not tell anyone of this idea it should be just between you two.'

Mburumba's acceptance of the term organisation in preference to Congress is reflected in subsequent letters to his correspondents at home using the title of SWAPO.

An urgent cablegram[19] that Mburumba addressed to Nujoma – on the eve of a massacre that would leave many dead and wounded in Windhoek – reveals his sense that his countrymen needed detailed tutoring and that he harboured hopes they would look to him for leadership.

'Mr Nujoma, continue to attack the Government openly in public. Do not stop. *In the meantime, as soon as I think of something important I will inform you* (emphasis added). Refuse to move to the new location. Tell the people not to move. I will send you a statement which you should read to them and translate it into Ovambo, Herero, Nama, etc.

Also try to organize Mass Public Meetings every Saturday. Talk to the people, tell them to stand together.'

---

[19] ICJ Source cited, letter dated 5 September 1959.

THE UNITED NATIONS

After breakfast Mburumba Kerina accompanied me to the UN to renew my application to be heard as a petitioner. It meant doing the rounds of international civil servants serving on the UN Committee on South West Africa. The first of these was an elderly German who appeared to have local knowledge of South West Africa. The second was a Latin American, followed by an American, Mrs Jacqueline Yarrow. She wanted to know if I was related to Jakobus Samuel Beukes of Rehoboth, whose correspondence with the UN she had been handling for years. I couldn't quite make out what was behind her smile as she put the question to me. Oupa Koes, my grandfather's nephew, had been a very insistent man with an undying faith in the promise of the UN and of the League of Nations before it.

We next buttonholed the African and Arab diplomats who had shown solidarity with our cause. On one occasion we found ourselves sharing an elevator with the familiar figure of Ralph Bunche, the Black American Under-Secretary-General whose criticisms of South Africa's policies had made his a household name at home. His forbidding visage deterred me from telling him this.

Having secured me access to the UN complex, Mburumba next acquainted me with its facilities where a multitude of hues and tongues presented the very image of what southern Africa might have been – had the interaction between its peoples been as civil. The next day I was sitting alone in the cavernous cafeteria overlooking the East River, scouting in vain for black faces with familiar features among the groups of people in earnest conversation at the tables around me. At that moment I could find no good words for the bigots whose policies disqualified my people from taking their rightful place in, and from interacting with, the world of which we were part – and from taking care of our own interests and the interests of our yet unborn generations.

A block away from the UN, in a tall building at 801 Second Avenue, the American Committee on Africa (ACOA) had their offices. The ACOA was founded by the clergymen George Houser and Homer Jack, the Reverend Scott's counterparts in the US. Like the Africa Bureau in London, it was the place where one went to read newspapers 'from home', to be provided with basic office facilities and assistance, or merely to drop in for contact.

As Mburumba and I stepped through the entrance on my first visit there it was to make the acquaintance of another harbinger of liberation in our region of Africa. With the morning sun reflected from his shining pate, a Black man of commanding presence rose from his desk in a corner office to welcome us by name. It was Eduardo Mondlane, the founder of the Liberation Front of Mozambique (FRELIMO), busy shaping plans for his country's liberation from Portuguese colonial rule and South African economic exploitation.

Thousands of Mozambicans along with natives from the surrounding colonies were gang-recruited annually to work in the South African mines as contract labourers who were barred from organising themselves into trade unions to negotiate for better pay and working conditions. Yet until that moment I had known of no one from either Angola or Mozambique fighting for their liberation.

We were still conversing with Mondlane when Joshua Nkomo and Kanyama Chiume happened by. They were making a detour to the UN on their way to Washington that day. 'Hello, Hans', was all Nkomo said, having no time for idle chat.

THE MAKINGS OF A NETWORK

In the days of waiting for the General Assembly to convene, I had plenty of time to become acquainted with the rarefied atmosphere in which international business is done. A bridge leading there was provided by representatives of non-government organisations (NGOs) who were accredited to the UN. Situated near the office entrance of the Secretariat Building, a room reserved for their use offered a meeting place and some office facilities. There I became acquainted with representatives of the Quaker organisation (the American Friends Service Committee – AFSC), and WILPF – the Women's International League for Peace and Freedom. All had been close observers of the years of plodding by the Reverend Scott at the UN to keep the issue of South West Africa alive.

Among the occasional visitors to the NGO office there was a French noblewoman, Anne-Marie Stokes, the widow of an American. Cultural displacement had left her wonderfully unsentimental about the vagaries of life, making conversation with her delightful.

Roger Baldwin, a co-founder of the American Civil Liberties Union (ACLU) and of the International League for Human Rights (ILHR), would occasionally turn up to follow the proceedings, discuss our situation and dispense advice. On such occasions he subjected me to a barrage of questions, demanding precise answers. The difficulties I had responding to such cross-examination alerted me to the seriousness with which anything I said would be considered by the UN panel I was hoping to address.

Mr Baldwin was also a devout churchgoer. During a critical phase in the UN debate, when we doubted that the resolution we were lobbying for would be passed, he invited me along with the Reverend Scott to his townhouse in Lower Manhattan for an evening of discussion. From there he assigned me to address a gathering of Congregationalists at his church the next day.

AMERICAN FRIENDS

Another member of Scott's informal support group was Winifred Courtney, the American wife of an English immigrant, Dennis. On Kozo's arrival in New York, Winifred had extended her care for Scott to us by inviting Kozo and me to spend a weekend at her home on the banks of the Hudson River outside New York. We learned that her family's engagement had begun during the very first year of the UN's existence, when Michael Scott arrived in the US to champion the cause for which the Herero chiefs Fredrik Maharero and Hosea Kutako had engaged him.

It was a time when very few Americans were concerned about political developments on the African continent, which, in general, was the playground of the European powers. Her family's interest was ignited by a tour her father had made through Africa in the 1920s. He was appalled by what he saw of the treatment of Blacks by Whites. When Scott attended the early UN deliberations at Lake Success, a New York village, Winifred's father mobilised the assistance of the Quaker community to sustain his efforts.

On Sundays, the Friends gathered in an unassuming village along the Hudson for a fascinating form of religious observance. The gathering sat down in quiet contemplation for half an hour or so. During that time anyone feeling moved might rise to say a few words, cite a spiritual reference or, usually towards the end, make an announcement. Winifred made a short announcement about our reason for being in New York, comparing it to the thirteen earliest US colonies' own struggle for independence.

During a subsequent visit to the Courtneys I was introduced to another couple, the Balassas, who were also part of the local community of Friends. Born in Hungary, Lesley Balassa had emigrated to the United States to pursue his post-doctoral studies and there met Alice Hussey, a descendant of a Mayflower family. Alice Balassa's mother, the 96 year-old Mrs Grace Hussey, was visiting them at the time. I was told that even at that advanced age she kept writing to her Congressmen and Senator to express approval or disapproval of their performance in Congress on matters of concern to her. Some weeks later, the Balassas invited me to join them and their college-age son, John, for a weekend's retreat on a New Jersey farm. The retreat was convened by the Friends Society to discuss contemporary issues of war and peace.

In pursuance of the Society of Friends' quiet, behind-the-scenes efforts to mediate debate between the chief adversaries in the Cold War, a Soviet UN civil servant from Belarus and an American Congressional staffer were invited to the gathering. As American public life had only recently been set free from the blight of McCarthyism, to bring such persons together was a courageous act. It backfired. The American promptly placed blame for all the political ills plaguing the world on the Soviet Union's ambitions for world domination. The White Russian turned red but refrained from replying in kind.

Feeling offended by a point of view that would deny the legitimacy of African protests against oppression, I thought myself entitled to make my own views known. I pointed out that up to a third of mankind had only recently won or were still fighting for their liberation – from Western, not Communist, domination. I further reminded the American of the grim legacy Western colonisation of the non-European world had bequeathed to generations of mankind yet to be born.

An elderly American professor of English rose to dismiss what his countryman had said in a most elegant way. He simply said before sitting down: 'Never before in my whole life have I heard anyone say anything with which I have been so utterly in disagreement on every single point.'

On the way back from the gathering, Alice passed on to me a request Mrs Hussey had asked her to convey: since my own grandparents were far away, she wanted me to regard her as my grandmother in the United States! On my return to Oslo, Alice wrote to tell me that 'my grandmother' had sent new letters to her representatives in Congress, and even to a presidential candidate, to ask for changes in US policy towards South Africa.

What I didn't have to worry about on arrival in New York was the question of where to sleep. Without my having to ask, on the day of my arrival, Mburumba – ever concerned about the welfare of his countrymen – let me know that he was taking care of my accommodation while in New York. However, as they were expecting Kozo from London, he had to approach good friends in the borough of Brooklyn to put me up. This involved travelling by subway.

On my way there in a crowded train one afternoon I happened to sit next to a woman reading a newspaper. A query about a train stop gave away the fact that I was a stranger, which quickened her curiosity. On learning where I was from, she showed me a small item in *The Daily News* that she had just been reading. It reported a threat against me that had been made by the South African Deputy Minister of Internal Affairs, P W Botha: If I were ever to set foot in South Africa again, the future president had told a gathering of his party, I 'would regret it'. The threat had been reported even in Norway. A few days later, a letter arrived from Oslo. It contained a clipping of a letter to the editor of a local daily with condemnation of the Minister's threat. The letter was signed Hals, whom I later learned might have been a marine biologist.

At the time I dismissed Botha's outburst as the churlish reaction typical of White South Africans whose paths had been crossed by Blacks. But his threat had nevertheless made it clear to me that my return home could only happen after South West Africa had become independent.

The time-consuming commuting between the city centre and the distant station on the Brooklyn subway came to an unexpected end. A couple of lawyers, Dan and Elaine Knickerbocker, living with their young son in Brooklyn Heights just across the river from Manhattan, offered me accommodation at their home. Both were descendants of the Dutch settlers of New Amsterdam and were proud of their heritage. Living with them, even if for some weeks only, alerted me to the subtle cues by which social life in that metropolis is lived. Their patronage of the visual arts enabled me to frequent the city's renowned Museum of Modern Art and to visit the Guggenheim Museum soon after it opened. What I found fascinating was that, since Dan was a member of the Republican Party and Elaine a Democrat, they cast mutually neutralising votes in elections.

My intermediary with the Knickerbockers turned out to be Mrs Elizabeth Landis, who went by the name of Betsy. She was also a member of the New York Bar and a staunch supporter of the American Committee on Africa. A native of the Midwest, by her own account Betsy Landis was among the first generation of White Americans to develop a professional interest in African affairs. Her interest had been kindled by a famous analysis by the American political scientist, Gwendolyn Carter, of the coming to power of the National Party on a racist platform in South Africa. Thereafter, she readily accepted when one of her law professors offered her the Herculean task of sorting out Liberia's case law as handed down by that country's Supreme Court through a century of rulings. To assist her, she had engaged Elaine Knickerbocker who, on hearing where I was staying, offered me the hospitality of her home.

The three-volume codification of Liberia's case law having been completed, Betsy Landis would transfer her interest in the continent's affairs to the situation in southern Africa. In 1962 she produced a comprehensive study of apartheid legislation that was published in the Yale Law Revue. For years, she sent urgent pleas to successive US administrations for disengagement from the apartheid regime. In due time, she would become the UN's adviser on the legal system of the apartheid state. On reaching retirement age, her husband Bill, himself a lawyer, became adept at cooking, thus relieving her of that household chore.

Gifts of tickets from Betsy and Bill enabled me to experience memorable opera and theatre performances. One play, *A Raisin in the Sun*, portrayed the raw reality of American apartheid, depicting what happened when a Black family inherited money that allowed them to leave a Black ghetto and move into a White area. The drama that ensued revealed the disfiguring effects on people, Black and White alike, of constantly having to defend either their dignity – or their privileges. I left the theatre shaken by the dismal familiarity of what I had seen.

The play was a first on several counts: both its author, Lorraine Hansberry, and the director were Black; and the lead roles were played by the Black actors, Sidney Poitier and Ruby Dee. The play's catalogue included Poitier's description of the event as 'the first step by the Negro to real participation in the American theatre' and a quote from actress Diana Sands that claimed 'This isn't just a play. It's history!'

Betsy and Bill's connections also allowed me to attend an eye-opening fundraising dinner, where the main speaker was the veteran diplomat Averill Harriman. Placed near the head table, I was able to observe the manoeuvring that decided who, among the many reporters present, would be allowed to ask their questions.

PETITIONER

At the commencement of the General Assembly, the ongoing tug of war between the world's two superpowers was given a public demonstration when the Soviet Premier, Nikita Krushchev, arrived for a visit to the UN that included the US. Days before Krushchev's arrival, placards appeared in the subway trains and on the walls of office blocks. They showed the Soviet Premier shaking a blood-splattered fist with a diabolical expression on his face and a speech bubble oozing from his mouth declaring, 'We'll bury you!' Finding my way barred to the Assembly Hall on the day he delivered the Soviet Union's policy speech, I watched the broadcast on a TV screen at Granson's. Afterwards I took up a position on a nearby corner alongside dozens of other spectators in the hope of catching a glimpse of the great man as he was being driven by. It would prove to be futile. The fleet of limousines with their tinted windows zipped by at considerable speed.

With regard to our errand at the UN, there were two things that gave us concern. The first was whether the three Americans would be granted a hearing; the second was whether we could expect a resolution 'with teeth in it':

one committing the world body to act in some decisive way against the Union of South Africa. From different well-meaning advisers we heard different accounts of why this was unlikely to happen. The British Commonwealth together with all the West Europeans would oppose any meaningful resolution; the UN, we were told, was a trade union of states, where no one would do more than scold or criticise another verbally. Afterwards their representatives would square up with one another over a drink in the Delegates' Lounge – where it was forbidden to take pictures of who was speaking to whom.

When Mburumba circulated the text of a legal opinion that he had obtained about the advisability of referring the conflict with South Africa to the International Court of Justice, we were told that the Soviet Union was said to have no great faith in that institution. Even though we could count on the support of the rest of the world, the possibility of an abstention from that quarter worried us a little. In view of this, the stand likely to be taken by the United States became decisive.

However, while we pinned our hopes on the three American citizens, Lowenstein, Bull and Bundy, being granted permission to appear alongside us as petitioners, we could take nothing for granted as far as the US administration was concerned. Still, we soon took heart when Mason Sears, the US chief delegate to the Trusteeship Committee, took his seat in the chamber. We heard that on a UN mission of inspection to the mandated territory of Tanganyika (now Tanzania) Sears, the scion of an aristocratic Boston family, had returned with a jaundiced view of the British administration of that mandated territory.

In the Assembly, the first order of business as far as the issue of South West Africa was concerned, was for the Fourth Trusteeship Committee to decide on giving the petitioners a hearing. While the admission of the three natives and the Reverend Michael Scott should have been a formality – in view of established precedent – the question as to whether the Americans could be heard as well became a major issue.

In previous years, the Union of South Africa had adopted an aloof posture whenever the issue of South West Africa came up for debate, because it had for some time discontinued the practice of submitting annual reports to the Trustee Committee about its administration of the territory. Now, however, they put up a strenuous fight to bar us from being heard. In a reversal of tactics a spokesman for the South West Africa Administration, a Mr van der Wath, was flown in to read a report about his administration's efforts to meet the needs of the territory's Black population. Much of it had to do with a number of boreholes for water that had been drilled in the reservations. The South African Minister of External Affairs, Eric H. Louw, joined the debate to defend his country's record in South West Africa. Louw used the occasion to launch a tirade against the would-be petitioners, charging the Americans with having obtained visas to visit South West Africa by fraudulent means, and charging me for having lied about the true purpose of my application for a passport. Making much of my father and grandfather's alleged disavowal of my departure from the Union, he called me a crook, albeit 'at least an honest one'.

The Americans reacted as if stung to the quick to Mr Louw's charges. However, familiar as we were with the South African politician's idiom, Mburumba, Kozo and I found nothing to be offended by in what he had to say about us. Contrary to the impression he had sought to create, that I had been disavowed by my family, I knew that they were deeply satisfied with what I had done. My father had sent me a letter to express the family's support of me – regardless of the possibility that I might never be allowed to return home. More difficult for me was hearing that the magistrate had demanded that my grandfather repay my student loan he had vouched for with a third of his farm as surety. As there was no way any of us could raise money, he had to sell off a piece of his land.

To counter the effect of the minister's charges, Al secured testimonials from four of the most distinguished Americans of the day: Mrs Eleanor Roosevelt, the mother of the UN's Universal Declaration of Human Rights; Pennsylvania Governor Adlai Stevenson; Senator Hubert Humphrey and Dr Frank Graham, past president of the University of North Carolina and a UN emissary. All testified to Al's integrity and expressed their support for the cause he and his companions had embraced. Yet, even with the backing of several of America's foremost citizens, we were not sure if the US would vote for them to be heard.

Al's doubt came in part from a chance meeting with a Congressman at the US Mission to the UN. The representative appeared oblivious to the political issues involved and informed him that the Americans would abstain from any vote.

When the debates started we soon discovered South Africa's most persistent and able opponent to be Angie Brookes, the representative from Liberia in the Trusteeship Committee. She demonstrated a fighting spirit matched with a familiarity with the UN's Rules of Procedure that was second to none. Supported by African, Latin American and Asian representatives, in addition to some from the East European states, she wore down all South African objections to us petitioners being granted a hearing. With the US delegation abstaining on a vote about their citizens being granted a hearing, the procedural hurdles were eventually cleared, whereafter the Chair put us on notice to appear on the morning of 13 October 1959. As to the order in which we would make our presentations, it was agreed that the Reverend Michael Scott would be first, to be followed by Mburumba, Kozo and myself, ahead of the Americans.

None of the others told me what they expected me to say, nor did any one of them mention what they intended saying. For weeks the question uppermost in my mind had been what I should say in my submission to the forum to which I had invited myself. When eventually it occurred to me that I needed help, I wrote a letter to Jack Simons at UCT. Less than a week later his reply arrived, with a list of themes to take up. Although terse, it was greatly reassuring as it referred to issues that I had been addressing in public statements since leaving southern Africa. Encouraged, I could finally begin to draft what I thought the UN needed to hear. The weekend before we were to appear, I finished the text at the Balassa home by the Hudson River and tried it out on an approving Alice Balassa, who was ironing a shirt for me.

On the way to the UN complex I stopped over by appointment at the ACOA offices where two secretaries quickly typed and copied my notes for distribution to the translators. However, as I was about to be called to speak I discovered that some of the paragraphs had been mixed up. With my heart in my throat throughout the delivery, I had to jump from page to page and back to keep the trail.

While we were waiting to be called by the Chairman, I noticed that Roger Baldwin had joined the audience. Afterwards he expressed his approval of what I had said. It made my day. On my departure from New York, he entrusted me with the improbable assignment of representing the ILHR in Norway.

Emory Bundy encountered a different problem. By the time we were called to take up our seats in the middle of the Chamber, Al had not arrived. With a lot of things to do and people to meet, spending more time with each than he ought, Allard Lowenstein was seldom on time for appointments.

This meant that Emory had to make a statement that he'd prepared to fill out what he expected Al to say. He was, however, still smarting from the personal slight that the South African Foreign Minister had directed at them, and prefaced his statement by rejecting the minister's accusations as falsehoods. The Chairman ticked off such language as inadmissible, whereupon Emory found himself defended by one after the other delegate present. When the last word was spoken, it was time for a break in the proceedings, which saved the day for Lowenstein.

The diplomats were noticeably moved by the damning evidence submitted by the Americans about what they had experienced and seen in South West Africa – at some risk to themselves. One of the emotionally most charged moments happened when members of the Trusteeship Committee gathered in the chamber of the Security Council to listen to a testimony on tape that Al and company had recorded at Hoachanas, an oasis in the Kalahari Desert. Earlier that year military planes had been sent to terrorise the inhabitants into making way for the well-watered place to be put at the disposal of White settlers.

A disembodied voice echoed from the Chamber's walls, calling out, 'Help, United Nations, help!' 'The dogs of Whites live better than we do', cried out another voice. 'Give our children the key, and they'll open the door', pleaded yet another who lamented his people's lack of schooling.

Most of the delegates expressed their appreciation of the accounts we had given about conditions in the territory, leaving us to wonder if that would translate into votes for the resolution we wanted the UN to adopt. Al was particularly impressed by the warm praise given in private by several delegates from states he hadn't considered to be friendly to the US. An inveterate anti-communist, he was touched when a diplomat from a communist country, he didn't say which, told him that he and his companions had earned their country credit.

At the conclusion of one debating session I caught the attention of the Uruguayan representative, Professor Enrico Fabregat, to obtain his signature on a photograph that showed us talking together. Some days earlier he had made the chamber chuckle at the South African minister's expense. After his allegations about my moral decrepitude, Mr Louw had turned to his colleagues' pronunciation of my surname. The old teacher retorted, 'It seems to me much better to mispronounce the young man's name and respect his rights than to studiously observe the correct pronunciation of his name.'

After putting his signature across his own image he turned the photograph around to scribble a message on the back, some of which I still find hard to decipher:

'I have listened to these boys and (illegible) of the hist. of my own country 100 years ago when we fought to (illegible) of the colonial (illegible).'

THE COMMONWEALTH THROWS IN ITS WEIGHT

Even while the Council was debating whether to hear us, we learned that we were pitted against not only Eric Louw and his officials, but against all of the British Commonwealth, minus Ghana and Ceylon. Incredulously, even India, until then a staunch supporter of UN action against South Africa – in protest against the treatment of people of Indian descent in the Union – would express reservations about the likely outcome of recourse to the ICJ. To join the British Delegation, there arrived from London Sir Andrew Cohen, until shortly before the British governor of Cyprus. A tall, heavily girded man, but strikingly energetic, we could observe him moving about in the complex, buttonholing delegate after delegate for what we assumed was a plea to vote down the Court resolution.

Seeing that my own presence in New York was related to a scholarship that the Norwegian students had handed out, the way the Norwegians might vote was of some interest to us. 'It's your people, make sure they vote the right way', Kozo teased me with a sardonic titter. That simple comment expressed the doubts I shared as to whether any European country could really be counted on to support our cause. It seemed unlikely that they would vote against a country where they had kith and kin, not to mention commercial interests, particularly in the maritime sector, and where South Africa's strategic location in the southern hemisphere was a matter to be taken into consideration.[20]

Soon after my arrival in New York in September, I had visited the offices of the Norwegian Delegation to the UN and been welcomed by the Ambassador, Mr Sivert Nielsen, and his councillors, Per Ravne and Arne Arnesen. Feeling uncomfortable at having become an issue in the relations between Norway and South Africa, I had nevertheless refrained from returning there until I was summoned to a meeting with the Foreign Minister, Mr Halvard Lange.

A few letters sent to me from new-found friends in Oslo had sounded encouraging. They informed me that the South Africa Committee, formed during my visit, had held meetings chaired by Mr Gunnar Jahn, the Chairman of the Norwegian Nobel Committee, and that they were urging their government to take a stand against South Africa at the UN.

In contrast to this, an alarm bell rang when a grey-haired Dane stopped me in a corridor with an apology. We had been getting on famously with one another before. Now he told me that unfortunately his government couldn't vote for the resolution that we wanted. No explanation given.

We sought comfort in the meetings Mburumba had arranged with the Arab and the African block and the encouragement from individual delegates from Eastern Europe, Ireland and the 'Third World', notably a Mexican, and a Ceylonese.

I reported to my two compatriots one evening: 'You know the Dane

---

[20] In a letter to Chief Clemens Kapuuo, dated 30 April 1959, Kerina expressed the same thought: 'I am a little worried because no western country will ever do anything for us to liberate our people'. ICJ source cited p 41.

– the one who last week told me that his government couldn't support the resolution that we want? Well, I've been avoiding him since then, but today he intercepted me with an invitation to lunch with him and his wife in the Delegate's Lounge tomorrow!' Mburumba and Kozo immediately agreed that it was an indication of the extent to which some Europeans were unhappy about the negative vote they had to cast on behalf of their governments.

Mr Peder Veistrup seemed to confirm this conjecture by extending to me an invitation to address the following year's annual meeting of the Danish United Nations Association, of which he was president, and to take a vacation with his family in Copenhagen. In June 1960 he renewed that invitation.

THE UN PETITIONS

In lieu of a facsimile of my statement to the UN Assembly, I translate passages from the Norwegian Government's annual report submitted to the Storting (St.meld. Nr 36 for 1959-60) under the heading 'Norway's participation in the UN's 14th ordinary General Assembly':

'As is customary the (South West Africa) Committee's deliberations of the issue (relating to the enforcement of apartheid in the Territory) was preceded by presentations from petitioners. In all 16 petitioners, amongst whom Hans Beukes, requested a hearing by the Committee, but only seven had occasion to meet in person. All applications were accepted by sizable majorities. For Beukes the number of votes were 57-2-10 (for, against, abstentions). The Nordic countries voted for the applications of the petitioners from South West Africa, who could be assumed to have first-hand knowledge of conditions there. They abstained on voting for petitioners with a looser attachment to the Territory. This applied in particular to three young Americans who had been there for only very few days.'

'During the debate about admissions the South African Foreign Minister, Louw, gave a declaration that contained very strong allegations about a number of the petitioners. Inter alia he stated that Hans Beukes didn't have any support as a petitioner from either his family or his tribe. The South African authorities had withdrawn his passport because they became informed that he had applied for and been granted a passport under false pretenses. Beukes' immediate purpose had not been to travel to Oslo to study with the bursary from the Norwegian Students Association, but to head for New York to appear as a petitioner.'

'Besides Hans Beukes there was also another young South African student, Jariretundu Kozonguizi, amongst the petitioners. It was the first time in several years that the Committee heard petitioners from the Territory who had arrived with fresh impressions. The petitioners' accounts brought few new facts. These did, however, illustrate material in the report from the South West Africa Committee with personal experiences and in that way underscored the human tragedy behind the racist policy.'

'Hans Beukes delivered a calm and factual account of conditions in the Territory and about events in connection with the bursary and the withdrawal of the passport. He declared emphatically that he had not at all thought about applying to the United Nations to appear as a petitioner. One of the American petitioners, Lowenstein, said that he could confirm this. Lowenstein had met Beukes in Cape Town after the retraction of the passport and suggested to him that he ought to submit a request to the United Nations to be accepted as a petitioner. According to Lowenstein this was something that Beukes himself had not at all considered.'

'Common for all the petitioners was that they had little faith in the pursuit of negotiations with the South African government. They went in for political and economic boycott actions and the submission of charges against the Union of South Africa at the International Court of Justice.'

'For the first time in many years the South African delegation, who used to absent themselves whenever the Committee heard petitioners, this time actively participated in the further deliberations about the case ...'

'The general debate showed that a practically unanimous Committee shared the South West Africa Committee's opinion about the internal developments in the Territory. From no side was there any attempt to defend the racist policy or the other conditions that had been condemned in the Committee's report.'

LOBBYING IN THE US

Press coverage about us had been limited to a few paragraphs in the *New York Times* and *The Herald Tribune*. In the absence of considerable press interest, there was of course no reason to assume that US decision makers would be swayed to make a significant break with their allies, the British and members of the Commonwealth. Moreover, an invitation from the CBS Television network studios to the American trio and me for a ten-minute interview by the famed Walter Cronkite, provided a reminder of the odds a thinly populated and hardly known territory had to compete against for attention in a world beset with problems of direct interest to the American public.

Faced with such a reality, Al was nevertheless not one to throw in the towel. His response was to drum up support from university students whose interest he had kindled at the annual conference of the American NSA. At a campus in Queens to which he asked me to accompany him, I could observe the way in which the student audience was moved by the eloquence of his pleas for solidarity with an oppressed people. When they asked the question, 'What can we do?' he urged them to phone or send messages to their congressmen, their senators, the State Department and the US Delegation to the UN. From the next day onwards, he sent me off on my own to campuses he couldn't visit.

My first stop was in an Upper Manhattan college for women, where I was struck by the warmth of my reception by both the students and their teacher. I departed from there feeling uplifted by the informed interest about southern Africa that they had shown.

Eventually, my speaking engagements took me as far afield as the twin cities of St Paul and Minneapolis in the Midwest, with a detour through Washington D.C. to Raleigh in North Carolina, before returning to New York. To venture that far into the American interior so as to engage people whose concerns were so different from my own, was to suspend credulity. To justify the venture to myself I recalled the injunction, as Al had stated it in Cape Town, 'to put the case of my people to the world'.

When the plane touched down at the airport serving St Paul and Minneapolis, there was no mistaking the alternatives available: whether it was likely to make a difference or not, the play had to go on. My host, a student named Dave Russell, proved to be most business-like. He presented me with the program drawn up for my one-day visit. It was designed to have me seen and heard by as many of the region's students and radio and TV public as possible.

My first assignment the next morning was to deliver a talk on South Africa to a class in Government at a college with the Norwegian name of St Olav. From there Russell drove me to a city TV station for an interview. Far from New York, the pace was laid-back: the personable newsman invited us to watch with him an entertaining newsreel that had just come in from Moscow. It showed the US Vice-President Richard Nixon in a heated exchange with an aroused Nikita Khrushchev about the relative merits of American and Russian-made fridges.

After the interview I was driven across the river for a quick sightseeing tour of a Ford Motor Company assembly plant, before I had to be back at the university campus, this time for an interview on a student radio station catering to the school's 40 000 students. There, a journalist who had emigrated from the Swedish city of Gothenburg engaged me in an hour-long discussion about apartheid in South Africa. At the debating session with a class of Sociology students that followed, a young woman on a scholarship from Cape Town introduced herself. She recalled for my benefit how the media had used 'the Beukes case' to rub salt into the government's self-inflicted wounds. A *Cape Times* cartoonist had drawn Eric Louw, the chief hunter of spies, followed by hooded minions, entering a room with an iron bedstead to lift the bedcover. The caption read: 'Where is Hans?'

When I could finally recline in a seat on a flight to Washington late that evening, a rush of emotions engulfed me. Although utterly exhausted, I felt both elated and humbled by the friendliness and encouragement of the people whom I had encountered in the twin cities.

Yet, while my day's sojourn there had been wonderfully free from anything to remind me of the scourge of racism, the very next day would bring me face-to-face with the paradoxical nature of the errand I was on: trying to win support for the destruction of apartheid in a country where its Black citizens were still treated as second-class by the White majority.

From a Washington airport where I had spent the remaining night hours in a waiting lounge, I took an early-morning flight to Sweet Briar to keep an assignment at a local girls' college. At the airport I found a liveried Black limousine driver waiting to take me there. My efforts to strike up a conversation with him drew no more than monosyllabic responses – a reticence that became understandable when he stopped at a pedestrian crossing for a flock of Black children on their way to school. The patches sewn onto their dresses and shorts spoke loudly of Black poverty – while he was taking me to a school for privileged young White women.

For my own sake I told him why I was there. Still, my discomfort grew when the sole male teacher at the school joined my table for breakfast alongside Jenny Lapham, the student leader who had sent me the invitation. The gentleman chose to allude, albeit in the most civil of terms, to the impediments to equality of the races – whether it be in the US or in South Africa. He seemed to believe that Black subservience to Whites was, even if ever so regrettable, an inescapable fact of life. It was the sort of innuendo one doesn't quite know how to tackle in polite conversation. However, a few minutes later, on being introduced in the college chapel to the packed assembly of students and teachers in nuns' uniforms, an opportunity to respond presented itself.

I opened with the story about a conservative professor who made his protest against the rising number of female students attending his classes in the most civilised of ways. When the onset of a war had drained away all but one disabled male, occupying a seat in the back of the hall, the old teacher put on his lorgnette and addressed him. Mimicking the inveterate male chauvinist's handling of the situation, I turned to the only other male present in the hall and said, 'Good morning, Sir!'

My target flushed as the largest bevy of beauties I'd ever set eyes on, including the nuns in charge, burst out in laughter. I then went on to extemporise on the illogical arguments that would have my generation of Blacks come to terms with a social system in which we'd forever be subservient to Whites. I commended my audience for inviting me to address them on the challenges both they and we faced in turning around our respective societies.

The students were said to be from privileged homes in both North and South America, a fact that made it all the more interesting that they had invited me as a speaker. When Jenny Lapham graduated a year later, she joined President Kennedy's Peace Corps to do service in one of the most out-of-the-way places on the African continent.

On the bus ride from the girls' college to the Charlotte campus of the University of North Carolina, I would unexpectedly come up against one of the ways in which apartheid was practiced in America's backyard: Unaware of the rule, I chose a seat some rows behind the bus driver, who promptly responded by ordering me to the back of the bus. My first impulse was to protest, but I backed down on reflecting about what I risked bringing upon myself by remonstrating – with New York so far away. My feelings would sink further the next morning when I opened the student paper to read the interview I had given on arrival: 'Refugee student ...' I had difficulty seeing myself as such. It was a headline that had clearly missed the point of my being there.

One of the students I met while at the university was Mohamed Sahnoun from Algeria, a 'refugee' himself. It was a strange feeling, encountering someone from the northern end of Africa who was in the same situation as I. The difference in our prospects would, however, become clear when Algeria shook off French rule three years later, while it would take a lifetime before I would be able to set foot in South West Africa again. Meanwhile, as a member of Algeria's diplomatic corps, Mohamed would become an international trouble-shooter in Africa.

The high point of my day's visit in Charlotte would occur that evening when my hosts invited me to a concert. The giant hall was packed with students who had come for a man and his guitar. He was the folk singer, Pete Seeger. I'd known nothing about the singer whose repertoire included workers' and protest songs from both the US and abroad, including one or two from South Africa which he sang in Zulu. His introductory remarks to the various numbers sounded intentionally seditious of US Cold War policy and in particular with regard to its policy on Cuba. After delivering a paean to the island's bard, José Marti, he led the giant audience in a rousing rendition of its unofficial national anthem, *Guantanamera: Con los pobres de la tierra / Quiero yo mi suerte echar…* With the poor people of the world/I want to cast my lot.

Later that evening I would meet Seeger and learn that he had indeed fallen foul of the House Committee on Un-American Activities chaired by the fanatic Senator Joe McCarthy.

There was another Black student at the private party that evening. He was from a college from even deeper in the South. It proved difficult to get a conversation going with him. I could get nothing out of him. He appeared hesitant to express any opinion. Where I was from and why I was there clearly did not interest him. Considering that the two of us were the only Blacks there, it was a disconcerting encounter.

THE POETRY OF RACE

Back in Washington the next evening I stopped off at the campus of Howard University – established for Blacks. I was told that a mixed group of South African 'community leaders' on a US tour would take part in an event. Among them would be S V Petersen, one of the two 'Coloured' poets to figure in the Afrikaans anthologies we had to read in high school. Even though there was no reason for our paths to have crossed in Cape Town, where he was the principal of a high school in Athlone, I was feeling the loneliness of exile and yearning to meet somebody – anybody – from my part of the world.

Alas, my enthusiasm would not survive the encounter. Limply shaking my hand, S V Petersen let me know that my remarks about Afrikaans in my presentation to the UN had been poorly received 'at home'. I was considered a renegade. His manner didn't make it clear whether that was also his own opinion. I took leave of the man who in one of his poems had prayed that the Lord ease his resignation to '*die vloekstraf van 'n donker huid* (the accursed punishment of a dark skin)'.

Even as a schoolboy in Rehoboth I had been taken aback by the self-abnegation implicit in that *bede* (prayer). In my presentation at the UN I had quoted a verse, in heroic meter, by the White poet, Jan F E Celliers, that we were required to read at school: '*Ek hou van 'n man wat die bastergeslag in sy siel verag.*' I admire a man who despises the bastard race in (the depths of) his soul.

This line appeared in a poem in which the poet called his people to greatness. To me, it exemplified the abuse of Afrikaans – the common linguistic inheritance of Blacks and Whites throughout southern Africa – to inculcate in us a sense of inferiority. It had not been explained to us at school that the term 'bastard race' would have been a reference to Boer renegades in the struggle between Boer and Brit for hegemony in South Africa.

Even the poem by Petersen might have conveyed a meaning beyond the comprehension of a schoolboy in Rehoboth, who knew of no reason why he should be lamenting the colour of his skin.

COLLEGE NEWS CONFERENCE – NATIONWIDE TV APPEAL

On my return to New York, I learnt about an alarming turn of events that had taken place. A conflict that had been brewing in the Himalayas between China and India had come to a head and a major war appeared imminent. India was seeking assistance from the Commonwealth of Nations. With regard to South West Africa, Indian diplomats were now dramatising the reservations that we were familiar with about having recourse to the ICJ: they were lobbying against 'our' resolution.

While our supporters from Ceylon, the Latin American and Arab countries and others remained steadfast, the position the Americans would take had become that much more crucial. At this juncture one of the regular guests at Granson's, Ruth Hagey Brod, offered the services of the TV network she was working for, to bring the South West Africa issue to public attention. On Sundays she hosted a forum for political discussion called College News Conference that was broadcast nationwide from New York at noon. The opportunity to be on the Brod programme was much sought after by public and international figures of the day.

It came as no surprise that two prominent members of the US Congress agreed to discuss the issues represented by South West Africa with the three Americans and the three South West African natives who had been in the news. The Congressmen were Republican James G. Fulton from New Jersey and the Democratic Chairman of the House Judiciary Committee, New York's Representative Emmanuel Cellers. Meeting with us in the foyer before going into the studio, the Republican heightened our insecurity by throwing one penetrating question after the other at us. For my first appearance on television, Al offered an instant course in comportment. 'Remember', he said, 'your image will be in people's living rooms throughout the country. Talk to them as if they have admitted you in person.'

In the studio it became clear that the Republican's aggressive queries had been simply the way a busy man acquainted himself with an issue he had had no time to study. Both politicians roundly condemned South Africa's policy of apartheid and its stance about South West Africa. The clippings in the 'Beukes file' (SA National Archives), of reports in two South African papers the next day, indicated that the programme had been widely reported 'back home'.

However, as was the custom, the thrust of foreign criticism was blunted by shifting the focus on to my person. The *Pretoria News* headlined its report (19 October 1959), 'Beukes Tells TV listeners: SA Pressure on America (… to restrict his movements and activities)'. It quoted me as saying that I had been tipped off by an American diplomat and that I was 'very glad that the United States Government did not acquiesce in the mockery of the things which its people believe in.' Under the heading of 'Hans Beukes on TV impresses Americans', *The Star* (Johannesburg) cited one of the Congressmen (Emmanuel Cellers) as stating that I was 'in the best tradition of our American patriots.'

In New York we had understood that extraordinary accolade as encompassing us all and expressing a plea, as strong as we could hope for, from a senior politician that his government should support the resolution we were lobbying for. The report further noted that 'members of the programme also discussed briefly the threat of communism in Africa and gave the view that it would reap its successes in countries where oppression was present and justice absent'. This was a formulation that summed up the thrust of Al Lowenstein's pitch in the discussion.

As we emerged from the studio into the foyer it was to join a small group of studio workers making way for two leading politicians of the day, NY Governor Nelson Rockefeller (Republican) and Governor Adlai Stevenson (Democrat) of Pennsylvania. They were about to enter the studio for a political joust but first shook hands all around. 'I think I must tell you, Mr Stevenson', I said when he extended his hand towards me, 'that something you wrote almost put me behind bars in South Africa.' Stevenson listened with evident enjoyment to my tale about how one of Major Heiberg's sidekicks had declared his political tract of the early fifties, *A Call to Greatness*, to be full of communist propaganda. He positively beamed as he recalled the visit he had made to the land of apartheid several years earlier and roundly condemned it.

Listening in, Nelson Rockefeller charged me with delivering greetings from him to his friend in Oslo, the UN's first Secretary General, Trygve Lie. Alas, an occasion to deliver that message never presented itself.

MASON SEARS CLINCHES VOTE

The next day at the UN an American diplomat caught up with me to make a pleasant comment about the TV programme. He also informed me that they had received a complaint from the South Africans about my appearance on it, referring to the fact that my visa to be in the US should already have expired.

The question of where I could expect to be expelled to now became a source of anxiety. There were, however, further appointments to keep. At Temple University in Philadelphia some students had arranged for me to address a meeting that evening. The packed auditorium would become as keen as I was to know the outcome of the vote in New York on the issue we were discussing right there and then.

As it proved, the visit to Temple made me miss out on what had been a climactic confrontation between the colonial powers and the rest of the world about the future of South West Africa – with an American diplomat, Mason Sears, voting for the text that would become G A Resolution 1361 of 1959,[21] the resolution that opened the door to an appeal to the ICJ.

Donald Grant of the *St Louis Post Despatch*, who alone among American journalists had for days been chronicling the debate about South West Africa's future, gave the following account of the final vote:

'The Africans ... have had the backing of the United States. Head of the American delegation in the committee is Mason Sears, a veteran of African affairs, who has followed the South West Africa case diligently. He is a Boston patrician who is becoming a symbol in African eyes almost as powerful as the Rev. Michael Scott, the Anglican priest who has been fighting for the people of South West Africa for 13 years. Members of the American delegation have been in close consultation with the Rev. Mr. Scott – but perhaps more importantly, also with the two Africans from South West Africa who escaped last summer to come to the United Nations. They are Fanuel Kozonguizi and Hans Beukes ...(b)oth under 30 years of age ...'

After returning to Grand Central Station from Temple University that night, I walked over to Granson's where Dr Lowenstein directed me to Angie Brookes' apartment in the Lexington Towers Hotel. There I was admitted to a party in full swing. People were dancing to a throbbing West Africa High Life recording on Miss Brookes' gramophone. The hostess, Al, Kozo and

---

[21] The Norwegian St.Meld.nr 36 for 1959-60 provided the following particulars with regard to the vote: Twelve Afro-Asiatic countries, joined by Haiti, submitted a draft resolution that drew attention to the conclusions of the special report about legal steps aimed at ensuring that South Africa fulfill its international obligations concerning the Administration of South West Africa. The proposal was passed by a vote of 52-4-7 in the Committee and by 55-4-16 in plenum. Australia, Portugal, Great Britain and the Union of South Africa voted against. The Nordic countries abstained, together with amongst others Argentina, Belgium, Canada, Brazil, France, Italy, the Netherlands and New Zealand. (A/Res/1361/ (XIV)).

Mburumba were celebrating not only the vote, but the honorary doctorate Miss Brookes' Alma Mater in Alabama had awarded her earlier that day.

As I'd arrived at too late an hour to make it back to Brooklyn Heights by subway, Dr Lowenstein ordered a room to be put at my disposal at the hotel for the rest of the night.

SENATOR KENNEDY IS INTERESTED IN THIS

When I awoke the following morning it was with Al's warning in mind: I had better secure an extension to my visa before action was taken on the South African complaint. That meant that I had to travel to Washington the same day. Before setting off for the Greyhound bus later that morning, I made for the US Delegation's offices to inform Mr Mason Sears about my reason for making a trip to the State Department and to ask for his advice. His response was unexpected, 'Oh good!' he said. 'You go down there and tell them what it's like in your country. I had to make twenty-four calls last night before they would give me permission to vote the way I did.'

It was an astonishing revelation, not only about the forces that were arraigned against us, but also about the haphazard circumstances that until then had seemed to govern the fate of the SWA Territory.

I left Sears' office as if on a cloud to catch the Greyhound bus for the ride to Washington. The two-day visit must rate among the more out-of-the-ordinary of my experiences in the US: I became the 'concern' of a future president, enjoyed a grandstand view of the comings and goings at the office of the US Vice-President, and spoke my mind to the men at the helm of US policy on southern Africa.

Al had given me the numbers of the offices of Vice-President Richard Nixon and Senator John F Kennedy, where he had friends from his days as a Congressional staffer. My first port of call was the office of the Vice-President, who right then was out of town on the campaign trail, as was his opponent, the Senator. The staff parked me in an easy chair with nothing to do other than observe the hectic comings and goings in the second most powerful office in the US. About half an hour later somebody could finally attend to me and then it was to suggest that I return the next day to give them time to make the necessary inquiries.

As it was clear enough that nothing would come of it, I made straight for the Senator's office. The level of activity there appeared no less intense, yet exuded a remarkably light-hearted atmosphere. While one secretary straightaway began to make the outside calls required (with an introductory,

'Senator Kennedy is interested in this …') another showed me around the Senator's private office where the memorabilia of his wartime service aboard a gunboat were prominently displayed. Having vouched for the Senator's personal concern for my welfare, they sent me off to an address across town.

A further call from there also began with the magic phrase, 'Senator Kennedy is interested in this'. This call appeared to be made to the point where the final decision was made. When, as advised, I phoned there for an appointment, it was to be reassured that I was free to return to New York without fear. The visa had been extended indefinitely.

Curiously, far from being elated at this I felt a tinge of discomfort. It worried me that what I thought were the laws of the Medes and the Persians had been bent to allow me to overstay my welcome in the USA. However, with the uncertainty about my stay resolved and with the exhortation of Mason Sears in mind, I next took a taxi to the offices of the men in charge of the southern Africa desk at the State Department, where I had been granted an appointment at the close of office hours.

At the appointed hour I was admitted to an office where two men were waiting for me, the senior one of stern countenance, his younger colleague striking a more accommodating attitude. There could have been no doubt that I was in front of the 'them' Mason Sears had been referring to. With that thought in mind I thanked them profusely for the vote that the US had cast in the South West Africa case. As if in confirmation of my hunch, the senior officer took issue with my view of the economic conditions in South West Africa, defending in particular the wages practice of US mining corporations. What he said showed greater familiarity with our circumstances than I had expected. Yet, to me it was quite clear that he shared the underlying assumptions on which the Territory's economy was based, namely that the natives had to be grateful for what they got, and that the system of migrant labour was quite in order.

Drawing encouragement from Mason Sears' advice, I thought to myself that, having been granted the opportunity, I should let the American official know how my generation of Africans looked at US policy. To dispute the notion that employment conditions for Black workers were tolerable, I referred to the most recent instance that came to mind, that of a stowaway from Walvis Bay who had been saved from taking his own life in the port city of Houston. He had preferred suicide to being sent back to South West Africa.

I lamented the fact that when Blacks opposed government policy in southern Africa, it was as if they were taking on the whole Western world, an impression that was reinforced when US warships arrived in South African harbours for so-called friendly visits. In Cape Town I had been aboard such a warship.

When the incongruous give-and-take that ensued finally drew to a close, I felt quite exhausted and not at all reassured, even when the elderly official adopted a more conciliatory tone and sent me off with kindly words of advice.

On seeing me out at the gate long after the other offices had closed, the junior official referred to a statement I had made 'in there'. He reminded me that I had said that, with regard to South Africa, the US was compromising with evil. However, he told me that they had recently concluded a treaty on Antarctica with fifteen countries to prevent, among other things, the continent from being used to test nuclear weapons. For that reason, South Africa had to be one of the signatories.

This was the first time I would hear that the apartheid regime was developing nuclear weapons, and that the US government would merely deny them a testing ground.

A LOST OPPORTUNITY

On my return to New York, Al listened with interest to what I had to report; but he was unforgiving about my having failed to seek out a congressman whom he had particularly wanted me to see. The man in question was one of only two Blacks in the House of Representatives at the time. I hadn't understood that looking him up hadn't been merely a suggestion. Al had evidently hoped to have the congressman involved.

The depth of Al's concern about US race relations became clear to me only two or three years later when the Civil Rights Movement built up steam. And in time I would learn that Al had become the chief link between liberal White opinion and Black America: 'Al Lowenstein's unswerving devotion to his fellow man will ensure him an impregnable niche in the annals of contemporary American history', no less a person than the Rev. Martin Luther King Jr., is quoted as having said of him.[22] 'He responded, a little earlier than the rest of us, to the bitter failures of the society – to racial injustice, to the Vietnam war, to the misery of the poor and powerless... A man without fear, he toured the fighting front from Mississippi to South Africa in the unending battle against oppression,' wrote Arthur Schlesinger Jr, in the foreword to *Lowenstein: Acts of Courage and Belief.*

---

[22] Cited in Editors' Note in *Lowenstein: Acts of Courage and Belief*, eds. Gregory Stone and Douglas Lowenstein, 1983

A STOWAWAY SAVED FROM THE GALLOWS

Like the good activists they were, Mburumba and Jane Kerina had developed an extensive network of contacts. The reach of that network was demonstrated forcefully some weeks after my arrival when Jane received a late-night call from her brother in California. As a lawyer specialising in labour relations, Jane's brother had been alerted by dockworkers in Houston about a stowaway from Walvis Bay who had arrived aboard a cargo vessel. On being told that he would be repatriated, the Ovambo stowaway named Gabriel, tried to hang himself – and would have succeeded but for the timely arrival of a prison warder.

Jane immediately went into action and for the next couple of days would keep the telephone lines busy between Los Angeles, Houston, the State Department in Washington, and New York. She orchestrated a campaign, in association with the International Longshoremen's Association, to save Gabriel from being sent back home to certain imprisonment.

At some point Miss Angie Brookes became aware of what was afoot. Very generously she offered to adopt the 26-year old Gabriel and pay his fair to Liberia, where he would join other young people for whom, on her personal salary, she was providing a home and education.

Four days after the matter had been settled, Mburumba and I could take the subway to a city penitentiary to see Gabriel off on his way back to Africa. He still bore the marks on his neck of his close brush with the hereafter on his self-made gallows.

TO TEA WITH MRS ELEANOR ROOSEVELT

That the Trusteeship Committee had adopted the resolution regarding the ICJ involvement in the SWA situation didn't mean that the General Assembly would pass it. Given the strenuous opposition to Resolution 1361 from the Commonwealth, what should otherwise have been a routine vote could still be blocked in the plenary session. Although there was little we could do about it, Mburumba and I kept on doing the rounds of the UN corridors. Kozo meanwhile had returned to London.

One morning Jane told us to be back early that afternoon as she'd been alerted by Al to expect an invitation to tea from Mrs Eleanor Roosevelt. It was a prospect that clearly thrilled Jane. 'The mother of the nation', Mburumba remarked as we left the apartment, 'and the only leading White US politicians to publicly identify American racism as the US counterpart to apartheid in South Africa.'

When Mburumba and I returned home at the appointed hour, it was to find Jane in a state of excitement: we were to present ourselves at Mrs Roosevelt's apartment in half an hour. It was the rush hour. Fortunately our taxi-driver, who became enthusiastic when he heard where we needed to be, hit a wave of green traffic lights that enabled us to get there just in time. Sherman and his fiancée, Marcia, and Emory with his wife, Mary, and their eight-month-old baby Rebecca arrived at the same time. Al turned up as we were on our way out. Only much later would I read about the special bond, as if between mother and son, that allowed him to be late at an appointment with 'the Mother of the Nation'.

The excitement of the Americans was palpable, all speaking in hushed tones as the elevator carried us up to the floor where Mrs Roosevelt's secretary opened the door to let us in. We didn't have long to wait before the hostess shuffled into the sparsely-furnished lounge, simply clad in a cotton dress and fluffy big brown slippers. Flashing us all a welcoming smile she sat down to start pouring tea into our cups, saying nice things to the ladies and their babies, Rebecca and Mandume, all the while.

Observing this grandmotherly figure sitting right across from me, I tried to recall what I had read about her from my schooldays onwards. The recollection was patchy, but the realisation that I was in the presence of somebody extraordinary crept up on me. When she finally leaned back to say, 'Now tell me all about South West Africa', I suddenly felt overcome by the occasion.

Speaking up, I said something about how great an honour it was for me to be in her presence. The other women in the room chimed in as of one voice, urging me to say it louder: 'She's hard of hearing'.

At this I took a deep breath and repeated what I had said in a voice I feared could be heard at street level. The discomfort that briefly flickered across Mrs Roosevelt's face confirmed my dismay. But she waved her hand as if dismissing what I'd said, rewarded my effort with a kindly smile and continued to ask about my plans. When I replied that I was bound for Oslo, she expressed her delight about what wonderful people the Norwegians were. She was also impressed by the cleanliness of Oslo's streets. 'Not a scrap of paper to be seen anywhere', she enthused.

That evening I dashed off a telegram to my mother, wanting it to be read by the South African regime's eyes. It said, in Afrikaans: 'Had tea with Mrs Eleanor Roosevelt today'.

Two days later Jane Kerina shrieked with pleasure on opening *The Post*. Naming us all by name, Mrs Roosevelt's personal column, *My Day*, was devoted to 'the brave young men and the gallant women' whom she had 'been honoured to meet...'

A PARTY IN NEW YORK DRAWS COMMENT FROM PRETORIA

At Granson's, the mood had been lifted by the US vote on our resolution. Imperial Ruth Hagey Brod declared that we deserved a party and that she was going to throw it at the prestigious New York Press Club. Deciding that I had nothing better to do, she promptly engaged me as social secretary, assigning to me the enjoyable task of drawing up a list of guests. There was not much discretion to exercise: a representative of the South African press had to be invited alongside our foremost supporters, in addition to the embassies from which we had derived most support, including the Norwegians.

It was a swell party and the South African press returned the compliment by duly reporting, under another lopsided heading, what the four of us had had to tell the dinner guests. In *Pretoria News* on 11 November, the story appeared under the heading 'Story told how Beukes fled Union'. They quoted me regarding my transit through Rhodesia, 'I don't know who pulled the strings but I learned along the grapevine that if I presented myself at the border once again I would be admitted... I went along and they let me in. I still do not know who was responsible, but I am eternally grateful'.

That report prompted a response from the South African Minister of External Affairs. They knew very well who had facilitated my passage, said Mr Louw, in a thinly-veiled reproach to South Africa's closest allies for having let me slip out of his Government's reach.

NEW NAME FOR SOUTH WEST AFRICA

I returned late one evening from a speaking engagement at a school to find Kozo (who was back from London) and Mburumba relaxing in the latter's apartment. I mentioned the difficulty I was experiencing trying to raise sympathy with local audiences for the people of a geographical region – South West Africa – rather than for a country with a name. Both had experienced the same thing, they said. That set us testing possible names for our country. We were only too aware that, in general, before their fate had been joined together by the colonial powers the relations between the people inhabiting the territory's different regions had mostly been adversarial. And, while at the UN the three of us were 'blasting' the apartheid regime (as Kozo would say), it was with the knowledge that beyond the statements we had been making on their behalf, representatives of the various groups had not even begun to discuss the issues of common concern to us all.

Nevertheless, wondering what name our country might be given, I tried combining words derived from the two most salient features of the territory, the Namib and Kalahari deserts: Kalnam, Kalanam, Namkal, Namikal ... only to have my two compatriots snigger good-naturedly at my efforts.

'Whatever was to be the stem,' Kerina chimed in, 'it would need to have an affix -a or -ia to it, as in Liberia or Ghana'. At this point Kozo cut short the game by stating that the country's title was an issue for its people to decide. And with that he abruptly withdrew to his room, breaking up the party.

Many years later, Mburumba told me that he, (Mburumba) himself, was the first to use the name Namibia. It was in a lecture he had delivered at the University of Jakarta in Indonesia, where he was awarded a doctorate.

A MASSACRE IN WINDHOEK

To honour the Reverend Michael Scott before his departure from New York at the end of his appearance before the UN, Al's brother, Larry, next invited all the petitioners for a farewell dinner at Hyde Park, a fashionable restaurant that he was running uptown. The main course consisted of lobster caught off the coast of South West Africa. The Americans exuberantly relived their adventurous ride into a desert land and their act of political abduction worthy of a Scarlet Pimpernel. And for once the stern countenance of Michael Scott – the embodied conscience of an enlightened international community – unfolded in smiles the whole evening through. We all agreed that the dinner had proven to be worth the while.

Alas, such moments of happiness seldom last long. Yet nothing could have prepared us for the telegram that would be delivered to the Kerina apartment around noon a day or two later. It told of thirteen people shot dead and forty-four others wounded by the police in Windhoek – on Human Rights Day. The victims were part of a crowd that had gathered to protest being moved from the 'location' for Blacks close to the city centre, to a township several kilometres distant. In the place they promptly named *Katutura* – no home of our own – Damara, Hereros, Ovambos, and others who had lived cheek by jowl with one another, would be separated into different sections, to comply with the dictates of apartheid. In Walvis Bay, the people living near the foreshore were moved towards the sand dunes of the interior where 'Coloureds' and other Blacks were settled in separated townships.

To us the carnage was nothing other than an act of state terrorism, committed to quench the flames of hope that had been kindled among our people by the success of our efforts at the UN – in particular the UN General Assembly's adoption of the resolution to have South Africa sent to court.

Throughout the weeks and months leading up to the horrific event, Kozo and Mburumba had been corresponding daily with their people in Windhoek. They exhorted their correspondents to unite the opposition against the expulsion of people from the foreshore in Walvis Bay and the old 'location' in Windhoek. A communication from Mburumba to Sam Nujoma had Gandhian overtones:

'We do not want to see one drop of African blood shed, but we must face that possibility and make the most of it. There is one thing which helps and which we suggest be commenced immediately. That is this. Each person whose house is evaluated and who is forced to sign should individually send a petition on behalf of his family (stating the number of people involved) to the UNO stating the date on which the evaluation is made, his determination not to go; the unreasonableness of the government; and his knowledge that African blood is about to be shed because the Administration is determined to move the people by force.

'You must stress the urgency of the situation and the fact that UN is being informed so that this ultimate conflict can be avoided. Several hundred petitions should flood the UN immediately!!! We leave the rest to you. Please also inform the people at Walvis Bay to follow the same course. As many petitions as possible should be despatched to the UN as soon as possible.'[23]

Mburumba and I were at his home when the devastating news of the massacre arrived. On our behalf, Jane sent a telegram to the governments of the two superpowers, the Soviet Union and the US, requesting their intervention to prevent South Africa from visiting further atrocities upon our people. A telegram condemning the massacre arrived from the Soviet Premier Khrushchev early the next morning; the US government didn't respond.

We located Kozo, who was in the city, and the three of us set off for the UN to submit an urgent request for a renewed hearing. On my way into the UN complex, I happened to reach the street entrance at the same time as Mason Sears, the US delegate to the Trusteeship Committee. I asked if he'd heard the news from Windhoek. He had seen it in the *Herald Tribune* while having his dinner, he replied, adding that it would be taken up in the Trusteeship Committee which was having its last meeting for the year that evening.

Again the South African diplomats put up a strenuous procedural fight

---

[23]   ICJ Source cited p. 43 letter dated 9 December 1959

to stave off debate about the events in Windhoek and to prevent us from being given a hearing. However, with Angie Brookes backed by loyal friends taking them on, the Committee eventually came around well past midnight. Having 'stopped the clock' – a device that allowed proceedings to continue beyond the allotted time – the Chair invited Mburumba, Kozo and me to take our places in the witnesses' seats. After Mburumba and Kozo had given their account of events leading up to the massacre, I could think of nothing to add and said so to the Chair. We knew of course that the body we were addressing had no power, even if it should have had the will, to undo what the South African Administration had done or intended to do.

What comfort we could draw came from the significance of being granted a platform to protest to the international community on behalf of our people. It meant the UN had extended to us the status of our peoples' representatives. As a precedent it also recognised that the issue of South West Africa, resting as if on a ratchet, could not be turned back – a minor but significant landmark. That the status we had been accorded would eventually prove fateful – when the UN extended to a guerrilla organisation the status of 'sole and authentic representatives of the Namibian people' – no one present in the Chamber that night could have foreseen.

PREMONITIONS

Later that morning, Kozo and I were walking in a UN corridor on our way to an appointment with African diplomats when I spotted Ruth Hagey Brod hastily approaching us. She was accompanied by the UN correspondent of the *New York Herald Tribune*, with whom I was acquainted. It was the first time I'd seen Ruth Brod there and it came as no surprise that they wanted to interview us about the massacre in Windhoek; Ms Brod wanted us to go to her TV studio.

My immediate response was that a follow-up interview to the half-hour programme she had so recently produced would be more than we could have hoped for. But in that case I thought that Mburumba ought to be on it as well, and offered to get hold of him at the nearby Liberian Mission to the UN, where he happened to be right then.

The disinterest with which Kozo had observed the two journalists approaching us could scarcely have been more obvious. Now the mention of Mburumba's name seemed to unleash an anger that he had been suppressing. Dismissively mumbling something about 'these Americans', he simply moved off – leaving me standing there speechless and embarrassed.

Whatever conclusions the journalists drew from this demonstration of ill humour, they found it pointless to pursue the matter and withdrew – leaving me to catch up with Kozo, who wouldn't even deign to give me an explanation for his behaviour.

Almost immediately afterwards, I myself would suffer a loss of self-control. At the end of the passage we happened upon the two Norwegian diplomats, Arnesen and Ravne. The latter began to upbraid me for failing to keep them informed about when I intended to return to Norway. He added that this inconvenienced the students who were expecting me. Given the reasons why we were in the building, the thought that the convenience of Norwegian students ought to be a consideration, riled me. I retorted that I would have no need to be in New York if they would tell their friends not to shoot at our people.

A few days later Kozo joined me for a more convivial re-connect, for him, with 'the Americans'. The students of Sarah Lawrence College, where I had spoken before, sent us an invitation to address the whole school at an end-of-term event. From Ms Brod's studio they had acquired a recording of the College News Conference programme. Screened in a packed auditorium, it provided me with an idea of the impact it must have made on student audiences who had tuned in when it was sent. After an animated debate the gathering trooped out into the streets of the Bronx to sing Christmas carols. When late that night Kozo and I could finally disentangle ourselves from the happy chorus to get back to Manhattan, it was with warm feelings for the Americans whom we had addressed as 'fellow students'.

The explanation for Kozo's ill-tempered outburst at the UN came unexpectedly a day or two later when the two of us were in a taxi on the way to the airport, from where he was to take a flight to London and I one to Oslo. Unasked, he now let me know that Mburumba had undone what he had laboured to get going. It concerned SWANU that he had been trying to build up with the likes of Sam Nujoma who, as his trusted lieutenant, had been 'the organiser of the Ovambos of Pokkiesdraai' – the compound for contract workers on the outskirts of Windhoek. I gathered that Nujoma had been persuaded to leave SWANU for an organisation of Ovambo tribesmen parading as a national organisation under the name of SWAPO.

This news fairly stunned me. Belatedly I realised that, when on the day of my arrival in New York, I suggested that Mburumba change the title of the Ovamboland People's Organisation to SWAPO I had, unwittingly, helped to undermine Kozo's project. It was with the knowledge that my two countrymen had become engaged in a tug of war for 'national' leadership, a conflict that bode ill for our common future, that I flew with Icelandic Air into the darkness of the North Atlantic. To me it was clear that Ovambo tribesmen entering politics would coalesce into SWAPO, while the Hereros and some other groupings would attach themselves to SWANU.

Personally, I found it significant that neither Mburumba nor Kozo had invited me to join their chosen parties. Until that evening I had enjoyed making life difficult for the apartheid regime alongside two of the most accomplished of my countrymen. Yet even if they should have asked, I couldn't imagine joining either of their enterprises. Years later I thought of what might have been when I came across a letter, submitted by the Agents for South Africa to the ICJ – to discredit the petitioners. Dated 12 October 1959, it was by Kozo and addressed to Louis Nelengani, then a member of OPO as well as serving as SWANU's National Treasurer. It read:

'Monday we shall be commencing with the battle at the United Nations. Louw made a statement but I don't think he will be present to hear us – he said he shall be leaving on Monday. But Van der Wath will stay on a little while. He is also going to make a statement. But we shall blast him. We have a team of seven. Rev. M. Scott, Mburumba Kerina, Hans Beukes, Emory Bundy, S. Bull, Al Lowenstein and myself. And we shall blast them like anything. Keep up the Light – Work, Work, and Work – that is what we have to do.'

Ironically, having been shown the way, Kozo's and Mburumba's correspondents 'back home' would soon demonstrate that they could do without their further services. Both would be denied having much more to say over the affairs of either SWANU or SWAPO during the years of exile that would ensue.

CHAPTER SIX

Hello again, Oslo

RENEWED ACQUAINTANCE WITH EDVARD MUNCH

It was dark when I checked in at the Icelandic Air desk for the flight back to Oslo. When the plane touched down for refuelling at its home base of Reykjavik early the next morning it was in the light of a bleary-eyed sun on the horizon. That afternoon it landed at a snow-covered Oslo airport where the sun had already set. The clock showed four pm. For me, geography had become palpable, and from then onwards a constant source of confusion.

This time, my reception at the airport was matter-of-fact. Two final year students were waiting to accompany me to Studentbyen, the university's student town, where I was to be assigned a room in a block of flats. One of the students, Asbjørn Eide, recently married, relayed to me an invitation from his parents-in-law to spend Christmas at their home in the town of Sarpsborg, south of Oslo.

All residents of Studentbyen, I was told, had gone home for Christmas. The place was enveloped in silence – a silence disturbed only now and then by cars passing on a nearby road and the screeching of tram-wheels some distance off every now and then. The cold and darkness made venturing outside uninviting.

My room was one of five in a flat with common shower and WC, a kitchenette and a telephone fixed to the wall of the connecting passage. On the wall above the couch that doubled as my bed, I made renewed acquaintance with the idiom of a familiar painter, Edvard Munch. This time it was in the form of a charcoal drawing, not of The Scream, but of a scene no less discomfiting: a man and a woman whose relationship had clearly come to an end but who appeared to be unable to sever the bond that held them together. It was so dismal in what it portrayed that I tried to avoid looking at it, but was defeated at least twice every day, in the mornings when making up my bed, and at bed-time getting into it.

I subsequently learned that my Munch was one of a collection lent by a collector to Studentbyen, this Spartan complex of red-brick apartment buildings originally built to house participants at a post-war Winter Olympics.

I was now farther away than I had ever been from family or friends, and more isolated than ever. A year before, I had been carrying drinks to a raucous crowd in a Cape Town bar. Afterwards I had mingled with the midnight revellers in Adderley Street and up Hanover Street on my way back to my digs in Eden Road. With nowhere to go, I made up my bed in the silent Studentbyen and sought oblivion in sleep.

A NORWEGIAN FAMILY

Asbjørn returned the next afternoon to accompany me for the two-hour train ride to Sarpsborg, where his father-in-law was waiting for us at the station. There was warmth in the welcome extended to me by Mr Barth, a quietly spoken man of medium build and deliberate manner – which, I would discover in due course, camouflaged a deadpan sense of humour. Mrs Solveig Barth and their daughter, Wenche, likewise made me feel welcome when we arrived at their home.

Showing me my room, Mrs Barth diffidently explained their reasons for inviting me. They had heard on the radio that I was on my way back from New York, and realised that I would be left on my own in a deserted Studentbyen. They thought I'd prefer to spend Christmas with a family. During the next three days they lavished attention on me. To allay the discomfort that I couldn't quite shake off at thus being taken out of my depth, I reasoned that it had little to do with my person, but with the opportunity it provided them – as all other people I'd met along the way – to show their feelings about the oppression of Black people in southern Africa. That would make me merely a stand-in for the people of the sub-continent. If only the people 'at home' which now, ironically, meant South Africa as much as it did South West Africa, could have known about such support and solidarity.

Even the media appeared to be interested in my comings and goings. The state television network, NRK TV, sent a two-man team to Sarpsborg to report on the African student's first Christmas in their country. But even if it had been possible to transmit the report across the continents, it struck me that an item of its kind – a Black celebrating Christ's birth in the home of Whites – would have had difficulty passing the apartheid regime's censors. Not to mention that the country's Minister of Posts and Telegraphs regarded the medium of television itself as subversive – wherefore South Africans would be able to enjoy its mixed blessings only from 1976 onwards.

Most unforgettable was my first Christmas dinner in a Norwegian home. For starters, an asparagus soup was served with a white wine, followed by freshly-caught cod flown in from Northern Norway, stewed and served with boiled potatoes, a cucumber salad and red wine. For dessert, strawberries from the Barth's own hothouse had been topped with fresh cream.

After dinner, the self-confessed agnostic family gathered in the lounge to observe an evidently revered tradition: holding hands while circling a Christmas tree singing carols, some of which I knew. When Mrs Barth sat down at the piano to accompany herself singing the German carol, *Er ist ein Ros entsprungen* (Lo, how a rose e'er blooming), I joined in to surprised acclaim. A call home from Else, the daughter who lived in Amsterdam, completed the family feeling and brought another surprise. Expressing her delight at hearing that I was at her parents' home, Else told of having discussed with her husband, Henk Misset, the report they had read in that morning's Dutch papers about my returning to Oslo from New York.

Mention of the attention that something as insignificant as my comings and goings had enjoyed in the Netherlands told me much more than Else had said. To me it spoke about the discomfort that some Dutch people must have been feeling about the pain that the masters of the colony they had established in Table Bay were still visiting on the descendants of those with whom some of them had intermingled. One of their most recent emigrants had been the Verwoerd family whose son, Hendrik, would both raise the Boers from the despondency they were still suffering after the British Empire had seized control of their republics – only to seek the perfection of apartheid for which the British had laid the foundations.

When I subsequently met Else – the first Norwegian woman to be appointed to a Chair in Philosophy anywhere, which happened to be in Amsterdam – she mentioned the difficulty many Dutch people had to relate to Afrikaans-speaking South Africans for whom the Universities of Amsterdam and Leyden were what Oxford and Cambridge were for English speakers.

On Christmas Day the Barths invited a local singer over for tea and a song. The performer's repertoire included songs made famous by the great American baritone, Paul Robeson, who had been barred from travelling anywhere outside the US to perform, or from appearing on US stages, or even from having his magnificent voice recorded at the height of his powers. These strictures had been delivered as punishment for his 'un-American' take on politics.

On Boxing Day they invited me along for dinner at the home of a colleague of Mr Barth's, who managed the town's major chemical plant. During the course of the evening the conversation ranged from cultural matters – for example, the mounds still covering ancient Viking graves that still awaited excavation in the district – to world affairs. I also learned something about the easy relationship between management and labour in the Norwegian economy, based on employer associations and workers organised into corresponding unions; and it became evident that the treatment of Black labourers in South Africa, denied the right to organise so as to be able to negotiate wages and terms of employment, was viewed by these convivial Norwegians with distaste. The host expressed his satisfaction that his company did not have any business dealings with South Africa. This left me wishing that South African employers could have known how they were viewed by enlightened businessmen elsewhere in the world.

With next to no information about either the family or the society in whose midst I had landed, I spent the days picking up clues that might enlighten me. Mr Barth would engage Wenche in games and word puzzles that required scientific knowledge to solve. I understood that it was the way a doting father had inspired his two daughters to choose academic careers – with Else in Philosophy and Wenche at the Faculty of Science in Oslo.

But the greatest surprise of my visit to Sarpsborg got sprung on me as I was about to leave the house to return to Oslo. Mrs Barth drew me aside and said in a soft voice that she and her husband would feel 'honoured' if I would regard them as my mother and father in Norway. Added to all I had experienced in the course of my three-day sojourn in Sarpsborg, this gave me much to ponder about concerning the people who had shown me such warm hospitality. Their homes, in Sarpsborg and in Oslo on Mr Barth's retirement, became oases where I found laughter and sustenance for years.

IN AT THE DEEP END

The day before my departure from New York, the Norwegian Ambassador, Sivert Nielsen, had assured me I would find many friends in Norway, and had sent me off with the advice to concentrate on my studies to the exclusion of all else back in Oslo. His 'many friends' prediction turned out to be an underestimate. As to his advice about focusing on my studies to the exclusion of all else, I was more than keen to catch up on all the reading I'd missed.

But in Norway the public had become interested in developments, not only in South Africa, but also in the political convulsions that the African continent appeared to be undergoing. 1960 was the year in which news from Africa kept arresting the world's attention – the year that began with Patrice Lumumba, independent Congo's first premier, fighting against mighty odds to hold his country together, and the British Prime Minister, Harold MacMillan, telling Parliament in Cape Town that 'winds of change' were blowing through the continent.

As the most readily accessible 'expert' I would be inundated by demands for talks and interviews – from schools, student bodies, gatherings of housewives, political organisations, Rotary Clubs, academic institutions, trade unions, the media, film makers, and so on, both in Oslo and further afield. I found myself either referred to in the media, or drawn into debate about perceptions regarding African affairs, the details of which were often beyond my ken.

If a marker was required from where public opinion in Norway had to be moved at the dawn of the sixties, it was provided by the country's chief diplomat in South Africa. On 7 January 1960, Fredrik Holtung, Norway's Consul-General in Johannesburg, used the platform of NRK, the Norwegian national broadcasting service, to express support for apartheid. It led to an expression of alarm by the afternoon paper *Dagbladet.* In an editorial it protested against 'the Norwegian Foreign Service having a man in this position … who says straight out that he is of the opinion that racial segregation is 'necessary' in the Union of South Africa … It cannot serve the interests of the Norwegian Foreign Service to have a man as Consul-General in Johannesburg who is so little in line with the outlook of the country which he represents.'

In a letter to the editor of the *Sarpsborg Arbeiderblad* published on 4 February, my 'Norwegian mother' Solveig Barth, ticked off a Mr C R Berg for having defended Holtung 'with the insinuating remarks that the South-West-African student Hans Beukes is spreading misleading propaganda'. She suggested that 'the truth from Beukes' own experience must sound bad in the ears of Mr Berg and those who share his opinions'.

The correspondence was picked up by the South African Minister in Stockholm who, in a covering note 'about the letter from Mr Solverg Barth (sic)', sent to the Secretary for External Affairs in Pretoria, explained:

'In case you should wonder why Mr Holtung's talk should have generated more interest and excitement in Sarpsborg than anywhere else in Norway, I should explain that Sarpsborg was the place where Beukes spent his Christmas holidays immediately after his return from New York. Mr Barth, who was responsible for the second letter mentioned above, is, I believe, a relative of Beukes' hosts. His description of Beukes as 'an exceptionally nice, cultivated and well-balanced young man' from all accounts I have received reflects the impression Beukes makes on most Norwegians on first acquaintance. (Signed Bruce), MINISTER.'

Some of the invitations I received opened privileged access to persons of unquestioned influence. Early on in the New Year I learned that the South Africa Committee that had been launched in Oslo in September the year before had become moribund, but that the interest that had persuaded Mr Gunnar Jahn, the chairman of the Norwegian Nobel Committee, to head it remained undiminished. He sent word for me to come and see him. Again I was struck by the modesty of the small, lino-floored office where he was writing the history of the Bank of Norway. Yet, on taking his outstretched hand, thoughts about his Spartan surroundings evaporated. After quietly regarding me from behind his heavily-lidded eyes, he expressed his dismay at the massacre that had taken place in Windhoek. Thereafter he wanted a report about what I had experienced in New York. His genuine interest immediately put me at ease. Conversation flowed easily with the old chieftain – as I inwardly regarded him – who spoke with sad resignation about the politicians in charge of our future.

The next call was from the head of the newly-established Norwegian Foreign Policy Institute (NUPI). Professor John Sanness introduced me to his co-workers and after a pleasant conversation asked me to write something about how I regarded the continent's future for publication in the institute's journal, *Internasjonal Politikk*. As the subject was beyond my ability in terms of background knowledge, all I could manage was a five page essay that expressed no more than my own hopes and fears. Sanness nevertheless placed it in the fledgling magazine alongside learned articles about democracy in Germany, and about peacekeeping and peace research, both issues of abiding interest in Norway.

From Torild Skard, a fellow student and the collaborator of a literary magazine *Fossegrimen*, I received a similar request. To get to know Torild, as I did on the day of my registration as student at the University, could be compared to having acquired a ringside view on a generation's struggle by Norwegian women for equality with men. In the years that followed, she would demolish one after the other the bastions of male privilege. She became a driving force in the politics of the country. She articulated women's causes in books like 'Half the World are Women'. She represented Norway as a diplomat and civil servant, and in retirement embarked on an encyclopaedic study of women in power world-wide.[24]

Other requests, with length requirements and deadlines given, I had to let go. Not only did I lack the time, the Security Police in Port Elizabeth had deprived me of the documents that could have been useful as references at the time.

---

[24] Torild Skard, Women of Power
     Half a Century of Female Presidents and Prime Ministers Worldwide, Chicago Press 2014.

On a walk in town one day, I would make the acquaintance of an earlier Norwegian generation's views on South Africa. Professor Jac Worm-Muller, an historian who had participated in the negotiations leading up to the creation of the UN, addressed me as we were passing each other in front of the university's Great Hall. In the hearing of other passers-by, he told me that he had been a 'mere seventeen' when he wrote his first book – a passionate defence of the Boers against the British during the Anglo-Boer War of 1899-1902. Sadly, he lamented, the Boers had become his *smertensbarn* (children of sorrow)[25].

My induction into the University was marked by a dinner invitation at the home of the Principal, Johan T. Ruud. The other guests were three or four local students. The conversation was wide-ranging and instructive; one of the items raised concerned the Samé, the indigenous peoples of northern Scandinavia whose territory had been colonised by Norway and Sweden. I gathered that the majority of Norway's Samé lived in Oslo, but that to escape acts of discrimination by the ethnic majority, they made themselves invisible by avoiding to go dressed in their distinctive national dress. It occurred to me that the bursary had connected UCT and the University of Oslo, and that I ought to submit a report 'home'. The impulse faded on recalling that I had put myself beyond the pale.

Whenever my name appeared in the media, which happened quite frequently that year, it was as 'the South African', one moreover elevated to a position as spokesman for the Black opposition. As happened when I was woken early one morning by a call from *Verdens Gang (The (World's) Passing Scene)*, the Oslo afternoon paper. The caller wanted me to comment on a statement by South Africa's Foreign Minister in Pretoria the evening before. I learnt that the minister had charged the Scandinavians with hypocrisy for attacking his country at the UN while trampling the rights of their own minority Samé populations underfoot.

Recognising that for once Advocate Eric Louw seemed to have taken on a good case, I pleaded ignorance about the situation of the Samé and suggested that the paper call the University's principal. The Louw 'attack' was reported on in war-like headlines in both Norwegian and Swedish papers. Ironically, neither the Norwegian nor the Swedish Samé appeared to have been very pleased by having the South African as champion of their cause – to judge from their demurrals.

---

[25] The occasion to relay this message came only a lifetime later. At the banquet for the Nobel laureates Frederik de Klerk and Nelson Mandela – that I could attend because wife Edel Havin represented the Norwegian section of Women's International League for Peace and Freedom – I approached President de Klerk to tell him what Worm-Muller had said. This seemed to agitate him. 'Yes,' he responded heatedly. 'People forget that we were the first in Africa to have risen against imperialism.'

On the day of the Sharpeville Massacre, 21 March 1960, it was the turn of the Norwegian Broadcasting Corporation to summon me for a comment – alongside Edward Hambro, the ex-Registrar of the International Court of Justice. Reminding myself that my listeners were the kith and kin of White South Africans, I said that the incident had no doubt given as much pain to Whites as it did to Blacks, but that the Verwoerd regime had shown its true character.

STILL DEEPER END

Being thus exposed in the media appeared to have lent me the aspect of a sure draw-card for organisers of events in the most varied venues. As it was known that I was the recipient of a Norwegian bursary, the expectation also appeared to have been that I was obliged to speak for free. The time required to prepare for every such request made it difficult to concentrate exclusively on studies. But as interest spanned from small children's in my hair – I remember one girl, today a doctor, who stole up from behind me to touch my head – to academic assemblies in my opinions, it was difficult to back out.

Such invitations struck me as motivated by a deep-felt need by a relatively isolated people to remain abreast of affairs in the world beyond the borders of their own country. An invitation of this kind came from the students at the Technical University in Trondheim, where the nation's engineers were educated. The last speaker to address their Union about southern Africa, I learned, had been Alan Paton, the author of *Cry, the Beloved Country*. On this occasion I felt surprisingly connected with the audience that filled the large auditorium – even though the beer was flowing as freely as it did in *Kroa*, the Oslo Student Union's pub.

Recalling Professor L M Thompson's characterisation of the architects of apartheid – as being of a Teutonic mind-set which valued classification and order – I sought to portray apartheid as the single-minded pursuit of a diabolical design for keeping Black people eternally subjugated to White supremacy. I referred to the distribution of land resources where 13% of the population claimed ownership of 87% of the land; a migratory labour system connecting 'White South Africa' and 'Black homelands' on terms literally worse than slavery; a Bantu education system where mathematics had no place, followed by Tribal Colleges where it was forbidden to criticise any aspect of government policy; the criminalisation of personal relations between Black and White men and women; the supremacist logic that made it tantamount to an offense for a Black doctor to give orders to a White nurse...

The audience spontaneously called for a boycott of South African goods. Interestingly, the chairperson, who was the son of a government minister, stepped in to prevent the resolution from being adopted. I wondered if he wanted to avoid yet another student body from full-heartedly supporting a boycott, as the Oslo students had done a mere half a year earlier.

It sometimes happened that such meetings revealed something about the hidden interest of members of the audience in the situation in southern Africa. Thus Sigrun Kaul, the editor of the Trondheim students' paper *Under Dusken* (Under the Mortar Board) made me aware of the trauma suffered by some of her generation, as a consequence of the five years of occupation by Nazi Germany between April 1940 to May 1945. After the war, those with parents deemed pro-German, or related to Germany in any way, carried a stigma. In due course I would encounter other individuals who bore the burden of imputed or real failure as good Norwegians during the years of occupation.

One of the most distinguished among these was the sculptor Wilhelm Rasmussen. In 1926 he won a commission to create a monument in honour of the Fathers of the Norwegian Constitution – drawn up in the village of Eidsvoll in 1814. The 40 metre tall column – with scenes depicting a thousand years of the nation's life in bass relief along its circumference – was meant to go up in a park in front of the Storting (Parliament) in Oslo. But to see the mighty work of art today, one has to travel to a narrow valley some 400 kilometres distant from the capital. Dark in winter, the valley leads into *Jotunheimen* – the home of the gods. Imprisoned and villified for alleged collaboration with the occupying forces, Professor Rasmussen was denied financing to finish the monument. Political Norway found any number of reasons to consign to the scrapheap both the finished and unfinished parts of the work. After Rasmussen's death in 1965, the monument was salvaged by a hero of the Resistance who happened to have been a friend of the late sculptor, and erected in the grounds of his tourist hotel in Bøverdalen. I had the privilege of interviewing Rasmussen, a man who, in his own words had been 'blackened' – 'in this country we say blackened', he excused himself to me – and ousted from the company of the good, but who retained a bitter-sweet take on the foibles of his fellow countrymen.

CATERING TO CONFLICTING POLITICAL PERCEPTIONS

A question that sometimes cropped up in discussions after talks I gave, was to what extent Scandinavian societies had benefitted from the exploitation of the European colonies' peoples and raw materials. To my surprise, even presumptively educated people were happy to deny the connection. However, early on in the New Year I received an invitation from a politician who had clearly concluded that the oppression of Blacks in South Africa was a moral challenge for her Norwegian constituency as well.

Mrs Aase Lionæs, a senior member of the governing *Arbeiderpartiet* (Labour Party), whom I had met at the United Nations, invited me home for dinner. She introduced me to her husband, a refugee from Hitler's Germany, her daughter Kristine and a handful of young politicians. For the next two years Mrs Lionæs would take me in tow when she spoke at meetings of the Norwegian Labour Movement in support of the boycott of South African goods on the Norwegian market.

To this end she mediated an invitation for me to address a meeting of the Oslo chapter of the Norwegian Labour Party Women's Network. There I was ushered onto the rostrum from which the then Prime Minister's wife, Mrs Werna Gerhardsen, had just addressed the meeting. The next thrust involved participating in a session of *Arbeidersamfunnet* (The Labour Union), the party's debating club. The text of the boycott resolution adopted was reproduced in all the party-owned newspapers nationwide.

A Labour Day demonstration in the west coast town of Stavanger, to which I accompanied Mrs Lionæs, turned into a fascinating encounter with the spirit of the labour movement in Norway. Falling in line with the marchers I found myself keeping step behind a banner touting '*Send Misjonærar til dei Kvite I Syd Afrika*' (Send missionaries to the Whites in South Africa).

I learned that the jibe was directed at Norway's Missionary Society, whose headquarters were in Stavanger, and grounded in the Labour Movement's uneasy relationship with the Lutheran State Church.[26]

Following on Mrs Lionæs' impassioned defence of the boycott of South African goods that had been launched by the Norwegian Confederation of Trade Unions (LO), I followed up with my first five minute 'appeal' in Norwegian – the text of which I had worked on late into the night on board the train and had translated by Mrs Lionæs at breakfast. In my opinion, it was in no small measure due to Mrs Lionæs that the issue of a boycott acquired a certain resonance in parts of the Norwegian Labour Movement.

On 1 May the following year, 1961, we trawled the industrial heartland of the country to address huge crowds in the Telemark towns of Porsgrunn and

---

[26] It might have been opposition to apartheid that brought about a rapprochement of sorts between Church and Labour movement in Norway. This became clear from the 1970s onwards when the Lutheran Church, after much soul-searching – no doubt influenced by the prophetic stand taken by the likes of Allan Boesak, Beyers Naudé and other South African clerics – came out openly in support of the South African liberation movement.

Skien. On the train that morning, Mrs Lionæs became interested in a quote from Dr Faust by the German poet, Goethe, that I had perused with some difficulty the night before: *He who would enjoy freedom as he would life, needs to fight for it every day*. For my birthday she sent me an English version of the classic.

At one point I received a dinner invitation from the Secretary-General of the Labour Party, the redoubtable Haakon Lie himself. Mr Lie picked me up in his modest automobile, a Volkswagen Beetle, and, after a convivial dinner prepared and served by his American-born wife, delivered me back at Studentbyen. Alas, given my limited acquaintance with the nation's political hierarchy, I didn't realise that it was Norway's most powerful political figure who had evidently wanted to take a closer look at me. Since he didn't follow up the visit, I assumed that he had satisfied himself that I was not likely to be of much use to him.

THE SHARPEVILLE MASSACRE

The Sharpeville Massacre of 21 March 1960 brought renewed calls for a boycott of South African goods. This in turn brought me urgent requests to speak at functions near and far. At the University of Bergen, a student, Rolf Schøder, had been moved to start his own campaign to support the liberation movement. He was collecting money to bring Black students to Bergen and sent me a plane ticket to come and launch the campaign. Picking me up at the airport after an early morning flight, he drove me straight to the city centre where a dais stood rigged up in the middle of the town square, with loudspeakers placed around the periphery. With the echo of my voice booming back at me, I delivered the message I had been asked to deliver, and afterwards answered the questions of journalists.

What sums Rolf Schøder's fundraising project had raised, I haven't been told. But to me it would prove richly rewarding. On the way to Bergen a fellow passenger, Dr Brun, wished me luck. On the flight back, we again shared seats next to one another. This time I shared with Dr Brun my worry about a student feast to which I had received an invitation. It was to start with a waltz, and I couldn't dance. Dr Brun promptly took out pen and paper and sketched the steps needed for a waltz. These I had to practice to the rhythm of *Ku-rum-Pah, ku-rum-Pah...* (the Cow's Tail). Such training in the art of the waltz, he explained, was the way in which the Norwegian military sought to inculcate a smattering of culture into the raw recruits from the countryside. Back at Studentbyen I found chalk and drew the markings on the floor for practice.

And on the Saturday evening I earned fulsome praise from my partner, Kari Sundbye, for the 'elegant' way in which I had led her through the only dance that I dared invite her to that evening.

Dr Brun also recommended a dentist from whom I would get free care; and he offered me a lift to Gothenburg the following week – where I was to take part in a debate about apartheid. It just so happened that he was due to drive there himself.

A few kilometres north of Gothenburg he stopped at the impressive Bohus fortress that once marked the border between a mightier Norwegian kingdom and Sweden. There was a wistful look in the doctor's eyes as he told me this. However fleeting, it betrayed the pain of generations whose ancestors had lost land over which foreign flags now flew.

GOTHENBURG

During a visit to the National Archives in Pretoria I came across a report sent home in 1960 by E M Malone, South Africa's Charge d'Affaires in Stockholm. He named thirteen individuals whom he identified as the 'prime-movers behind [the] anti-South African Movement in Sweden'. About them, he wrote, *'It can be broadly said that, had they never existed, the average Swede would have heard relatively little about South Africa and have cared less.'* In Gothenburg it would be my privilege to meet the Reverend Gunnar Helander, who headed the list. Having served as a missionary of the Swedish Lutheran Church amongst the Zulus of Natal and in Johannesburg from 1938 onwards, he was fluent in both Zulu and Afrikaans – the language of his wife. For having published articles, books and plays critical of the South African regime's policies in the Swedish media his South African visa was withdrawn in 1957 while he was on his first vacation home in Sweden.

Another distinguished member of the group of thirteen was Herbert Tingsten, the chief editor of *Dagens Nyheter*, Stockholm's liberal newspaper. After a visit to the land of apartheid in 1953, he set the tone for Swedish reportage about South Africa. The collection of articles published under the title of *Problemet Syd Afrika* – the South African Problem – presented as concise an analysis of life in the racist state as can be found in any language to this day. By the end of the fifties practically all Swedish journalists were *personae non grata* in South Africa. A dispatch by Malone, penned on 23 November 1959 and quoting from a report by a hired Australian public relations consultant, summarised the effects of the negative press attention being received by South Africa:

'The poison had been spread throughout the country and we had 90% of the population thoroughly against us and in a state of mind where they were prepared to believe any slander against the Union.'

On arrival in Gothenburg I found myself received in a manner worthy of an official representative of his people. A frightfully formal young student met me by appointment in the city's premier hotel where they had put me up. From him I learnt that I was the only student from Black Africa enrolled at a Scandinavian university and that my opponent in a debate about apartheid the next evening would be one Per Engdahl, the wartime leader of the Swedish Nazi Party, but that I would have the Reverend Gunnar Helander by my side. He also told me a journalist would come around the next day to conduct an interview with me. With that he left me to my own devices.

The interview took place at a restaurant overlooking the impressive headquarters of the Swedish East India Company that now houses a museum. The exhibits, the journalist explained, were from a time when the Swedes were participating in the plundering of Africa, Asia and elsewhere. To me he offered his apologies.

In the evening, the confrontation with the Swedish *gauleiter* proved much less challenging than I had feared. Engdahl put in a plea for a place for Whites under the African sun, the argument which Hendrik Verwoerd had used to counter Harold MacMillan's challenge in Cape Town. Engdahl's opinion about Black people, reported to be objectionable, he kept to himself that evening.

The chairman of the meeting, Åke Holmberg, had served as a missionary in South Africa from 1947 to 1951 and in Tanganyika from 1954 to 1956. From there he had returned to take up a Chair in History in his home town. His decision to invite Engdahl proved controversial: nearly half the audience demonstratively marched out on the man. To my surprise, they trooped back into the auditorium after Engdahl had spoken. Holmberg defended Engdahl's right to speak by referring to his own practice of playing tapes to his students of speeches even by the likes of Adolf Hitler '*och sådana där gubbar* (and such types).'

The meeting adopted a resolution decrying discrimination on the basis of colour, creed or gender. The local papers published copious reports of the proceedings.

'YOUNG' LIBERALS

Some three months later I received a second invitation from Sweden. This time it was from the Swedish Liberal Youth who would be hosting an annual conference of the so-called World Federation of Liberal and Radical Youth (WFLRY). The conference was held in the holiday resort town of Falkenberg situated along the coast south of Gothenburg.

To welcome me at the railway station was Hans Blix, then still a university lecturer. To my surprise, the majority of the 'youth' in whose company I'd be spending the next several days turned out to be well advanced in their professional careers. The conference introduced me to the issues exercising the minds of some of Europe's leading politicians-in-waiting. The British expressed their undying faith in the pendulum movement of the electorate that periodically made it possible for parties to remedy each other's excesses. The Swedish were hoping to oust the Social Democratic Party that had grown hegemonic. Their difficulty was that the Social Democrats had transformed their nation from a poverty-stricken class-ridden society to a welfare state. It had built on what would become the successful three-legged Nordic socio-economic model of equality, powerful trade unions and government participation in the economy. The Germans were defending the Erhard doctrine that threatened sanctions against the recognition by other states of East Germany; the Italians agonised over the influence of the communists in Italy's affairs; and the nascent European Common Market dominated discussions.

A plenary session was devoted to a discussion of southern African affairs following a talk that I had been invited to make.

In time, the hopes of the 'young' Swedish liberals would be fulfilled. The majority of those I met in Falkenberg would move on to serve their country in various positions in government and academe. To his own surprise, Hans Blix would immediately afterwards be recruited as legal adviser to Sven Undén, Sweden's then Foreign Minister and his opponent in politics. One of the participants declared himself to have no higher ambition than to become the editor of the society page at *Dagens Nyheter*. It represented, he explained to me, the pinnacle of power in all his nation's media, endowed as it was with the privilege of deciding what to publish about whom on any particular day.

During the week, arrangements were made for an interview with Mrs Segerstedt-Wiberg, an elderly journalist who appeared to be revered by the young Swedish liberals for her staunch support of their party. She also happened to be the daughter of Torgny Segerstedt, the editor of the borg *Göteborg Handels Och Sjöfarts Tidning*, the paper made famous for its unwavering opposition to the Nazi regime in Germany. Writing for the *Göteborg Posten* Mrs Segerstedt-Wiberg wielded a sharp pen in her own right.

She surprised me with greetings from a friend of hers who had interviewed me on the student radio station at the University of Minneapolis. I was stunned by such testimony to people talking to each other – across a continent and an ocean – about the suffering inflicted on their fellow human beings by a 'Western' regime. And I wondered how long that regime could withstand the force of their opposition to its policies.

Accompanying me to the interview was Lena Ohlin, the daughter of the Liberal opposition leader in the Swedish Parliament. The caption of Mrs Segerstedt-Wiberg's article read: 'We are discussing matters charged with dynamite ... Swedish and African youths ...

COPENHAGEN

At the conclusion of the conference in Falkenberg, I hitched a lift with a Danish participant to Copenhagen where Mr Peder Veistrup, one of the representatives I had become acquainted with in New York, had invited me to spend a fortnight's vacation at his home. The *quid pro quo* was that I had to deliver an address at the annual meeting of the Danish United Nations Association, of which he was the president. Prior to the meeting Mr Veistrup introduced me to the political editor of the country's leading Liberal paper, *Politiken*. The paper published an extensive interview about conditions in the land of apartheid.

My sojourn at the Veistrups' proved doubly rewarding. Neither Mrs Veistrup nor their four-year old granddaughter, Lise, with whom I spent the days in the housefather's absence at work, spoke English. This compelled me to listen carefully to what Lise had to tell me. Her clear pronunciation and infinite patience helped me to distinguish the words. Combined with the fact that there appeared to be little difference between written Danish and Norwegian, this opened the door to an understanding of both languages, with the related Swedish thrown in as a bonus in due course.

My contribution to the discussion at the annual conference of the Danish UN Association earned favourable comment from all participants. Although much sympathy was expressed for the cause they associated me with, it struck me that the Danes were not quite clear as to what, if anything, they could or should do to support the 'liberation struggle' – as was observed by political commentator Friis in the Association's yearbook. When a year or so later I submitted an article to the editor of *Politiken*, I received a reply stating that their readers were 'sick and tired of reading about apartheid'.

As the Nordic foreign ministers used to meet in one of the capitals so as to coordinate the policies they would be espousing at the UN General Assembly, Friis' apostrophy fairly summed up the situation in Norden – in 1960. Still, as to the several approaches to the South African challenge, there appeared to be considerable differences between them. Presumably constrained in their foreign policy by the Peace Treaty with the Soviet Union, the Finns showed no great activism with regard to apartheid. Neither did the Danes, as I had already become aware at the UN the year before.

In contrast, a group of Swedish journalists were denied access to South Africa – because of the negative image of the apartheid state their reports had helped to create in the minds of the Swedish public.

As to Norway, History major Ole Kristian Eivindson summed up his findings about *Norge og raseproblemene i Sør-Afrika 1945-61* ('Norway and the race problems in South Africa', Univeristy of Oslo, 1977) as follows:

'From 1945 to 1960 ... Norway pursued a policy of compromise. The race problems didn't cause any glowing Norwegian engagement during this period ... The Beukes case (1959) ... brought the student body and public opinion into direct contact with the policy of apartheid ... increasing awareness in Norway about (that policy) both amongst the public and in the government. The Norwegian Students Association succeeded also in pressuring the Foreign Office to take up the issue of race in education at the UN.'

What next shook up public opinion in Scandinavia and worldwide, was the Sharpville massacre of 21 March 1960. It would, however, take yet some time before the revulsion caused by the excesses of the apartheid regime, would elicit support for efforts to undermine it.

INTERNATIONAL STUDENT SEMINARS AND FESTIVALS

As mentioned, the swelling tide of political emancipation on the African continent set the agenda for international debate in 1960. The blocks involved in the Cold War set in motion programmes to influence the political choices the new African elites would make. In Europe, both East and West, African students were wooed with festivals and seminars, free transportation to and first-class accommodation in places few, if any, would otherwise have been able to visit.

Approaching Easter 1960, I received an invitation to join a gathering of African 'youths' in Tunis. The organising body this time was an agency called World Assembly of Youth (WAY). Some months later, this was followed by an even larger festival in Accra. Administering WAY from an office in Amsterdam was a Swede, David Wirmark, with an Indian politician as his deputy. Since Sweden was neutral and India a member of the non-aligned states, the impression given was that attendance at a WAY event would not be compromising one way or the other. It would merely enable participants to make useful contacts. In the belief that I would be able to create awareness about South West Africa, I accepted the invitations to both events.

The flight to Tunis went via Amsterdam where for the first time I could meet up again with a fellow student from UCT, Vernon Afrika. The last time the two of us had been together was just before my departure from Cape Town, when we had a lively discussion about our situation as Blacks in southern Africa. I had been displeased at the time by what I'd regarded as his defeatist attitude in the land of his birth. Now, in possession of a valid South African passport, he was pursuing an academic career at Leyden University that would land him far beyond the limits that the apartheid regime had preordained for the likes of him. This pleased me. We shared a *rijsttafel* (an Indonesian dish) and a beer and parted.

In Tunis, it amused me to meet again with the physically towering figure of the future Zimbabwe's Joshua Nkomo, mingling with the other long-in-the-tooth 'youths'. From Lesotho a future Prime Minister, Leabua Jonathan, took part. And then there was another South African student named Geffen, a NUSAS official with whom I'd become acquainted in Johannesburg.

From the beginning to the end of the gathering, South Africa dominated proceedings. On the opening day came reports from Johannesburg of a near successful attempt on the life of the chief architect of apartheid, Dr Hendrik Frensch Verwoerd, the South African Prime Minister. On the closing day, Mr Oliver Tambo, the ANC's secretary-general, arrived to deliver the closing speech. Following the Sharpeville Massacre he had crossed over the border into Botswana to lead the ANC from abroad, whereupon David Wirmark had intervened to make it possible for him to come to the seminar.

Although Mr Tambo's address to the gathering was measured, it struck me that his flight abroad, like a latter-day Paul Kruger's, signalled a chilling message. It was that civil war in South Africa was in the offing. From Tunis he left for New York to submit his advocate's report to the UN about the massacre in Windhoek the year before.

At the seminar I thought I could discern a sharp difference in the presentations made by the Anglophone and Francophone Africans. The latter had a penchant for Gallic verbosity, complete with grand gesticulation in the manner of the French president Charles de Gaulle. They would expound on the ideological problems facing Africa. The Anglophones, in contrast, were down to earth and factual.

The agenda also included cultural diversions and insight into the region's political tensions. Of special interest was a meeting with Habib Bourguiba, the leader of Tunisia's fight for freedom from French colonialism. At the venue for the meeting – a countryside village – we found ourselves engulfed by ululating women throwing rose petals over their president and over us all.

This excursion into North Africa also brought with it a brief encounter with representatives of the Algerian Liberation Army that were stationed in Tunis at the time. The precarious balancing act that Tunisia was obliged to conduct was quite clear: they needed to offend neither the French nor Tunisia's potentially more powerful neighbour to the west.

A morning's excursion to the impressive ruins of Carthage, destroyed by Rome, provided a mute reminder of a fateful early defeat Africa had suffered at the hands of Europe.

THUYNSMA AND LEFTWICH

In Accra, the drama unfolding in the Congo overshadowed the proceedings at WAY's 'Africa Youth Festival'. A day or two after our arrival, a distracted Patrice Lumumba, the Congo's first and hitherto only democratically elected prime minister, landed at the airport for consultations with Dr Kwame Nkrumah, Ghana's president and the senior statesman of Black Africa. The 'Congo Crisis' had made it clear that the African peoples' liberation from colonial oppression had become hostage to the Cold War. African leaders striving for real independence from the ex-colonial masters were the primary targets of Western states fearing loss of control over the continent's natural resources and political orientation. Not long after the Accra Youth Festival, Patrice Lumumba would be imprisoned, tortured and killed – the victim of collusion between the Eisenhower administration in the US and the Belgians.

My brief sojourn in Accra provided a link-up with other South African exiles. Almost immediately after Ghana achieved independence in 1957, Black South Africans, for whom apartheid had closed the doors of opportunity, left for Accra to find work – as teachers, medical practitioners and in other occupations. I was therefore not surprised to run into Dr Thuynsma, the doctor with whom I had become acquainted in Serowe. We spent an evening together reflecting about the whys and wherefores of the choices in life that we had been making, or had been compelled to make.

The only other participant from South Africa at the Youth Festival happened to be my old classmate from UCT, Adrian Leftwich. With his encouragement I ventured an opinion at a plenary session – to call attention to the peculiar problems facing the liberation movements of southern Africa, and what this would require from our brethren in the rest of the continent. The reception I received was one of yawning indifference. It was difficult to know why, but sobering for what I suspected the reasons might be, namely that I was not Black enough. This indicated to me that Black Africa was, and perhaps remains, unaware – if not downright dismissive – of the resistance of the Khoisan peoples to European colonialism.

It was a noticeably subdued Adrian with whom I would spend most of the time. Little did I know that he had become involved in a body known as the ARM, or Armed Resistance Movement. With activists drawn mainly from university students they blew up power installations and carried out other acts of sabotage in hopes of 'bringing the apartheid regime to its senses'. That campaign would end with several of Adrian's comrades having to serve many years in prison – because he had cracked up under police interrogation.

It would take years before Adrian and I could meet again. On a visit to England I travelled to York, where he had settled, ostracised by the exiled South African community in London. I found him weighted down by unrelenting remorse. On my return to Oslo from York, I had an opportunity to mention this meeting with Adrian to John Sanness at the Norwegian Foreign Policy Institute, himself a veteran of the Resistance Movement against German occupation. It was not uncommon for people to break down under stress, remarked Sanness. That was why, he added, even History majors were denied access to some files of the Resistance Movement. This was done to protect the reputations of people who had done great service for their country but who might have made the sort of mistakes that could only be understood by those who themselves had faced extreme danger.

In York, Adrian had told me of a recurring nightmare: while he was *rowing* from Cape Town to Southampton in England, his two police interrogators kept circling his boat in a fast speedboat, taunting him all the while.

AN UNCOMFORTABLE EMBRACE

At the request of the National Union of Students in Norway, on my flight back from Accra I stopped over in Zurich. From there I took a train to the Swiss

Alpine resort of Klosters to attend a conference of the western world's university students associations. The conference was convened by the Coordinating Secretariat of National Unions of Students (COSEC), with headquarters in the Dutch city of Leyden. (The organisation was disbanded in 1964, when it became known that it was run on US Central Intelligence Agency funds.)

At Klosters I was registered as a member of NUSAS alongside two White South Africans. Yet I soon discovered that while sharing the NUSAS bench my 'colleagues' would not take a chance on letting me make a statement. This struck me as odd, as the only reason for my accepting the invitation was to put South West Africa on the agenda.

When I sensed that the other Black Africans seemed to be avoiding me, I collared one of them, a Zambian, to hear why I was being ostracised. 'You are regarded as a stool pigeon for Whites who are representing South Africa to the exclusion of its Black students', he told me. So it had to do with my colour, I realised, recalling my experience in Accra.

On hearing this I promptly told both a Norwegian as well as a US representative, persons whom I had thought of as friends, about the invidious position this put me in. Later the same day one of the South Africans, Magnus Gunther, born of German parents in Swakopmund, called me in for a private talk. Quietly but bluntly he told me that if I wanted 'to make trouble' for them, they'd suggest that I leave Klosters immediately. Realising that my Zambian interlocutor had a point, I assured Magnus that I had no intention whatsoever of causing his delegation any embarrassment.

From that moment, however, I had only one thought in mind: to break away from NUSAS in as dramatic a way as I could, and at a moment of my choosing. The opportunity presented itself at the last evening's closing session. In order to get through outstanding business, the Danish chairman of the conference had limited speeches to a minute. At some point close to the end I raised my hand. The chairman asked me to speak.

I rose to plead for ten minutes to put the case of the people of South West Africa, about which, I emphasised, I had until then been offered no chance to say anything. I had to wait until the predictable protests from the already sorely tested gathering died down, before offering a compromise: 'All right,' I said, 'five minutes.' Whereupon I told them that I had simply wanted them to adopt a resolution to put together a report on the situation in South West Africa – about which I gave the briefest summary – and to disseminate the findings to all the universities represented at the conference. The motion was promptly seconded and carried unanimously.

The next morning I was sitting in a park waiting for the train's departure from Klosters, reflecting on the treacherous embraces from which I had been obliged to free myself, when a woman from Turkey came to sit next to me. She wanted to let me know, she said, that while my intervention the previous night hadn't been the most eloquent, it had certainly been the most moving. With these comforting words she rose and left. Some four years later, COSEC published a factual Research and Information Committee report on the situation in South West Africa. Magnus Gunther was the editor. By then, the agents for Ethiopia and Liberia at the ICJ were presenting argument that apartheid was at conflict with international law.

CHAPTER SEVEN

Student days

RUTH REESE AND PAUL SHETELIG

In 1960 there were only a few foreign students enrolled at the University of Oslo (UiO), practically all of them involved in post-graduate research. For this reason our paths seldom crossed. The various humanities institutes were spread throughout the city, and the science faculties moved to an out-of-town campus. Only anatomy, law and economics remained in downtown Oslo. So my daily contact even with the Norwegian students turned out to be thin. People I met 'off-campus' and at the University library would provide what insight I gained into the society in which I had landed.

Soon after my arrival from New York I received an invitation for dinner from the singer Ruth Reese, who the year before had dedicated the spiritual *Joshua fit de battle of Jericho*, to the Reverend Michael Scott and me. Ruth's husband, Pål Shetelig, ran a bookshop in Oslo. The war had interrupted his career as a sportsman. Even so, he boasted Norway's light-heavyweight boxing championship to his credit. We therefore never lacked things to talk about. Even I knew my stuff about boxing's greats: Joe Louis, Max Schmelling, Primo Carnera, Sugar Ray Robinson. He hadn't heard about Jake Ntuli and Jimmy Carruthers, respectively South Africa's and Australia's greats in the fly-weight division.

Ruth had feared the worst, she told me, when after my passport had been retracted nobody knew what had become of me. She had exhorted the students association to organise a South Africa committee and to raise more stipends to get Black students to Oslo. She couldn't understand why on earth they absolutely had to have as chairperson of the committee Gunnar Jahn, an opponent of boycotting South Africa.

In due course I would also learn that Ruth had herself fought the proxy battles all Black Americans had to fight to gain a place in the sun. The opera world would have stood open to her if she had been White. Winners at the annual Chicago classic music festival used to be invited to all the major operatic scenes of the United States. In 1948 something sensational happened when a unanimous jury picked her, a Black alto, as the best of 27 contestants in that division from all over the US and Canada.

However, in her case, the invitations to other performances which could have consolidated her triumph never materialised. In hopes of improving her chances, Ruth boarded a passenger liner for Europe. There she found that prejudice against Black performers of classical art was as prevalent as in her home country, while she had to be on guard against unwanted attention. 'Have you had a Black woman in bed yet?' she heard a Frenchman say to her agent in the taxi on their way to her hotel after a night's performance in Paris. Assuming that she knew no French her agent replied, 'Not yet, but I intend to do so tonight'.

'Would you believe it?' Ruth burst out, telling the story.

She discovered, though, that she could make a living with her art in cabaret performances with a repertoire of Black American music interspersed with jewels from the European treasury of songs. She also found that a wider audience could be reached through that medium – in schools, in churches, in neighbourhood halls – and that audiences were avid to hear her tell about the contribution Black people had made to the US cultural heritage – in science and in the arts, as writers and performers, or as champions of human rights.

Ruth's account reminded me of an afternoon in Cape Town in 1954. I had just returned to my room from school when the unmistakeable voice of a Black baritone coming from one of the three SABC channels arrested my attention. It was extremely seldom that one could hear a Black voice broadcast by the country's public radio. The singer performed a fifteen-minute recital of German *lieder* and English songs that he concluded with a sweet lullaby in Zulu. The announcer explained that he had recently returned home from Europe where he had attended music academies. That broadcast was the only time that I would ever hear that magnificent voice. A flood of protests from White fanatics put a stop to further broadcasts of performances by him.

In time, Ruth would become like an aunt to whom I would turn for advice when I felt unable to relate to 'the natives'. Returning from her frequent tours of the country and abroad, she would call me to share with Paul meals she cooked like no one else in Oslo.

In 1961 she offered to throw a dinner party for my birthday to which I could invite friends. I could think of no one else except Freddy Reddy, a recently arrived student from Durban studying Medicine, my adopted 'sister' Wenche Barth Eide and her husband Asbjørn. But then I recalled that on a Marine Biology excursion to Northern Norway, Wenche had sent me a postcard co-signed by another Biology student to whom I had briefly spoken at a leap-year event at Kroa, the students' beer hall, the year before. Wenche assured me that it would be okay to call her fellow student, Edel Havin, and let me have her telephone number.

With our acquaintanceship reinforced by Ruth's pungent Southern cuisine, going steady became easy. And when Edel invited me home, the normalcy with which I was received by her family – mother, father, sister and brother – dissolved what anxieties I might have felt about our relationship.

TORBORG NEDREAAS

The years of German occupation of Norway were never absent in the discussions that followed the talks I was asked to give. Ridden as I was by my own anxieties and fears, if not the insularity of youth, initially I didn't really comprehend the pain that the occupation had wrought in the lives of practically everyone I came in contact with. Understanding began to dawn on me only through becoming acquainted with families that had experienced the divisions of the war years when loyalties within individual families were often on opposing sides.

Author Torborg Nedreaas had escaped being sent to the extermination camps to which the great majority of Norwegian Jews were shipped during the German occupation of the country. She had found a hideaway for herself, her mother and her two sons on the offshore island of Stord. Married a second time she settled with her second husband, Aksel Njaa, in a timber cottage situated on the shore of the Bundefjord arm of the Oslo fjord.

My acquaintance with Torborg Nedreaas and Aksel Njaa began when I was invited one weekend to their home, together with a few other foreign students and friends of the family. We boarded a ferry for the short voyage up the Bundefjord arm of the Oslo fjord to Blylaget. During the course of the evening, Torborg sought me out with a protest poem that she had written, seven or eight years earlier. It had been in reaction to a commentary on the state of the world just then, read on NRK the Norwegian State Radio on Christmas Eve. The commentary followed a news bulletin telling among other events, of the shooting of eleven Africans by the police in Johannesburg. With the exception of the war in Korea, the commentator thought that the world was at peace. The fact that eleven Blacks had been killed by White, Christian police evidently wasn't able to impress on him the fact that a different kind of war was being waged, a race war leaving Black people dead, maimed and deprived. The complacency of this important news medium had destroyed the Nedreaas appetite for a feast.

Torborg was a little apologetic about the weaknesses of the stanzas she had written. An angry letter to the editor might have been better. But it had been one of the first and only times that she had felt tempted to express herself in verse, she said. This was the beginning of a series of many excursions to the Nedreaas-Njaa residence at Blylaget.

In addition to established fellow authors and individuals involved in the publishing business, Sunday dinners there drew many younger authors and artists still at the beginning of their careers. Most of them were from the left side of the political spectrum, people with a cause, and in time I would recognise the battle-scars – on both Torborg and Aksel – of a lifetime of struggle against bigotry, in private as in public life. Norway's post-war strategic re-orientation – from neutralism to membership of the North Atlantic Treaty Organisation – had marginalised many individuals for whom it was difficult to reconcile with the militarisation of their society.

For Aksel, a sworn communist, who had been a Civil Servant before the war, employment opportunities seemed to have vanished. He appeared to experience what in Germany was called *berufsverbot* (an occupational ban). For a living he had turned to the translation of books. I recall with fondness our Sundays on skis when we would discuss world affairs.

Some little time after my making their acquaintance a tragedy hit the family. Torborg's younger son, Kaare Kieding, broke his back in a motor car accident and was taken to hospital. On regaining consciousness, a hospital nurse pressed slices of orange against his parched lips. His mouth moved and when the nurse listened it was to hear him say, 'Are they from South Africa?' When she replied in the affirmative, having made inquiries, he weakly shook his head.

There was pride in her voice as Torborg related this to me. But her indignation was ignited by the thought that disabled persons are seldom consulted about their preferences.

THE CLAUSEN FAMILY

A week before Norway's Constitution Day, celebrated on 17 May, I kept an appointment in town with a businessman, Jørg Clausen. He headed the festivities committee of his local community in the suburb of Bærum, he explained, and wanted me to deliver the five-minute homily with which such events are customarily solemnised. The reason for inviting me, he emphasised, was to remind people that the oppression my people were opposing was related to that from which they themselves had emerged a mere fourteen years earlier. The venue was a park by the fjord where families in festive mood gathered for the day's celebrations. These turned out to be like nothing I could have imagined: colourfully clad children of all ages merrily waving the national flag, with their parents keeping themselves in the background.

I spent the night drafting and redrafting seven or eight sentences on the theme as suggested by Jørg, and had them translated by Kari Sundbye. But, surveying the celebratory scene in the park, the incongruity of what I had to say made me wonder about Jørg's reasoning for wanting me to say it here. Yet, by going there to deliver the briefest remarks on the theme of freedom, I won the friendship of a family who had been actively engaged in the Resistance Movement. Jørg Clausen was modest about his role in the high-risk job of transporting Jewish Norwegians to safety across the Swedish border. To save his own life he eventually had to follow the same route with his wife Thea. Pointing out a place where he once had had to seek cover, he confided to me that he had received training in methods of silent killing and served in the military after the war, but that he was pleased about never having had to take the life of another person.

This commitment to non-violence, and compassion for the less fortunate appeared to be an imperative for a family that had known the diverging loyalties of the war years.

Thea's mother, the widowed Mrs Sigrid Larsen, had seen the devastation wrought by war and become dedicated to pacifism when shortly after the First World War she travelled to Paris through Germany and the Benelux countries on her honeymoon. Her opposition to Norway's membership of NATO, articulated in a constant stream of publications, earned her the sobriquet of Fredslarsen – Larsen for Peace.

Yet there was disquiet in the Larsen-Clausen home, when it became known that the wartime's seamen, some suffering the symptoms of post-traumatic distress, were being forgotten and neglected. The Norwegian seamen sailed the ships that had supplied Great Britain with the oil without which the war with Germany could hardly have been sustained.[27] Thea's response was to enrol in a college of social affairs so as to acquire the skills wherewith to come to the assistance of the survivors. Her elder sister, Gunvor Sæther, also married to a businessman, continued their mother's activity as an anti-war publicist.

Even though the Clausen home had become another oasis for me, I never heard them speak about a family connection with one of the most

---

[27] Commenting on the contribution of Norway's merchant fleet to Britain's war effort, King Haakon VII mentioned the supply of fuel in the Battle of Britain, 'without which the Spitfires could not have brought the German Air Force its first defeat'. He quotes the then Parliamentary Secretary to the Ministry of War Transport, Mr Noel Baker, as saying, 'The Norwegian tankers were to the Battle of the Atlantic what the Spitfires were to the Battle of Britain in 1940'. And a British shipping paper, 'The British Motorship', as writing that, 'the Norwegian Merchant Fleet was worth 1 million soldiers'. (Speech 7 June 1944)

invidious instances of the post-war squaring of account between the 'good' and the presumed tainted Norwegians: Knut Hamsun was married to Mrs Larsen's sister, Marie, an actress and the fêted author in her own right of children's books that were widely read in Germany as well. After the war, Hamsun was charged with having provided moral support to the enemy's war effort, stripped of his possessions and subjected to a pre-trial course of base humiliation. A psychiatrist called upon Marie Hamsun, herself imprisoned, for questioning about her husband, whereupon he declared Hamsun to be feeble of mind. The diagnosis saved the Norwegian judiciary from having to sentence the world renowned author for having exercised his right to free speech – even if the enemy might have drawn comfort from his letters to the editors. Broken down in health and financially ruined, Knut Hamsun would 'not go gentle into that good night'. In his swansong, entitled *Paa gjengrodde stier* – On Overgrown Pathways – he delivered a resounding indictment against his antagonists in the judiciary and in a psychiatrist's overcoat.

One of the more curious requests I received was to deliver a valedictory address at a confirmation ceremony for youths. The organisers were the Norwegian Humanistic Society with the immense expanse of the Oslo City Hall as venue. To add to my misgivings about being associated with an anti-religious grouping in a country with a State Church, Kristian Horn, founder of the Society, listed the names of people who had preceded me as valedictorians. The previous year's speaker had been Arnulf Øverland,[28] the poet who in the thirties had caused an outrage for decrying Christianity as 'the eleventh plague'. He also formulated what could go for the 'eleventh commandment': '*du skal ikke tåle så inderlig vel, den urett som ikke rammer deg selv*' (You shall not tolerate so very well the injustice that does not harm you).

After days of considering what to say, I finally hit upon the obvious. Taking my cue from Øverland, I suggested to the candidates that while they had chosen an alternative source of moral authority than one predicated on religious beliefs, this did not relieve them from an obligation towards the less privileged members of their society.

My inspiration had also come from visits to three rehabilitation centres for young children: two outside Oslo and one outside Stockholm.

---

[28] Some time later one of my teachers at the university, Johan Vogt, introduced me to Arnulf Øverland. Øverland wanted to hear me say some words in Nama, so he could hear the distinct clicks of the language that he had only read about. For some reason it occurred to me to ask his opinion about the biblical parable of two sons who had been asked by their father to do him a service. The first one had refused the request but then repented; the other had agreed, but then failed to keep his word. Øverland reflected a moment before responding that it was a question he hadn't considered before but that he liked neither of the sons' behaviours. Moreover, he added, he '*hadde heller ikke sans for*' (didn't care much either for) the notion that children owed their parents unquestioning obedience. In this remark I finally found relief from the nagging guilt I had been feeling about having left home without parental sanction.

The first happened when a social worker insisted that I address a group of juvenile delinquents for which she had responsibility at a closed, correctional institution. I couldn't quite understand how the situation of the boys could be related to the struggle for liberation of people in a distant land. I imagined it to require an order of awareness about the notion of a society beyond what the waifs could be assumed to possess. Yet the sociologist, who had worn down my resistance, thought that it might be good for the boys to be informed about a world beyond their own, where people were also struggling for a better life.

At the UN one of the journalists who had interviewed me for their papers in Norway was Ingegjerd Galtung, then the doyenne of the organisation's press corps. With an introduction to her sister, Dagny Galtung Oftedal, in Oslo I made acquaintance with the work of the city's first school psychologist, who also had responsibility for the care of juvenile deliquents. I accompanied her to a rehabilitation centre for boys that the city maintained on a farm with cows and horses and by all appearances a kindly 'uncle', to engage them. But what struck me was the disinterest with which they appeared to regard our arrival there.

A lift to Stockholm with Ms Galtung-Oftedal enabled me to make the acquaintance of Barnbyn Skå, a village for neglected children situated on a lakeside near the city. The village was run by her colleague, Gustav Jönsson, for whom care for society's most vulnerable members was an ideological imperative. It provided children of the ages between 7 and 15 with the love of substitute parents. The spontaneity with which a little girl broke loose from a group to throw her arms around the visiting 'aunt' brought a tear to the eyes of somebody who 'had seen it all'.

DAGBLADET

Dagbladet, the liberal daily, reported my speech to the agnostic youth as if something significant had been said. Shortly afterwards the paper's foreign editor, Ragnar Vold, called me in for a meeting. Shoving aside the papers cluttering the guest chair in his office, Mr Vold stated that, as I would have noticed, there weren't many journalists with insight into African affairs in Norway. He wondered if I'd be willing to pick books for regular review, for which *Dagbladet* would pay.

I think I did four books in all, before realising that I had taken on a bigger task than I could manage. To review a book on issues with which I myself was not familiar, such as one on the Kenyan leader Jomo Kenyatta, I had to read three or four others so as to acquire the necessary background.

It was with regret that I had to drop out of a newspaper column that was as much a privilege to write as it should have been rewarding. The association did, however, leave me with access to a newspaper that would seek to keep its readers updated on developments in the apartheid state.

A FILM AND AN EXTRAORDINARY ÉMIGRÉ

A request that intrigued me, was to appear as foil in a promotional film about Trondheim: '*Trondheim, en by i vekst*' – a developing city. I was to act the part of a visitor and have the city's spokespersons extolling the ancient city's attractions to me. Expecting to be financially rewarded for my participation, I would discover that the film company was operating on a shoestring. But I was glad for the participation, which provided me with some insight into the concerns of town planners.

And then I made the acquaintance of a remarkable woman, a Russian émigré named Viktoria Backhe, the widow of a Norwegian consul, whose contribution to the city's cultural heritage had been second to none. Together with her husband she built a museum to honour Peder Tordenskiold (1690-1720), the nation's most renowned sea captain. To this she added a magnificent collection of musical instruments from all over the world.

As her contribution to the Trondheim film project she lavished a dinner on a delegation that included city dignitaries in addition to the film crew. There she treated us to a hilarious account of how she had bent the arm of a French Minister of Culture to secure for her collection one of three priceless precursors to the piano-forte that she had spotted in a Paris museum. Showing us around the music collection she pointed out the guitar's emulation of the female body and, stroking the contours of her own barrel-like torso, uttered a sigh and said, 'Regrettably I am not classic. I am more or less baroque'.

I still treasure the copy of *Tordenskioldiana*, a tome she had edited and had presented to me that evening.

CHIEF ALBERT LUTHULI AWARDED NOBEL PEACE PRIZE

In October 1961 Mr Gunnar Jahn of the Norwegian Nobel Committee announced that they had awarded their prize for 1960 to Chief Albert John Luthuli of South Africa and the prize for 1961 to UN Secretary-General, Dag Hammarskjöld . Hammarskjöld had lost his life in Northern Rhodesia earlier that year – under circumstances that suggested he was killed to thwart his efforts at resolving the conflicts around the fledgling Congo's future.

Oslo received Luthuli as if he were a Head of State. In leopard skin headgear at formal occasions, and exuding dignity as befits a leader, he looked the part. Public interest in the Luthuli couple's movements about town knew no bounds; the media followed their every move. To hail him, a great throng one cold evening gathered in front of the City Hall carrying lit torches. At his departure, a headline succinctly summed up his stay, 'Zulu Chief took the Prize. Peace Prize Laureate Albert John Luthuli conquered Norway with his worthy demeanour and wise speech'.

Chief Luthuli's presence in Oslo briefly turned the Norwegian capital into the headquarters of the Anti-Apartheid Movement (AAM) abroad. In addition to members of his family who had accompanied him from South Africa, his entourage included the leaders of the ANC-in-exile, headed by Mr Oliver Tambo, Robert Resha, advocate Duma Nokwe and others. Canon John Collins of St Paul's Cathedral in London represented the British AAM. Having boarded his plane from London in Gothenburg, the tall figure of the Swedish missionary, the Reverend Gunnar Helander, scooped the Swedish press with 'An interview with Luthuli, conducted in his own language'. From the US, Al Lowenstein turned up to honour him.

President John F Kennedy sent the Chief a letter of congratulations, an act of recognition that for a time might have shielded the ANC from being branded a terrorist organisation – but did not save a fugitive Nelson Mandela's whereabouts from being divulged by American agents to the South African Police.

The undoubted high point of Luthuli's visit occurred at the conclusion of his acceptance speech in the University's Great Hall. Overcome by emotion the great man intoned *Nkosi Sikelel' iAfrika* (God Bless Africa). Seated in the front row, King Olav V of Norway rose smartly to his feet ahead of all others in the hall, and from their various places those of us who knew the words joined in a thin chorus for the very first public rendition in Norway of South Africa's future national anthem.

One of the younger members of Luthuli's entourage was the Zulu poet Mazizi Kunene. Sharing dinner with him one evening, I told him of my meeting with the laureate on the day before my departure from Cape Town and of his patient response to the queries that an American journalist put to him about the ANC's policies. Kunene heard me out and then drily remarked that the line of policy represented by 'that man' had run its course. He added that Luthuli's successor as leader of the ANC, Nelson Mandela, was busy organising a military wing of the ANC, *Umkhonto we Sizwe* (Spear of the Nation).

At that moment – even as he had been anointed an African Prince of Peace – tragedy for me became personified by Chief Albert John Luthuli.

FATHER IN BOTSWANA

'Is it your father who has been arrested in Botswana?' a journalist asked, stunning me with a call from NRK – the Norwegian Broadcasting Corporation – early one Sunday morning in August 1963. He had just read a wire message stating that my father, Hermanus Beukes, together with three companions, had been abducted from Botswana and returned to South West Africa in order to halt their planned flight to the UN in New York. While I was unfamiliar with Paul Smit and Andreas Shipanga, Kenneth Abrahams was an acquaintance from UCT who married a fellow student, Otillie Schimming from Windhoek. And while I knew nothing about the circumstances that had compelled my father to risk exile, it was clear to me that, quite mistakenly, he must have thought that a complaint lodged in person at the UN would be of consequence. That for at least one of his companions it was quite literally an escape from the gallows, I would learn only much later.

This situation concerned Kenny Abrahams who at UCT had become involved in a so-called National Liberation Front alongside the philosopher Neville Alexander. Meanwhile Rehoboth had lost its only medical practitioner when, in compliance with the town's classification as a Reservation, the White Dr Laubscher was compelled to uproot his practice. To fill his place, Kenny Abrahams was persuaded to establish a practice in Rehoboth, rather than in Windhoek, his wife's hometown.

THE ABRAHAMS CASE

Long after the event, my sister Anne-Marie related the details to me.

Returning from a doctor's errand in the northern town of Otjiwarongo in the late afternoon, Kenny responded to a call from an outlying farm named Duineveld – against his wife Otillie's advice. That observance of a doctor's calling might have saved his own life. That evening a girl living at their place, which happened to be situated next-door to my family's, turned up to tell Father that the Security Police had come to look for Kenny. Father instructed her to call him immediately at whatever the time, should the police return – which they did, at daybreak. This time the girl was frantic, pleading with Father to hurry, even while he was getting into his clothes as fast as he could. Mother woke up my younger brothers and sent them out to wake Grandfather and other burghers of the community.

Shortly afterwards both Father and Grandfather took up position outside Kenny's bedroom. Facing the officer in charge, Grandfather pointed at his own forehead and challenged him to shoot him – before he would allow Kenny Abrahams to be arrested.

With a crowd forming outside the doctor's residence and tempers rising, the officer in charge attempted to prevent the confrontation from getting out of hand. Speaking up, he gave his 'word of honour' that nothing would befall Kenny. In response Father reminded the gathering that Dr Verwoerd had given his word of honour to the UCT student, Phillip Kgosana,[29] who had led thousands of Black workers peacefully to Parliament to deliver a letter of protest. If Phillip would lead the demonstrators back to their township of Langa in as peaceful a way as they had come, Phillip was reassured, Verwoerd would meet with him the next day to discuss the workers' complaints. When Phillip turned up for the audience, he was promptly put under arrest and jailed. If Verwoerd's word of honour could not be trusted, Father asked how much worth could be attached to that of a fifth-rank officer.

At this point the police officers withdrew, whereupon Father instructed Barend de Klerk, a neighbour and childhood friend, to bring my grandfather's car around to Kenny's house. To Kenny, he suggested that he collect what clothes he would need for some days absence. With Barend at the wheel they next 'smuggled' Kenny out of town to a farm south of Rehoboth – to consider the situation.

That night a large number of people, including some from Windhoek who had heard about the commotion, congregated at the Methodist church in Rehoboth to vent their feelings. Breaking the rule against teachers expressing political opinions, the teacher Paul Smit let it be known what he thought: 'When this country becomes independent, we'll hang up the Boers by their heels'.

Unhappy at the turn of events, Grandfather, with memories of his own earlier scrape with South African forces, sent my brother Hermann Ludvig to keep the refugees informed. But he soon let himself be driven to the farm to advise them to return. There he was reminded that 'interfering with the Police in the execution of their duties' was a criminal offence carrying a heavy jail sentence. In view of this he dropped his objections to my father's idea that he and Kenny make their escape from the country to lodge a complaint at the UN. Father next sent George to summon Paul Smit, on whose vehicle they travelled to Windhoek via a roundabout route. In Windhoek they were joined by Andreas Shipanga, an associate of the Abrahams' as one of the founders of the organisation that had taken the name of South West Africa People's

---

[29]   Phillip Kgosana, a UCT student, found himself compelled to take on the leadership of the protest march on Parliament from the township of Langa that swelled into the tens of thousands along the route, when the senior officers of the Pan African Congress movement of which he was a member, was arrested by the Police.

Organisation (SWAPO). The same evening they crossed the Botswana border and made for the town of Ghansi. However, having reached the safety of the then still British Protectorate of Bechuanaland, my father's companions relaxed their vigilance and accepted a lift aboard a truck that was supposed to go east. The helpful drivers turned out to be South African agents who returned them to prison in the town of Gobabes, grievously assaulting Father along the way. The British Government now stepped in to demand the release of the men who had been abducted from a British Protectorate.

On their return to Botswana the fugitives sent word to Kenny's wife Otillie, to join them. When she arrived in Francistown, where the group had been housed in a refugee camp, things quickly turned sour between my father and his companions. With their escapade, known as 'the Abrahams Case', having become a diplomatic *cause célèbre*, the fact that Father had saved the good doctor from serving time on Robben Island – if not worse – was promptly forgotten. Father was informed that his idea of presenting a case at the UN was bizarre – in view of his decrepit take on the politics involved, not to mention his non-existent command of English. The enmity he subsequently experienced during their months-long sojourn in a refugee camp made him fear for his life. This eventually became a matter of concern even to the locals. Doctor Thuynsma, the surgeon with whom I had become acquainted at the Khama home in Serowe four years earlier, secured for him a place away from the refugee camp where he had been staying. Next, Mburumba Kerina who happened to be in the country called on Father with a warning that the people with whom he had associated himself 'were not his friends' In conversation with Kerina (November 2012) he said that at the time he was assisting Seretse Khama to get the political party he had formed in shape for the elections for independent Botswana's Constitutional Assembly. Kerina had arranged for Father to be picked up by Mrs Ruth Khama, who was canvassing in Francistown, and to be transported to the safety of Serowe.

On the morning prior to his departure for Serowe, Father received a summons from the District Commissioner in Francistown. Directing him into a soundproof room, the official informed him that the Botswana authorities were aware of the circumstances that had motivated the South Africans. They had wanted to question doctor Abrahams concerning acts of sabotage that had been either perpetrated or planned. If my father would make a submission concerning threats to his life from his companions, the commissioner stated, the Botswana authorities would be ready to take appropriate action.

Father responded that he was not one to dig holes for other people to fall into. This response earned him the official's praise and the reassurance that his safety was a matter of concern to the Botswana authorities.

Father remained in Serowe for a short while before giving up the idea of travelling to New York. In consultation with Seretse Khama (my source here is again Mburumba Kerina) he decided to present himself to the authorities in Pretoria – in hopes of being permitted to return home. Although committed to prison 'for his own safety', on arrival in the capital, the police officers treated him with unexpected deference. The ensuing exchanges went both ways. The officers showed him documentation that portrayed Kenneth Abrahams as the mastermind behind the group associated with the more well-known Neville Alexander. They informed him that while the latter was sentenced to imprisonment on Robben Island, Kenny would have been sent to the gallows. The source of their information about Abrahams was said to be a prisoner whose jail sentence had been curtailed on condition that he infiltrate an alleged secret cell of ten at the heart of the Armed Resistance Group.

During the three weeks he spent in prison Father unburdened himself of every objection he harboured about the apartheid regime's policies with regard to South West Africa. Among the complaints he raised was the disregard of the terms of the mandate by which South Africa was obliged to advance the education of the Territory's youth. That this particular demand had made an impact was discovered by my brother Kehat. On submitting an application for a bursary to the Administration in Windhoek, so as to complete his medical studies at UCT, he was told that it was due to his father that a bursary was his for the claiming – as it was for all others.

VISITING THE SINS OF THE FATHERS ...

Unaware of all of the above, in distant Oslo I received a letter from Otillie Schimming, writing from Dar es Salaam, in which she spouted gall about 'the betrayal' of his people that my father had perpetrated. The people would never forgive 'Enemies of the Revolution' like him, she let me know. What I could do to reverse the damage that she claimed had been done to the 'liberation movement' the letter did not make clear to me.

Otillie's rage deterred me from sharing with her my relief at the return of the family's breadwinner to their embrace. If he had not returned I should have had to face the grim prospect of finding a job to help sustain them at home, and to help him abroad. This would have meant being obliged to terminate my enrolment as a student at the Faculty of Economics in Oslo.

Back home in Rehoboth, meanwhile, Hermanus Christoffel Beukes remained concerned about the condition of his people. In due course he would throw all the energy he was capable of generating into a campaign to conjoin the country's diverse groups of people so as to be able to present a united front behind calls for an end to the occupation regime. It was the first time such an effort had been made. It resulted in the formation of the short-lived National Convention.

All along he opposed the transformation by Pretoria of Rehoboth into a Bantustan-model statelet, a fight that he would lose and that would result in the further loss of the community's self-government to central authority. This time Father's adversaries were not 'the enemy' but members of his own community.

SWA ON THE FOREIGN POLITICAL AGENDA IN SCANDINAVIA

My first thought, on being told that my father had escaped into Botswana, was that he and his companions would need money. But I could not imagine who to approach for assistance. I did, however, agree to the journalist's request to come over to the NRK studio to provide some general background for the midday news bulletin.

Reasoning that the event required as much publicity as possible, I boarded a train to Stockholm that evening to make contact with the Swedish media. Nils Treving, one of the 'young liberals' with whom I had struck up a friendship after the WFLRY conference three years earlier, introduced me to Per Wästberg, an author who had published influential books about apartheid, and to Anders Ehnmark, another Africa specialist on the editorial staff of *Dagens Nyheter*. Wästberg offered me tea and sympathy. Ehnmark wrote a two-column report about 'The case of Dr Abrahams'. From Stockholm I took a train to Gothenburg and, recalling the *Göteborg Handels- och Sjöfartstidning's* (GHST) reputation as a champion of freedom, spoke to a desk reporter who duly wrote a column about the case.

Having done what I had travelled to Sweden for, on the train back to Oslo I was suddenly struck by the pointlessness of the errand. Appealing to people in foreign lands, for some reaction to a situation about which they could do as little as I, appeared to me as an absurdity that I had been engaged in for far too long. Back at Studentbyen I noticed with scant interest a message that had been left at my door. It was to call Doctor Fred Lange-Nielsen, a surgeon whom I had met some weeks before at the opening of the University's Summer School.

When I returned his call, Fred, as he wanted to be called, told me that he'd heard the interview with me on the radio and was keen to do what he could to help his colleague, Dr Abrahams, and my father. He invited me to a dinner on Saturday evening at the house of one of his friends to discuss what could be done to help the refugees in Bechuanaland. My girlfriend would be welcome, he added.

I accepted Fred's invitation merely out of courtesy. I fully expected to have to address yet another group that would politely listen to what I had to tell, only to wring their hands afterwards at the inability of their small country to do anything to influence the situation. It was in this state of mind that I asked Edel to join me at the house of Architect P.A. Mellbye (known as Pim-Pam by his friends), where a group of fifteen guests, all middle aged, was assembled.

After a meal served by the hostess, Fred invited me to address the gathering. I made it brief, no more than twelve minutes, emphasising that the nations, including Norway, that had entrusted the Union of South Africa with the administration of South West Africa had taken upon themselves a moral obligation to be concerned about how that trust was being observed.

The silence that followed was finally interrupted by an elderly figure of commanding presence, speaking in the unmistakable voice of a man from Bergen. He said, 'It is clear we cannot just sit here and listen to a story like that without doing anything about it.' A chorus of murmurs confirmed that Egil Tresselt, a public relations consultant, had expressed what everyone was thinking. They soon reached a consensus that if they didn't exercise what influence they, with their standing in society could wield, no one else would. But what were they to do?

At this point Mr Tresselt took charge of a brainstorming session where all possible courses of action were considered. It soon led to a second consensus: the people of Norway ought to be persuaded to demand that South Africa be divested of the right to govern South West Africa. Somebody recalled that the Nordic foreign ministers were due to meet in Stockholm later in the coming week for their customary annual consultations prior to setting off for the GA of the United Nations. That made it clear that the Norwegian foreign minister had to be 'instructed' as it were, to put such a demand before his colleagues so as to make it a Nordic initiative.

To generate the public opinion required a short, sharp campaign to reinforce such a call – from the following Monday to the Wednesday evening. To make the desired impact, it had to be an unconventional campaign, one where people were asked *not* for their money, but merely for their signatures in support of an easily comprehended text. Even as he was explaining all these considerations, the campaign's text took shape in the fertile mind of an Egil Tresselt in top gear:

Nå gjelder det Syd-Vest Afrika.
Brennende spørsmål: Er det gamle mandat et eksklusivt privilegium eller en
internasjonal forpliktelse?
Ta fra Verwoerd formynderskapet han forvalter forbrytersk.
Vårt krav er, at FN overtar mandatet som en internasjonal forpliktelse.
Vi ber utenriksministeren fremme for Nordens utenriksmøte tanken om FN-
aksjon i høst.

(This time the focus is on South West Africa. Burning issue: Does the old mandate stand for exclusive privileges or for an international obligation? Take from Verwoerd the trusteeship he administers in criminal fashion. We demand that the UN take over the mandate as an international responsibility. We request the Minister of Foreign Affairs to present at his meeting with his Nordic colleagues the proposal that the UN take such action this autumn.)

In order to lend weight to a campaign about which many Norwegians might have reservations, it was thought prudent to obtain the support of the nation's leading citizens – from across party and other dividing lines.

To get such a campaign off the ground anywhere calls for certain practical measures, such as obtaining permission to put up a stand in the Eidsvoll Square in front of the parliament building. Then we needed to engage the press, and so on. Tasks having been assigned, it was well past midnight when the group broke up with the understanding that they would meet again later that Sunday afternoon, to finalise the details.

By the time we got together later that day the required permissions had been obtained; group member Bernhard Rostad, a journalist from *Dagbladet*, had alerted his press colleagues; Fred's wife Vesla had transferred the campaign text onto a banner of the required size; the stand was being seen to; all that remained was to draw up a roster of attendance and errands to be run by the members: an opera singer, two architects, a housewife, three art and textile designers, a physiotherapist, a stage actor, a film actress, a medical specialist, a businessman, a journalist, an Olympic ski-jumping medallist and film-maker, a biology student, and the city's premier public relations consultant.

For me it was simply a thrill to observe at privileged close quarters a squad of the Norwegian capital's burghers making ready to launch nothing short of an assault on the sensibilities of their townspeople. I felt thoroughly chastised about the spirit in which I had approached them.

Demonstrations and marches are not foreign to Norway. Even so, it could have been socially risky for some of the individuals to be involved with a political action of the kind spelled out by our text. However, by presenting a common front, the fifteen attracted considerable attention and their involvement certainly lent a measure of gravity to their demand. It was the first of its kind by the citizens of any country whose representatives had given South Africa its mandate to govern South West Africa at Versailles in 1920. The demand was for that mandate to be revoked.

The stand was rigged up on Monday morning, 2 September 1963. One of the first to affix his signature to the text was the principal of Oslo University, Johan T Ruud. He was followed by the philosopher mountaineer, Arne Næss. Having arrived in town a little late, Næss hurried to the stand, pulling his little daughter behind him, before dashing off to his class.

The afternoon papers, *Dagbladet* and *Verdens Gang*, competed that day with the breadth of coverage that they lent to the campaign. *Verdens Gang* devoted its front page to Professor Ruud signing the protocol with the heading '*Rektor Ruud protesterer*'. *Dagbladet* used his picture with a story under the heading, '*Verwoerd carries out apartheid ruthlessly in UN's Trust Territory*'. The subheadings read: '*Wants to systematically wipe out native population; spontaneous action started in [the city centre] in protest against abuses*'. It further highlighted the abduction of Dr Abrahams and his companions as the '*sheer Wild-West Methods used by the South African Police*'.

While the implication of Dr Verwoerd's genocidal intentions was regrettable, I felt no compulsion to correct it. I reasoned that the journalist might have been misled by my pointing out the discrepancy in the life expectancies of Blacks and Whites – three score and ten plus years, against a mere 45. To me this showed the cost to the Black population of their subjugation to White domination. I reasoned that any attempt at correcting Dagbladet's heading would merely have invited digression. What was more disturbing was the failure of *Aftenposten*, subscribed to by a majority of the city's households, to make any mention of the campaign. On Tuesday, *Dagbladet* reviewed the media's coverage of the campaign as follows:

'Two afternoon papers had it on their front pages yesterday; it was sent in the television news casts at 8 pm and at 10 pm. The NTB [Norwegian Telegraph Bureau – news agency] sent it out and all morning papers had it this morning: that yesterday a spontaneous campaign started in Studenterlunden (the central city square), with the demand that the Verwoerd regime be divested of the trusteeship of South West Africa, that the UN take it over as an international responsibility, and that the Foreign Minister present a proposal for such action by the UN this autumn at the meeting of Nordic foreign ministers in Stockholm. But the country's largest circulation newspaper has hitherto not found any space for it; the campaign has hitherto not been mentioned with as much as a single line, either in yesterday's afternoon edition, or this morning's. We merely mention this.'

It was explained to me that this comment was an oblique reference to the *Aftenposten's* failure to take a stand against the persecution of the Jews in Nazi Germany during the 1930s. To underscore the message, a photographer from Dagbladet accompanied Edel and me to the home of the poet Arnulf Øverland with a protocol to secure his signature – at his request. It was an assignment that greatly pleased me.

DOCTOR HENDRIK FRENSCH VERWOERD

A document I found in the file under my name at the National Archives mellowed my view of Dr Verwoerd. It revealed to me the patriarchal mindset of the man who had assumed charge of even the minutiae of government business – in the execution of which he showed anxiety about making any mistake. Marked 'Confidential' the document refers to correspondence between the South African diplomatic stations in Stockholm and New York, and the departmental heads of Internal and External Affairs. An opinion expressed by 'His Excellency the Prime Minister' about a passport for Hans Beukes is cited as follows:

'Since I had no firsthand knowledge about Beukes after his departure overseas, I could only have made my assertions on what had been committed to me. I therefore don't know from where the wrong impression comes. If it is true though that Beukes is now only devoting himself to his studies, and there is no reason to think that he would come to make trouble here, a passport could be given to him if he asks for it – with a reminder that his departure without a passport is in contravention of the law, but that with a view to his youth and reports about good behaviour the Government had decided that, if he asks, he will be treated with clemency.

'In other words I am <u>not</u> in favour of the initiative of our Honorary Consul-General. As far as we are concerned, matters remain as they are and our standpoint is that the Government is prepared to hand out the passport, but that the person concerned must of course ask to get it. If, therefore, he should complain abroad that we don't speak the truth, our answer will be that he ought to know that, after my statement, the passport is available but that it stands to reason he must show that by asking for it he wants it. Theoretically it is thus given back to him, but not in practice until he asks for it. If he again misbehaves, we might retract it – whether he has it or not. Inform the Minister of Interior Affais about this my opinion.'

(The memo is undated but appears to have been written in late August 1962.)

GETTING TO KNOW OSLO

Manning the stand soon revealed to us the sympathies and antipathies of the city's denizens. Many were surprised to find that we didn't want their money. Others were not prepared to give their support; they merely stopped by to let us know what they thought about the ability of Africans to govern themselves. During one of my shifts a man from Iceland approached us in a foul mood to vent his spleen about Blacks in general. After he left, one of our group's members explained his outburst by reference to a sore matter in Icelandic politics: the presence of Black servicemen at the US military base at Keflavik. On another occasion an elderly gentleman stopped by to chide opera singer Anne Brown about her concern for the welfare of Blacks – when she ought to have been concerned about the threat they represented to the White race.

'*La oss nu anta, kjære fru* (Let us now suppose, dear Madam),' he began, 'that you have two daughters.'

'That's not difficult to suppose. I am in fact the mother of two lovely girls,' Anne Brown replied.

'Ah, Madam, there you have it. And let us suppose they were students at the university.'

'They are not there yet, but it is not impossible that they might want to enrol once they've finished school.'

'And when they get there,' the elderly gentleman went on, 'they might meet the young Blacks who have begun to study at our university.'

'You certainly cannot rule that out.'

'And let us suppose that soon they bring them home to you.'

'Yes?' asked Anne Brown.

'To tell you that they want to get married.'

'Oh, but that's not a choice for parents to make, it would be their choice.'

'And having married,' the gentleman said, 'they started to get children.'

'That would be quite natural, I'd think.'

'But, Madam wouldn't it be a tragic thing to happen?'

'What do you mean?'

'I'm referring to the mixing of colours …'

'Well,' said Anne, barely able to maintain her composure, 'It's not for me to have an opinion about the matter. You see, I'm the offspring of such a union.'

At this point the gentleman took a closer look at the person he had been addressing and said, 'Is it Anne Brown I'm talking to? Is it Anne Brown herself? So good to have met you, Madam!' Whereupon he saluted smartly and sauntered off.

Many people stopped by merely for the chance to talk to somebody. The things they chose to talk about at length, the minutiae of their lives that they aired, betrayed the loneliness many single-person households must bear: the widows and the widowers, the divorced, the unattached living by themselves, the country folks who left their villages to make a living in town. Some did while others didn't eventually sign the declaration before moving on.

In the meantime I became better acquainted with the group of people with whom I had become associated. In time I would discover that as noted young musicians of their day, Fred and Pim Pam played a part in renewing their nation's musical fare at a time when, as in Nazi Germany, the cultural trendsetters viewed jazz as 'uncivilised Negro music'. To escape notice during the years of occupation, jazz clubs were registered as sewing clubs.

Some years later I asked Fred about a painting for which he had paid the then sizable sum of seven thousand kroner, and driven all the way to Gothenburg to hand over as a present to the American musician, Duke Ellington. It turned out that during an Ellington band's visit to Oslo in the 1930s, Fred, then a student, had invited the band leader to lunch at the city's premier restaurant. After the war, Fred was in New York on a research grant when he heard that Ellington was performing in Harlem. Against the advice of Whites, he made his way there. Anxious about whether Ellington would even remember him, he was overwhelmed by the great musician's response on being informed that he was in the hall. Ellington called him to the stage and introduced him to the audience as the first White man ever to have invited him for a meal at a restaurant anywhere.

With a voice as sandy as called for and with a guitar or bass at hand, Fred was in his element wherever jazz was performed. I therefore assumed that he had joined the band for a jam session that night.

On the morning of the campaign's closing, *Aftenposten*, as if to make amends, quoted verbatim the demand being put forward, and listed the names of the citizens who had taken the initiative for the campaign: Thorleif Schjelderup, Fred Lange-Nielsen, Arne Korsmo, P A M Mellbye, Egil Tresselt, Bernhard Rostad, Anne Brown Schjelderup, Moyen Egede-Nissen, Thoralf Maurstad and Per M. Skavlan. It reported that over 1 000 people had signed the petition on the first day.

If there was any doubt about what the campaign had achieved, it was laid to rest by a front-page headline in *Dagbladet* on Thursday, 5 September: '*En opinion er reist for Sør-vest-Afrika* (An opinion has been raised for South West Africa)', with the subheading, '*Også svensk krav om reaksjon* (Even Swedish demand a reaction)'. The paper noted that in spite of dismal rain throughout the last day, interest in the campaign had been on the rise towards closing time; and it published the text of the telegram sent to Norwegian Foreign Minister, Erling Wikborg:

'In a protocol laid out for 36 hours at the Wergeland Statue 3 549 women and men, prominent representatives of all political opinions, of the courts of law, of schools and the Church, of Arts and Science, of labourers and employers in industry, shipping, agriculture and forestry, handicrafts and trade, the Civil Service and public services in Norway, and of youth engaged in sports have signed the following declaration.'

It then included the full text of our campaign. And added that the footage shot for the Norwegian national television service had also been broadcast over the Swedish network; and that in an editorial the *Göteborg Handels – Och Sjöfarts Tidning* (GHST) had lent the campaign its support in the following terms:

'It cannot be disputed that the Territory has an international status. The only question is what preparations are to be made for independence … Whatever the UN decides or doesn't decide, democratic countries are fully in their rights to make direct approaches to the South African government. It would be interesting to see what they would answer to such an action in favour of the distressed inhabitants of South West Africa.'

Even more telling proof of the hardened attitude towards the South African regime was to be experienced by a hapless member of the South African parliament, Leif Egeland, a man of Norwegian extraction. He arrived in Oslo to test the waters after a right-wing coalition had come to power. Ending 28 years of rule by a Labour Party government on 28 August, John Lyng, the leader of the Conservatives, became the country's Prime Minister and the Christian Democrat, Erling Wikborg, its Foreign Minister. In terms that couldn't have been more dismissive, the Christian Democrat newspaper *Vårt Land* (Our Country) reported from a press conference held by Egeland. Under the headline, 'Verwoerd politician on a visit', it printed a photograph of the politician with the caption, 'Mr Leif Egeland, who wants to give Verwoerd even more time'. The report read:

'A Verwoerd politician has found it timely to visit us – Norwegian-speaking Leif Egeland. He has been sitting in parliament for ten years for what he calls the opposition party, The United Party, but at a press conference in Oslo yesterday it was the old, well known Verwoerd arguments he put forward.'

'It would be first and foremost the workers on the fruit farms, in the canning industry, in the fisheries and other export trades that would suffer under a boycott of South African goods,' he said. He could also tell us that

South African Blacks enjoy a higher living standard and a better standard of education than those in neighbouring countries.

'And whilst a whole world looks on with foreboding at the way in which Verwoerd tightens his iron grip on the opposition with Acts against sabotage and like measures, his appeal to Norwegians and the world at large reads: 'Give us time! A forced acceleration of equality will create conditions in South Africa that will make the Congo tragedy to look like an idyll.'

Even *Aftenposten* now made mention of the issue. Its morning edition for 6 September carried the caption, 'No common Nordic initiatives on South Africa issue, but the foreign ministers agree to coordinate Norden's attitude.' It went on to report that the South African issue had dominated discussions at the Thursday meeting, where attention was paid in particular to the problems raised by South Africa's mandate to govern South West Africa and the situation in the Portuguese colonies.

In a further story about a mysterious mishap with the plane that had been sent from Dar es Salaam to pick up the Abrahams group, the newspaper's correspondent gave prominence to a statement on the political demands my father had intended to address to the UN.

CRISIS FUND ESTABLISHED

It was with a sense of achievement that half a dozen or so members of the squad turned up to witness the last stragglers arrive to give their signatures and to help fold up the stand at 8 pm on the Wednesday evening. But at the same time there was a nagging realisation that the group stranded in Botswana remained in need of the money that we, in the interest of making a public relations impact, had renounced.

Very early on, Fred could tell us that his colleagues at Rikshospitalet, the National Hospital, and at Ullevål Hospital had contributed over 1 100 kroner to help pay for the legal assistance that their African colleague and his companions would need. At the party he threw to celebrate the success of our campaign, Fred spoke up to comment that it would be a pity for a group that had worked together so well to simply dissolve.

'*Man kunne jo få abstinens symptomer av det,*' quipped Per Skavlan, saying that it would be to court symptoms of abstinence. Skavlan was a businessman with a lively interest in the arts and theatre and with a sense of humour that made him great company. Fred, playing the role that Egil Tresselt had played the week before, had an easy task persuading the rest of the group to establish a so-called Crisis Fund. It would raise money to provide assistance to the current and future victims of the apartheid regime.

However, while the signature campaign had called for the participation of all who could give of their time, it was equally clear that the creation of a fund called for volunteers prepared to put in a long-term effort to organise the collection and administration of funds. At this point, enthusiasm flagged somewhat. Eventually Vesla Lange-Nielsen got cajoled into taking over the chore that would soon take complete charge of her life, with Edel by her side at the start of the journey.

The Crisis Fund was duly registered with the financial control authorities. As leader of the fund-raising committee, Fred Lange-Nielsen set out to recruit people from across the political spectrum as members of the Board: a bishop, a bank director, a shop steward, a medical doctor, an architect and the head of the Norwegian Federation of Trade Unions, Tor Aspengen – and me representing the African students in Oslo.

With indefatigable energy Fred Lange-Nielsen sought to secure the engagement of both right-wing and left-wing political youth organisations. To this end he had us draw up a manifesto that expressed an obligation to defend the human rights of all people in southern Africa, regardless of race and colour.

In what must have been quite unique in the political history of the country, Fred secured the support for the Crisis Fund's statement of purpose from a cross-section of the nation's leadership. The list bears mention: Frithjov Birkeli, Bishop of Oslo; Johan T Ruud, Rector of the University of Oslo; Einar Gerhardsen, ex-Prime Minister (Labour); Astrid Rynning, Justice of the Supeme Court; Gunnar Jahn, Chairman of the Norwegian Nobel Committee; Kristian Schjelderup, Bishop of Hamar; Nils Langhelle, Speaker of the Storting; Hans Vogt, Ruud's successor at the UiO; Konrad Nordahl, Leader of the Norwegian Federation of Trade Unions; Terje Wold, Chief Justice; A.P. Østberg, President of the Norwegian Employers Association. (See photo section.)

Edel Havin undertook to address requests for contributions to municipalities and organisations nationwide. She also organised the sale of candles by an army of engaged youths in the bitter cold outside the parliament and about town. The design of the Fund's logo and the production of pins, to raise money, were left to the artistic talents of Vesla Lange-Nielsen, who also mobilised support among the artistic community of which she was a member.

Although it never commanded much money, the Fund would become a bastion of support for the liberation movements of southern Africa. In a report, dated 22 January 1964 and submitted to the Board of Management, Fred summarised the work that had been done until then.

'The first period of money raising, from 11 December to Christmas Eve, has been used for such short-term measures as time would allow: short items on Radio and TV; joint gatherings by the Labour Party's Youth Organisation and their Conservative Party opposite number at the Sjølyst [Exhibition Hall]; speeches and films in the University's Great Hall; the sale of candles in front of the Storting; and talks in the larger towns outside Oslo, etc.'

'In parallel, work was done with an eye to preparing for the longer term: examining the possibilities of countrywide support from labour and employer organisations, the sale of pins, and other activities by the member organisations countrywide, etc.'

'It has been a great pleasure to experience that a number of towns on their own initiatives have arranged the collection of money.'

The other South Africans at the University, the medical students Freddy Reddy, Maxwell Mlonyeni and Isaac Mgmane, as well as chemist Mazwi Reshane, were also called upon to make presentations at various places in support of the campaign.

FIRST TRANSFER OF MONEY

I have a warm recollection of Tor Aspengren,[30] leader of the LO and one of the most influential men in the country, coming on foot from town one day to Dr Lange-Nielsen's surgery at the Ullevål Hospital. He was there to oversee that the appropriation of our limited resources would be in accordance with the rules governing registered funds. It must have been the smallest fund for which he had oversight. A giant of a man who had started his career as a metal worker, Aspengren was said to have been particularly incensed by the South African regime's denial of the right to organise to Black workers. The first funding request we were asked to approve should have given him satisfaction. In a letter dated 28 March 1964 Lange-Nielsen had written:

'Advocate MANDELA, Luthuli's right hand man, is currently standing trial together with nine others, of which four are White. Advocate MANDELA is a man of great real and symbolic value, and this case is being followed by the

---

[30] Some years ago I was conducted around the grounds in Oslo's industrial district where a foundry named **Spikerverket** (The Nail Works) had once stood. Its general manager for many years had been Vesla Lange-Nielsen's father. I was told that Tor Aspengren's father had worked there and lost his life when he slipped and fell into a container holding molten metal. While I could not know whether either Fred Lange-Nielsen or Tor Aspengren had been aware of such a link in their lives, it provided me with an explanation for the commitment that had made Aspengren walk several kilometres, to sanction the transfer of a small sum of money for the defense of men charged with treason for fighting for the liberation of their people.

whole world, not least by the Blacks. Its outcome will be of great importance and be known everywhere.'

The case referred to was the so-called Rivonia trial of nine leaders of the non-parliamentarian opposition who were charged with a number of counts that could have resulted in their being sentenced to die. The accused were Walter Sisulu, Nelson Mandela, Govan Mbeki, Lionel Bernstein, Ahmed Kathrada, Raymond Mhlaba, Dennis Goldberg, Elias Motsoaledi and Andrew Mlangeni. Their defending counsel was Bram Fischer.

The request for support from the Crisis Fund had come from Canon John Collins of St Paul's Cathedral in London who was also chairman of the British Defence and Aid Fund (BDAF). He requested £1 000 to ease the burden of £60 000 they thought they would need in the next six months. Canon Collins also extended an invitation to the Fund to become associated with the BDAF.

This invitation opened the way to wider contact with the international anti-apartheid movement and with representatives of southern African liberation movements, the ANC foremost among them. Among the South Africans we would receive as guests of the Crisis Fund – whose title was soon changed to embrace all of southern Africa – was the journalist Ruth First who had revealed the enslavement of 'pass offenders' on the potato farms in the Transvaal. She had been held in solitary confinement for 117 days before being released with permission to leave South Africa (the title of her harrowing account in prison was titled *117 Days*). Despatched to meet her at Oslo airport, I wondered if she recalled her description of my father as resembling a character out of a novel by John Steinbeck.

Another was the poet Dennis Brutus, who had offered me a meal and a bed after Major Heiberg and his minions had impounded my passport in Port Elizabeth. Dennis showed me the still-healing wounds on his torso from the attempt on his life by the police in Johannesburg. His errand in Norway was to raise support for the campaign he was waging to have South Africa excluded from all sports competitions worldwide.

The Crisis Fund also played host to a number of Zimbabweans as well as to Eduardo Mondlane, the founder of FRELIMO. But the activist that stole most hearts was the singer Miriam Makeba, whose rhythms warmed up a cold winter's night.

The South West Africa campaign had thus both reinvigorated public interest in southern Africa, and established a platform from where the work of building up public opinion could be done – with Norwegians carrying the major burden: a development I found deeply gratifying.

EXPANDING THE ANTI-APARTHEID CAMPAIGN

The recently arrived students from South Africa – Freddy Reddy, *et al* – and a growing number of other Black Africans also began to make their presence felt in the public exchange of opinion about the interaction of Whites, including Scandinavians, and our people 'at home'. An example of such exchanges happened soon after Freddy's arrival in 1961. The newspaper *Aftenposten* gave space to a representative of the Norwegian colony in Natal Province for a patronising account of their treatment of Blacks. Since it was a matter about which Freddy had personal experience, the two of us collaborated in a blunt rebuttal .

In 1963, I joined up with Mazwi Reshane who had arrived the previous year, to participate in the Labour Movement's May Day parade through the city centre. Alongside us we had Jimmy X, one of a group of Kenyans sent for training by Tom Mboya's Labour Union. With a chain around our necks and the names of the White-dominated territories written on sandwich boards, our political statement made the next day's front page of *Arbeiderbladet*, the governing Labour Party's mouthpiece, with the comment that it had been the most moving of all the day's appeals.

From now on, too, our efforts had the backing of a great number of activists in student and various other youth organisations which straddled party-political divisions from Left to Right. Such contacts were formalised when in 1964 the Crisis Fund joined with practically all the country's major youth organisations to establish *Fellesrådet* (The Norwegian Council for Southern Africa). The founders of the Crisis Fund would, however, form the nucleus of the Council's administration for some years yet. From the member organisations there came a constant stream of volunteers who gave of their time to organise the raising of funds and the dissemination of information about developments on the African continent as a whole. Participation in the ever expanding work of the Council would provide a great number of young people valuable organisational practice, and a springboard into public life. Some of them, indeed, would move on to positions of influence in politics, the media and public affairs generally. Sailing on the sympathy that 'the cause' enjoyed, even allowed Freddy Reddy to stand for election, and be voted chairman of the prestigious Norwegian Student's Union – the first time a foreigner had been granted such a privilege.

A consequence of all this was that the public debate about colonialism became much more informed than it had been only a few years earlier – with concomitant pressure on policy makers in government.

NOT ALL PLAIN SAILING

As often happens, some people are slower than others to notice changes taking place in the political temper of the times. In May 1964, this was demonstrated by the Norwegian Tennis Association when they ignored advice from the Norwegian Sports Federation to drop a Davis Cup tennis match against a South African team. News about the upcoming event spread like fire in dry grass among the city's politically wide-awake youth. On the evening of the South African team's announced arrival, a group gathered at the airport to demonstrate, only to discover that the flight had been re-scheduled.

The next day, with numbers swollen, they met at the Madserud Tennis Courts, where the matches were to take place. In what was promptly dubbed The Battle of Madserud, the police engaged with demonstrators to clear the courts and carry away the most persistent.

At the time I was employed as an intern at the Bank of Norway and could not attend the happening. However, even though I had not taken part in the Battle of Madserud, I became one of its casualties. As it happened, one of the stewards at the tennis court was the son of my landlady. I was therefore not surprised when soon after the event she served me with notice to find another place to stay. In a city where there was a housing shortage, this sent me moving from one short-term accommodation to the next, until Edel and I got married two years later.

TRIBUTE TO VESLA

I wish to end this chapter with a special tribute to Vesla Lange-Nielsen. My tribute to her appeared in the *Arbeiderbladet* on 10 October 1994.

'For Vesla Lange-Nielsen, work towards the freedom of South Africa's people became her life's task. It is with veneration and gratitude that we recall her tireless labour during the dark sixties. Her efforts laid much of the basis for Oslo becoming a bastion in the fight against apartheid and oppression. It was not a matter of there being a lack of support for the cause of the oppressed. Nor were there no dedicated persons around who wanted to put in an effort. But it was Vesla – as we became accustomed to call her – who struggled tirelessly, day in and day out, year out and year in, in the rain and in the cold, to secure the means and the persons needed to get the campaigns off the rails. It was she who recruited the artists – Norwegian, Scandinavian and African – to make their outsize contributions to the work of solidarity, first through the Crisis Fund, subsequently through the Council for Southern Africa.

'It was not difficult to see that Vesla's engagement happened at some cost to her – she allowed herself little time to cultivate her own artistic interests – and that it must have laid some burdens on her family. At the same time it was clear that she couldn't have kept it going without this family's warm traditions of social and artistic engagement.

'No one went in earlier and with greater zeal than she in the demand that Nelson Mandela be set free. It was, therefore, most pleasing that she could welcome him during his visit to Norway last year. She handed him some wild flowers that she had picked in the woods of Nesodden, where she lived. It is such flowers that we should like to strew on her memory.'

CHAPTER EIGHT

Changes

CONSIDERING MARRIAGE

During the summer of 1965 I was cycling along the Bundefjord arm of the Oslo fjord when I happened upon the hamlet of Svartskog (Black Forest). Passing a cottage I fell into conversation with its owner, an elderly lady, and learned that she would be moving to her apartment in town at the end of summer. This turned out to offer a solution to my housing problem for the coming winter.

In Svartskog I found the air sweet, the neighbours friendly, while the bus into and out of town stopped right outside my door. But as the days grew shorter and darker, the life of a hermit began to bear down on me. Days could go by during which I'd exchange words only with the bus driver, paying for my fare, and with the woman running the University Library's refectory, paying for my coffee. With the last bus out of town leaving early in the evenings, my contact with student life practically came to a standstill. Without a telephone or a radio to listen to I was wrapped in silence once I entered the cottage, particularly after the snow cut out the view to the neighbours' dwellings.

The winter was severe that year and the cottage poorly insulated. It was cold when I got up in the morning and when I got back in the evenings. A little iron stove had to be fired up to provide heating. It was when the temperature rose to above 12 degrees Celsius that I became aware of other life in the place. Flies that had lain supine, apparently dead on the windowsills, one by one began to come alive with a buzz. Fascinated, I ignored the lessons learnt at school, namely that flies were the carriers of diseases. Instead, when one of them fell into a cup of tea that I was drinking, I carefully fished it out to save its life. And when one of them had drunk its fill from the foam that had seeped from a glass of beer that I had filled, I was amused by its uncertain gait as it moved away. It began to bother me that, in longing for the voices of a family around me, I should be developing concern for the welfare of flies.

By contrast, Edel at this time was busy testing the effects of ionising radiation on living organisms. To this end she carefully bred, irradiated and thus caused the death of literally thousands of fruit flies, known by the imposing name of *Drosophila melanogaster*. Although we had been going steady for some time, the thought of asking her to marry me now posed problems. I lacked the financial means to sustain a family. I also reflected that the institution of marriage united not only the couple involved, but their families and their societies in terms of whose mores and legislation their union was to be recognised. While I expected no objections from either her or my immediate family, there was sufficient reason to be dubious about subjecting her to the indignities inflicted by bigots in either society. On further reflection, however, I dismissed the idea that I should be bound by the bigotry of racists in my choice of my life's companion – if she would have me as such. When I had finally scraped together enough courage to 'pop the question', Edel's response evaporated my fears. We decided to get married in May. At the beginning of the New Year I could also move back to a room in Studentbyen.

AFRICAN VISITORS

Although staying in Svartskog had put constraints on my movement into and out of town, I maintained contact with the affairs of Fellesrådet with which the Crisis Fund for Southern Africa had merged. As one of the founders of the Crisis Fund, Edel had moved on to serve as deputy leader of the Council while I served on the Board. Like the Africa Bureau in London and the American Committee on Africa in New York, we regarded the provision of hospitality and support to political activists from Africa arriving in Oslo as an obligation. Thus we had made the acquaintance of activists from the future Zimbabwe, including one Hamadziripi who years later would be linked by Zambia to the assassination of Herbert Chitepo.[31] And on one occasion I was called on to extend the hospitality of the freezing cottage in Svartskog to a Zimbabwean lawyer, Simpson Mutambanengwe, when he visited from London. Many years later I would learn that he was serving as a judge on independent Namibia's Supreme Court.

This calls to mind another visitor of note with whom we had to deal in our Crisis Fund days, namely Kenneth Kaunda. Some months before Zambia was to become independent, the Fund heard that the leader of the United National Independence Party of Northern Rhodesia was due to arrive for a two-day visit. His mission was to seek contact with politicians and members of the trade union movement with a view to securing moral and financial

---

[31] Herbert Chitepo was one of the most impressive men I have ever met. Asked to deliver the closing speech at a 1973 UN-OAU conference in Oslo, in five minutes he put the liberation struggle in Africa in a context and in a style of delivery that to me was riveting. His assassination in Lusaka soon afterwards robbed not only the future Zimbabwe, but Africa, of a leader of stature.

support for a campaign of peaceful demonstrations – to compel Great Britain to respect African demands for a break-up of the Central African Federation. NUPI – the Norwegian Foreign Policy Institute – undertook to organise a meeting for him and at short notice Edel, representing the Crisis Fund, was asked to find a venue and invite people so Kaunda could address a larger section of the Norwegian public.

Mr August Schou, the then director of the Norwegian Nobel Committee graciously put the Institute's meeting hall at her disposal; she was on the phone a whole day to mobilise an audience. In spite of the short notice, we were relieved when something like two dozen individuals turned up to listen to Kaunda make his presentation.

GETTING MARRIED

Some days before Edel and I presented ourselves at the Bærum Town Hall to be declared legally wed, I received a reminder of my precarious economic status. Returning from my day in town, I found a letter in my mailbox informing me that I was in arrears with taxes due to the city of Oslo. I hadn't known that the small stipend I'd received during my internship at the Bank of Norway, where I no longer worked, was taxable. I mentioned this to an elderly gentleman with whom I always had a pleasant conversation on the tram to and from town. His response surprised me greatly. There was nothing wrong with the claim I had received, he told me, adding that he had handled it himself. But he did advise me that I could apply for forgiveness at the City Hall. Only years later would I learn that I had been speaking to the chief tax collector himself. At the tax office there awaited a further surprise.

'So you can't pay a red øre, as you say?' said an official. 'Then we have no choice but to declare you bankrupt', he said as he clubbed the decision with a gavel on the desk behind which he and a colleague stood. I didn't know whether to laugh or to cry, but decided to spare Edel the embarrassment of knowing that she was getting married to a bankrupt.

For the same reason I had pleaded and Edel accepted that we keep the wedding a modest affair, inviting in addition to Freddy Reddy and her childhood friends Bjørg Aagre and Ellen Blankson, only the elderly couples with whom we had enjoyed the closest contact: the Barths, the Clausens, the Lange-Nielsens and Moyen Egede-Nissen – the latter friendships established during the Namibia campaign.

After our wedding, we stayed for the summer months at the home of my parents-in-law. At the beginning of the school year in August, we moved to the village of Ski where Edel had landed a job as a teacher while I got ready to finish my studies.

ICJ THROWS OUT SOUTH WEST AFRICA CASE

To combine a belated honeymoon with attendance at the wedding of a French childhood friend of Edel's, we travelled to France in July. Due to a breakdown of our car, an ancient Citroen 11, we arrived in The Hague on the way back a day after the ICJ had handed down its judgement in the South West Africa cases (1960-66).

In New York in 1959, I had shared the hope of many people that the Court would find that the enforcement of apartheid in South West Africa violated international law, and that this ruling would lead to the abrogation of South Africa's mandate to govern the Territory. The Court's decision put such hopes to shame. And it was with foreboding that I would soon learn that the leaders of SWAPO, an organisation with predominantly Ovambo membership, saw bloodletting as the proper response to the ICJ's decision.

THE SOUTH WEST AFRICA CASES 1960-66 OF THE ICJ

The GA Resolution 1361 of 1959, for the adoption of which the Reverend Michael Scott, Mburuma Kerina, Jariretundu Kozonguizi, Allard Lowenstein, Sherman Bull, Emory Bundy and I had lobbied did in the end, as had been feared, result in an adverse decision by the International Court of Justice. The circumstances nevertheless merit a short explication.

Sovereign states cannot be dragged to court to answer charges laid against them. Cases brought to the ICJ therefore have to go through two phases: a preliminary phase during which the complainant(s) have to prove that the defendant(s) are obliged by international law to respond on a matter brought to Court. Only then, in a second phase, can the Court be asked to deliver judgement on 'the merits of the case'.

It took the ICJ two years to decide that South Africa was obliged under international law to answer to the charges laid against it by Ethiopia and Liberia – the only African members of the UN that had also been members of the defunct League of Nations which had created the mandates system. This decision was handed down by a majority of eight of the Court's fifteen members.

It next took the Court four years to hear argument about the merits of the case. This was whether apartheid, as enforced in the internationally mandated territory of South West Africa was in accordance with South Africa's obligations under international law, and if not, that South Africa be divested of its mandate to govern the Territory.

Before the Court could come to a decision, the removal of judges – both fortuitously and by political intervention – reduced the majority that had handed down judgement in the first phase. With the technical majority of a presiding Australian judge casting a double vote, the Court dismissed the case. Ignoring dissenting opinion that the Court could not act as an appeal instance to a prior decision of its own, it decided that neither Ethiopia nor Liberia had established their interest in the matter in hand, and that therefore the Court did not have to deliver any opinion.

The decision caused worldwide embarrassment and uproar, except in South Africa, where it encouraged the regime to go full steam ahead with the implementation of apartheid in South West Africa. At the UN, the immediate reactions were fairly predictable, and momentous. An enraged majority of members voted to revoke South Africa's mandate to administer the Territory and to establish a UN agency empowered to assume *de jure* control of the Territory's affairs. In charge would be a UN Commissioner.

The unhappy decision was not without consequences for the Court itself. By failing to deliver judgement in a matter of deep concern to all ex-colonised countries, it damaged the perception of the Court's avowed independence as the principal judicial organ of the UN system. For years subsequently, Third World countries shied away from making use of the ICJ's services. Even though in 1971 it again reversed its stance – in a judgement about the 'Legal Consequences for States of the Continued Presence of South Africa in Namibia (South West Africa) notwithstanding Security Council Resolution 276 (1976) – the UN system's chief judicial organ would only be rehabilitated when in 1986 it delivered a judgement against the United States in the so-called Nicaragua case.[32]

NATIONAL UNION OF SOUTH WEST AFRICAN STUDENTS

On the way back to Oslo from The Hague, Edel and I stopped over at the offices of COSEC, the (western world's) international student organisation in Leyden. There we were invited to an upcoming gathering of South West African students scheduled to take place in Uppsala, the Swedish university city. The gathering was to be financed by both COSEC and its eastern

---

[32]   See essay by Georges Abi-Saab in *Fifty years of the ICJ*, eds. Vaughan Lowe and Malgosia Fitzmaurice, Cambridge University Press 2007.

counterpart, the International Union of Students (IUS), as well as by the Swedish government and Scandinavian students' organisations. The purpose was to facilitate the formation of a South West Africa Students Association. Although this was the first time that I heard about the planned event, I welcomed the prospect of meeting up with countrymen of mine abroad for the first time.

To highlight the importance that the Swedish government attached to the event, it was opened by Olof Palme, then Sweden's Minister of Education. Present, too, was Zedekia Ngavirue, Kozo's successor as leader of SWANU together with other members, as well as SWAPO's Sam Nujoma, Solomon Mifima and Andreas Shipanga. As the only independent, I was elected to chair the meeting, and subsequently to act as General Secretary of the National Union of South West Africa Students (NUSWAS) that was formed.

To build up and serve an organisation of exiles residing in many different countries – the US, Western Europe, Scandinavia and Eastern Europe – proved to be a thankless task. The difficulties were exacerbated because I tried to perform this demanding task while also preparing for my final examinations at the Institute of Economics in Oslo.

As I saw it, the first order of business was to construct a database of our membership and what they were studying. The idea was to be able to advise future students about fields of study which would match the likely needs of an independent country. I would soon learn that all this was easier said than done. Very few members bothered to respond to the circulars I sent out. In Eastern Europe, Hamuteni Kaluenja, SWAPO's Secretary for Youth Affairs, developed anxiety about NUSWAS' political orientation in a world divided between East and West. My deputy in the US, Linekela Kalenga, similarly met a lack of enthusiasm. Soon it emerged that the SWAPO leadership all along had doubts about an organisation in which their opponents in SWANU were represented as well. They appeared to fear that the organisation could grow into a contending mouthpiece for the South West African 'liberation movement' – at a time when they were gunning for the monopoly over that title.

NUSWAS was thus doomed to expire, quietly. While still under the impression that we had a future, I accepted an invitation from the IUS to represent the organisation as an observer at a conference in Ulan Bator, the capital of Outer Mongolia. Sandwiched between the Soviet Union and China, the Mongol republic evidently lived in fear. A short while earlier a re-ignition of a border conflict along the Amur River between its two mighty neighbours had led to the discontinuation of work on Chinese building projects in Ulan Bator. For the duration of the weeklong conference the student delegations were transported by a fleet of taxis from their hotel to the refectory and the parliamentary complex – each situated merely a few hundred yards distant.

That this was intended to make contact with the locals impossible, I would learn on taking a stroll on my own down the main street one day. A Buddhist priest whom I ran into astounded me by recognising that my English was South African. He explained that he had returned from a fourteen-year sojourn in India, where he had met South Africans. Alas, the possibility of conducting a meaningful discussion with an evidently erudite native was snuffed out no sooner than it had commenced. Two men in uniform promptly approached us with what was clearly a command for the priest to make himself scarce. From their attitude I understood that the command applied to me as well. When a journalist turned up the next day with a request for an interview, I gave him my well-rehearsed account of South West Africa's precarious situation – wondering how he would pitch it to his readers who, as far as I could tell, didn't enjoy much freedom either.

FAMILY AFFAIRS

Edel completed her degree in Biology in 1964 and went on to do research in her field before deciding to abandon it for teaching. When a post became vacant at a school in the village of Ski, we moved there in 1966. Finishing my own studies in 1967, I landed a job at the National Budget Office of the Ministry of Finance. The office coordinated the budgets of all government departments and thus provided insight not only into the workings of the Norwegian government in general, but in particular into the practical application of the imperative of equality that informs every aspect of Norwegian society. Nowhere was this more visible than in the salary scales of the departmental staff.

The salaries of all departmental employees were entered into a ledger that was open to inspection. The figures showed that while the Minister of Finance at the time drew a monthly salary of somewhere above 6 000 kroner, the wages of the messenger delivering papers from office to office was in the region of 1 700. Thus, the official responsible for the economic health of the nation drew a salary not much more than three times that paid out to the lowest functionary. I doubt whether there was, or is, any other country on earth that could surpass that measure of equality – one of the keys to the wealth subsequently enjoyed by the people of Norway. It needs to be added that the Minister, Ole Myrvoll, was a member of the Norwegian Liberal Party in a right-wing governmental coalition.

JON ARE ARRIVES

Our firstborn, Jon Are, saw the light of day in midsummer at the National Hospital in Oslo. During her pregnancy, Edel developed a condition that made it necessary for me to assume the baby care normally left to mothers. In due course I learned that babies have only a few needs which they communicate with variations in the pitch of their cries. I also discovered that far from being innate, a 'mother's instinct' was something acquired. Thus the slightest sound from Jon Are's cot woke me from the deepest slumber, while his mother could sleep on.

After the three months maternity leave mothers could enjoy at the time, we came up against the problems all nuclear families are familiar with: finding caretakers for their infants while earning an income. After a succession of temporary nannies we could finally leave Jon Are in the care of a well-run day care centre in Ski for the working day.

Exposure to a working mother's problems with childcare would in due course lead to Edel's growing involvement in local politics. Elected to its parents' association, she had to deal with town councillors who had not yet accepted that female tax-payers have special needs. This engagement got her elected to the municipal council, where she made her debut with an environmental case that would prove to be the starting point of a lifetime's engagement for her.

It started late one evening when two of her pupils arrived at our home with a jar of water that they had collected from a stream flowing out of the grounds of a nearby dynamite factory. The stream joined a river that emptied into a lake from which the town of Moss some forty kilometres away drew its drinking water. The boys had been shocked by the acidity of the water. The following day Edel's class in Chemistry analysed the water and found a heavy concentration of nitrates and sulphates, and a pH value of $1,0$ – a very high level of acidity.

This prompted Edel to ask what the municipality of Ski intended to do about the pollution by the dynamite producing company of the water supply upon which a large number of people downstream depended. The response was a classic study in denial by administrations and polluters the world over.

A subsequent joust with the administration concerned the effluent from the municipality's sewage treatment plant that went straight into the Oslo fjord. A cross-party alliance of women in which she next became involved, put an end to the municipality's practice of discriminating against women in its pay scales. Thereafter they took on the fire department for refusing to hire women as firefighters.

It was an engagement that would prove as instructive to Edel's pupils about Norwegian politics at the local level as it was to me. But at times it could be costly. As when the 'housewife', as the only female participant, insisted on joining a delegation of the Norwegian Polytechnic Society on a study tour to the United States, to gain insight into issues relating to energy supply. All other members of the delegation had their costs carried by their employers – but Edel's trip had to be financed from our family budget

JOINED BY OTHER EXILED COUNTRYMEN

On a Wednesday evening in August 1972 I returned from a weeklong cycling tour in the mountains to find Edel in a state of desperation about having been unable to get in touch with me. Four of my countrymen had arrived illegally at Oslo airport aboard a weekly flight from Budapest and were to be returned there on the same Hungarian flight that Saturday. Pending their return, they were imprisoned for having entered the country without visas. With the visiting hours for prison inmates set at 6 pm, the whole of Thursday was lost before I could speak to them.

The four men, Joe Murangi, Menason Murangi, Usiel Muruko and Usiel Nguarambuka, had studied Electro-mechanics in Budapest on Hungarian scholarships. On completion of their courses they were ordered to leave the country. As Hereros and members of SWANU, this placed them in the invidious position of having to apply to the rival Ovambo organisation SWAPO, recognised by the UN as 'the sole and authentic representative of the Namibian people' for an endorsement of their application for a renewal of their UN passports. Assuming that as Secretary-General of NUSWAS I could be of assistance to them, they had approached the Norwegian Embassy for visas and been received with sympathetic attention. However, while still awaiting a response to their visa applications, the Hungarians informed them that their time was up and that they had to choose where to be sent. They chose Oslo.

Early on the Friday I knocked at the door of the immigration authority. Before I even had a chance to utter a word, the man behind the counter told me, 'Their appeal against expulsion has been reviewed and rejected.' 'By you?' I asked – and his reply confirmed that the same officials who had made the expulsion order, had reviewed it. Realising that it would be a waste of time to plead I turned around and made a beeline for the Foreign Office a mile across town. There I asked for Arne Arnesen, a diplomat with whom I had become acquainted in 1959, and left the matter in his hands. The expulsion order was annulled, but fully six months would elapse before the immigration people would issue the four men with work permits. Once these had been granted, the men were employed by a telephone company. There they promptly slashed to a third the time it took the local Norwegian workers to install the company's telephone exchanges in office buildings. Joe in particular kept pace with the company's digitalisation of its technology, and soon became one of their most valuable workers. He installed their hi-tech systems in countries all over the world, diagnosed faults online from headquarters in Oslo from where he advised technicians on site about maintenance.

It gave me great pleasure to visit my Herero countryman at his place of work one day, to find him on the phone in front of a monitoring unit, giving directions to an engineer in Germany – of all places – about how to sort out a problem with a unit he had installed there.

Even the Norwegian Defence Force benefited from Joe's services – in circumstances where the term *force majeure* literally applied. An uncommonly ferocious winter's storm had put out of commission the communications system of a military base in North Norway. In Oslo the company received an emergency call for at least three engineers to replace the system that had been disabled. At such short notice the company could offer only one engineer, with the assurance that he could be counted on to do whatever was needed. As if such news was not bad enough, the generals also learnt that the engineer in question was an African, that he had been trained in a Warsaw Pact country, and that he had travelled extensively in the Soviet Union.

When they finally arrived at a decision, things happened with impressive speed. A police car, blue lights flashing, arrived at the company offices to pick up Joe. With him aboard they sped to the military airfield outside Oslo, where a big transport plane was waiting with its engines running. Making a brief stop at an airfield midway to pick up replacement equipment, they flew northwards into the darkness of winter.

Having familiarised himself with the equipment on-board, when the plane landed Joe hit the ground running. To his surprise, and some irritation, he now found that every move he made connecting wires was being followed by two men who had clearly been put under orders not to let him out of sight for a moment. On the second day he received an invitation to lunch from the officer in charge of the base. When he returned to resume work he was astonished to find that his guards had been withdrawn, finally leaving him alone.

'I worked through the night and all of the first day and only went to my hotel for a short nap before returning to finish the installation and testing', Joe recalls, adding that on his return the office was very pleased. 'We didn't believe that we had all the parts needed, but I managed; you make friends that way', he said.

DOMINEE AND MRS BEYERS NAUDÉ

Edel's and my membership of the Youth Council kept us in touch with a stream of representatives from liberation movements and other individuals from Africa arriving in Oslo with their concerns. One of our most distinguished guests was the theologian Dominee Christiaan Frederick Beyers Naudé and his wife, Mrs Ilse Weder Naudé.

As leader of the most powerful Dutch Reformed Church and as leading member of the Afrikaans *Broederbond* – the secret society with a political agenda – Beyers Naudé had been a candidate for leadership of the White political elite, when he found that he could no longer reconcile support of apartheid with the faith that he professed. This turned him into a renegade and an outcast from White society but embraced with admiration and compassion by the opponents of apartheid Black and White.

On hearing that the couple was in Oslo, I called their host, a Norwegian clergyman of my acquaintance, to express my wish to pay my respects to them. As the clergyman had an engagement out of town that day he would be pleased, he said, if Edel and I were to entertain his guests at dinner.

From Oslo the Naudés travelled to Uppsala in Sweden for a church conference. On their return to South Africa we were appalled to hear that the apartheid regime had served an order of house arrest on one of the most impressive individuals that it had been our privilege to welcome into our house. In terms of the order, he was to meet with no more than one other person at a time. This meant that Mrs Naudé had to make herself scarce whenever he received a visitor. On the next occasion when we would be able to meet with them, Dominee Beyers Naudé had just been released from house arrest and his passport returned. At a church where he was to deliver a sermon, I told him of our concern for his welfare during the years of his detention. 'Oh, no', he replied. 'House arrest was good for me. I longed so much for the company of people and for what they had to tell me that for the first time in my life I found myself listening to others.'

His sermon was equally memorable. As the text for the day he read Matthew 21:22: 'And all things, whatsoever ye shall ask in prayer, believing, ye shall receive.' In the sermon he referred to the doubt that Christians must have felt through the ages when their prayers went unanswered. To which he asked rhetorically how people could expect miracles to happen unless they were to end their supplications to the Almighty with a prayer that he use them as his instruments.

AN AFRICAN SAFARI

After two years in the government office of a foreign country, I felt isolated from developments in and concerning my country of birth. With overseas phone calls a luxury on our income, and with no other regular contact with my countrymen abroad, I got to know about events only after their occurrence. Letters from my mother dealt with family matters.

What exercised my mind was where the processes set in motion by the ICJ judgement were leading us. At home, the apartheid regime pursued its policies as though the World Court had given them the right to tighten their hold. In New York a scandalised UN peremptorily abrogated the mandate and declared *de jure*, albeit illusory, command of the Territory, which it now named Namibia; the world body further established a post of Commissioner for South West Africa to assert that illusory control. And SWAPO had begun to send guerrilla units across the border.

I never shared the illusions that a guerrilla war could possibly succeed against South Africa's Defence Force whose foundations had been laid by the modern world's premier guerrilla warriors. One of the views Mburumba Kerina, Jariretundu Kozonguizi and I had unreservedly shared, was that for demographic reasons alone our people were in no shape even to think in terms of a military confrontation with the South African regime. The people of the central and southern regions were the second and third generation survivors of a genocide that had left us with a population density of less than one person per square kilometre. Confined to impoverished reservations, the people would be even less able than their recent ancestors to confront a military force that in both absolute and relative terms was incomparably mightier than the German garrisons that had laid the country waste.

As for the people of Ovamboland and the Caprivi, we were faced by groups divided by tribe, living in isolation from the rest of the country – with the possible exception of the dispersed army of 'contract labourers' employed on farms and in other menial occupations. In addition, since pre-colonial times, there had been no discourse among the native peoples about their shared interests. This was why Mburumba and I had agreed upon 'organisation' as the name for the political party he had exhorted his correspondents at home to form.

Moreover, I was sceptical about warriors on foot being able to survive, find any popular support, or be able to inflict significant damage on the SADF with the means at their disposal. At most, I reasoned, guerrillas crossing the thousand kilometres long borders without being caught, could deliver only pinpricks to which the regime would predictably overreact. On the other hand, military reaction by the South Africans would further undermine the legitimacy of their occupation of the mandated Territory.

'What are you concerned about?' a teacher of Economics at Yale University, asked me at a small party to which Betsy and Bill Landis had invited me during a visit to New York in 1970. 'The future belongs to you', he continued and pointed out that on every relevant count the odds were tilted against the survival in the long run of the apartheid regime in South Africa.

However, even though it appeared obvious that the regime could not survive the pressures building up – growing isolation and an expanding boycott movement being the prime – time went by without the end appearing in sight.

NORWEGIAN CITIZENSHIP

Earlier that year (1970) the Ministry of Foreign Affairs in Oslo granted me a stipend to make a tour though East Africa, with stopovers in Ethiopia, Kenya, Tanzania, and then into southern Africa to visit Zambia and Botswana. I had been feeling the need to become updated on developments in the post-colonial republics. In the belief that the new discipline of peace research developed by Johan Galtung might help me to deepen my understanding of the forces at work in southern Africa, I approached him at the International Peace Research Institute in Oslo (PRIO) for academic guidance.

For travel through a series of African countries I also required a passport, instead of the travel document that had served me well for ten years. To this end I also applied for and was granted Norwegian citizenship.

In Addis Ababa I happened to meet a Black American diplomat who expressed surprise about this – wondering where my loyalty as an African lay. I told him that I hadn't been required to state an oath of loyalty as precondition for being issued with a passport and that I could say whatever I wanted to say without fear of reprisals.

ETHIOPIA

In Addis Ababa, the Ethiopian capital, an acquaintance from my early days in Oslo met and assisted me to find my way about his city. Beggars, occupying the sidewalks, were a new experience. It didn't take long before I realised that there was some risk in giving money to an outstretched hand. It would cause all the others down the street to reach out their hands in urgent expectation. Realism, laced with shame, made me suppress sympathy. Thus, within hours of my first day in Addis, I came to see first hand how the world's privileged go about their business amidst its misery.

I nevertheless was struck by the irony of it all: this was the Ethiopia in which, alongside Liberia, we had invested our hopes when the UN had passed the resolution to charge South Africa with the violation of our human rights at the International Court of Justice. I had to remind myself that Ethiopia was the only African country that had withstood the ignominy of being colonised and that Haile Selassie, its leader, had early recognised the need for collective security of the world's states – the cornerstone on which the UN is built. In 1960 he had reminded the UN that even the fate of the powerful is not fully in their own hands. As to South Africa, he had identified himself with all aspects of the struggle for liberation, exhorting African statesmen to follow suit.

My destination was the OAU headquarters and the UN Economic Commission for Africa (UNECA). At the OAU I had an informative chat with Mohamed Sahnoun, with whom I had become acquainted in 1959 on an American campus. In Addis, he was on his way to becoming one of the OAU's troubleshooters.

At UNECA I met the Norwegian economist Erling Nypan, who had done service in Ghana and other African countries. He shared with me accounts of the work he had carried out to make the Ghanaians aware of the losses they were likely to suffer if they were to remain economically tied to their erstwhile colonial masters.

On my way from Oslo I transferred to Ethiopian Airlines in Rome, where I discovered Sam Nujoma boarding the same aircraft. We had met each other in Uppsala for the first time in 1966. However, although I went to greet him, he showed little interest in deepening that acquaintance. This didn't bother me as I had chosen to remain independent of both SWANU and SWAPO.

It was altogether a different matter to run into Phillip Kgosana in Addis. In 1960 the amiable UCT student had prevented a bloodbath from taking place in the heart of Cape Town when the leaders of the Pan Africanist Congress (PAC) were imprisoned after calling for a demonstration, whereupon he had to step in. Starting from Langa, a Cape Town township, demonstrators made their way to Parliament. By the time they were a stone's throw away from the centre of power, their numbers had swelled to an estimated 30 000. A panic-stricken Chief of Police, who had had Phillip arrested, now begged him to call off the march – with an assurance that would prove to be false. He told Phillip that the Minister of Justice would see him later the same day to discuss their grievances. After escaping from South Africa, Phillip was welcomed by Emperor Haile Selassie, who opened the portals to Ethiopia's military academy to him and afterwards financed his university studies.

KENYA

From Addis Ababa I headed for the Kenyan capital Nairobi, a city and a country about which I was somewhat better informed. In Oslo at the beginning of the 1960s, Black people were seldom seen. Thus when an African arrived in town, he was very visible – and accessible. As I happened to pass the Hotel Continental one day, I caught sight of a man who presented himself as Joseph Murumbi, a Kenyan. Though I didn't know it at the time, Murumbi was one of the British colony's leading politicians. I noticed that he was reading a travelogue of East Africa by Teddy Roosevelt. To me this was a reminder of our dependence on foreign sources for knowledge of our continent's history. Assuming that Murumbi was on business, I didn't ask why he was in town. Much later I learned that he had been looking for money to buy a large number of transistor radios that could be used to spread his party's messages in the period leading up to Kenya's first parliamentary election. For fear of offending Kenya's British masters, the Norwegians had turned down his request. During the week or so of Murumbi's presence in Oslo, Jørg and Thea Clausen hosted us for a dinner – as they often did when my friends and acquaintances from abroad happened by.

Some time after Kenya attained its independence, the Oslo Students' Union, chaired by Freddy Reddy, invited another Kenyan, Tom Mboya, to deliver an address at the Union's Saturday evening debates. Mboya was a name with which I was familiar from my first year at UCT when Mr Stanley Trapido, our lecturer on African affairs, had predicted that the charismatic trade union leader would lead his country to independence. During the run-up to independence, Mboya persuaded the Americans to provide scholarships for Kenyan students at US universities. Plane-loads of them, among whom notably were Onyanga Obama and Wangari Maathai, departed from Nairobi to various cities in the United States.

On the Sunday after Tom Mboya's lecture, Freddy and I accompanied him to the airport for his flight back home. Homesick, the two of us had difficulty taking our leave from a man who exuded optimism about our continent's future.

It was with these memories that, having landed in Nairobi, I went to the spot in the heart of the city where Mboya had been shot and killed some ten months earlier. According to some rumours the British had been responsible; according to others it had been the Kenyatta family, keen to secure their grip on power. Mourning for Tom Mboya, I reflected on the grim prospects his murder portended for the country's future.

I next went in search of Jimmy X, one of the ten or so Africans in Oslo whom Ruth Reese had welded into a chorus to back up her performance of Negro spirituals on the radio. On his return home, Jimmy had won a seat in Parliament, only to be ousted in the next election. He was, however, not giving up hope of returning. When he took me on a tour of a township, he was warmly greeted.

DAR-ES-SALAAM – HARBOUR OF PEACE

In Dar-es-Salaam, where SWAPO had established its headquarters, I wanted to form an opinion about the group that had started guerrilla pinpricks against South Africa. On arrival I was met by old acquaintances Andreas Shipanga and Solomon Mifima who introduced me to Peter Nanyemba, said to be in charge of the guerrillas. Nanyemba responded readily to my inquiries about the organisation's foreign policy. Given the Western powers' inherent resistance to supplying them with arms, the guerrilla movement was sustained by the OAU's Liberation Committee. This committee supported OAU-recognised liberation movements with military hardware and training. As to the Soviet Union and China, although both accepted SWAPO cadres for military training, his organisation resisted being pressured into declaring allegiance to either. It was a reassurance that appealed to me. I left Dar-es-Salaam impressed by my countrymen whose optimism appeared undimmed, even though it was clear that it must have taken an effort on their part to sustain – given geographic distance and the circumstances under which they had to make do.

LUSAKA

In Lusaka, the penultimate stop on my safari, I met up with Emil Appolus and Moses Garoeb, the only southerners amongst the organisation's senior membership. Emil had been a journalist before leaving the country in 1960. The group he joined had spread to different countries to build support bases for the cause that they represented. He went to the Congo's Katanga province where, he told me, he had served as a press assistant to the rebel Moise

Tshombe. He laughed heartily when I asked why they had chosen Nujoma as their leader. He then told me that on arrival in Dar, they were asked who their leader was. Compelled to choose, they said it was Sam Nujoma, for no reason other than that Sam was the eldest among them.

From some of the people staying at the house Appolus was occupying, I heard a disturbing story. It concerned Moses Groeneveldt from Keetmanshoop, one of my classmates at high school in Rehoboth. Moses was said to have been killed by his own countrymen soon after his arrival in Lusaka. It proved impossible to discover any further details.

Rebel movements from all over southern Africa had offices at the so-called Liberation Centre in Lusaka. There I was received by Moses Garoeb, whom I had met at Mburumba and Jane Kerina's apartment in New York some eight years earlier. In the meantime the ambitious young man had become SWAPO's secretary-general and appeared quite pleased to see me. In his student days he had circulated a list of members of government for an independent South West Africa, in which my name appeared as Minister of Foreign Affairs. I had recognised Mburumba's hand behind it, clearly intending to show that we were ready to take charge of our country – under his leadership. With Mburumba since side-lined, and Moses now part of the group with ambitions about their role in an independent Namibia, I refrained from reminding him of his youthful excesses.

Nevertheless, I found conversation with him interesting. He expressed his admiration for an Arab diplomat whom I had also observed in action at the UN. This diplomat had served as UN representative for a number of Arab countries. Moses contrasted this with our own proclivity for remaining imprisoned within our tribal boundaries. This was clearly what had inspired him, a Damara, to serve as right-hand man to Sam Nujoma, an Ovambo tribesman. Given the change of mood at the UN after the ICJ's disastrous judgement, Moses confidently expected Namibia to become independent by 1974.

While waiting for Edel and Jon Are to join me at the end of the school year, I spent the evenings with a Polish engineer who was also staying at the block of flats where I had found accommodation. He made no secret of his opinion about the communist regime that had sent him as an advisor to the African country. He had developed an improvement to diesel engines that could have put Poland in the forefront of their technological development, he told me. The planners had resisted his pleas that they take out a patent. He found no comfort in my corresponding tale about a Norwegian iron smelter that was started after the Second World War. It could have become a world leader in electrical furnace technology. But a parliamentary decision had delayed by several years the iron smelter going into operation. By then, the advantage had been lost.

A FAMILY REUNION AND A POLITICAL SEMINAR

Finally the day arrived when I could go to Lusaka International Airport to welcome Edel and Jon Are. When I left them at Ski two months earlier, Jon Are couldn't speak properly yet. As they emerged from the plane, I could now hear the two year old's high-pitched voice rising and falling with the cadences of his mother tongue. It struck me that, incredibly, I had become the father of a Norwegian.

As Edel's and my marriage prohibited us from entering South African controlled territory, Botswana was the nearest we could get to my home. My family arrived by train. While we were waiting for their arrival, I availed myself of an opportunity to visit the capital, Gaborone, in hopes of seeing my erstwhile host, now independent Botswana's first president, Sir Seretse Khama. It turned out to be a poorly chosen day as Kenya's president, Daniel arap Moi, happened to be in town on a state visit. While I stood outside parliament, not quite knowing what to do, Quett Masire, Botswana's vice-president happened by and invited me to his office. We had met each other at the home of a mutual friend, the journalist Nils Treving, in Stockholm. Treving had subsequently assisted the Botswanans with establishing a newspaper. After a few pleasant exchanges with the vice-president, I felt it unnecessary to prolong my stay in Gaborone.

On the way out of town I thumbed a lift from a travelling salesman of Indian descent from South Africa. He became visibly anxious on learning that his passenger had unfinished business with the regime in Pretoria. I was glad that there was no place on the deserted road back to Palapye where he could have dropped me off.

We had expected my parents to arrive alone for our first ever get-together for eleven years. Great was our pleasure when they arrived with my three youngest brothers Dirk, Tony and Leon, my sister Anne-Marie, and my father's brother-in-law, Dirk van Wyk. As they alighted from the train at Palapye, Jon Are surprised us all by going straight to his grandfather and taking him by the hand.

My brothers had been small when I left home, and I could observe the difficulty they had relating to an elder brother who had disappeared out of their lives. Uncle Dirk, a distant relative of my mother's, was imbued with a sense of humour that had us all laughing a great deal. A few years later I heard that when a prolonged drought completely wiped out his stock of animals on the farm, Aunt Martha upbraided him one day for remaining in bed till almost noon. His defence: 'I didn't know poverty felt this good. I now have absolutely nothing to worry about.'

The political future of our country dominated the talk during our short family reunion. My parents were interested in my view of our country's situation. I told them of my worries since 1959, when Mburumba Kerina and Jariretundu Kozonguizi had launched competing organisations, SWANU and SWAPO. Even though SWAPO pulled in individuals from smaller groups such as Moses Garoeb, Theo-Ben Gurirab, Hage Geingob – all Damaras – and a few others like Evald Katjivena, a Herero, and Peter Katjavivi, from the Mbanderu wing of the Hereros, in my experience it basically pitted Ovambos against the Hereros and the rest of SWANU. As far as I knew, groups in the southern districts, the Rehobothers and the Namas, had not joined either organisation.

Comparing the merits of SWANU and SWAPO, it nevertheless seemed to me that the former had lost out to the latter in terms of political influence abroad. Moreover, my recent visit to Dar es Salaam and Lusaka had left me with a positive impression about the dedication of the SWAPO crowd.

In view of all this, I put forward an argument the consequences of which I wouldn't learn about until much later. I pointed out that the Basters of Rehoboth were not required to carry passes moving from place to place, and were thus free to visit the various other groups that were confined to their reservations. And I argued that the Basters ought to be exploiting this freedom to impress upon the representatives of the various tribes the importance of getting together to deliberate upon our common future, and to steel them for effective opposition to the regime. This was that much more important since the arrest and imprisonment of Toivo Ya Toivo and others had paralysed what political activity there had been inside the country.

URGED TO SUPPORT SWAPO

On the way back from Botswana, Edel, Jon Are and I stopped over in Dar es Salaam and were again well received by both old acquaintances and new arrivals. This time we met Ben Amathila, who was soon to take up appointment in Stockholm as the SWAPO representative in Scandinavia, with an office situated a stone's throw away from the Ministry of Foreign Affairs. Ben set about in all earnest to sign me up as a party member. Referring to the positive role the party was playing in the struggle for Namibia's liberation, he thought that they deserved my support.

This was the first time such an invitation had been extended to me. Although I had abjured membership of either SWAPO or SWANU at their inception, my reservation about accepting the invitation had waned. Since I had recently given my own family the advice to facilitate contact between the various groups at home, I accepted Ben's invitation. In practice membership didn't bring me any burdens nor did it provide me any opportunity to influence party decisions either. Considering the reasons advanced for my joining the party, I found it interesting that there never was any attempt to involve me in any deliberations about its future. In time I would learn that decision-making power was the monopoly of a triumvirate comprising Sam Nujoma, Peter Mueshihange and Peter Nanyemba – all Ovambos – with the Caprivian Mishake Muyongo as Sam's nominal deputy president.

Mishake had led of a group from Caprivi who had joined SWAPO. He comported himself as if he were the equal of the party's Ovambo triumvirate, which well he might have been – considering that joining his party to SWAPO had gone some way towards augmenting its claim to representing the Namibian people. But he was there only for as long as they had need of him. For allegedly having led a post-independence attempt at secession, he was charged for high treason in Namibia. By the inability of the Courts to come to a decision, his alleged co-conspirers are held in juridical limbo – which speaks volumes about the infirmity of the post-independence Namibian judiciary.[33]

HOPES AND FEARS

Our second son, Sven Tanab, was born in early 1972. This time too it became my task to supply all the care – sans feeding – that babies need. With experience baby care came easy and we had fun observing both the newcomer claiming his place in the group amidst which he had arrived, and his elder sibling having to be reassured that he was getting no less attention.

Outside the family circle we were facing new concerns, particularly when later that year the stipend that had made it possible for me to do research at PRIO dried up and I had to begin the search for paid employment. Countless applications were returned, with the message that the vacancy had been filled. I waited in vain for a response from others. Eventually I found myself compelled to return to teaching – a profession that I had sought to escape by enrolling at UCT.

---

[33] *analysisafrica.com/reports/**caprivi**-secession-trial-still-haunts-namibia/*

A summer course in education to qualify as a teacher was offered in the town of Kristiansand. When schools reopened in August, the local primary school in Ski needed a part-time assistant. On my first visit to the teachers' lounge I became a witness to a scene that made me wonder what I was letting myself in for. A teacher, visibly upset, was giving a colleague a blow-by-blow account of the battle he had just waged in a classroom in order to do his job. The class he spoke about was the one I had been hired to instruct in Maths.

It didn't take me long to understand the teacher's reaction. It was a class in which the major preoccupation seemed to be to have fun at the hapless teacher's expense. Having learnt to live and let live, this didn't bother me. However, one boy soon overdid it, leaving me no alternative but to break the rules myself by chucking him out of the classroom.

A week later, I was surprised by one of those changes that can be experienced in all classrooms. The school had arranged for the class to acquire a week's practice at different places of work. The boy I had disciplined now expressed the wish for me to act as his contact teacher. I found it a reassuring indication that I was accepted for who and what I am.

With two incomes to cover our household expenses, two small boys as company, and caring neighbours, Ski provided the simple comforts we had need of. It could not, however, stem my longing for the company of my own people. In spite of my reservations about the direction that the liberation struggle had taken, led by guerrillas seeking 'liberation through the barrel of a gun' in the forests of the Caprivi Zipfel, I couldn't free myself from the thought that I ought to be making a contribution to their 'struggle'. With the insights that I had acquired, particularly in government, it occurred to me that, in collaboration with party members, I could draft position papers about issues that would need to be addressed as priorities once apartheid was consigned to the world's scrapheap of obnoxious ideologies.

The urge became stronger when in 1974 I wrote a report for an Oslo paper about the reign of terror with which the South Africans had responded to the Ovambo contract labourers' countrywide strike. It turned out that the strike had been organised by Ovambo youths who had gone on to organise a SWAPO Youth League. Floggings and other abuses had compelled the youths from Northern Namibia to leave their homes in droves to join 'the fight for independence' – as they thought.

In distant Oslo, their plight had put me under considerable private pressure. Here I was, earning my keep by taking part in the education of young Norwegians, while these young patriots proved themselves ready to make the supreme sacrifice for the independence of our country.

Edel understood my needs. The course we settled upon was that she would apply for a vacancy on a Norwegian Development Agency (NORAD) funded programme to supply Zambian schools with qualified teachers, while I would freelance for Norwegian media.

Having been involved in the development of a new curriculum for Norwegian high schools and having published two instruction manuals on environmental and resource problems, Edel's qualifications could not be questioned. It would, nevertheless, require political intervention before the Africa specialists in NORAD would back down from their view that, due to Zambian sensibilities, a woman could not be sent to Zambia.

As a measure of the extent to which our desires reflected wishful thinking, we imagined that our sojourn in Zambia would be brief, and that within a short time we would be able to cross the Kalahari Desert into a liberated Namibia.

FOREWARNING

At Easter in 1975 I had made a trip to London to get updated about the situation in Zambia. In Oslo I caught a lift aboard a road-hauler to Rotterdam. From there I took a ferry to Dover, before making the last lap by train to London. Emerging from Victoria Station I called Peter Katjavivi, SWAPO's representative in the city. I was hoping that he could recommend a cheap place for me to stay. Instead, he surprised me by the warmth with which he greeted my call. He advised me about the way to the centrally located Bloomington Hotel, where a room was reserved for me at the party's expense, adding that Theo-Ben Gurirab and Hage Geingob, respectively SWAPO's representatives in New York and the United Nations, as well as Ben Amathila from Stockholm were all there, including the SWAPO representative in Algiers.

This left me guessing. What would be discussed at the 'conference' about which I had not heard a word before my arrival in London? And it made me wonder about the way the affairs of the organisation that Ben Amathila had talked me into joining some five years earlier were being conducted. Although I had fairly frequently been in contact with both Peter and Ben, I couldn't recall either of them mentioning any serious discussion of the party's affairs.

In the course of a cold and windy afternoon, even Kozonguizi turned up to join the six of us for dinner in the hotel's restaurant. It turned out that Kozo, who had been living in London since 1959, had gotten wind that his countrymen would be in town. Once a pathfinder for Namibia's liberation, he had become a spectator to the tug-of-war about its future. Still, he had lost none of his good humour and belly-shaking laughter. He left us when the SWAPO members hinted that they wanted to start their meeting – a sad reminder of the divisions that had developed among Namibians both inside the country and abroad.

Our conference, I now learnt, had been convened on the instructions of the office in Lusaka. Sam Nujoma had charged his lieutenants with organising a long-overdue party congress to renew his long-exhausted leadership mandate. The congress was to be held in Algeria. The intention was clearly to limit participation to a small number of hand-picked participants.

But this would effectively bar the SWAPO Youth League (SYL) from having much of a say. These were the young political animals who in 1971 had managed to paralyse Namibia's economic life by organising a nationwide strike of Ovambo workers. In Lusaka, Andreas Shipanga would show me a confidential note that had been lifted off an official desk in Windhoek. It revealed that the regime's officials had become aware of the failure of their policies: imprisoning and meting out punishment on the youthful activists, merely turned them into heroes, raising their stature in their own communities.

The strike of Ovambo workers in Namibia had breached the first line of defence of all oppressive regimes: the oppressed people's fear of reprisals. It electrified the trade union movement in South Africa itself, as I would be told by the photographer Omar Badsha, one of their organisers in KwaZulu-Natal.

At our conference in London, my SWAPO colleagues were in a bind. If Sam Nujoma thought they had failed him, he could decide to drop them. There was no lack of candidates with college training and ambition among the Ovambos who could replace them. By loyally carrying out his orders each and every one of them would strengthen their credibility in his eyes. But if they were to snub the SYL and Sam was to lose control of SWAPO to his opponents, their jobs would in any case be in jeopardy.

During the second day of our conference, I could observe what they stood to lose. As we sat down for talks after breakfast, an animated Theo-Ben Gurirab charged into the conference room with news about what London's agile cat burglars had done to him. They had slit open his suitcase and, he informed us, helped themselves to cash and traveller's cheques worth several thousand dollars. Having hitch-hiked to London, and given my almost empty purse, I had some difficulties commiserating with Theo-Ben.

Next it was Peter Katjavivi's turn to demonstrate what prominence he had achieved in London. We received an invitation to tea from Mrs Barbara Castle, one of the Labour government's most highly respected members. Although afterwards I could not quite recall what, if anything of significance, she had said to us, we were in an elated mood as we walked back to our hotel that afternoon. I felt good about the satisfaction Peter could draw from the event. I had a high regard for him on account of the courtesy with which he invariably responded to any calls I made on him from Oslo.

Returning to our discussions at the hotel, it struck me that none of Sam's men wished to recommend what message to send back to Lusaka. This emboldened me to venture an opinion that reflected my own needs, but seemed to resonate with them as well. I pointed out that the unravelling of the Portuguese empire in Angola and Mozambique had resembled a tectonic shift in the political landscape of the whole region. This meant that if we were to do an effective job in the places where we were stationed, we needed to have gathered where the effects of this tectonic shift had been most dramatic. I concluded that the unity of the movement made it imperative for the party congress to be held in Zambia. Nobody raised any objections. Instead they urged me to draft a letter to headquarters setting out the arguments.

Much later, in 2011, I found out from Andreas Shipanga that the letter had been sent to him. It had been prefaced by a plea (that I did not write) that he do all he could to persuade his colleagues about the importance of our recommendation. This further strengthened my hunch that the SWAPO representatives meeting in London had been anxious about failing the instructions they had received. In view of subsequent events it also revealed the confidence that Andreas Shipanga had inspired in them.

IN REHOBOTH – AN ILL-FATED NATIONAL CONVENTION

As before, it was difficult to be in contact with my family on their return home from our reunion in Botswana. Confirmation by my mother in Serowe, that our correspondence was in fact being read by the South African Police, made us even more distrustful of the postal services. 'What a pity it is that Hans had gotten married to a Norwegian woman', the local Police Chief had told her on handing her my letter with our wedding photos, 'now he will never be able to return home'. I had no idea, therefore, of the extent to which my father had taken to heart the opinions I had expressed at our family reunion.

My argument, that it was imperative to organise political resistance against the regime, also implied that common cause had to be made with the domestic members of SWAPO, who with a few exceptions, including my sister Martha Ford, represented the Ovambos of the north almost exclusively. When I next heard from the family it was that my father's tireless efforts had led to a gathering in Rehoboth on 13 November that year (1970). The organisations represented were the following: the National Unity Democratic Organisation, the tribal organisation lead by the Herero Paramount Chief, Clemens Kapuuo; SWANU, led by Gerson Veii, a Herero; SWAPO, represented by Johnny Ya Otto and other young Ovambos who subsequently left the country; the Damara Tribal Council, represented by Max Haraseb; and the Volksparty, of which my father was the leader. In addition there were Nama participants such as Captain Samuel Witbooi of Gibeon.

Although several tribal groups from the non-Ovambo districts in the north such as the Caprivians, were absent, it could nevertheless be claimed that for the first time in the history of the Territory, representatives of its various native groups had come together to deliberate its future freely from their various points of view.

As expected, the participation of two Herero groupings led to certain complications: Kapuuo and Veii refused to sit under the same roof. My father shuttled across the street dividing the rooms that they occupied to update them, while exhorting them to join the process fully for the sake of the peoples' unity.

Meanwhile, the gathering concluded with the formation of a National Convention. On my father's motion it was decided that the next gathering of the Convention be held in the southern town of Gibeon. The purpose was to secure the full participation of the region's Nama population.

Inevitably, by dint of his position and commanding personality, Chief Kapuuo became a leading member of the National Convention. In 1974 he was delegated to travel to London and New York, accompanied by Johannes Karuaihe, his counsellor. In London they were to consult with Peter Katjavivi, SWAPO's representative, about joining forces. Katjavivi poured cold water on their expectations: the UN, he informed them, had designated SWAPO as 'the sole and authentic representatives of the Namibian people'.

Thus did the Herero Chieftain come up against postcolonial African elites' acceptance of borders that corralled together people who, in historic times, had been independent from one another. This meant that the representative of a self-appointed Ovambo-dominated junta could call on higher authority to stymie his errand on behalf of a fairly representative assembly of the Territory's people.

However, Clemens Kapuuo wouldn't be deterred. As a teacher in Windhoek he had been the contract labourer Sam Nujoma's instructor in English. And he could only have felt deeply offended by thus being repulsed by Katjavivi – a member of the Mbanderus, the other Herero tribal group – who had gone into Nujoma's service. Kapuuo next proceeded to New

York, where he was received with due respect at the UN. (My source here is Mburumba Kerina). From New York he flew to Kingston in Jamaica, where the Commonwealth of Nations had its annual meeting. For my information as to what transpired there, I refer to newspaper clippings that Peter Katjavivi had handed me in 1975, prior to my departure for Zambia later that year.

Normally reticent of manner, Peter was ebullient when I dropped by his office so soon after our Easter conference – where I had demonstrated my commitment to SWAPO. He told of having been received as a guest of the Jamaican Government in a style no less opulent than any of the Commonwealth heads of state. As it was the sort of reception I myself wasn't quite unfamiliar with in Scandinavia, I didn't take a second look at the documents, mainly newspaper clippings, that he handed me but put them in my handbag. The result was that it would take a long time before I would discover that Peter Katjavivi had in fact sabotaged Chief Kapuuo's errand by calling into question his integrity and describing the National Convention, convened by my father, as pro-South African. A newspaper quoted him as follows:

'Mr Katjavivi explained that the National Convention which Chief Kapuuo claimed to lead was not representative of the interest of the people of Namibia, and as a political organisation was defunct because it's pro-South African stance had been rejected by Namibians. He explained that … Chief Kapuuo's possession of (a passport) was indicative of the Chief's political inclinations.'

To Sam Nujoma, Katjavivi wrote a report dated 5 May 1975:

'Dear Bwana President,
Chief Kapuuo arrived here having obtained his Jamaican Visa in New York under false pretences. He claimed to have had an appointment to see Sir Seretse Khama. This was denied by a spokesman of the Botswana Delegation here. So far, Kapuuo's trip here ended in a fiasco. The Jamaican Government decided to withdraw the Visa he got in New York and made it clear to him that they do not recognise him, nor the organisation he claimed he represents, so he had been ordered to leave Jamaica not later than the 6th of May. The Chief was accompanied by Mr. Karuaihe and Mr James Endycott. The last-mentioned gentleman is the Chief's Representative in London. Yours in the struggle.'

It was a disillusioned Herero Chieftain who returned home to tell my father that the National Convention 'wouldn't work'. Whether he had told him that his bane had been a young man who claimed that they were pro-the apartheid regime, I haven't heard. As nobody in Namibia read Jamaican newspapers, even the domestic SWAPO people remained ignorant of Katjavivi's view of them. My sister Martha Ford, who spoke Nama fluently, took it upon herself to trawl the southern towns and reservations to recruit members for SWAPO that, after Kapuuo's withdrawal from the National Convention, remained part of the rump organisation they called the Namibian National Convention (NNC). Among those she recruited was Lukas Stefanus, who in 1983 would lose his life in Lusaka, allegedly at SWAPO hands. Another was the Nama Chief, Hendrik Witbooi, who would be elected as Namibia's first vice-president. My brother Hewat took on the central and coastal towns in a similar manner.

Thus, while the people of the territory had resumed a discourse among themselves, a discourse that had been stifled for nearly a hundred years of colonialism, two external parties contended to undo what they were striving for. Abroad, the SWAPO junta feared for their status as the UN annointed 'sole authentic representatives of the Namibian people' – as did the diplomats from various countries who enjoyed sinecures at the largely toothless UN Commissioner's office.

TURNHALLE CONFERENCE

Nearer at home the apartheid regime took a page out of the National Convention's book by backing the White farmer Dirk Mudge's call for a Constitutional Conference. It would take place in bouts between 1975 and 1977 in a building known as the Turnhalle in Windhoek. The conference was provided with what the impoverished participants of the National Convention could not match: unlimited cash and booze. Many of the original participants were those who had been absent at the formation of the National Convention, particularly the Ovambo tribal chiefs, some Damara chiefs and self-appointed spokespersons of immigrant communities. Its legitimacy would, however, remain questionable without the participation of the Paramount Chief of the Hereros, Clemens Kapuuo, and the Nama chief, Hendrik Witbooi. While the former had been deeply embarrassed by a SWAPO agent abroad, the untravelled Witbooi had been won over to the SWAPO cause by the eloquence in Nama of my equally untravelled sister, Martha Ford.

It could not have been easy for Clemens Kapuuo to risk being called a stooge of the regime that had been frustrated in its desire to annex South West Africa by the wisdom of his own illustrious predecessors. I have been told that to explore his options, he had carefully consulted legal opinion – in New York and closer at home – before committing himself. He no doubt hoped that once in a position of power he would be able to defend the interests of his people.

Kapuuo's march to national leadership was cut short by the bullets of assassins on 23 March 1978. In the belief that SWAPO was responsible for his death, Herero tribesmen set upon and killed a number of Ovambo workers.

In Rehoboth, members of the community participating in the Turnhalle Conference became enamoured by the promise of wielding power in a 'self-governing Basterstan' – as had been bestowed upon willing tribal heads elsewhere in the Territory. In the process, however, they would play dice with their community's say over their own lands.

CHAPTER NINE

Husband of a 'development expert'[34]

LUSAKA

If our experience on arrival in Lusaka on a Sunday in August 1975 was a harbinger of things to come, we were properly forewarned. By Edel's contract with NORAD, we were supposed to be provided with a place to stay. Instead, a representative of the local NORAD office met us at the airport, drove us to a rundown hostel in town and set off before we could have a look at the single room we had been assigned. Liquid oozed into the passage from under the bathroom door. The two iron-framed bedsteads that took up most of the cement-floored room were covered with rough bedding and sheets that had not been changed after the previous occupants.

Our first thought concerned the health of our boys. The proprietors had no other room to offer and no telephone available. Constrained by my status as merely the accompanying husband to the development expert who had been hired, and mindful of the fact that it had been my need that had landed us there, we settled for Edel taking on NORAD the next day.

They found us another room at a government hostel called Highland House. However, within a short while my wife would come down with amoebic dysentery which her doctor ascribed to the unhygienic conditions of the hostel's kitchen. Yet Highland House was not all grim. We enjoyed the companionship of other expatriates that also happened to find temporary accommodation there. We became particularly close to two couples, Patrick and Joan Anim-Addo – he from Ghana, she from the Caribbean island of Grenada – and Mick and Val Bell, both English. Patrick was a lawyer and interested in chess, which he taught to Jon Are. Mick was an economist. In due course we would get to know Joan and Val as accomplished teachers and excellent cooks – once they too could move into their own dwellings.

---

[34] Individuals sent out by aid organisations invariably carried the honorific of 'expert', regardless of how inadequate was their prior instruction about the people they were supposed to serve, or how foreign they were to the kinds of problems they would be encountering. The term expert was clearly meant to impart status, and power.

From the sixties onwards Lusaka had become a refuge for many of the region's revolutionaries, including a number of South Africans. Among those I had great pleasure meeting again was Phillip Kgosana, who in 1960 had led a demonstration of 30 000 Black workers to parliament and prevented a bloodbath from taking place in Cape Town that day. I now chided Phillip about having withheld a command that could have ignited the revolution – like the French storming of the Bastille. 'I was young and inexperienced,' he defended himself.

If the true revolutionary lives as if the reality he fights for already exists, nowhere was this more evident than in the case of the South Africans. At home they had cultivated intellectual and social intercourse with one another – as if the racist regime's strictures didn't apply to them. I saw this at play when I went for dinner at Jack Simons' and his wife Ray Alexander's house just before my departure from Cape Town in 1959. I learned about the work that the hosts were carrying out. They raised awareness of social issues among those who didn't enjoy the privilege of formal schooling. That was where I first met Solomon Mifima from Ovamboland who, by all appearances, was a regular visitor to the couple's home. Solomon was one of the founders of the Ovambo People's Congress in Cape Town.

Placed under restrictions that no academic could live with and the threat of further measures against them, Simons and Ray Alexander chose to leave the country. Unlike others, who made for Europe and elsewhere, they moved no further away than to neighbouring Zambia, from where they could remain in contact with other opponents of the South African regime.

While dropping in at their home in Lusaka, I wasn't surprised to find there both Solomon Mifima, now nominally in charge of SWAPO's labour relations department, and Andreas Shipanga. With Simons I discussed the UN Institute for Namibia (UNIN) that was being formed, expressing my reservations: it was a microcosm of the UN's hierarchy, complete with assistants to assistants and functionaries in subordinate positions, all at UN scales of remuneration. He shared my reservations but encouraged me to seek entrance so as to be able to exert influence from the inside.

Another couple who lived and breathed for a different South Africa was the pathologist, Norman Traub, and his wife Marianne. They had left Johannesburg to settle with their three young sons in Lusaka. Dr Traub diagnosed the condition that had afflicted Edel at Highland House. Some months later he watched over her health when she came down with a second affliction, this time hepatitis.

At the Traubs' we became acquainted with yet another couple of revolutionaries, I.B.Tabata and his companion Jane Gool. With a track record as a leading intellectual, Tabata's writings had for decades influenced the political debate among the opponents of the racist regime. His pamphlet *Education for Barbarism*, about the consequences of Bantu Education, was banned shortly after its publication in 1958.

MEETING A NEW GENERATION OF NAMIBIANS

Years in exile had left me yearning to become acquainted with the new generations of my own countrymen. After having made a dramatic impact on labour relations throughout southern Africa from 1971 onwards, in 1973 they began to leave 'the comfort of their homes' to fight for independence from foreign oppression. During our months at Highland House, we had little contact with them. After moving into a house of our own just before Christmas, things changed. Evidently motivated by the same need for contact, if not by hunger – which they were too polite to mention – they became regular visitors. Two young women, Ndeshi Uyumba and Soini XX were most helpful when Edel fell ill a second time.

I was struck by the confidence of the youth leaders, their insecure circumstances notwithstanding. Their accounts of the lessons they had learnt mobilising mass gatherings in Windhoek were fascinating. They had come to realise, they told me, that to have four or five interpreters – who would render the main speeches at gatherings that they organised into Afrikaans, Herero, Nama, Ovambo and Tswana – was the way to generate a sense of belonging among members of diverse ethnic communities.

On discovering that certain individuals would sell SWAPO membership cards and pocket the receipts, they devised strict rules of accounting to ward off corruption from tainting the organisation that they had founded. Being Ovambo, they never failed to express their unease at which 'a clique' from within their own ethnic group, had acquired absolute control of the political party which was supposed to represent all Namibians.

On 26 August shortly after our arrival in Zambia, we attended a commemoration of the Battle at Ongulumbashe. Observed as signalling the start of the guerrilla war, the circumstances were apparently less auspicious. South African forces eliminated a group of PLAN – People's Liberation Army of Namibia – guerrillas together with their commanding officer, Tobias Hainyeko. After his release from imprisonment in Tanzania, Philemon Leonard Nangoloh, who claims to have succeeded Hainyeko as the chief commander of PLAN, charged Sam Nujoma with having compromised the operation. For reasons unexplained, Nujoma, together with Hifikepunye Lucas Pohamba, had flown from exile to Windhoek prior to the momentous encounter – and returned unharmed. Nangoloh, on the other hand, was captured a few days after the confrontation with the South African units at Ongulumbashe. On his release and return to Dar es Salaam, Nujoma had him imprisoned on charges of having betrayed his comrades.

The day began when Andreas Shipanga arrived at Highland House to give my family a lift to 'The Old Farm', located in the bush some forty kilometres outside Lusaka. Once an agricultural property, the farm had been acquired to provide space for refugees from Namibia. The venue for the commemoration proved to be a patch of land that had been flattened for a football field. A roof that ran along a long side provided shade for rows of plank seats.

Young women and men emerged from the nearby huts, clad in what was clearly their best attire, newly washed and colourful. Some of the women, carrying babies in their arms, made their way on platform shoes. I wondered how they could have crossed the Kalahari on them. The majority, I was told, had arrived at the camp shortly before from a regular refugee camp elsewhere in Zambia, where they had been handed agricultural implements and seeds. Fearing that SWAPO's leadership intended to have them settle in the camp, they sent a letter of protest to party headquarters. When Zambian soldiers by mistake delivered the letter to a guerrilla camp, it caused uproar. The guerrilla fighters promptly sent a message to Lusaka demanding that the matter be immediately cleared up.

Not familiar with this background, I ascribed the nervousness I sensed that day to the fact that for many of the camp's inmates, it would be their first meeting with the senior leadership of their party. These arrived in a cavalcade that included the Swedish diplomat, Anders Bjurner, his wife and their small son, as well as the Bishop Richard Wood, who had stepped in for the Right Reverend Colin Winter as Anglican Bishop of Damaraland after the latter had been expelled. Wood was subsequently also expelled from Namibia.

Flanked by Peter Mueshihange and Peter Nanyemba, the other two members of the triumvirate in charge of the party, Nujoma took his place on the first row of seats alongside the Swedish diplomat Anders Bjuner, his wife and small son. In a back row Edel and I, together with our boys, found ourselves alongside the Reverend Salatiel Ailonga and Anita, his Finnish missionary wife.

The events of the day commenced with a group of young Ovambo women in traditional dress performing a dance. Following them, Nujoma delivered a speech that he concluded by handing over a handgun to a guerrilla that was said to have taken part in a skirmish with South African forces.

Saluting his chief, the soldier fired a couple of rounds into the air. Next Peter Nanyemba rose to deliver a broadside against those among the new arrivals who thought that war was a game. He warned them that their parents would mourn them if they were to be sent to the front, as they claimed to want.

Apparently not at all fazed by this stern warning, the spokespersons for SYL stepped forward to speak. With charming innocence, young Taati Ithindi reminded all those present that behind every successful man there stood women. She was followed by Keshii Pelao Nathaniel, SYL's president, who presented a resounding challenge to the party's old guard: they had been away from the home country for far too long; their absence was felt. Reminding them that by standing together one gained strength, he informed them that the youth had taken it upon themselves to take them home.

The unease with which Nujoma and his lieutenants responded to being thus addressed was palpable. Their discomfort struck me as mirroring that of the colonial administration in Windhoek, whose violent response had driven the youngsters into exile.

Before the arrival of large numbers of youth, the guerrilla forces had mainly been recruited from so-called contract labourers, grown men hired by the mining recruiting agency Witwatersrand Native Labour Association. They were sent off to work for exploitative wages in the mines, industries and on the farms of central and southern Namibia, and in South Africa itself. Now former 'contract labourers' were facing a new generation of their countrymen who came right from the schools they themselves had never had a chance to attend, some of them even from universities in South Africa. Their exodus had been in breach of their parents' and their tribal chiefs' authority. The events of the day made it clear to me that the relations between the two generations of Namibians were fraught with conflict.

After Nathaniel's speech, Sam Nujoma had apparently had enough. Together with his lieutenants he left the arena and headed towards the vehicles in which they had arrived. They disappeared in a cloud of dust. After their departure Andreas Shipanga, uncharacteristically mute, drove us back to Highland House.

Radio Zambia's news-bulletins were a fixed lunchtime feature at the hostel. That day it surprised us with the news that the SWAPO leadership had decided to call a congress for the exiled organization. It struck us as odd that the decision should have been taken so shortly after Nujoma had left the Old Farm in a huff.

KAUNDA-VORSTER CONFERENCE AT THE MUSI-O-TUNYA FALLS

The very next day a conference took place at the Musi-O-Tunya falls (The Smoke that Thunders) that would drain that question of interest. South Africa's Prime Minister, John Vorster, and Zambia's president, Kenneth Kaunda, met as hosts for a conference between Zimbabwean nationalists and Ian Smith, the farmer who had declared Rhodesia independent to prevent Blacks from taking their rightful place in its affairs. The outcome of the Vorster-Kaunda 'détente' would prove fateful for the hopes of the young Namibian revolutionaries.

Before our departure from Oslo in early August, I had entered into an agreement with the NRK to act as a stringer during our sojourn in Zambia. To that end I had been supplied with a considerable quantity of 16mm film for a camera I had bought second-hand. When I learned about the conference between the Zimbabwean liberation movements and the Ian Smith regime in the Crown Colony of Rhodesia, it was clear to me that I needed to be there. The chance to observe at close range some of the major actors in the region's political drama was too good to miss. The evening after the gathering at The Old Farm I took a train out of Lusaka to Livingstone. Early the next morning a train coach was shunted from the Rhodesian side to midway onto the bridge that spans the mighty Zambezi River below the majestic Musi-O-Tunya Falls. Accompanied by Vorster, Smith boarded it from the Rhodesian side; Kaunda, with the Zimbabweans led by the Reverend Muzorewa, joined them from the Zambian side.

Shortly afterwards, Kaunda and Vorster emerged from the Zambian side of the coach and started to walk towards the bank of the river. Flanked by two of his top officials, one of which was the tall figure of General Hendrik van den Bergh, Vorster was surrounded by a sea of Black security personnel. It was a scene so striking that, addressing a South African journalist standing next to me, I wondered who had scripted Vorster's performance. 'He has scripted it himself', he replied.

For their own negotiations Kaunda and Vorster headed for the Musi-O-Tunya Inter-Continental Hotel, a short distance from the bridge. Sitting down in a small ante-room, they admitted journalists who had been instructed to ask brief questions. Loaded with cameras, I was duly called in to take my shots of the host and his guest: the man holding South Africa in an iron grip, now striking a convivial pose with an arm slung over the backrest of his settee.

Afterwards I joined the half dozen or so foreign journalists, in company with the British ambassador, by the poolside – all waiting for word about the outcome of the meeting. It would prove to be a long wait. By my watch Kaunda and Vorster were in each other's company for close to twelve hours. Their officials continued for another three or four. Close to midnight a Zambian official gave me a wan 'report' of what had transpired. On the train back to Lusaka a Swedish colleague, Anders Johansson from Dagens Nyheter, with better contacts than I, related to me an exchange that was said to have occurred between Vorster and Kaunda.

Vorster had shown Kaunda two sets of pictures of a particular military base. Before the attack there were various structures; after the attack, none. Vorster was then supposed to have asked Kaunda if he had such powerful weapons in his arsenals. At this an evidently embarrassed Kaunda promptly gave orders for SWAPO forces based in Zambia to be disarmed and confined to their bases.

The news that SWAPO's guerrillas had been disarmed in Zambia caused uproar among the solidarity movement abroad. It was silenced only when Sam Nujoma appeared at the UN and denied that that was the case.

On 22 September I went to the Liberation Centre in Lusaka to look up Moses Garoeb. When he finally emerged through the gate of the wall surrounding the complex, I reminded him that he owed me a briefing about the situation we were in. For once Moses took some time to bring me up to date: the news reports about SWAPO having been hamstrung were true; Sam's denial of the fact was a diplomatic move; the Zambian Ministry of Defence was responsible for the pressure on SWAPO; a *coup-d'état*, about which rumours abounded, would be from the right-wing and would spell the end of Zambian support for liberation movements; SWAPO was trying to strengthen its military capability so as to augment its independence and influence; Tanzania and Mozambique supported the struggle but expected this to be kept quiet and especially away from the Press. I noticed that Moses was stressed, so I let the urge pass to follow up on any of his statements for an explanation. When I ran into him again sometime later, he told me about SWAPO's dissatisfaction with Andreas Shipanga who had met the German foreign minister, Hans-Dietrich Genscher, while the latter was on a visit to Lusaka. Even though his colleagues decided to boycott the meeting to protest Germany's policies regarding Namibia, Shipanga had gone to see the man on his own, on the pretext that Genscher was one of his old political contacts in Germany. Near the end of October, Shipanga disappeared from Lusaka on an unannounced trip abroad.

When I next saw Moses Garoeb (on 5 November) he informed me that they had decided to isolate Shipanga, as they found the circumstances of his trip abroad to be mysterious. He commented that Andreas was an 'unreliable figure'.

Considering that Nujoma was constantly travelling but seldom, if ever, gave an account about whom he'd met and what they had discussed, I didn't feel too disturbed by Andreas following suit. I did, however, feel aggrieved by his failure, despite the fact that we seemed to be on the best of terms, to inform me about developments that I suspected were happening.

A DOMESTICATED HUSBAND'S ROUTINE

As long as we were confined to Highland House, with all meals provided, my tasks as domesticated husband were fairly light. In the mornings the boys had to be taken to school and day care centre, where they both very quickly developed a command of English. The seven-year old Jon Are acquired a heavy Zambian accent and three-year old Sven Tanab a Scottish tang from the lady in charge of his day-care centre. What's more, in a class of forty, Jon Are, who hadn't yet been admitted to school in Norway, speedily caught up with his classmates. In the course of the next six months he would even be permitted to leapfrog two classes in succession. We were filled with admiration for the teacher, a woman of Indian descent, who could produce such spectacular results in a class of forty pupils.

After taking the boys to school, I would go on my daily round in town, in search of bytes of information. In a town where rumour flourished, the local media were thin, and foreign newspapers several days old by the time they went on sale, if they got to us at all. This gave me the feeling of picking up nuggets. Back at Highland House I noted down the day's harvest:

'Tuesday 28.8: Got a lift into town. Made an appointment for a meeting with Anders Bjuner at 3 pm. He was expecting Sam Nujoma. We spoke about this and that: the country's precarious economic situation; SWAPO and Zambia; rumours of an impending coup; rumours about a loan of 2 billion Rand from South Africa; rumours of a South Africa-Zambia-UNITA triangle; stories about a South African encouragement of Ovambo self-exertion in Namibia. Pleasant bloke.'

'Afterwards I dropped into the office of the IUEF – International University Exchange Fund – financed by Norway and Sweden that supports students throughout southern Africa. It is being represented locally by Zanele Mbeki, Thabo's wife, as paymaster.'

'13.09. Spoke to Justin and Rob, journalists I'd become acquainted with in Livingston. They mentioned that their colleague M was at H.I.C. I called him and got invited up. His answers were one-sentenced. Asked me what I thought about Rhodesia. What could I say? Mentioned that I'd heard a rumour that the ANC had been forbidden here. He thought the ANC ought to be careful about maintaining a good working relationship with the host government – be it in Zambia, Tanzania or Mozambique. Thought the situation we were in was like the darkness before the break of day. So he was optimistic about Namibia. He responded pedantically to my effort to get him to say something about Zambia's financial problems. They were extreme problems, he admitted. 'He who already is lying down cannot fall. People are eating maize porridge.' Asked me to say hello to Edel.'

'Monday 24.09. Went to the UNHCR's office after having delivered the boys. After waiting for three quarters of an hour was informed that the Commissioner's representative is going to a meeting and that I could get an appointment Thursday at 9.45.'

'Ran into George Silundika in the street. (Silundika is one of the men who put Robert Mugabe in charge of their political party.) He was on the defensive when I asked him about the split in the Rhodesian ANC, which weakened their common position. 'No one can press us together,' he said. Handed me his telephone number.'

'Just after him I ran into another Zimbabwean, a lawyer, and make an appointment to see him on Thursday at 3 pm.'

'Dropped in at Libertine Appolus' place earlier in the day. She showed me a list of things she had run around the two previous days to organise. She had dragged Sam to the office to write a letter to the OAU. It concerned indispensable medical equipment that was urgently needed.'

'I had a long conversation with the Kenyan diplomat Kinuti, who told me that the Zambian authorities were registering all South Africans under their real names and tribal affiliation. He didn't have to mention that this practice could pose a risk to the individuals concerned as well as to their families. He also mentioned that millions had been given to the struggle for liberation in the south, but that nothing had happened since November last year.'

'Met Mrs Shamenas [wife of Namibian priest] and Maxwell, who runs SWAPO's transport service. There had been a bad confrontation between the youth movement and the SWAPO leadership yesterday. A meeting is to be arranged with me soon. What it would be about they didn't mention. I called Mueshihange twice to find out – but couldn't get him on the phone. Sent a telex to the harbour in Oslo. Asked them to send the car to Dar es Salaam, instead of to an Angolan harbour.'

'Thursday 25.09. Went to town for the appointment with the UNHCR representative, who turned out to be a Greek woman called Anne-Marie Demmer. Got served generalities, but invited for breakfast at her home tomorrow, where I would be meeting a mutual acquaintance, on a visit to Lusaka, who wanted to see me.

'Returned to town after lunch with the boys for an appointment with the Zimbabwe lawyer who had taken over the office of the Israeli ambassador. Inside wall heavily reinforced with steel plates. Pleasant conversation. He is also an opponent of Nkomo's, whom he takes for granted will enter into a compromising agreement with Ian Smith. We shall see after Smith's Rhodesia Front and Nkomo's ANC hold their congresses at the weekend. I sensed that the stay in Zambia is stressful, but he confirmed that the Zambian version of last week's bloodshed in a guerrilla camp, where 11 Zimbabweans were killed, is factual – a feud was said to have erupted – and that no attacks [against the Smith regime] were currently taking place. The guerrillas had no arms. Armed fights to take place at the earliest in a year's time – but then from Mozambique territory. There are, however, indications that Nyerere and Machel are supporting Kaunda, but that Tanzania might be engaged in a double game. UNITA is involved in a 'triangle deal' whose contours are not quite clear. He confirms that the Zimbabweans in jail, among them Hamadziripi – to whom we had provided assistance through the Crisis Fund in Oslo – were responsible for the death of Herbert Chitepo.'

Ran into Peter Nanyemba immediately afterwards and invited him home. Both Edel and I enjoy his company. I used the opportunity to let him have the second bottle of Black and White scotch I had purchased in a tax-free shop on the way to Lusaka. The first had been polished off when Bishop Wood and a friend visited us last week. Expressing his appreciation, Nanyemba confided to us that he and others had been inspired by my flight from South Africa to fight our case abroad.'

This was the finest expression of our common purpose that I have ever heard from any of my compatriots. We discussed societal matters and it sounded as if we were of the same mind on a number of issues. During our conversation Nanyemba admitted to sins of omission by the party's top leadership. He revealed that he was responsible for 3 000 guerrilla soldiers of which half are very well trained, and that 500 newly trained ones are in Tanzania on their way to be trained by Chinese instructors.

Before he left I asked Nanyemba for assistance to get our car out of the harbour in Dar, where it had arrived. He promised to write a letter to Lukas Pohamba, SWAPO's representative in Tanzania, which he would bring to me the next day.

At A-M D's house I was greeted by Cedric Thornberry, a lawyer from Northern Ireland who I had first met at Peter Katjavivi's house in

London. Both hostess and her guest wanted to talk about the Namibian situation, which they described as dire. They shared the opinion that SWAPO's head had been chopped off, while the Namibian National Convention, it's political counterpart, was showing itself to be viable. A-M D expressed strong negative feelings about Nanyemba and Nujoma, whom she described as incompetent.

Thornberry was very interested in my opinion that the military wing is viable. He wanted to know the number of guerrilla forces. They told me of a rumour that about 1 000 Zimbabwean guerrilla soldiers have been killed and then drew a disturbing picture of what could be expected.

I found myself uneasy about the opinions expressed by a Greek diplomat and a Brit with, it struck me, an all-too-keen interest in our affairs. Back at Highland House I drafted a memo which I addressed to SWAPO's leadership, where I expressed my concern at the general lack of information at the level of the party's rank and file – particularly at a time when all sorts of rumours about developments in the region flourished.

As he had promised, Nanyemba the following evening arrived with the letter to Pohamba. He thanked me for the confidence I had shown him by letting him have a copy of the memo I'd sent the office. Just as he was about to say more, Cedric Thornberry knocked at the door to collect a letter I'd wanted him to post for me on his return home the next day. As he entered the room, Nanyemba suddenly got into a hurry to leave. Both Edel and I were struck by the tension that had risen. It was as if they knew each other.

When some time later I ran into Moses Garoeb and mentioned the memo I'd sent them, he defended the leadership by reminding me that information was Andreas Shipanga's responsibility, and that he had neglected it. To this I suggested that since the matter was of some importance, they ought to take it up at their weekly meetings and decide what ought to be published. He then mentioned that they had discovered that Shipanga had sought a job as adviser to an international church organisation in Geneva during his visit abroad, but that SWAPO had made sure he didn't get it. There was a self-satisfied smirk on his face as he said this.

Later that day I visited Nanyemba and Mueshihange at their dwelling. I was cordially received and we chatted loosely about this and that. With reference to the memo I had sent the office, Nanyemba made the comment, without being specific, that there were several interesting suggestions, adding that he liked a man who put things straightforwardly.

I departed from them with a depressing feeling of the wordless patience they had cultivated – a wordless waiting, waiting, waiting with few encouragements – having become inextricably involved in an unending struggle, shifting like chimera into the distance with every new assault they had to parry. 'It is now that it counts,' Nanyemba said with emphasis on the 'now', as I took leave of them.

It didn't fully occur to me that the reserve I had noticed could have had something to do with my contact with Thornberry, or with my memo to SWAPO headquarters which might have struck them as supporting the demands of the youth and guerrillas.

BUREAUCRACY TRIUMPHS

On Saturday, 11 October, Maxwell drove me to the airport for a flight to Dar es Salaam where the car we had sent from Oslo had been offloaded. I thought I'd be able to collect it on the Monday and be back in Lusaka the following day. I took with me the letter from Peter Nanyemba to Lucas Pohamba in which I was described as 'part and parcel of SWAPO' and in which Pohamba was asked to assist me in getting the car out of the harbour.

At the office, Lucas thought the matter uncomplicated, so I took it upon myself to go get the car myself – only to become ensnared by a kind of muddle for which I was unprepared. While it took us half an hour to have the vehicle and its load cleared for shipping in Oslo, it would take a fortnight before I could finally leave Dar es Salaam. First, I was told that the officials empowered to sign the bills of lading were away for the week. The following Monday when I returned to the port, I made the mistake of taking pictures of the goods – occupying two or three football fields of real estate – waiting to be shipped out. The film was impounded, whereupon I had to wait another week for it to be developed. Only when I signed the papers that finally secured the release of the car did it occur to me that greasing a palm on arrival could have had me on the road as planned.

Having become motorised, back in Lusaka my chores as well as keeping contact with my compatriots became much easier. However, during my absence, Edel was informed by the Zambian immigration officials that they had dug up the order, issued in 1959 at the Rhodesian border town of Plumtree, which declared me to be a prohibited immigrant. Even though the Central African Federation had become defunct, they considered it still to be valid. They would, however, let the matter rest for the duration of my wife's engagement as a 'development expert'. I would nevertheless be prohibited from writing anything or doing any other paid work until such time as I could apply for a work permit from outside the country.

SWAPO/SWANU INTERLUDE

Towards the end of the year Edel and I unexpectedly became host to Zedekia Ngavirue, a countryman whom we had last seen in 1966 when we formed the National Union of South West African Students in the Swedish university city of Uppsala. After graduating from Stockholm and obtaining a doctorate at Oxford, Zed had moved to Papua New Guinea where he taught history. While still a student in Stockholm, he had replaced Jariretundu Kozonguizi as head of SWANU. On his arrival in Lusaka he had made his way to the SWAPO offices whereupon Moses Garoeb, who had never before favoured us with a visit, brought him to our house for accommodation. In my absence Edel made no objection as she knew that I would be as pleased as she was to see Zed again.

The reason for Zed's unexpected visit turned out to be extraordinary. It would make us privy to what could only have been the last attempt to bridge the gap between SWANU and SWAPO. In Botswana, Zed informed us, there were a hundred Herero youths, SWANU members, in detention for having entered that country illegally. As their leader, he had been summoned to assist them. On his return from Francistown, Zed now revealed to us that his charges had left Namibia with the sole purpose of joining the guerrilla army under SWAPO's command. Because of SWAPO and SWANU's rivalry, he was unsure what SWAPO's response would be. In Nujoma's absence, Moses Garoeb had invited him to a formal meeting.

Due to a previous arrangement, I had to leave home on the morning after Zed's return from Francistown. When I returned several days later, it was to learn that he had had to return to Papua New Guinea without having seen any of the SWAPO leaders. Two days of effort on his part to make contact with them had been in vain. Even at Lusaka Airport, Esmé Shipanga and Edel had observed the strenuous efforts made by both Peter Nanyemda and Peter Muesihange to avoid getting close to Zed. Sam Nujoma's closest associates were checking in to board the same plane.

THE NEW SWAPO REFUGEE CAMP

As a party senior (I appeared to have been considered a senior member by virtue of my age), I transported Andreas Shipanga and the Reverend Salatiel Ailonga on a visit to the new camp to which the Namibian refugees had been moved from The Old Farm. It was situated some 500 kilometres west of Lusaka. The visit would allow me to experience three days and four nights of the conditions that my young compatriots had exchanged for 'the comfort of their homes'. It would have been cruel to ask any one of them whether they had anticipated what they were experiencing, and what hopes they were entertaining for their futures.

For the first time, I had the opportunity for quiet conversations with two other members of the party that I had joined some six years earlier. They were Libertine Appolus and Linekela Kalenga, the former trained in medicine in Poland and married to Ben Amathila, the latter my deputy as general-secretary of the South West Africa Students Association that we had formed in Uppsala in 1966. Here I quote my notes of the tour:

'Wednesday 7.1.76. We left Lusaka at 9.15 for the 470km drive to the farm. We were Andreas Shipanga and the priest Ailonga. Among the things they mentioned was that Ezekiel and Nana – neither of whom I know – were suspected as working for the CIA. (As president of the US branch of NUSWAS, Kalenga was the first to warn me about the interest in SWAPO of this beast.) Just before we reached the camp we encountered a lorry that had become stuck, surrounded by about 100 ineffective helpers. Tried to help with the Range Rover's pulling power – to no avail. Heard later that the lorry had been pulled out with the aid of a tractor. The road of approx 15km from the nearest Zambian village, had been made by our people. But there are still a number of stumps that gave the undercarriage of the RR some bad knocks.

'On arrival we were shown around by Andreas, a type with a speech impairment that didn't dim his eagerness to talk. Among the things he showed us were Libertine's clinic and her quarters. A row of hitherto unfinished huts had been raised. We were given a tent for eight where Andreas S and I were provided camp beds belonging to some chaps who were currently in Lusaka.

'When Libertine dropped in, I handed over letters I had brought with me. We had a little chat. She will soon be starting a kindergarten with 4 assistants who will handle the hygienic aspects of toddler care. The mothers tell her that they boil the water, as she tells them to do, but she doubts that they do. *En passant* she asks if I had seen some of the other chaps in the leadership, mentioning Nanyemba. No, I have almost given up meeting with them, even though I often go to the gate of the Liberation Centre. But I do believe they all are currently in Dakar. She shares some of Esmé's chicken, declaring that it is the first time in 2 weeks that she had tasted any meat! (How could this be as she has been here for only a week). The camp's meals are said to be poor. Porridge is cooked in a great iron pot.'

'At 7 I share a bowl of porridge and sour milk, locally acquired, with Andreas S. At 1.05 am I am woken by what I should have foreseen, and again an hour later.

'This morning I greet Linekela Kalenga who arrived with two cars, a minibus and a Land Rover. He is thinking of staying here for a while before going to 'the front'. We were served tea. Andreas handed out newspapers and copies of Namibia Today, which he edits and has brought a number of – all of which were snapped up. They descend on him for copies. They are starved of reading matter. Bedtime-talk last night, with the camp's commander participating. There is a Zambian military camp in the vicinity. It had been put up a fortnight before the arrival of the SWAPOs. The soldiers are bachelors without families – something of concern considering that young women are in the majority among the camp's inmates. Their total numbers are difficult to determine as the men are frequently shifted out.

'Libertine warned me against using my camera. I replied that I had costly experience of that, but that I had intended to do a 'low-key' report on the work she is doing at her clinic. With a crèche it would be super. This appealed to her. 'Oh yes,' she enthused, 'if it is shown in Sweden, they will recognise me,' she added, suggesting that I could take the pictures when the hut had been furnished.

'While we are talking, a couple of girls in tribal kilts walked by. Libertine lowered her voice and told me that they were from Caprivi – the part of the country that stretches eastward towards Rhodesia between Zambia and Botswana. The folks from there have had very little contact with the rest of the country – or with the liberation struggle – until Mishake Muyongo joined SWAPO and was rewarded with the position of deputy to Nujoma. Many of the girls from there were very young when they left their parental homes, something which posed a problem when they reached maturity – when girls and boys were geographically segregated before undergoing certain rituals. To provide assistance with regard to the girls was something Libertine has taken upon herself. Admirable!

'Parade with the whole camp in attendance was called at 6.50 am. Group leaders were called out and handed the tasks for the day. The visitors (the four of us) were duly presented, to be followed by a reading of the day's news bulletins. Following that an elderly gentleman demanded to speak. The eloquence of his speech, with scathing irony underlying it, was evidenced by Shipanga's embarrassed laughter and the audience's glee at the verbal barrage directed at him – on behalf of 'the office' in Lusaka. The old man had referred to the reports – carried in the papers and on radio – about all the aid that was flowing to SWAPO from abroad. The answers they always got from the camp commanders when they wanted to know what had happened to all the things they needed, were always the same: 'ask the office' … Now he was very pleased for the chance to put the question to a representative of the office: 'What has happened to the food, where is the medicine, and the tobacco?' The fact that the old gentleman was a minor tribal chief, lent extra weight to his intervention.

'Thursday: Was knocked out by stomach trouble yesterday and had to remain in bed for the rest of the day. Late in the afternoon Libertine again arrived for a visit, this time chatting with Andreas S. Thoroughly false when she confided to me that 'One can never know when Andreas speaks the truth.' She invited me for a cup of tea and to show me her not yet finished clinic. She revealed a remarkable duality: with reference to Zed's errand, she rejected the participation of a Herero contingent in the liberation army. One of PLAN's top leaders had been of Herero descent, another had deserted and joined the South Africans and was now a top BOSS (Bureau of State Security) agent. I defended the participation of people from the southern part of the country with the same reasoning that I always used, namely to unify the people politically – but without making any visible impression on her. But then also our conversation was constantly interrupted by the sick, and by the girls staying with her. I must pursue this theme with her. 'It is a matter – referring to Zed – the leadership will have to discuss two or three times before coming to a decision,' she said dismissively, 'I am from Zed's people; I know them.'

'A little later she mentioned some of the unreasonable complaints coming from some of the newly arrived. Notwithstanding this, she followed up with a defence for the idea that a reshuffle at the top of the organisation could be of benefit! 'People have become without fantasy' she added! Although I realised that she might be laying a tripwire for me, I nevertheless used the occasion to have my say: 'I am not in favour of shifting out anybody. But what I'm thinking of is that everyone needs to make a useful contribution.'

'I'll return to my meeting with Linekela Kalenga. We had seen each other last in Zurich in 1968, when we gathered with some other members of the NUSWAS Representative Council.

'Friday: Kalenga now told me that he wanted to be here, but that he would also be going to "the front". He was married and had two children of three and six years of age. His wife and children are in the USA – they would not be able to tolerate an existence without any income, as would be the case here. In the US he was earning well doing jobs like carpentry and the like. Theo-Ben had requested him to take over Hidipo Hamutenya's job as Educational Coordinator. But there had been a divergence of opinion in the party, with Moses having another candidate, one related to the farm here. I mentioned the UN's Namibia Institute that I had been encouraged to apply to for a job by several persons, including Jack Simons – even though I had reservations about it and described it in a note as a Trojan horse. He hadn't wanted to apply; thought there was something fishy about the whole thing; called it MacBride's baby. (Interesting remark: In October Simons said to me that the way he saw it, the institute was part of a great power play, but he nevertheless advised me to apply for a position there). Kalenga mentioned 'some strange people' interested in a job at the institute. With regard to other party business he revealed the same duality that Libertine had shown. On the one side he criticised the youths' radical wishes for a shifting out of leaders: 'Those who are presently in the leadership know the channels to diplomatic influence; this is something we cannot afford to experiment with now.' On the other hand, he revealed impatience with the inefficiency and moral decay of some leaders he mentioned by name. He is particularly upset by the regular exploitation of young women.

'I repeated what I had told Libertine: Am not interested in helping to unseat people. But am interested in whether the people at the top are prepared to make it possible for me, and for others, to make a contribution to the movement.

'I'm asked to drive Sheeli Shangula (SYL secretary-general) to Kaoma to buy paraffin. We had another passenger along, a woman by the name of Elizabeth, who was married to one of the guys at the radio station in Lusaka. According to Elizabeth, the camp commander doesn't want her to travel to Lusaka to visit her husband. He told her to wait until he has had the matter cleared with the office in Lusaka.

'Food was evidently a major problem. Tea was served at 6 am. From 12.30 to 13.00 they had maize porridge with small dried fish with beans – when available. The same dish was served at 18.00. The food was cooked in big ironware pots in a communal 'kitchen' – merely a corralled space. The youth and the older men ate right outside. Some women appeared to be preparing their own meals. The basic diet was augmented with sour milk and cassava – nearly pure starch – bought from local farmers, something only a few with money can afford. Here and there some had scraped up the soil to plant maize. But it looked as if the plants were being attacked by insects. The soil bore no indication of having been worked before. A marshy hollow meandered below the incline on which the camp lies.

'It was said that there were 31 pregnant women here; pregnancy would appear to be a strategy to which the girls resorted, to be taken off hard work and frontline duty. For the men, it meant that SWAPO took over responsibility for the children – with the reasoning that because Namibia was sparcely populated, more children should be produced. Another reason for the high pregnancy rate was that many of the older children have fled from very puritanical homes. Here they feel free. There are many very young mothers in the camp, with prominent party members said to be among the fathers. According to Shipanga, teachers are also involved with their pupils.

'Saturday. I followed the "bridge gang" to the bridge they are constructing some four kilometres away from here. Coordination of the work was difficult, suggesting that supervisory experience was lacking.

'I found something that looks like a nugget of copper, and a large orchid. My compatriots plucked twigs off a bush familiar to them , which they use to clean their teeth.

'I had a final conversation with both Libertine and Kalenga – without making any progress. I told Libertine that rejecting Zed's proposal would imply that they risked a red line drawn right across Namibia north of Windhoek. The northern part would be accorded to SWAPO, the rest to South Africa. Even if they had experienced bad things before, they now needed to provide people in the south with a basis for identification and shared experience. South Africa would find war material among those who had lost their familial and social roots in the south, and particularly among those who were being excluded from the idea of a unitary Namibia.

'Linekela's laconic response to my effort to draw him into a discussion of plans about our future: "We are fighting for a country, Hans, not for an ideology!"

'Four young men came to me on their own account. They are all fathers and unhappy with their circumstances. I note down their names: Filemon Moongo, Emmanuel Engobe, Gottlieb Nakaamboh and Tulipohamba Ngidinwa'. (The first three of these four young fathers would lose their lives in the massacres that would commence later that year. Linekela Kalenga died in Angola of causes unknown to me. Libertine Appolus would become a member, alongside her husband Ben, of independent Namibia's first cabinet and gain respect as one of its more capable ministers.)

'Not much was said on the way back from the refugee camp. Pastor Salatiel Ailonga remained behind. In his place we had Keeshi Pelao Nathaniel, the president of the SYL. Keeshi had a list of items the camp greatly needed.'

Andreas was visibly affected by what we had experienced. It couldn't have been easy for him to be held responsible for the refugees' parlous state. We had seen young people who couldn't have been able to imagine what they were walking into when they chose to go to Zambia. Some of them hoped to be sent abroad to schools and for military training – for what that was worth. In contrast to refugees from other countries, the SWAPO leadership had complete control over their countrymen. This meant that no international organisation had access to SWAPO camps.

Elizabeth van Wyk and Hermanus Christoffel Beukes with Hans Johannes.

My mother, Elizabeth.

Father with helpers at shoemaking factory.

Grandparents Johannes Timotheus and Anna Beukes.

My younger brothers Kehat,
Hewat, Dirk, Tony, Leon.

My sister, Anne-Marie.

Bushbuck for Khama pot. Photographer Seretse Khama.

*Oslo 12 September 1959, welcomed by
Mariken Vaa of Norw Student Assn.*

Oslo airport interview on arrival by NRK reporter.

Welcome to Hans' condemnation for apartheid.

Verdens Gang gives prominence to call for boycott

Thank you, freedom tastes fine – Gunne Hammarström of Billedbladet Nå quoted me as having said

Petitioners Scott, Kozo, Mburumba, Sherman Bull, Hans, Lowenstein.

With Professor Fabregat of Uruguay in UN corridor.

U.S. Policy on Africa Reported Moving Away From Colonialism To Support People's Aspirations

Change Taking Place in U.N. and Is Reflected in Guinea President's Visit — Surprising Opposition by India in World Court Dispute.

By DONALD GRANT
A Staff Correspondent of the Post-Dispatch.

UNITED NATIONS, Oct. 26.

UNITED STATES POLICY on Africa is moving to a perceptible degree away from a cautious desire to please the Union of South Africa and the colonial powers who are our European allies. It is moving toward positive support for the emerging peoples of the African continent.

No formal announcement of this change has been made, and perhaps there will be no formal announcement. The United States seeks to disturb its relations with the European powers as little as possible.

In the United Nations, however, a considerable change has taken place in American policy.

BRITISH OPPOSITION seems to be explained by the hope by British diplomats

domination of a small "white" minority over a vast African majority.

No Africans were allowed by the Union to leave South West Africa to protest. An Angelican priest, the Rev. Michael Scott, became the champion of the South West African people, however, and it was the Rev. Mr. Scott who, several years ago, got the idea of a World Court decision of the type now being sought.

At first American diplomats not only opposed such a World Court action, but even opposed to speak for the South West African people. This year, however, the American delegation voted in favor of the Rev. Mr. Scott's right to appear, and have consulted with him on the World Court measure.

As long ago as 1950 the World Court in an "advisory opinion" held that South West Africa had an "international status" which the Union of South Africa could not alter. What is contemplated now would be, in effect, an order holding the Union of South Af-

Tape Recordings Carry Africans Pleas to U.N.: 'Today We Are Like Animals Under the Boers'

Efforts to Silence Appeal Fail — Three Americans Made Recordings, Smuggled Out Interpreter — Union of South Africa Stands Accused.

By DONALD GRANT
A Staff Correspondent of the Post-Dispatch.

UNITED NATIONS, Oct. 26.

THE VOICE OF AFRICA, pleading its own case before the United Nations by tape recorder, has defeated efforts to silence it as the trusteeship committee meets to consider the plight of south-

Donald Grant of St Louis Post Despatch chronicled developments at UN 1.

U.S. Switches Policy to Back Africans in U.N. Debate on Future of South West Africa

Many Diplomats Believe Elimination of 'White Domination' in Trusteed Territory Could Be Start of Peaceful Solution in Colonial Areas.

By DONALD GRANT
A Staff Correspondent of the Post-Dispatch.

UNITED NATIONS, N.Y., Oct. 30.

THE DEBATE on South West Africa in the United Nations Trusteeship Committee, which a week ago appeared to be a fruitless repetition of a diplomatic exercise that has gone on for the last 12 years, has developed into a full-scale struggle which some diplomats think may involve the future of the entire continent of Africa.

Members of the American delegation have been in close consultation with the Rev. Mr. Scott—but perhaps more importantly, also with the two Africans from South West Africa who escaped last summer to come to the United Nations. They are Famuel Kenengeisi and Hans Beukes. Both are under 30 years of age and are believed to be significant for Africa as the United States Supreme Court school segregation decision was for this country. In the end, as a result

U.S. Scores Victory in U.N. By Identifying Itself With South West Africans' Hopes

Mason Sears Takes Initiative and Russia Is Forced to Support His Position — Native Leaders Convinced of Washington's Sincerity.

By DONALD GRANT
A Staff Correspondent of the Post-Dispatch.

UNITED NATIONS, Nov. 2.

THE UNITED NATIONS today moved into a new series of debates on problems relating to the continent of Africa. Whatever the outcome, the United States has won the first round—in the only sense in which victory is possible in the U.N.

Mason Sears, the American representative on the U.N. Trusteeship Council and head of the American delegation in the U.N.

would mean keeping Union of South Africa control over the territory, but with some international supervision. It means

Donald Grant's chronicles 2.

Daily MAGAZINE

27th Nov. 1959. Friday.

My Day By **ELEANOR ROOSEVELT**

The other day I had the pleasure of meeting two young men from Southwest Africa. One said that some years ago he forged his way out because he wanted to study in this country. He has been studying here for some time and now would like to go back to his own country as soon as it is safe for him to do so, for he wants to work for his people.

In the meantime, he is trying to become a lawyer, as he feels that will fit him better than anything else for usefulness.

The other young African was smuggled out with the help of some young Americans who had got themselves into Southwest Africa posing as tourists. They were deeply interested in the situation as it existed in that country and came home to appear before the committee of the General Assembly of the UN on trusteeships.

The three young Americans who made this hazardous trip were Al Lowenstein, Emory Bundy and Sherman Bull. The two young Africans are named Hans Beukes and Mburumba Kerina. All five showed great courage. The three Americans took with them recording material so they could take down what the natives said as they traveled from tribe to tribe. They must have made an impression when they testified before the committee, for they were kept much longer than the average person, and their recordings were played before the committee.

* * *

Apparently our representative on this committee was so impressed that for the first time the U. S. voted in favor of a resolution which dealt with this situation, a thorn in the flesh of the UN for a long time.

These young men all came to tea with me. One of them was accompanied by his wife and young baby, and another by his fiancee. I was very happy to meet two such gallant young women. I call them gallant because I feel it is harder to see those you love do something that you know is dangerous than to do it yourself.

Doris Fleeson is on vacation.

They were all very much excited the day I met with them over the case of another young Southwest African, Leonard Gebliel, a 27-year-old contract laborer who was a stowaway in a ship to America as a fugitive from aggression in his homeland.

Gebliel was not allowed to land in New Orleans when he arrived and they put him on a boat bound for Capetown, South Africa. He tried to commit suicide and was rescued and taken to a hospital. He had been on a hunger strike and was finally sent to a hospital in Galveston, Texas, on Oct. 20.

On Nov. 6 he was flown to New York, from which port he was to be sent back to South Africa, where he knew he would be put in prison. So he is deeply grateful for the fact that Angie Brooks, Assistant Secretary of State of Liberia, got her government to give him asylum there.

Somehow this does not seem to reflect any credit to us, for it seems to me that in view of what our young people had done in Southwest Africa our government might have had the courage to help another refugee.

I want to congratulate the three young Americans for what they have done. They made me feel proud of the people of my country, and I am sure many other people will be proud that there were young men with sufficient idealism to risk their lives to get the facts about other human beings so far away.

My Day by Mrs Eleanor Roosevelt in New York Post.

With Mrs Aase Lionaes at Oslo
Labour Party Debating forum.

Arbeiderkvinnene vil ha boikott av Sør-Afrika-varer

De to foredragsholderne på møtet, stortingsrepresentant Aase Lionæs og den sør-afrikanske studenten, Hans Beuken.

Et møte av Oslos arbeiderkvinner i Samfunnssalen vedtok i går en resolusjon som oppfordrer alle forbrukere til ikke å kjøpe varer fra Sør-Afrika-Sambandet.

Resolusjonen inneholder en skarp fordømmelse av raseforfølgelsene og antisemittisme og henstiller til myndighetene å stanse slike nedverdigende og farlige handlinger i Norge gjennom lovgivningen.

Møtet var arrangert av Samorganisasjonens kvinnenemnd og Oslo arbeiderpartis kvinneutvalg.

En fullsatt sal hørte foredragene av den sør-afrikanske studenten Hans Beukes og stortingsrepresentant Aase Lionæs.

— Det er utrolig at vi i dag, 15 år etter avslutningen av verdenshistoriens blodigste krig, finner det nødvendig å samle til møte for å protestere mot rasehat og raseundertrykkelse, sa Aase Lionæs.

I Franskmennenes krig mot befolkningen i Algerie drives tusener på flukt. 300 000 algirske flyktninger, blant dem 160 000 barn er drevet over grensene. Røde-kors-rapport forteller om tortur overfor algirske soldater.

I Tyskland skjender Hitlers onde gjenferd, hakekorset, jødenes hjem, synagoger og kirkegårder. Og i andre land over hele verden har den antisemittiske smitten bredt seg.

I Sør-Afrikasambandet forfølges og mishandles 10 millioner afrikanere i sitt eget land av et lite hvitt mindretall.

Jeg syns det er all grunn for Norge til å følge det engelske arbeiderpartis eksempel og boikotte Sør-Afrikas varer. Hver eneste husmor i Norge kan være med i denne hjelpeaksjonen. På den måten kan vi her oppe ved polarsirkelen hjelpe den forfulgte befolkning i Sør-Afrika.

Aase Lionæs kom så inn på de siste utslagene av antisemittismen og mente at vi her i Norge kan foreta oss en hel rekke ting for å drepe antisemittismens frø.

— Har vi en lovgivning som kan verge oss mot dem som organiserer hets og rasehat mot andre? spurte inn. — Og hvor-

STORBRANN I ELVERUM

Arbeider som levende fakkel ut av bygning

Fra Arbeiderbladets korrespondent
Elverum, onsdag.

Femten arbeidere ved Jønsrud bruk i Elverum var i alvorlig fare under en eksplosjonsartet brann som herjet for 1,5 millioner kroner i lakkeringsverkstedet i går formiddag. De var nær blitt sjerret inne av flammene og fem av arbeiderne måtte berges ut fra 2. etasje. Den 40 år gamle Egil Brenden fikk klærne antent og kom styrtende ut fra verkstedet som en levende fakkel.

Brenden fikk kastet seg overende i snøen og fikk slokket ilden. Han er nå lagt inn på sykehus. Det er ikke fare for livet. Brenden var oppfylt med å ruse et

OVER TIL SIDE 2

OVER TIL SIDE 2

Labour's women vote for boycott of South African goods.

Fra Kafkas verden

*From Kafka's World, Dagbladet's Cartoonist Gösta
Hammerlund's and journalist Karl Emil Hagelund's take.*

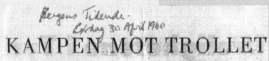

KAMPEN MOT TROLLET

*Bergens Tidende's headline –
The fight against The Troll.*

... og 6 år senere kom *Hans Beukes*
som talte om «sit elskede land».

Inger Mikkelsen Røsoch,
den første kvinnelige lambe-ridder.

Trondheim Tech. U. Six years after Alan Paton, Hans
Beukes arrives to talk about his Beloved Country.

Ekonomiska bojkotten
mot Sydafrika ej nog

Studenterna
i rasdebatt

DET ÄR inte nog med en ekonomisk bojkott mot Sydafrika. Alla demonstrationer från den övriga världen, allt stöd är värdefullt. Även i sportsammanhang som t ex i den kommande olympiaden kan protester mot deltagande av representanter från den sydafrikanska unionen vara verksamma. Vi bör komma ihåg att även om de styrande försäkrar att de inte tar hänsyn till opinionsyttringar så gör de det. Om de inte gjorde det skulle de ha fortsatt den påbörjade massakern mot de infödda.

Den som framlade ovanstående synpunkter var infödde studenten från sydafrikanska mandatet Sydvästafrika Hans Beukes vid en debatt om rasfrågan på Göteborgs Universitets studentkår på söndagskvällen. Beukes

Infödde sydafrikanen Hans Beukes tillsammans med sydafrikakännaren kyrkoherde Gunnar Helander på studentkåren.

Fortsättning på sista sidan (3)

Protest mot Engdahls medverkan
vid studentdebatt om Sydafrika

With Pastor Gunnar Helander at Gothenburg
University – Economic boycott not sufficient.

Easter 1960, WAY's Africa Youth Seminar in Tunis.

«Dere har valgt et alternativ –
i motsetning til det tradisjonelle»

Hans Benkes talte til de unge ved borgerlig konfirmasjon

*Humanist Association's conformation
ceremony in the Oslo City Hall.*

Dagbladet

*Varm velkomst på
kald vinterkveld*

**Nobelprisen har styrket
vår sak, sier LUTHULI**

*Nobel Prize has strengthened
our case, says Chief Luthuli on
arrival at Oslo Airport.*

Gunnar Jahn mellom Hans Beukes (til v.) og festens «seremonimester» Maxwell Mlonyeni.

Afrikansk-norsk forbrødring på Sogn

.frika-studentene i Oslo har nå ;anisert seg, og i går kveld mar-te de dette med en tilstelning i .dentbyen på Sogn. Om lag 80 ske gjester var invitert, venner a på forskjellige måter har vist npati og fellesskap med student-ene under oppholdet her. Det var en meget hyggelig og vellykt fest som sikkert vil bidra til å knytte båndene enda sterkere mellom afrikanske og norske venner.

Formannen i African Students Association, Hans B ǫ u k e s, øn-sket velkommen på prikkf norsk, og takket for all velvilj vennskap de hadde møtt her i det. Han opplyste at forenin hadde utnevnt følgende æresn lemmer: direktør Gunnar J a professor Gustav L i n d e b e Ruth R e e s e, direktør Au S c h o u, dr. Cato A a l l og gramredaktør Lauritz J o h n s Beukes takket spesielt Gun Jahn for alt han betød med store hjerte.

I en menneskelig og varm takket Gunnar Jahn for æresbe ningen og fordømte i sterke o lag det Hitler-tyranniet som vi d lig ser så brutalt demonstrer Sør-Afrika. Og som drives så la at vi kanskje må se i øynen Lutulis linje, den passive stands vel, ikke fører fram. takket de afrikanske stud for den verdi de har gitt som ikke har noen fremme oss har så mye å lære av

Torborg N e d r e a a s afrikanske studentene i visert tale. Hun minnet var 8. mai — dagen sor vår egen frigjøring fr

Afro-Norse fraternisation – Dagbladet.
With Gunnar Jahn and Maxwell Mlonyeni at
formation of African Students' Association.

MORGEN POSTEN

IOO ÅR

LØSSALG 60 ØRE — OPPLAG A   OSLO NYHEDS- OG AVERTISSEMENTS-BLAD   NR. 286 — 101. ÅRGANG

nde Luthuli og frue charmerte ved Oslo-ankol

A smiling Luthuli and wife charmed Oslo.

NÅ GJELDER DET SØRVEST-AFRIKA:

Verwoerd gjennomfører hensyns- løst apartheid

To som står midt oppe i studenterfestlighetene i disse dager.
Universitetets rektor, professor Johan T. Ruud underskriver
appellen mens 25-års jubilanten Torleif Schjelderup ser på.

*2 September 1963, Professor Ruud, UiO, signs
South West Africa campaign protocol.*

*Citizens of all ranks including
future mother-in- law followed.*

Sørvest-Afrika - -

Poet Arnulf Överland was sick at the
time, but wanted to sign the protocol.

Vi gir vår støtte til krisefondet for Sør-Afrika

● **Rasediskriminering**

forekommer ikke bare i Sør-Afrika. Også i andre deler i verden ser man manglende respekt for menneskets elementære rettigheter.
Men Sør-Afrika er likevel det eneste land i verden som har bygget opp sitt samfunnssystem på en bevisst undertrykkelse av noen enkelte befolkningsgrupper som har landet som sitt eneste fedreland.

● **Dagens situasjon**

I Sør-Afrika er beskrevet med to gjennomsnittstall: De hvite lever til de er 72 år, — de fargede dør når de er 36. Fargede barn dør av sult og nød, — i et av verdens rikeste land.

● **Terror er dagens kalde virkelighet**

i Sør-Afrika. Regjeringen der vil bygge samfunnet på prinsipper som er forkastet i alle andre vestlige land. Da den fargede befolkning i 1960 protesterte mot de nye passlovene, gikk politiet til aksjon ved Sharpeville. Resultatet ble 67 drepte og 200 sårede, menn, kvinner og barn, som bare hadde gått til fredelig demonstrasjon mot lover som strider mot alminnelig rettsbevissthet. Fra april til september 1963 ble det bare i Johannesburg behandlet 360 politiske rettssaker. 40 ble dømt til døden,[1] 6 fikk livsvarig fengsel, 620 fikk til sammen 4020 års fengsel.
Dette er apartheid i praksis.

Frithjov Birkeli

Johan T Ruud

Einar Gerhardsen

Astrid Rynning

Gunnar Jahn

Kristian Schjelderup

Nils Langhelle

Hans Vogt

Konrad Nordahl

Terje Wold

Walter R Rostoft

A. P. Østberg

● **Kampen for de fargedes rettigheter**

føres både av hvite og fargede. En av lederne er høvding Luthuli. For noen år siden ga Stortingets Nobelkomite ham Nobels fredspris. Dengang ga vi nordmenn ham moralsk støtte i kampen for menneskerettighetene. Han måtte sympati i alle leg. I dag ber Luthulis folk oss om praktisk hjelp. Er vi rede til å gi dem hjelpen?

● **Det er bydende nødvendig**

å skaffe de tiltalte i Sør-Afrika juridisk assistanse. Gode jurister tar seg villig av deres sak. Men disse må kunne dokumentere at de blir regulært betalt. Kan de ikke det, kan de bli gjort «medskyldige», og de tiltalte mister sine forsvarere. Bare til de pågående saker medgår £ 60.000 (kr. 1.200.000,—). Det sier noe om sakenes antall, — og er ikke uttrykk for den enkelte jurists fortjeneste.

● **Apartheidpolitikkens ofre —**

både hvite og fargede og deres familier, må sikres eksistensmidler. De som klarer å flykte til de britiske protektoratene, må også ha hjelp til underhold, til videre transport til et sted de kan bo og få arbeid, og de trenger utdannelse. Skal verden unngå kaos og unødige tap av menneskeliv må de fargede få dyktige og kunnskapsrike ledere.

Nation's leadership in support of Crisis Fund's charter.

KRISEFONDETS KJEMPESHOW PÅ SJØLYST

PROGRAM:

Konferansier: JOHAN VIGELAND

Medvirkende:	EILIF ARMAND
NAT RUSSEL	SIGVARD WALLENBERG
KARIN KROGH	JORUN KIRKENÆRS JAZZBALLETT
KARI og IVAR MEDAAS	KJELL BÆKKELUND
LEIKARRING	ROBERT LEVIN
MATS BAHR	EGIL KAPSTADS TRIO
THORLEIF SCHJELDERUP	HELGE HURUMS STORBAND
RUTH REESE	THE KEY BROTHERS
HANS BEUKES	THE QUIVERERS

SHOW – DANS – SHOW
FYRVERKERI

INNGANGSPENGER KR. 8 OG KR. 5 — ARRANGØR: KRISEFONDET FOR SØR-AFRIKA

Crisis Fund fundraising show with distinguished international cast.

Crisis Fund's Vesla, Freddy, Edel, Trond Romstad, Hans.

Crisis Fund's Johan Thorud, Per Eggum
Mauseth, Vesla, Lars Alldén, Edel.

*Guest Ronald Segal, Crisis Fund's Fred
Lange-Nielsen, Edel, Lars Alldén.*

*Nobel laureate Martin Luther King launches
Crisis Fund's national fundraising campaign.*

Anti-apartheid-mann hos Lyng og andre politikere

ORIENTERING OM STOR INTERNASJONAL KONFERANSE — SYMPATISK MOTTAKELSE

Norge har en del av skylden for Sørvest-Afrika

Abdul Minty, fotografert av Dagbladet

— Jeg ble meget hyggelig mottatt hos utenriksminister Lyng og han hørte med sympati på alt jeg hadde å si, sier Abdul Minty, en eksil-sør-afrikaner bosatt i London som er på skandinavisk reise for å samle støtte til og muligens deltakelse i en stor internasjonal konferanse om Sørvest-Afrika som skal holdes i Oxford i England 23.—26. mars neste år.

Minty, som bare er 26 år, men som likevel har rukket å være med på å danne boikottbevegelsen i Storbritannia i 1959, den som nå er gått over i anti-apartheid-bevegelsen, har ikke vært her for å få noe endelig svar på anmodningen om å delta i konferansen. Han har hatt kontakt med representanter for politiske partier og for LO, foruten Lyng — Fortsettes 17. side —

Anti-apartheid - -

— Fortsatt fra 1. side — og andre representanter for Utenriksdepartementet. Norges standpunkt hittil har jo vært at man ikke deltar med regjeringsrepresentanter i konferanser som ikke holdes på regjeringsnivå, men det er utelukket ikke at politikere kan reise og at regjeringen kanskje kan sende en observatør.

Minty hadde

EN SPESIELL APPELL

med til Lyng og de andre norske politikerne. Han hevdet at Norge hadde vært med på å undertegne mandatet som gav Sør-Afrika råderett over Sørvest-Afrika, og at vi dermed faktisk har en del av skylden for de rådende tilstander. Dette er jo et viktig argument og Lyng skal ha sagt seg enig i det. Seinere vil det komme innbydelse til regjeringen om å delta i konferansen, om det blir svart ja er et åpent spørsmål.

Minty har vært i Stockholm

Abdul Minty arrives with a reminder to Norwegians about their obligations towards SWA.

Baerum Town Hall, 7 May 1966. Marriage witnessed by Bjørg Aagre, Jørg Clausen, Henry Havin, Borghild Havin, Odd Havin Solveig Barth, Jacob Barth, Aashild Havin.

Seriousness of moment.

*Father-in-law Henry Havin in oratorical flourish
delivering his daughter to the man of her choice.*

Expressing thanks for having been admitted into the family.

*Uppsala, August 1966. NUSWAS formed with Sam Nujoma,
Olof Palme, Zedekia Ngavirue, Bengt Carlson, Hans Beukes,
AdelaideTjijorokisa. Tunguru Huaraka on the podium.*

Participants at formation of NUSWAS.

Serowe, June 1970. Family reunion, Oom Dirk to right.

Family pays respects at Khama family's grave.

Serowe, June 1970. A session of the Khotla – democracy in action.

GUARDIAN MARCH 8, 1979

Martha Ford

The South West Africa People's Organisation has been fighting for the liberation of Namibia from South African occupation for twelve years. A social revolution in the country brought women into key roles in the independence struggle. Martha Ford, who runs SWAPO's women's campaign, talked to Martin Walker.

Freedom fighter

SIX MONTHS ago, Martha Ford fled from her country. To get out, she and her seven-year-old daughter were taken north to the border by various friends. Then they walked for eight miles through the South African patrols and reached Angola.

She left behind in Rehoboth, one of the bigger towns in the part-desert, mineral-rich expanse of Namibia, her two other children, aged 16 and 13, and her husband, a carpenter. She hasn't heard from them since. She hasn't tried to send a message to them, afraid that it would provoke retaliation from the South African authorities.

Martha Ford is secretary of the SWAPO Women's Campaign, a member of the central executive of this most unusual of liberation movements. Unusual, because SWAPO is involved in a complex campaign for national independence. On the one hand, SWAPO believes in the armed struggle, and claims to have fought a military campaign against the South African occupying forces for the past twelve years. But SWAPO itself is not illegal and not banned from political work inside Namibia.

"I was campaigning, organ-

ness of foreign exploitation." And yet she has had no political education as such. She says she has "no time to read Marx" and her further education was limited to a year in commercial college.

She is in Britain "to mobilise support in the organised women's movement," and her diary is crammed with speaking engagements at universities and at the new circuit of women's conferences. There is a session with women MPs, the Brixton Black Women's Conference, the conference of the National Association of Women in London, the Women's TUC conference in Folkestone.

"We are oppressed not only by White South African domination, by foreign capital, but also as women. We have to struggle from within against our own attitudes, the way we were brought up as girls, and against our male comrades' attitudes. But we don't see the struggle of ourselves as women as being outside the national struggle. Liberation for our country, our people will have to include liberation for women. Our men have been contract labourers, our women have raised the new generation of our people. We have a

"I was campaigning, organising and speaking openly up to the time that I left for Angola," she says. "But although this was legal in the strict sense, it involved regular harassment and intimidation. I was arrested three times, held and interrogated for two and each time and then released. I was never beaten or ill-treated. It was a matter of permanent pressure. Searches of my home, papers confiscated, sudden arrests."

For her last few months inside Namibia Martha Ford worked full-time for SWAPO. But most of her political life had been a spare time effort, her mother looking after her children while she spent her evenings and weekends travelling to public meetings, speeches interspersed with hundreds of miles of driving. And then back to Barclays Bank and then to other commercial jobs until she was fired for political activities.

"We would leave Hehboth on a Friday night, travel to a meeting, speak and then drive on through the night to another meeting the next day, and more meetings, more speeches. We would drive home on the Sunday night, getting back just in time to go straight to work. It was more militarising than just the response at the public meetings made up for the lack of sleep."

She is a woman of remarkable composure and self-control. Her answers are short and disciplined. Her phrasing is Western, she talks of "levels of consciousness" and "political aware-

raised the new generation of our people. We have a strength there."

Martha Ford acknowledges that SWAPO is "male-dominated at the national executive level and at branch level." She carries pamphlets about the SWAPO women's campaign with photographs of SWAPO women, carrying machine guns, wearing camouflage uniform, posing in front of an ambulance. The pamphlets quote a SWAPO woman political commissar saying: "We now have female commanders. In the beginning, some men were trying to disobey or get around their orders. In these cases, we had stern discussions with the militants involved and told them that these women were given such responsibilities by the Party because of their intelligence and capacity. Through open criticism and self-criticism, we are able to deal with these problems."

In Britain, the overused metaphors about women's "struggle" and "the fight for rights" clearly have less meaning than they do in a liberation movement where people are being killed, where refugee and training camps are hit by air strikes, and where the role of rural women still means acquiescing in polygamy in some parts of Namibia.

"I never regarded it as a choice between being a mother and bringing up my children, and becoming politically involved," Martha Ford stresses. "We are in a process which has a long way to go, to develop—but it has come far already."

Sister Martha Ford on a SWAPO mission abroad, 1979.

With brother Kehat on a visit to Windhoek.

*Kehat on his last visit to us with Edel. He died,
aged 55, after an operation for a brain tumour.*

Joe Murangi, Mburumba with his daughter, Emory Bundy, his wife
Noel Angell, and Edel at grave of Herero chieftains in Okahandja.

Andreas Shipanga and Hans at Nam Human
Rights Assn office, Windhoek 6 November 2010.

Anita and Salatiel Ailonga, Umbalantu,
Namibia, Nov October 24 2010.

NORAD officials: Agnete Eriksen, Arne
Arnesen and Øyvind Lyng in Lusaka.

Sons Jon Are and Sven Tanab.

*Vesla and Fred L-N and Edel taking leave
of Ruth First at Oslo Airport.*

CHAPTER TEN
Strange times

ANDREAS SHIPANGA – BATTING FOR HIS OPPONENTS

In the days that followed I didn't see much of Andreas, except once when he passed me by as a passenger aboard a government truck, with Keeshi sitting by his side. When I could finally make contact with him again, it was to learn that he had been going from office to office – including to the Lutheran World Federation's (LWF) representative – for funds to buy maize meal, sugar, salt, cooking oil, tobacco and medicines. The Zambian Ministry of Defence had made available two trucks for the transportation of the food that he had purchased, while a third was filled with used clothing that he had obtained from aid agencies.

A little later Shipanga dropped by our place in an upbeat mood. Sweden's ambassador in Lusaka had urged him to meet with the overseers of the Swedish International Development Agency who would be visiting soon. One of the overseers was known to be very critical of the aid extended to SWAPO. The ambassador thought that Shipanga was the only one from SWAPO's executive committee who could be trusted to handle the questions likely to be asked.

Andreas knew what the ambassador was getting at and took along Oscar, a man with a strikingly pious visage. He instructed Oscar to remain mute, as if he didn't understand a word of English, if questions were directed at him. As expected the first question related to SWAPO's supposedly Marxist beliefs with regard to religion. With his commanding presence, effortless charm and deep voice, Andreas Shipanga could lead most people down the garden path. This time he didn't have to stretch the truth much. He replied that his countrymen were brought up in the church to be God-fearing and – with a nod in the direction of Oscar sitting by his side – added that that was why SWAPO made sure they had the service of religious advisers in the camps.

The next question was about the very expensive Mercedes trucks for which the organisation had a predilection. Shipanga now told them about the primitive roads that had to be traversed once one had left the tarred roads leading in and out of Lusaka. They had experienced axles breaking and the like from other kinds of trucks, but the Mercedes trucks never gave any trouble. Nevertheless, he invited them to go see for themselves.

The hearty handshake he got from the ambassador afterwards told Andreas that he had passed the test.

Next I would learn that Andreas Shipanga's concern for the welfare of his countrymen had been turned against him. Batting for his colleagues had already been rewarded with vengefulness. On a street in Lusaka, where we ran into each other, Moses Garoeb informed me that they had found out where and why Shipanga had mysteriously gone abroad in November. He had applied for a position as advisor at one of the international church organisations. SWAPO had seen to it that his application was rejected. The smirk of self-satisfaction on Moses' face as he told me this, warned me of ever becoming dependent on his goodwill. I nevertheless accepted the 60 Kwachas he fished out of a pocket and handed me – towards the assistance, he explained, that all party members were entitled to.

Concerning the supplies that Shipanga had secured, we heard that the trucks had been stopped before reaching their destination. The camp inmates had been told that Shipanga had sent them poisoned food that had to be destroyed. What had become of the supplies nobody seemed to know.

LOCAL CASUALTIES OF COLD WAR

On account of the depressed price of Zambia's copper exports, soap and washing powder, toilet paper, cooking oil and other necessities were often not available. Every morning I joined the city's housewives who queued outside the city's supermarket. The moment the doors opened there was a scramble to check what might have been put on the racks during the night. Often the racks proved to be as empty as they had been the previous day.

From Edel's diary:

'12.01.76. Went to town first, got hold of a can of cooking oil at CBC. Happened to be standing in the right queue.'

Another page in Edel's diary showed how our daily lives were being affected by events around us:

'Wednesday, 14.01.76. Zanele [Mbeki] came by. She wanted to make sure that Hans would be available to meet with Lars Gunnar Eriksen [the Swede in charge of the IUEF] on Saturday. Students at the University of Zambia are demonstrating in favour of the MPLA in Angola.'

The students were demonstrating against the Kaunda government's support for the UNITA movement. Instead, they wanted Zambia to deepen its relationship with the People's Movement for the Liberation of Angola (MPLA). President Kaunda closed the university, dismissed and jailed two political science lecturers, the Brit Lionel Cliff and the South African Robert Molteno. Some days before his imprisonment, Molteno had arranged with the dean of the faculty for me to be offered a position as a lecturer. Kaunda's dismissal of Molteno and Cliff had in fact caused a crisis in an institution that was already suffering a shortage of staff.

We had the privilege of having Molteno over for dinner the night before he was imprisoned. In a letter to Professor Johan Vogt, my mentor at the Institute of Economics in Oslo, I wrote on 6 April :

'Regrettably it would seem that the authorities have killed the institution. They have in any case shown such cynicism about the teachers' human and academic rights as would make it altogether irresponsible of me to report for duty there.

'Two of the lecturers who have been thrown in prison together with a journalist who is still sitting there, were my personal acquaintances. They have in common that they are highly competent and take their tasks seriously, both professionally and humanly. Besides, they have expressed their opinions with honesty and fearlessness. The journalist Robinson Makayi thus was the only one to openly state on television that Zambia was making a mistake by not recognising the Angolan regime.

'The lecturers did not, as far as I know, take part in any public debate but were known as radicals at the University and were said to have instructed in Marxism. 'This I will not have,' said the President, who is also the University's Chancellor.[35]

'Robert Molteno last year participated at a UN seminar in Dar-es-Salaam with a paper about the CIA's efforts to establish listening and observation posts at the University here. He published names and internal correspondence of the University in support of his statements. Rumours flourish here, but from a second-hand source I have it that CIA agents were let into the country early last year to provide the President with advice and help to deal with Soviet agents who, it is said, are crawling all over the place.

'From being a disillusioned White South African who wanted to carve a future for himself and his family, Molteno is said to have become an agent for a foreign power.'

---

[35] This was a reference to an experience Vogt liked to recount. He had been invited by the University of Cairo to deliver a talk on Marxism – only to be informed on arrival that the invitation had been cancelled. He had looked forward to a presentation to Muslim scholars of the critical distance that he had developed towards the ideology he had embraced in his youth. An unsurpassed essayist, Vogt published a stream of most insightful analyses of world affairs in publications like 'Det Trellbundne sinn'(The enslaved Mind), Memorandum to H.M. Kongen om den dårskap hvormed verden regjeres (Memo to H.M the King about the foolishness with which the world is governed).

NOISES OFFSTAGE

The '1968 European Students Revolution' had not passed Oslo by. Dropping by at Professor Vogt's office one day, he drily recounted to me a visit he had been paid by a firebrand who lashed out at 'bourgeois' economists like himself. After patiently letting the student have his say, Vogt wordlessly went to a bookshelf and fished out a yellowed offprint of an article that had been published in 1928. Opening it at a page, he placed it in front of the young man with the invitation that he take a look at it. I could well imagine Vogt sitting back and lighting his pipe as he studied the young man's reactions on encountering the self-same epithets that he had just been using. 'Did you write this?' the student, evidently stunned, asked. When it was suggested that he take a look at the author's name on the title page, the student rose from his seat and took his leave.

In contrast to the SWAPO seniors who, with the exception of Andreas Shipanga I seldom saw, my young countrymen – hungry for a chance to talk and to argue – often came to visit us. On one occasion I questioned two young women, Ndeshimona Uyumba and Monica XXX, who had more or less moved into our place, about what they knew of the party's leaders. I was surprised to learn that without exception they had not known anything about SWAPO's leadership before their arrival in Zambia. They made no exception for Andreas Shipanga, whom they regarded as one of the old guard.

Around that time there was much talk about a letter that the SWAPO Youth League had addressed to the party's leadership. It expressed anxiety about reports that had come to them from the front, where SWAPO guerrillas had been disarmed. Moreover, after South Africa had entered the Angolan civil war on UNITA's side against the MPLA, they could no longer count on the loyalty of their former Angolan allies.

Shortly after my return from the refugee camp, Solomon Mifima, who had been absent from Lusaka for some weeks, dropped by our house. He confirmed the SYL account. Without going into detail he indicated that relations with UNITA had become very bad. As to SWAPO, he complained that four men – Nujoma, Mueshihange, Nanyemba and Garoeb – had taken absolute power in the organisation. The Central Committee, to which he had been elected at the party's last congress in the Tanzanian town of Tanga, had never been convened.

Edel's notes, often cryptic, give a feeling of a situation around us that gradually became more difficult to interpret, even while our house was used by many key people as a thoroughfare:

'20.1. (1976) : Ndeshi and Monica both look unhappy. Ndeshi left at

2 pm in Moses' car to visit a pregnant friend. Hans visits (Professor) Jack Simons. We dropped by Andreas and Esmé. Esmé told us that Ndeshi is very depressed. Libertine had been there and roundly ticked off the SYL for the letter they had written. Andreas and Esmé are being boycotted by the hard core, but don't take it too seriously. Punch [the half-Labrador we'd inherited from a departing British couple] barked the whole night.

'Wednesday 21.1. Hans and the boys drove to a farm with 150 cows, three giant bulldogs (Rhodesian ridgebacks) and a halting sheep. Monica claims that Andreas Shipanga has proof that Sam Nujoma had been bribed by South Africa. Ndeshi has visited Hage Geingob (Head of newly established UN Institute of Namibia) who apparently now has changed his tune and wants matters to be discussed. Libertine doesn't want Ndeshi to work for Ben, her husband, as was the idea. Andreas ought to be careful. They want to punish the SYL.

'Sunday 25.1. The MPLA does well. South Africa must pull out of Angola. They do not get support from 'the free world' in the war against communists.

'Monday 26.1 Wina kicked out by K.K.(Kenneth Kaunda) Reason given: alcoholism. Probably has to do with the MPLA/UNITA/FNLA (National Liberation Front of Angola).

'Tuesday 10.2. Monica to Peter Nanyemba. She assumed that he wanted to question her about Andreas and Hans' activities and eventual contact with the youth movement.

'Thursday 12.2. Hans had a conversation with Andreas yesterday. Solomon Mifima is back from Angola. Some guys came here this evening. About ten. Solomon, Zacharia, Keeshi, Joe, Katana, Sakki and one more. Eight. Hans served beer and soup. Something is afoot within the party. The old guard is hopelessly compromised. It is not easy to be a foreigner in this country.

'Sunday 15.2. Peter Nanyemba, Moses Garoeb, Hidipo, Mueshihange are said to be more and more isolated – according to the girls. PN and Mu dare not sleep at home: they fear for their lives.

'Tuesday 17.2. Took a walk to the Hotel Intercontinental. Met Margaret Valentin[36] there. She had kept away from us for fear of compromising us. MacBride's secretary had been ticked off for lending her apartment to Margaret. She was sitting at the hotel waiting for an opportunity to meet with

---

[36] Margaret Valentin was married to Jorge Valentin, with whom we had become acquainted at the COSEC office in Leyden in 1966; subsequently she worked for a while at the IUEF – International University Exchange Fund – that had been created by the Norwegian and Swedish Governments, with the Swede Lars Gunnar Eriksen in charge at offices in Geneva. The fund provided support for students from southern Africa and Latin America until it was discovered that Lars had taken into his employ a South African, one Craig Williamson, who turned out to be a South African Police Agent. Entrusted with the clandestine transfer of money to South Africa, Williamson set up a scheme to divert money to fictitious individuals and addresses, for the use of his colleagues at Vlakplaas, a place where opponents of the regime were murdered.

UNITA's foreign minister. What is she to do? Husband in the bush. Travels home to England tomorrow. She doesn't have an easy time of it.

'Friday 20/2. Margaret Valentin for dinner. She didn't look happy. Later in the evening Hans and I hear a BBC report. Her husband is said to be responsible for the massacre of 100 people in Angola. Poor girl. Hans will take her to the airport tomorrow.

'According to Radio South Africa 150 SWANU members have returned to Namibia.'

We wondered if those were the young men whom Zedekia Ngavirue had come for all the way from Papua in New Guinea, to negotiate assimilation into the PLAN, only to be spurned by SWAPO's operatives.

WORRIES

From the end of February onwards, our housing problems were compounded by my precarious status within the country. Once I got called in by immigration officials who appeared oblivious to the irony of their wanting to execute the will of a long since defunct colonial agency – the Central African Federation that Kaunda had helped to kill in 1964. They wanted me to know that my designation as an undesirable alien still stood. An endless round of visits to offices to have this as well as our housing situation clarified eventually began to take a toll on Edel's patience and health. On Saturday 28 February she wrote in her diary: 'We have decided that I shall go on strike.'

The following week she fell ill. Dr Traub diagnosed a kidney infection. In the subsequent three weeks Edel notes down the comings and goings of people and what they have to tell:

'In Moscow, Peter Nanyemba is said to be UNITA's man. Thought he was on his way to Angola with the military. But he is now said to be hiding somewhere in Lusaka. Moses Garoeb is in London. Something is expected to happen this weekend. I wonder what.' All that happened that week was that the man who had come around to ask us for a job parted a poisonous snake while cutting the grass around the house with a scythe. This gave us something other to think about than the political developments in the region.

No less worrying were robberies that the Zambians ascribed to rogues from the Congo. Our nearest neighbours, a Zambian family, awoke one morning to discover that while they were asleep their bedroom had been emptied of all their clothing. Shortly afterwards we found that our kitchen door had been unlocked from the inside. A windowpane had been taken out to reach the key. Since nothing was missing, I concluded that the robbers had been disturbed by a light that I had turned on in the toilet in the middle of the night, the consequence of a watermelon we'd had before going to bed.

And then, on a morning in November, we woke to find that Edel's colour had turned the sickly yellow of hepatitis, which Dr Traub confirmed. I now had to take on the additional duties of a nurse for a patient that had to be kept in isolation. It became a challenge to prepare food that didn't get rejected the moment I entered the bedroom. Avocados and fruit juice proved to be Edel's lifesavers.

OMENS

Among the South Africans with whom I had become acquainted in Zambia was Bax Nomvete, an economist who headed the UN's regional office in Lusaka and was Esmé Shipanga's boss. Nomvete suggested that I attend an upcoming UN Conference on Trade and Development (UNCTAD) in Nairobi as an observer on behalf of SWAPO. As I knew of no other SWAPO members trained as economists, I immediately sent Moses Garoeb a letter to ask that he forward my name for an invitation to UNCTAD. In spite of a reminder I sent, I received no reply.

Some weeks later Nomvete came to me with a new invitation. This time it was to attend a regional UN conference about economic cooperation in sub-tropical Africa that he was organising in Mbabane, the Swazi capital. The precondition was that I paid my own fare. The conference would take place during the latter part of April. Encouraged by Mifima, who transferred to me an unused return air ticket to Maputo, I decided to accept the invitation, not bothering to inform 'the office' about it.

Shortly afterwards Andreas Shipanga and Solomon Mifima dropped by our home and spoke about the difficulties they were experiencing at the Liberation Centre. Both had returned from tours to find their offices emptied of typewriters and telephones. Having received reports that the guerrilla bases lacked basic supplies, they were worried about the situation of the PLAN fighters. At one of the bases, Nujoma and his associates were said to have been bodily threatened by the fighters. What had prevented things from going very wrong was an intervention by the Zambian Army, who had previously disarmed the guerrillas. From their nearby base they kept a watch on what was happening in the Namibian camp.

Early on Sunday, March 28 1976, Ndeshi Uyumba turned up with the news that the police had carried out a raid at Mueshihange's and Nanyemba's home, and found 'a lot of weapons'. 'A lot of weapons' was also said to have been dug up outside a SWAPO base – while guerrillas were sent out 'on missions' unarmed. Letters from the guerrillas also claimed that Nanyemba, PLAN's political leader, had handed SWAPO weapons over to UNITA.

On 6 April Andreas Shipanga paid me another visit, this time with a new letter from the guerrillas that he asked me to transfer to a stencil for copying. The letter told of unbearable conditions, including lack of food, and put forward demands for a change of leadership. Noticing that Shipanga was disturbed, I assumed that he wanted to take up the matter with the OAU's Liberation Committee, which I understood kept some sort of oversight over guerrilla organisations. I could not imagine what other alternatives he had.

It struck me that the letter-writers appeared to be ignorant of the fact that they had been disarmed on orders from the host government. Their only alternative would be to be sent to Angola. At that time, however, SWAPO's alliance with Jonas Savimbi's UNITA stood in the way of an approach to the MPLA government in Luanda, where Agostinho Neto was in charge. It was no secret that there was no love lost between Neto and Nujoma. For Nujoma there was the added risk of letting guerrilla soldiers, who had demonstrated their enmity towards him, precede him to Angola. As Andreas offered no indication of his plans, I kept my reflections to myself.

MPLA DIPLOMAT BEMOANS LACK OF SWAPO CONTACT

Andreas Shipanga was not the only one whose conduct that week would reveal to me that a crisis was brewing in SWAPO. On Friday 9 April, Keshii Pelao Nathanael and Sheeli Shangula dropped by to tell me that the day before they had seen André Miranda, the Angolan representative in Lusaka. They had gone to his offices with Ndeshi and a guerrilla by the name of Ndali Kamati, together with whom they had established SYL before their departure from Ovamboland. Acting on behalf of SYL, they had requested the Angolan diplomat to mediate contact for cooperation with the MPLA's youth movement in his home country.

Miranda had expressed his pleasure at this very first time members of SWAPO had approached his government. He referred to both the MPLA government and SWAPO receiving military training and arms from 'the same people', while remaining estranged from one another. On the spot, he issued Keeshi with a visa to Luanda, and promised to transmit their request to his government.

The background to the SYL's desire to speak to Miranda was intriguing. Here I must provide some details that would have given me a deeper insight into the situation than I had possessed at the time – had the SYL leaders been more forthcoming. It was only years later, on my closely questioning him, that Keshii Pelao Nathanael would admit that they had been less than candid with me, if not kept me completely in the dark about what was afoot. Regrettably, it would not be the only such instance – as I discovered after Sheeli had come to our house late one evening with the urgent request to drive Joe Mueshikela, one of their members, to the airport.

When the next day I learned that Joe's true destination had been London and not Luanda, as they had made me believe, Sheeli brazenly admitted that they had purposely misled me – to test me! He appeared to regard this as quite in order, which made me wonder what he had learnt about ethics at the theological college he was said to have attended in South Africa.

From Keeshi I learnt that Solomon Mifima had returned from Angola in company with one Kamati, whom he had then taken to Keeshi's and Shangula's place. There they could update each other about events in the year that had passed. Kamati had taken a certain risk in returning to Lusaka, which he had left in January 1975 together with the PLAN commander Dimo – 'to open up a front in Angola'. This had happened after violent disagreement between Dimo and Nujoma. In Angola they received supplies of arms from Savimbi's UNITA. Their position became precarious after Savimbi later that year entered into an alliance with the apartheid regime in South Africa. In this way, the need arose for them to approach the MPLA, from whom the SWAPO leadership was estranged.

Understanding the Dimo group's situation, Solomon Mifima had quietly left Lusaka to make contact with them in Angola. Returning with Kamati he had hoped to persuade his colleagues in the leadership to see that it was high time to leave Zambia and establish their base in Angola, in cooperation with the MPLA regime. This had also been in line with the youth league's demands.

There is reason to pay Kamati a little more attention. For three weeks, according to Keeshi, both Kamati and Mifima had been denied any meeting with the SWAPO office which, during prolonged absences from town of both Nanyemba and Nujoma had been run by Mishake Muyongo, Peter Mueshihange and Moses Garoeb.

On Nanyemba's reappearance in the city, Kamati was picked up by a SWAPO vehicle and driven to Nanyemba's home, where he remained.

After some days, he returned to his comrades with advice they had found disturbing. He told them that they had 'to change tactics', that they were risking their futures and that their lives were in danger. Asked if he had bought his own freedom by selling them out, he hadn't said anything. He nevertheless kept the appointment they had made to meet with them outside the gate of the diplomats' compound where Miranda resided.

According to Keeshi, the time spent with Kamati had opened his eyes to the brutalisation war leads to. His erstwhile companion had enjoyed talking about the bestial manner in which he and his companions had set upon and killed an innocent Ovambo villager – who had crossed the border into Angola on some regular business.

THEO-BEN GURIRAB ARRIVES IN TOWN

Unaware of just how inflamed relations between SWAPO's leaders had become, I drove to Shipanga's home early on Saturday 10 April, two days before my departure for Mbabane. To my surprise I found Theo-Ben Gurirab from New York there, elegantly dressed in a blue blazer, grey flannel pants, a broad-striped silver and blue tie, and polished black shoes. The party's observer at the UN looked the part.

While Shipanga was busy with other people, I took Theo-Ben aside to express my joy at seeing him there. Referring to the situation about which they had informed me in London the year before, I told him that matters had become much worse. To my surprise this made Theo-Ben recoil. In an accusatory tone, he told me that Moses Garoeb – whom he referred to as 'the General-Secretary' – had questioned them for having allowed me to co-sign the letter that they had sent from London. Theo-Ben appeared to have forgotten that he was referring to a letter that he and his colleagues had requested me to draft. The implication was clear enough: had I known my place they wouldn't have been in trouble.

At this moment I realised that the man in front of me was gripped by fear. With that I said to him, 'Theo-Ben, you are a big man. Besides that you have built up a reputation for yourself as the party's spokesman in New York and at international forums. Your colleagues are not so stupid as to want to do you any harm. I plead with you to sit down at Ridgeway Hotel and let them know that you are not returning to New York before they exert themselves to solve the problems that now threaten to do us great damage.'

Theo-Ben's response was to ask who my allies were. I found this to be a strange question, as the idea of partisanship was foreign to me. As we returned to Andreas' lounge, I invited him for dinner on the next evening.

At home, Edel noted the following update of the situation, as had been reported to her from various visitors that day:

'Mueshihange has been sent to Angola to fetch Peter Nanyemba and

Sam Nujoma. The Zambians had taken Moses Garoeb to the eastern front for a confrontation with fifteen military personnel – who had signed a letter. The Zambians had taken along a medical doctor. The men were in bad shape for lack of food. A safe with money for Nanyemba's use had been dug up. It was always guarded on shift by eight men. The weapons were buried on 19 December – and unarmed men sent out to meet the enemy. The decision had been taken by Hidipo, Sam, Peter Nanyemba, Mueshihange and Moses. Andreas has recently had a talk with MacBride about all this. He had been very bitter, especially because some of the men at the Namibia Institute had been among the compromised.'

At lunchtime on Sunday I walked over to the Ridgeway Hotel to look up Theo-Ben. There I found a room full of SWAPOs, some of whom I knew, others whom I had not met before. Assuming that they were there to say hello to our man in New York, I merely reminded him of the dinner I would be preparing for him and left. We waited in vain for him that evening.

The next morning Andreas Shipanga drove me to the airport for my flight to Swaziland. When I told him about my brief encounter with Theo-Ben at the Ridgeway the day before, he upbraided me for leaving a political meeting before it had ended.

FOLLOWED BY HENRY KISSINGER

Listening to the radio programmes about the victory of the Soviet-backed MPLA under Aghostino Neto over his rivals, Roberto Holden and Jonas Savimbi, for control of the capital Luanda in Angola, we could practically hear the alarm bells set ringing not only in Western capitals, but right where we were. Kenneth Kaunda gave orders for left-wing Zambian students to be arrested and had two university lecturers imprisoned. Ironically, in Washington the US Congress, on discovering that the CIA had supported the apartheid regime's foray into Angola, pulled the rug from underneath the agency's engagement there. Left high and dry, South Africa found it advisable to call off its own campaign – at a time when its forces were poised to take control of Angola.

In Lusaka we were, therefore, not surprised by the announcement in April 1976 that the US Secretary of State, Henry Kissinger, would be setting out on an African safari that would encompass the Zambian capital. When I ran into Theo-Ben Gurirab at Andreas Shipanga's house, I assumed that he had arrived in town to brief his colleagues for an eventual meeting with the man charged with American foreign policy. On our way to the airport, Andreas had volunteered nothing about what he and Theo-Ben had been talking about.

I had therefore taken it for granted that Theo-Ben had informed him that nothing worthwhile could be expected to come out of a meeting with the US official – the default position in dealings with the West.

SWAZILAND

The kingdom of Swaziland lived in the shadow of its mighty neighbour, South Africa. Its economy was dependent on the export of workers to South African mines and industries. Within hours of rolling off the press, Johannesburg newspapers were on sale in the Swaziland capital, Mbabane. Even though the theme of the conference was regional trade, it was clear that the country's relations with South Africa were a sensitive matter.

I nevertheless got a sense of the hidden feelings on a visit to a restaurant. A burly man at a neighbouring table wanted to know where I was from, what I was doing in the country and, on being told, whether I was a member of SWAPO. My confirmation of this instantly had him declare his love of me. 'Well, not in that way, but I love you', he insisted. My countrymen's armed insurrection had clearly touched a chord in that Swazi's heart.

The sense of security I enjoyed after that declaration would disappear like dew at sunrise the next morning. Even before I was out of bed, Bax Nomvete knocked at my door with the news that Andreas Shipanga had been arrested in Zambia on a charge of espionage. Two others were arrested with him, but then released.

The details were unclear, Bax said, but he had a very urgent plea to address to me. It was that I should not mention anything about the matter to Esmé Shipanga, his secretary, who was at the UN regional conference with us. Her mother, whom she had not seen for ten years, was due to arrive from Johannesburg that day. If Esmé were to know that her husband had been arrested, she would want to return to Lusaka straight away.

My first reaction was one of utter disbelief. It simply made no sense that Andreas, as a member of SWAPO's executive committee charged with the organisation's publicity, should be stealing information to which he was not entitled – so as to pass it to the enemy. I reviewed in my mind what sort of information Andreas could have sold to, presumably, the regime in Pretoria. The most obvious possibility – the difficulties SWAPO's guerrilla army was experiencing in Zambia – was the direct result of the collusion between John Vorster of South Africa and Kenneth Kaunda of Zambia. As every journalist in Lusaka knew the facts, it would not take a spy to give a detailed report. Unable to think of anything else that could seriously compromise Andreas Shipanga,

I concluded that he was in no real danger and would be released in due course.

It was difficult to have lunch and dinner with Esmé that day and talk about everything else but. The next day, when she discovered that I had known about what had happened, her wrath would make me regret having acquiesced to Nomvete's request. She was unimpressed by my plea, that it was her boss who had requested me to say nothing to her.

Wondering why Nomvete had bothered to inform me at all, it occurred to me that he might have wanted to warn me that I myself could be in danger on returning to Lusaka. Unable to think of anything I might have done wrong, I put that thought out of my head. At the conference I joined a working group to draft and co-sign a statement on behalf of SWAPO.

For me, too, the conference in Mbabane provided an opportunity to get in touch with family, even if only by phone. From the hotel room I called my younger brother, Kehat, who was busy specialising as a surgeon at a hospital in Cape Town. We had last spoken with each other seventeen years earlier when he was still in his early teens. When he answered the late night call I could notice the effect of many years of separation. Kehat didn't sound surprised to hear from me, but expectant. I found myself casting around for something to say that wouldn't sound sentimental.

HEARING THE BELLS TOLL FOR THE APARTHEID REGIME

After so many years of absence from South Africa I could find nothing in the newspapers that told me anything about what changes had taken place in society. For that reason I became transfixed by a short news item in one of the papers. The story was banal but stunning for what it portended. A quarrel between a Black and a White man about the right of way at a road crossing had resulted in the White man's death. The Black man got off with the most lenient of sentences. This told me two things: the country's judges had developed doubts about the righteousness of the cause they were charged to uphold. And Blacks had lost their fear of getting into scraps with Whites.

Instilling fear being the first line of defence of police states, I tried to convey my excitement about what the story portended to some of the participants. They reacted with scant interest. But it didn't surprise me when a few weeks later the Soweto uprising happened. It started as a revolt of school children in the Johannesburg 'township' of Soweto against the impoverishing curricula that were foisted on them and it spread like fire through dry grass across the country. By all accounts it heralded the beginning of the end for the apartheid regime.

IN LUSAKA A 'LIBERATION MOVEMENT' IMPRISONS ITS MEMBERS

On the bus back from Mbabane to Maputo a Zambian civil servant named Simonda took me aside to inform me that several of my countrymen had been jailed in Lusaka and that more arrests were expected. For a moment, I wondered if he too was warning me about returning to Lusaka. In that case, he might have been tipping me off that Maputo might be a good place to discontinue my journey back to Lusaka. But as I could think of no reason why anyone could accuse me of 'spying' I instead gave Simonda my view of developments in SWAPO since my arrival in Zambia. I emphasised that if the Zambian authorities could not provide hard evidence that Andreas Shipanga was in fact a traitor, his arrest and detention would have been a terrible mistake.

Immediately after our landing in Lusaka, while I was still standing in the passport queue, Simonda came over to hand me his card, whispering that I should call him at ten the next morning. He would then tell me what he had been able to find out about the matter.

I was not even half prepared for the news with which Edel and Agnete Eriksen, the Norwegian consul, met me when I got into Agnete's car close to midnight. On the way into town the seriousness of what they had to tell hit me like a sledgehammer. Andreas Shipanga and eight others, in addition to 42 guerrillas, had been spirited off to unknown destinations.

I now saw that the situation had nothing to do with spying, and that I had probably only that night to make sure that the truth be known – should I be imprisoned as well. What I therefore needed to do was draft a document that would be damaging to Kenneth Kaunda if it were published. I there and then decided to write him a letter and to deposit a copy with Reuters' representative in Lusaka to be used in the event of my arrest.

More surprises were waiting for me back at 7 Saise Road, where we lived. In addition to Soini and her new baby, there was Jimmie Ampala, who had worked for the SWAPO radio, Gottlieb Nakaamboh, the father of four with whom I had become acquainted on the SWAPO farm, as well as a younger man named Peter Nunguuluh, who walked with difficulty after a car had run over one of his legs.

Edel informed me that Gottlieb and Peter had slept in the house from the night of 21 April onwards, when they had escaped the swoop on their fellows. Gottlieb alternated, sometimes sleeping over at other friends' places, while Peter had been staying put.

In disregard of the danger they were said to be in and even though passers-by in the street could hear every word they spoke through the slatted window panes, my three countrymen were talking to one another as if they didn't have a care in the world. Basking in the warmth of their welcome, I nevertheless felt obliged to let them know that while I felt honoured to have them seeking refuge in our home, it would be prudent if they lowered their voices. Ms Eriksen consented to return early the next morning for the letter that I was going to write.

When we could finally withdraw to our bedroom, Edel had another disturbing story to tell me. A Finnish diplomat, Kari Karanko, accompanied by his Swedish colleague Anders Bjuner, had 'dumped' Jimmy Ampala in her care the night before. Having attended a Finnish missionary school at home, Jimmy had often visited the Finns in Lusaka. To escape arrest on the fateful night he had sought refuge in Karanko's house. Edel had been struck by the fear in both Bjuner's and Karanko's bearing, she thought that the Finn, a powerfully built athletic type, must have been reprimanded by his superiors for giving refuge to an opponent of Nujoma and his henchmen.

If so, we didn't need to speculate much: To strive for UN top jobs for their diplomats, I had learnt in Oslo, was the way in which Finland sought to gain international visibility, and to sidestep the constraints that its peace treaty of 1939 with the Soviet Union had put on its foreign policy. The only inference we could draw was that both the Finns and the Swedes had made investments in Nujoma that they were not prepared to forfeit by lending succour to any of his opponents. The prize was SWAPO's support for the appointment of the Finnish diplomat Martti Ahtisaari to the UN Council for Namibia.

What made an indelible impression on me that evening was the fortitude my wife had shown throughout a frightening ordeal, all the while suffering from a debilitating condition. With compassion for my countrymen, she had let them into our home in their hour of need, and shared with them what she could provide of sustenance and comfort. She happily told me of long conversations she had had with both Jimmy and Gottlieb. Gottlieb had given her his parents' address, in case something should happen to him.

Edel's diary, noting what she had been told by her fearful visitors, provides an account of the build-up to the tragedy that was unfolding. I here summarise the diary's contents:

'On the morning of 21 April Pastor Salatiel Ailonga and Anita arrived with shattering news. In the dark of night, the Zambian police had arrested Martin Taneni, Rubin (Sheeli) Shangula, Andreas Shipanga and Solomon Mifima. Nobody knew where Jimmy Ampala was. Keshii Pelao Nathanael and Ndeshimona Uyumba – who had departed for a course on trade unionism in the Netherlands – were also being searched for.'

Salatiel and Anita mentioned those responsible for the arrests as Moses

Garoeb, Theo-Ben Gurirab, Mishake Muyongo, George Kalomo, Libertine Appolus Amathila, Hidipo Hamutenya and Peter Sheehama. It was unknown whether the triumvirate, Nujoma, Mueshihange and Nanyemba, were in town. It was not known, therefore, whether they were also responsible for the appeal to the Zambians to imprison the Namibians.

After Salatiel and Anita's departure Edel worries:

'Now it will be problematical to get hold of food, etc. I wonder how long they will be held in prison. Does MacBride have a role in it? What's with the Zambians? Where are they imprisoned, here or in Kabwe? What could have happened?'

At ten in the morning on the Friday, a couple of Soini's friends turned up. With Andreas' help we had engaged Soini, a trained nurse, to take care of the household chores during my absence. Soini's friends had had no contact with the prisoners, but they were optimistic. One of the men hardly spoke. He had witnessed that guerrillas were sent out on operations unarmed. They told Edel that I was probably not involved in Shipanga's group.

This was news to me. From what I had observed since our arrival, it was hard to give credence to the notion that there existed 'a Shipanga group' capable of turning the tables on Sam Nujoma, or even that Andreas was considering such a prospect. In my opinion, Andreas Shipanga was too much of a realist even to consider unleashing a struggle for power in a foreign country with disarmed guerrillas confined to military bases in the bush as his potential supporters. Moses Garoeb's own story about Andreas having applied for a job in a church organisation in Geneva, had revealed to me that Andreas was trying to get out of a set-up that had become the conduit for filling the Swiss bank accounts of the men in charge – without his doing damage to the greater cause. The most he could subsequently have hoped for, with his escape route blocked, was for the guerrillas' unrest to strengthen his hands in a show-down, at a party congress, that he seemed to consider unavoidable.

Ailonga and Anita had something even more ominous to impart to Edel. They had told her that 'the clique couldn't stand' me. 'This was a fine compliment', she noted – without having asked what the cause might have been.

On Saturday 24, Edel penned the following:

'The men still seem to be in prison. Last night Jimmy said that he knew Hans' father and sister Martha very well. They were both militant, he said. It seems he liked them, from the way he said it. I joked that nothing was so bad as to be not good for something. Andreas won't be getting any whiskey in prison. He is going to come out in good shape.'

LETTER TO KENNETH KAUNDA, PRESIDENT OF ZAMBIA

Lusaka,

29 April 1976

H.E. Dr. Kenneth Kaunda,

President of Zambia,

I wish to plead with you to address yourself to the contents of this letter.

I know that the liberation of Namibia is a matter that is of great personal concern to you.

Your concern for the liberation of Namibia, Zimbabwe, and South Africa, has been so great – and it has been naturally shared by the people of Zambia – that no sacrifice was ever deemed too great for the country to bear.

Economic development in this country is retarded as a consequence of the invidious position in which your country has found itself since independence and because you were never willing to compromise on matters of basic interest to Zambia and Africa.

In recent years you have even risked personal popularity and misunderstanding of your motives by extending the hand of friendship and assistance to the Whites of southern Africa, in order to help them to overcome the threat that by their own choice(s), they have become to the life and happiness of millions of their, and our, people.

It is because I know all this that I have no doubt that whatever you decide to do or sponsor in matters relating to Namibia, is done in good faith and with the ultimate welfare of your and our people in mind.

It would therefore be a pity if Zambia were ever to decide to undertake a course of action that is in fact based on wrong information and for that reason could prove to be fateful to our future political development.

Mr President, it is a matter of experience, renewed again and again, that the affairs of our neighbouring brothers, will baffle and sometimes even exasperate us. In my own experience, the affairs of Namibia have often proved to be complicated, even to some of our best friends.

The past two weeks I have been out of Lusaka, where I am resident with my wife and children since August last year.

Very painful developments would seem to have come to a head in our party during the fortnight.

The Zambian police are said to have arrested leading members of SWAPO, among them Comrades Andreas Shipanga and Solomon Mifima, founding members of our party. Forty-two of our guerrillas are also said to have been 'rounded up'.

I should like to set out here, Mr President, my reasons for stating that this could prove to have been a terrible, terrible mistake – something that could prove to have the most tragic consequences for our party and the prospects of Namibian independence in the near future.

It is of course presumptuous of an individual to make such a claim towards a head of state who has recourse to vast information-gathering facilities. Under the present circumstances, it could even be regarded as foolishly arrogant.

I should be terribly unhappy if as a consequence of this letter I were to find myself either in detention, or branded as an unwanted person in Zambia. It would be a stigma that I for one, would prefer to do without.

I shall therefore assume that the orders under which my comrades had been deprived of their freedom, and whereby others have been turned into fugitives, have come not from you – although the responsibility will of course be that of the President of Zambia.

SWAPO was formed in 1960, after having started off as the Ovamboland People's Organisation. Its founding members were Herman Toivo Ya Toivo, Solomon Mifima, Andreas Shipanga and others. Sam Nujoma and other members joined after the inception of OPO.

The name change of SWAPO, after OPO, was decided upon in recognition of the fact that no one tribal or language group, could engage in a campaign for national liberation from the springboard of a tribal platform.

In the case of the Ovambo-speaking people, the reasons were and are only too painfully obvious. They form the majority of our people, the other groups having been greatly reduced by the German colonialists seventy-odd years ago.

But the Ovambo-speaking people are concentrated in a part of Namibia that right up to the present, is separated from the rest of the country, *from the part that is the one basically at dispute*, namely that known as 'the White man's land' in Namibia.

This is the point that is constantly being made by people such as Chief Clemens Kapuuo who not long ago tried to brand SWAPO as an 'Ovambo Organisation' and stated that the Ovambos had never lost land to the Whites.

It would be politically unwise to discount the potency of this situation in the political prospects of Namibia. Indeed, recent reports from Namibia can inform us of a new political grouping provisionally called the Okahandja Conference, with mainly Nama, Damara, and Herero support.

It might be useful in this context to recall that a historical bond was forged between the Herero and Nama Chiefs of Namibia in their hour of greatest peril, namely when the Germans were about to unleash their genocidal campaigns against those groups of Namibia's people.

The Herero and Nama speaking groups have thus had the oldest alliance in the struggle against colonialism, and, being minority groups in the population of the country as a whole, they will be sensitive to the 'danger of domination by SWAPO', where the Ovambo-speakers form the majority of members. This indeed forms the constant pith of the regime's propaganda campaigns directed towards our people.

Many non-Ovambo-speaking Namibians, myself included, have through the years joined SWAPO, because it was the one organisation with potential for becoming a truly national one, one around which we could seek to mobilise the strength of our people.

I should like, however, Mr President, to underline that joining SWAPO has not only been an act of political affirmation of the motives of the founders of the party. It has also been an act in the nature of a concession to the political dominance of the Ovambo-speaking people. SWAPO sprang from their numbers and the top leaders are predominantly Ovambo-speaking.

Thus an alternative to SWAPO as national organisation, was SWANU which had and still holds to the same goal, namely the independence of Namibia. But the founding members of SWANU were predominantly Herero-speaking.

The following quotation, translated from the Afrikaans of a secret South African evaluation of the political situation in Namibia (May 1974), is of relevance to the point made. It is an accurate opinion, in my view:

'Because of SWANU's anti-tribal nature, it has never enjoyed great support. One could put forward the thesis that SWANU had lost much support because it had not taken into account the realities in South West Africa'.

In 1966 the South Africans arrested all the outstanding leaders of SWAPO, Herman Toivo Ya Toivo amongst them. Toivo's plea in his own defense in that trial remains the most eloquent expression of the Namibian spirit of resistance, in recent generations.

In the defense he there delivered of the right of his younger countrymen to fight for the liberation of their country, even though he himself had chosen to remain unarmed, he spoke in the tradition of our great Nama and Herero leaders. He was the first Ovambo-speaker to join their ranks in Namibia. He showed himself a Namibian of stature.

We have never had any occasion to observe the leadership qualities of any of our leading men abroad, Mr President. In fact, all of us have tended to regard ourselves as the mere voices of our people, sent to mobilise international support for their cause. And if we should have begun to imagine otherwise, the lack of healthy grass-roots contact in the years of exile, has certainly become evident in the grievous failure of our present leadership to meet the needs of our fighting men and ordinary ranks and file the past two years.

After the arrest of and sentencing of Toivo and his thirty-seven colleagues the party inside Namibia went into eclipse.

It was then that a new generation of people entered the picture. Members of SWAPO's Youth League went about building the party from the ground up. Before even they were forced to flee the country in droves, from the middle of 1974 onwards, they had managed to place it on a firm and uncorrupted footing. They were the ones who had organised the strikes that swept through the country and into South Africa itself in 1972; they were preparing for a national strike to take place last August, when Chief Filemon Elifas was murdered and the regime provided cause for eliminating a new crop of leaders.

As far as I have been able to determine, the secret of the success of the Youth League in expanding the party's base, was their sensitivity to the basic problems facing us, namely those stemming from our inability to speak each others' language. SWAPO meetings became ungainly affairs, with seven to eight interpreters on the podia, so as to ensure that the party's message reached the members of each group in their own language. It was only then that people started to come to meetings.

But, while our young people were thus struggling to establish our party, they could get *no support and guidance* from our leadership abroad. On reaching Zambia and elsewhere after leaving the country, their demands have continued to be for the formulation of a *political line*, with capital letters.

What they have instead experienced, was to be branded as 'rebels'. It has come to light recently that such 'rebels', if they manifest themselves at the front, are sent to their deaths at the hands of the enemy through being deprived of proper arms while being ordered to go and fight.

Similarly, in December last year a number of twenty of our very fine young persons resident here in Zambia, were denied leave to travel to Britain to avail themselves of study and training opportunities offered to us by the British Government. The decision was made by SWAPO officials on the pretext that the persons concerned had shown insubordination and lack of discipline.

According to my information, these were veteran party workers and guerrilla fighters who had joined the call for democratic direction and a re-organisaton of our party.

On 13 September, last year, a large meeting of Namibians living at a farm owned by SWAPO near Lusaka, wrenched from the Executive the undertaking that a National Convention of the party was to be held by mid-December ...

(The final page of my copy of the letter has gone astray: I pleaded with the president to bring the parties together at an isolated place somewhere in Zambia to compel them to sort out the problems that were rending the party.)

I FINISHED the letter to Kaunda at three in the morning and decided to remain home that day so as not to be seen in Lusaka. At ten, though, I sneaked out through the backyard to find a phone booth from where I could call Simonda. He wasn't at his office. I never heard from him again.

In the afternoon Gottfried Nakaamboh, who had co-signed the letter, accompanied me to the house of Lily Monse, a minister of government. As chair of the UN regional conference in Mbabane, she had made a positive impression on me. Mrs Monse welcomed us with tea and cakes. After reading the letter at my request, she agreed that the matter deserved the President's interest, adding that even though he didn't like to be disturbed on Sundays, she would make an effort to get it to him.

On Monday morning President Kaunda was admitted to hospital for his annual check-up, only to be discharged on the Wednesday. On the Thursday evening two men in a white Mercedes approached our house with a letter handwritten by Mrs Monse. It stated that the President regretted that he could not attend to the matter before he had been discharged, but that I would soon receive an invitation for an audience with him. This never came.

MY MOTHER PAYS US A VISIT

The following Monday we received a telegram from my family in Rehoboth with the message that my mother wanted to visit us. She arrived on the Friday, two days before Keshii Pelao Nathanael of the SYL would return from Holland to defend his innocence and that of his comrades.

Thus it came about that around the lunch table on the Sunday, there were my mother, Edel, Soini, Keshii, Jimmy, Nakaamboh, Peter Nuunguluh, Paulus – a new acquaintance – and our two boys in addition to myself. Mother entertained us with anecdotes about the 'freedom movement' in Rehoboth and Windhoek, and about the hard times the Baster participants in the so-called Turnhalle Conference were given. Truckloads of demonstrators left Rehoboth for Windhoek singing SWAPO songs as they rolled down the Kaizerstrasse (after 1990, renamed Independence Avenue). She had us laughing with a story about my aunt Martha van Wyk, who had never before taken part in any political activity. Finding herself imprisoned along with youngsters who moaned about the turn of events, she sought to lift their spirits by calling out, 'Isn't it wonderful to be imprisoned for fighting for the freedom of your country?'

For a short while we could forget the bizarre situation we were in: at risk not from the police of a racist regime, but from our own 'brothers' wielding the forces of a foreign power as their weapons. (Word went round that 'the dissidents' were no longer to be addressed by the honorific of Comrade, but at most as brothers.)

On an impulse to find out how other people were looking at our situation, I left the lunch table to drive around to two or three addresses in town. One of those I found at home was Godfrey Gaoseb, a Namibian who had studied in Stockholm and with whom I had been on good terms. He had recently been appointed to a position at the United Nations Institute for Namibia (UNIN) where, as a member of SWANU, he became an impartial observer to the deteriorating situation in SWAPO. Godfrey now calmly informed me about the new strategy that the Nujoma loyalists had hatched in early April at the home of Hage Geingob, who headed the UNIN. The plan was to arrest Andreas Shipanga as the leader of a subversive group. Their problem was that the Zambians would want evidence against Shipanga that could be presented to the OAU's Liberation Committee. The conspirers' contact on the Zambian side was one Major Malupa, an officer in the Zambian Army who was in charge of the Liberation Centre. Peter Mueshihange had been sent to Angola to inform Sam Nujoma and to persuade him to return to Lusaka post haste, but had had no success. Nujoma remained in Luanda.

Godfrey's account squared with what Edel had been told by one of the girls: that Andreas had confronted Sean McBride with the complaint that the Namibia Institute's leadership was involved in a conspiracy against him.

Godfrey had also met a guerrilla from a SWAPO base named Oshatotwa, where the forces were said to be loyal to Nujoma. According to this man Richard Kapelwa, a Caprivian and Nanyemba's deputy, had visited the base and whipped up feelings against Shipanga. When he had done, many of the guerrillas were ready to do away with Shipanga. At the so-called Central Base, where the fighters had become mutinous against the leadership, measures had been taken to starve them – with the taunt that they were free to do whatever they wished to do: they could go home, or start a new party since SWAPO had no need of them. This had, however, led to complaints from the Zambians that the camp inmates were killing off their animals to feed themselves.

This news thoroughly depressed the group at 7 Saise Road; Jimmy

Ampala was especially worried about the situation of the women at Liberation Centre. I next drove Jimmy, Keshii and Paulus to the hideout in the countryside where they had an appointment with Sheeli Shangula and Martin Taneni – who had escaped to make known the situation of the group that had been arrested along with Andreas Shipanga. They wanted to call for an Habeas Corpus appeal to be submitted to the Zambian High Court. Taneni complained about chest pains, something none of us could do anything about.

For dinner that evening, we were again nine around the table, reviewing a situation that had become all but inspiring. Afterwards I drove Keshii and Paulus to the part of town where they lived, while Jimmy chose to sleep over at our place.

OTHER VISITORS

The next morning, during my absence in town, Keshii and Paulus returned to inform Jimmy that the Zambian Police were keeping an eye on their house and that it was therefore safe for him to sleep there as well. After having dropped him there I visited Esmé Shipanga, whom Edel and I had not seen for days. She had been to see both Aaron Milner, the Minister of Justice, and Rupiah Banda, the Foreign Minister, she told me. Milner had claimed that Andreas was neither arrested nor in detention, but that she had to see the Minister of Defence, Shinguli. The Minister made her wait for hours before calling her into his office, merely to inform her that he had given the order for her husband to be taken into 'protective custody'. He didn't want a replay of the Herbert Chitepo affair. Besides, he added, SWAPO's own leaders had requested it of them. He couldn't do anything further about the matter until Sam Nujoma arrived, something they had been waiting for in vain for some time. To us, Esmé revealed that she had considered writing an appeal to Sam Nujoma, but on reflection had given up the idea. She had lost all faith in Namibians, she said.

A little later, the Finnish diplomat Kari Karanko turned up, this time in company with a Finnish radio reporter by the name of Joini. Karanko informed us that the Foreign Minister, Rupiah Banda, had been fired earlier that day. This led to speculations about the real reasons for his dismissal. Karanko thought it had to do with Banda's close contact with a bank director who had been arrested. This brought out a revealing account of Karanko's own confrontation with Hidipo Hamutenya, whom he had warned that Nordic aid could dry up if it became known to what extent corruption had become rife in SWAPO. In response, Moses Garoeb had lodged a complaint with the

Zambians about Finnish interference in an internal SWAPO conflict. The Finnish Ambassador thereupon received a summons, not by the Department of Foreign Affairs, but by the Ministry of Defence. In retaliation, Kari again contacted Hidipo with the warning that SWAPO risked a complaint to the Zambian Ministry of Defence – about his leaders first impregnating young women before sending them to Finland.

Both Karanko and his companion expressed curiosity about where Shipanga stood in the power game that was clearly being played out in SWAPO. I aired my opinion that the case being made againt Shipanga as the leader of an internal opposition group was groundless.

Among the visitors that day were Jack Simons and his wife Ray Alexander. They told me that I could expect a job offer at the University of Zambia as an assistant teacher. A precarious situation had arisen there after two lecturers were fired at the behest of President Kenneth Kaunda. I would guide students on District Development, a theme Simons didn't think could involve much political risk. The next day Professor Brody, the Dean of the Faculty of Social Science, confirmed that they wanted me. Some days later I received a letter of appointment at the school. It required my signature of acceptance.

GRIM NEWS

In the meantime the conflict within SWAPO kept smouldering. Early in the week we found out that while we were all gathered at our house to celebrate my mother's presence on the Sunday after her arrival, the Zambian police had raided the house of Salatiel Ailonga and Anita when they were away on a long-postponed weekend's retreat. The police had searched for weapons and ammunition.

On a tour into town I ran into the Swedish diplomat Anders Bjuner. From him I now heard that Sam had arrived in Luanda some days earlier and that Peter Katjavivi was in Stockholm with Ben Amathila. Peter had decided to keep the situation 'under observation'. I let Bjuner know what I had been told about Shipanga's situation. He hadn't heard much since the arrests had taken place. Concerning the Zambians, Bjuner didn't think they had any strong opinions about SWAPO, though the president's adviser, Mark Shona, had reportedly said that the Namibian presence had become a burden Zambia dearly wanted to get rid of. Besides that, Anders thought Nujoma was not very close to Kaunda, especially when compared to Nkomo from Zimbabwe. The question remained, however: what kind of pressure was being put on Zambia from abroad?

Angola's position towards SWAPO was more ambiguous, he thought. As late as January, Neto's government hadn't taken a stand concerning SWAPO. Near the end of March and into the beginning of April, the consequences of this could be seen and felt. But now, Bjuner said, it seems that they had decided to give SWAPO their full support.

As to Sam Nujoma, he thought it a safe assumption that Andreas Shipanga had been hoping for a new leadership to emerge from within the military and that the problem regarding Sam Nujoma could be solved internally. How the developments of recent weeks had influenced the situation, he didn't have a clue.

The Swedes had decided not to make any changes in their programme of aid for SWAPO. To cut aid could be interpreted as support for a certain faction, while it would not affect SWAPO's leaders. They were in control of the money, Swedish taxpayers' money. Anders Bjuner criticised his Finnish colleague, who had confronted Moses Garoeb directly about where Andreas Shipanga was and why he couldn't be set free – as well as about internal corruption.

I asked what possibilities there might be for Andreas to obtain asylum abroad, Bjuner pointed out that the rules governing immigration into Sweden were very stringent and that it was also doubtful that Angola would be willing to have him.

Back at 7 Saise Road, Esmé arrived in company with Anne Marie, Andreas' niece who was living with them. For once Esmé showed optimism about her husband's prospects. Zambia's High Court was expected to deliver judgement that Friday about his application for Habeas Corpus – to have the Court determine the lawfulness of his detention. One of the judges had reportedly expressed his irritation at the military for not having learnt yet that no one could be deprived of his or her freedom before certain procedures had been observed. As the freedom of individuals was protected by the Constitution, he was looking forward to hearing what they had to say.

After Esmé's departure we drove to the Ailonga's home to update them. There we met a priestly couple who projected the very image of suffering Christendom. Anita in particular bemoaned the health of prisoners whom she knew to be suffering from asthma – a condition we learnt that afflicted a good number of people in Northern Namibia. From there we visited Fred Bridgeland, Reuters' representative, for what we could learn from as informed a source as any in Lusaka. Bridgeland's take on the conflict in SWAPO was simple: Sam Nujoma's position had been strengthened – what with the support he enjoyed from the Russians, the Cubans and the Nigerians.

Ironically, what this meant was quite clearly that the coup, staged with the aid of 'anti-communist' Kenneth Kaunda, had landed SWAPO firmly under the control of the Soviet Union. In addition, the operatives who had conceived the operation – Theo-Ben from the US, *et al* – were now, even more firmly than before, in Sam Nujoma's pocket.

A MIDNIGHT RAID

The Zambian police descended on us in the middle of the night, or to be precise, at ten to four on the morning of 12 May 1976. We woke to the sound of a large vehicle entering our yard followed by heavy footsteps approaching the house. Hammering on the door with his fist, a man called out, 'Police, police,' and, without being admitted, threw open the door and pushed me backwards into our bedroom.

Standing a head taller than me, he waved a badge that showed him to be from the Criminal Investigation Department (CID) and announced that he had come to ransack the house. He demanded to know if Ndeshimona Uyumba was in the house.

At that moment I was more concerned that the brutal entry would have shocked my mother and our two boys, who were sleeping in the adjacent room. Speaking with a low voice I asked the man to please leave us in peace as we were in Zambia by the terms of an agreement between the governments of Norway and Zambia, and that I couldn't allow him to do anything in our house without a court warrant.

This appeared to make an impression on the man, who now queried my knowledge about Zambia's laws. To this I merely responded that he had already broken the law by barging into our house and that he needed to produce a legal writ before he proceeded further.

To my surprise the bluff worked. Giving brisk orders to half a dozen of his men to take up positions around the house, he entered his vehicle and drove off. His parting words to me were that nobody was to leave the house before he had returned.

It was of course impossible to sleep after such a rude awakening, even though there was nothing to do other than to wait for government offices to open at eight. At seven an idea occurred to me and I asked Edel to let me have our copy of the contract with NORAD. With the paper in hand I walked towards our neighbour's fence.

Three or four men who had been standing watch at the back of the house immediately left their posts and approached me. The only one in uniform aimed a Lee Enfield rifle at my legs. Two slightly-built men had running shoes on; anyone trying to make a break from the house wouldn't have gotten far. That night, however, we had no guests other than my mother.

'What will happen if I were to crawl through here to speak to the neighbour?' I asked the man with the gun. 'I don't know', he replied, leaving me to imagine swinging a stiff knee walking for the rest of my life.

At this I lifted the paper and read in as loud a voice as I could command from the text of NORAD's contract with Zambia:

'In the event of the detention or arrest of a person [supplied] by the Government of Norway to the Government of Zambia, in terms of the agreement between the Government of Norway and the Government of Zambia the Norwegian authorities are to be informed immediately.'

Still clad in his pyjamas our neighbour stormed out of his house to ask what it was all about. Giving him the number I requested him to kindly call the Norwegian representative, which he promptly did.

A little after eight the CID man, accompanied by a further two types in civilian dress, returned with a warrant for my arrest and an order to ransack our house. Without further ado the two men made their way into our bedroom where Edel was still in bed, and began to examine our papers and books.

It was a scene that was familiar to me, from the day, seventeen years earlier, when three South African security policemen went through my reading material in Port Elizabeth in search of 'subversive literature.'

While the South Africans had spent their time looking for interesting material, the Zambians confiscated practically everything they laid hands on. They even took our correspondence with our bank and with other official bodies in both Norway and Zambia.

It gave me some satisfaction to see with what interest they perused a copy of the letter I had addressed to their president and one to Tanzania's ambassador in Stockholm for whom I had done a service in Oslo.

They also became interested in a placard put up on the inside door of the toilet. Portraying a social pyramid, it depicted the decadence of the moneyed classes. Did it reflect the situation in Zambia? one of them wanted to know. With the patience of a school teacher, Edel explained that the placard was printed in Chicago, probably in the 1930's.

It next amused her to observe the speed with which one of the snoopers closed a cardboard box in which she kept plastic models of the human reproductive organs for use in her Biology classes. Nothing is as fascinating as the prudery of people who have no compunction about invading the privacy, violating the rights and mutilating the bodies of their victims.

Shortly after eight Agnete Eriksen, responding to our neighbour's call, approached the house in her car. This caused the CID man to break out in a fit of rage at the guards who had not done their work properly. He blocked Agnete's approach.

A little before eleven another policeman drove into the yard with his car. Dressed in an officer's uniform he gave orders, whereupon the two ransackers collected their booty and all of them left. The warrant for my arrest appeared to have been forgotten about. It didn't take long though, for the mystery to be cleared up: as if personifying a deus ex machina, the Norwegian diplomat, Arne Arnesen, had landed in Lusaka that morning. As head of NORAD he led a delegation that was to negotiate a new aid agreement with Zambia. Edel and I assumed that confining me to prison without good reason, while expecting a Norwegian official to hand over new sums of money, would have caused if nothing else a media storm in Oslo. Later that afternoon Arnesen arrived at our house in company with Agnete Eriksen. As Edel was formally in his employ, it was a visit that lifted our spirits.

The reaction of our two boys to the events of the morning was moving. Both had noticed the policemen helping themselves without permission to the fruits of the avocado tree in our yard. Sven Tanab showed us a message he had written to the police. Even though the words were written phonetically and some letters were backwards, the meaning was not difficult to divine. The four year old had pleaded with the policemen not to take his father away.

What grieved me was the insult of the treatment to which my family and I had been subjected.

The next day the need for supplies compelled Edel and me to undertake a trip into town, a place where a sense of insecurity had become impossible to shake off. At the NORAD office, where we dropped by for mail, we ran into two representatives of the Lutheran World Federation, a German by the name of Gussing and a Norwegian, Gunnar Rygh. They led the Federation's emergency operations. Since the LWF provided aid to SWAPO's refugee camps, I thought it proper to brief them about the situation that had arisen and about my observations at the SWAPO refugee camp. They listened without making any comment.

Outside the office block we met Esmé Shipanga. From her we learned that Keshii had also been picked up. That was the last for a long time that we would hear anything about a young man for whom we had developed a certain regard.

On Friday, Edel, my mother and I joined the Ailongas to attend the hearing at the High Court of Andreas' Habeas Corpus appeal. In disregard of the spirit of the institution that requires the release 'forthwith' of individuals who had been arbitrarily arrested and detained, Zambia's High Court again postponed a decision so as to give the prosecution further time to present evidence of wrongdoing by Shipanga.

Following advice from the NORAD office, Edel proceeded to the 119 Central Police Station, to get our papers back. There she was stonewalled and had to withdraw – for the time being. Back home she gave vent to her anger, which made my mother look at her with concern. I remembered the efforts on behalf of the Crisis Fund for Southern Africa that Edel had gladly made, on short notice, one day in May 1964 – to provide Kenneth Kaunda with an audience to address while on a visit to Oslo. The Norwegian Nobel Committee had put its conference room at her disposal. I could very well understand the sense of betrayal she now felt.

ADVISED TO LEAVE ZAMBIA

On Monday, 17 May, I dropped by the office of two acquaintances at the Kenyan embassy. I wanted to hear what they knew about the drama that seemed to involve not only SWAPO, but the host country and certain foreign powers as well. They professed to be as much in the dark as I was. Both advised me to leave the country until the dust had settled. One of them, Kinuti, with whose family Edel and I had begun to exchange friendly visits, offered me the use of his house in Nairobi, promising to keep an eye on my family – even though he assumed that the Zambians would see to it that no harm befell them. I thanked them for their concern, but pointed out that if I was to abscond, it would be said that I had fled from the consequences of my wrongdoing.

Later the same day, Edel and I ran into a man who knew the names of Namibians who had been in Zambian prisons for the third year running. He was keen for us to know who they were: Tobias Job, Willipat Katangolo, Nduna Philip Haita, Andreas Shimvafeni, George Bootseng, Christopher Ipito, and Kanfilipo Napelilo. He didn't know the reasons for their incarceration; neither did we get a chance to inquire about their fate.

The next day, another young Namibian dropped by our house wanting to speak to me. In my absence he told Edel that there had been plans to kill Peter Nunguuluh and Gottlieb Nakaamboh the night when they fled to our house. Their would-be assassins had been three guerrillas who had come to town to eliminate 'Shipanga supporters' whom they believed were working for the South Africans. 'The clique' had said that I was the only one with brains still left to roam free. The message the visitor wanted to impart, was that I 'hold back a little'.

When I returned home, my mother, who had listened to the conversation, pleaded with me to leave the country forthwith. I tried to reassure her with the same arguments that I had used with the Kenyans.

The next day, Wednesday 19 May, Peter Nuunguluh appeared and stayed for lunch. He mentioned a diary he kept, written in a language he claimed that none at the SWAPO office could read. I encouraged him to keep writing, and then asked what was being said about me. Peter's response was to confirm the message Edel was given the day before. He had been a passenger into town aboard a vehicle driven that morning by Maxwell, SWAPO's transport chief. Maxwell had dropped a comment that I was the sole 'big fish' still left swimming freely.

On hearing this I immediately excused myself from the lunch table, telling Peter I had forgotten an errand that Edel and I had to run before the NORAD office closed for the day. At the office I requested Øyvind Lyng, the representative, to find out from the Zambians what they had against me. Lyng responded that he too would have liked to know the causes of the uproar in SWAPO, but that he would strongly urge me to leave Lusaka for a while – until things got back to normal. I reminded Lyng that I had nearly exhausted my resources on my recent trip to Mbabane and that I would face ruin if I were to flee. To this he coolly replied, 'Would you be less ruined if you were thrown into jail?'

That did it for me: in the preceding thirty-six hours I had been advised by four adults, including my mother, to leave the country. If I chose to ignore them all, I reasoned, I might risk having to regret it at leisure. When even Edel concurred with Lyng's argument, I agreed that the office messenger could be sent to purchase me a ticket for the same evening's flight to London. The unstated assumption was that the Zambians would have an interest in seeing to it that nothing befell my family.

While waiting for the messenger to return with the ticket, Lyng entertained us with an anecdote from his own experiences during the occupation of Norway by Germany (1940-45). He had run errands for the resistance movement in his hometown of Trondheim until he was tipped off that the Gestapo was on his trail and that he had to escape to Sweden. Together with a friend he made his way to the railway station where a train with German troops aboard was about to depart. There they sought out the carriage where the commanding officer had his coupé, entered it and requested permission to join him. The officer warmly welcomed the company of two personable young men – who spoke German to boot! He offered them schnapps and threw out the inspector who came around to check their tickets.

At the airport that evening I ran into an old acquaintance, Robert Resha of the ANC. Robert was waiting for a flight to Angola. He also expressed his surprise at the developments in SWAPO, but thought that it had to do with the well-known rivalry between Nujoma and Shipanga.

CHAPTER ELEVEN

The name of the game is play safe

SWAPO'S LONDON OFFICE

Humiliation engulfed me as I boarded the plane for London that evening: humiliation at having to flee from Africa for a second time – this time not from the apartheid regime, but from a 'liberation movement' that had become a threat to the very life and liberty of its members. I also felt humiliation at the realisation that I could not say this as loudly as I did when I arrived in London and Oslo the first time – to testify against the apartheid regime. I reasoned that to do so would do damage to that first cause, to my family and to myself and thus to any sympathetic hearing for the release of my imprisoned countrymen.

In good time I would have most of those fears confirmed, but I have often wondered if things would have turned out for the better if I had disregarded my fears. With hindsight, I think I grew demoralised by embarrassment.

Of more immediate concern, since I intended to avail myself of the facilities of the SWAPO office in London, was to what extent Peter Katjavivi, one of Sam Nujoma's most trusted men, had been involved in the coup that his colleagues had staged in Lusaka. On his way back to Lusaka from Holland, Keeshi had stopped by the SWAPO office in London. On his departure Peter had asked him to take along a large sum of money for the Lusaka office. Suspecting it to be a trap, Keeshi had refused the request and taken an earlier plane than the one he had been booked on. Some hours after landing in Lusaka the Zambian police informed him that SWAPO operatives, evidently expecting him to be aboard the later plane, had arrived at the airport after his arrival.

Peter welcomed me with a nervous little smile and a stunning story. At the office they – himself and his secretary Jane XXX, a South African woman – had been worried about me and tried to get in touch with me in Mbabane. They wanted to warn me about what was happening in Lusaka, he explained. He did not say, however, what he would have advised, or expected me to do. Since he evidently knew that I would be arrested along with Shipanga and the others, I didn't ask. Evidently he had been either a willing party to the coup, or been given an ultimatum to support it or get lost.

During my time in London, on and off through the latter part of 1976, Peter would maintain a formal distance that left me in the dark as to where he stood. Until I received a telegram from Lusaka later that year, an unexpected courtesy signed by Moses Garoeb, to say that my membership of SWAPO was terminated, Peter would provide financial support towards my accommodation in London. And he didn't object to my using the office facilities either. All of this spoke well of him, I thought, as it obviated confrontation.

In 1959, after my first escape from southern Africa, I had met my countryman Jariretundu Kozonguizi on arrival in London. We could laugh about the almost preposterous goal we had set ourselves: to protest the excesses of colonialism in the citadels of colonialism. I had next met Joshua Nkomo, on the war path for the independence of his country as Zimbabwe.

At this time I met with a Zimbabwean aged somewhere in the mid-twenties. He had as fine a physique as I had seen on anyone, but his bearing could not have been more expressive of the dejection that he felt. In a toneless voice he responded to my queries as to why he was in London. He spoke of the mass slaughter of his comrades that he had miraculously survived. It had taken place in a camp not far from Lusaka – with his own countrymen as the perpetrators. Evidently it was the massacre that I had heard about in Lusaka. The fugitives Sheeli Shangula and Martin Taneni had spoken of having seen dried blood and bits of flesh on the walls of the huts to which they had been confined. Still, I was not ready to believe that Namibians were capable of such excesses and persuaded myself that the prisoners weren't in that sort of danger.

Although London was populated with political activists from southern Africa, many of whom I had become acquainted with through the years, I did not expect any of them to want to become involved in a conflict among Namibians in Zambia. Interfering in the affairs of a co-liberation movement was not practised. One of those who did express an interest in seeing me was Randolph Vigne, a former leader of the South African Liberal Party, who also had to flee South Africa. A Norwegian diplomat had secured him passage aboard a Norwegian ore-carrier bound for a Canadian harbour. In London he headed a support group for SWAPO. At a lunch-hour meeting I told him all I knew about what transpired in Zambia. However, the feeling I had when we parted was one I would come to experience often. It was of having handed representatives of 'the solidarity movement' something more than they could handle.

Exceptionally, a young journalist, Roger Murray, who wrote about Namibian affairs and was often at the SWAPO office, appeared to have felt challenged by something I had said about 'solidarity movements'.

'You must not think we are not concerned,' he told me once, without elaborating.

Even Jane, Peter Katjavivi's closest collaborator, appeared to be confounded by the unfolding events. Her uncertainty about where I fitted, if indeed, in the gallery of rogues that had been unmasked and incarcerated in Lusaka, came to the fore on receiving a call from the British Students Association. They wanted the office to send somebody to speak on behalf of SWAPO at their annual meeting. It was the sort of opportunity that they didn't want to miss, as it was a great way to gather support for the 'liberation struggle'. In Peter's absence from town, she was in a bind.

I noticed Jane's uncertainty when she asked me if I could oblige, with the unstated request that I would stick to the script. As I was still entertaining the hope that the prisoners would be released in due course, I decided to present the events in Zambia as an unavoidable consequence of a long exile.

Arriving at the venue I discovered that SWAPO's internal problems had barely been noticed and that the agenda was full of national issues. Padding my talk with the obligatory references to the apartheid regime's record, I blandly stated that the movement still deserved the British students' consideration. It surprised me, and I am sure it pleased Jane, to find my appeal mentioned in the conference report.

Somebody who would make me feel unreservedly welcome on arrival in London was Margaret Valentin. Having recently passed by our place in Lusaka – after a fruitless attempt to meet up with her husband in Angola – she was now employed as a secretary by Colin Winter, the exiled Anglican Bishop of Damaraland. On Margaret's advice I approached the offices of Amnesty International, the organisation co-founded by Sean McBride. There I submitted a briefing about the events that I had observed in Zambia, with the plea that they do what they could to secure the release of the prisoners. What Amnesty had done to pursue the matter I have not been able to determine.

SITUATION IN LUSAKA

Access to the SWAPO office enabled me to phone Edel who continued to sound optimistic. It had been of help that my mother had stayed on for a week after my departure; our friends constantly dropped by to offer their assistance; the University of Zambia had approached her with the request to present a course in her field of interest, Ecology and Resource use; and she had even begun to take driving lessons.

However, in letters, she expressed anxiety about the unresolved situation. The boys understood a great deal, she wrote. 'What is wrong with Zambia?' the eight year old Jon Are had asked.

Edel could also inform me that Andreas Nuukwao and Ndeshimona Uyumba had been arrested on their return from Amsterdam. Before joining the youths' exodus from their homes from 1973 onwards, Andreas Nuukwao had been attached to the administration of the Lutheran Church in Ovamboland. In Lusaka he had acted as Nujoma's paymaster. An article I had written for the Oslo magazine *Billedbladet NÅ* in 1974 carried an illustration of a Black man's buttocks. Two broad white stripes showed where the skin had been ripped off by the whips with which the police had flogged the man. In Lusaka I learned that the owner of the maltreated body part was Andreas Nuukwao. Now, with Ndeshimona as the only female, he was imprisoned at the camp where Shipanga and the others were held.

THE 'YA-OTTO COMMISSION'

In her letter, Edel further informed me about a visit by a delegation of SWAPO officials. The delegation comprised Libertine Appolus, Peter Shehama, Nahas Angula and Johnny Ya Otto, a recently arrived ex-Robben Island prisoner. They had handed her a letter that identified themselves as members of a commission of inquiry, the Ya Otto Commission. And they solemnly declared that their task was to collect evidence from witnesses about the recent conflicts within the party. Such evidence would be submitted in a report with a view to correcting mistakes that had been made.

After they had left the house, my mother, who had observed the mendacious charade in silence, expressed her relief at my being in a safe place.

When the 'Ya-Otto Commission's' report arrived in London, Peter Katjavivi obligingly let me have a copy. One of its conclusions was a quite astounding admission, but only by implication, of guilt: the movement '*had lost its goal orientation*'. As this had been precisely the complaint of the party members whom they themselves had imprisoned, I looked for an indication of what they would recommend to set matters right, and found none.

ON THE HORNS OF A DILEMMA

At night, Mother heard sounds that she believed came from guards that were assigned to keep an eye on the house. From the Kenyan diplomat Kinuti, who in my absence had stepped in to give Jon Are a lift to his school, Edel heard that he had also observed a guard stationed in the street outside the house.

Although this was reassuring, it also gave rise to some concern: we could not expect it to last.

Our situation looked grim no matter how I looked at it. Moving on to Namibia was out of the question; the thought of returning to the hostile labour market of Norway held no appeal for me; migration elsewhere was not something Edel and I had ever considered. Moreover, on a short visit to Oslo, to reassure my parents-in-law that there was no need for concern, I would find they weren't at all reassured. Even though they didn't say it, it was clear that they expected their daughter's contract with NORAD to be terminated, and that she would then return home.

Back in London I began to look for paid employment. This time Peter Katjavivi graciously obliged by putting me in contact with a South African couple who ran a school and needed a teacher. However, before I could follow up on their invitation, Edel, Anita and Salatiel Ailonga were served expulsion orders from Zambia. With no arrangements in place to receive or to sustain my family in London, to postpone a return to Ski, where Edel could claim back her job, was impossible. In the months that followed, I returned to London several times in efforts to keep abreast of developments.

THE SHIPANGA GROUP

When the Zambian High Court finally came to a decision on Shipanga's Habeas Corpus appeal, it was to find that there was no evidence to justify his incarceration. It ordered that Shipanga and his eight companions be set free. Tanzania's Julius Neyerere now came to the SWAPO junta's aid. He sent a military transport aircraft to fly the group to Tanzania, where they were imprisoned like common criminals in conditions that made their survival a matter of chance.[37] A letter from Solomon Mifima, a copy of which I received from Salatiel Ailonga read:

'29.8. I am certain that you will be surprised about not having heard anything from us. The situation in which we live has become unbearable. Even though it is forbidden for us to write letters to the outside world, we used to receive some from family and friends. Now the authorities have put a full stop to that. All letters to us are sent to the prison authorities' headquarters in Dar-es-Salaam. Comrade Shipanga was sent a registered item that we thought was from his family, together with books, but everything was sent off to Dar. The situation is really bad. We are finding ourselves in a complete blackout, no information, nothing.

---

[37] See Keshii Pelao Nathanael's *A Journey to Exile*.

'One of the things that is rather disturbing, is the clothes that we have been sent. The government refused to pay the customs duty, whereupon the clothes were sent back. Now you can imagine the rags we go in. We have nothing at all to change into. We feel that this is too much. Even prisoners of war have the right to receive presents and post from family and friends.

'Food and medical care is very poor. We are being treated by other prisoners. I am suffering from PB and my comrade has a skin condition, but we get no treatment. At the least my comrade's case ought to have been attended to, he is in need of a specialist. But all the time we are told that no doctors are available. This is something that we regard as a deliberate decision, to let him suffer. Concerning this matter, we desire that you inform The International Red Cross, with a request that they intervene on our behalf. There are many prisoners who on account of this sort of treatment – bad food, etc. – suffer nervous breakdowns.

'Dear brother. Our immediate need is for money – to be able to buy some soap and a few other things such as tea and sugar. When one has access to money, one can always buy something for oneself. Inform comrade Beukes and all others that you know.'

From Andreas Nuukwao came the brief note:

'We ask that you try to make this known to an international public through different news media. Some, or rather international organisations, namely Amnesty International and Church Organisations, such as the LWF or the WCC, that could put pressure on these governments (Zambia and Tanzania). Inform people at home together with Hans Beukes. We really don't know why these governments expose us to these injustices. With all our best wishes. Yours in the struggle. Andreas T. Nuukwao (on behalf of the group).'

In Dar es Salaam's prison for women, the slightly built Ndeshimona Uyumba was traumatised. Bishop Colin Winter, the Anglican Bishop of Damaraland, told me about a visit he had paid her during a church conference held in the city. Asked what she wanted him to say to President Nyerere, Ndeshi answered, 'I have nothing to ask of that man. I didn't leave Namibia to land in his prison.'

Esmé Shipanga moved to London to be near her son from her first marriage, John Matshikisa, who was studying drama. Acquaintances of hers, a couple whom I only remember as Hussain and Daphne, put at my disposal a flat that I could use while in London. We often met in cafés in town to keep each other updated about our efforts to gain support for the release from imprisonment of her husband and our friends. Esmé was dejected; she felt herself caught in a Namibian web of intrigue that as a South African she was unable to fathom. Testimony to the trust in me that my Ovambo countrymen had expressed, in contrast, inspired me to approach all institutions that could conceivably put pressure on SWAPO: church officials, the Red Cross, the Lutheran World Federation, the Foreign Offices of Norway and Sweden.

As to the 'solidarity movements', my experience with their representatives soon made me lose faith in them while recourse to the media, I feared, would do more damage than good, and therefore I long resisted that possibility.

At the SWAPO office in London I came across an appeal that Kenneth Kaunda had submitted to the colonial court in Northern Rhodesia. In it, he complained of having been arbitrarily deprived of his freedom and sent to a concentration camp in Kabompo:

'Since my arrival here I have suffered terribly. During the first week I was attacked by dysentery. After a couple of weeks I was attacked by malaria fever. This was followed by a bad cold and cough from which I am just recovering.'

The complaint was signed K.D. Kaunda, 25/4/59.[38]

LORDS TEMPORAL AND SPIRITUAL

Colin Winter, the Anglican Bishop of Damaraland, had been expelled from South West Africa on account of his outspoken opposition to apartheid. On his return to England, a noble family offered him the use of an abandoned monastery near Oxford. There he established the Namibian International Peace Centre, turning the place into both a temporary home for his family and an oasis for youth from Namibia and elsewhere who needed accommodation and support. Among the youths occasionally staying there was a son of the Pastor Siegfried Groth, a similarly engaged German priest, who bravely challenged the SWAPO junta to release the prisoners – *and was ostracised for his pains by his fellow Christians in Germany.*[39] Margaret Valentin proved to be the Bishop's indispensable help.

On a couple of occasions I availed myself of an invitation to spend a weekend at The Monastery. One Sunday I accompanied Bishop Winter to a village named Whitchurch where he had been invited to deliver a sermon. It happened to be the country seat of Lord Denning, known as Master of the Rolls and the Lord Chief Justice of England's Court of Appeal for civil cases. In keeping with his stature, the Bishop was invited for breakfast at the Dennings', prepared and served by Lady Denning.

I cannot recall ever sitting in at a breakfast table with as fascinating a

---

[38]   African Archives File2/Document 22, Published by Oxford University Press and Neczam.
[39]   See Siegfried Groth: *Namibia: The Wall of Silence.*

discourse as took place between representatives of the realms Spiritual and Temporal that day. Lord and Lady Denning had recently returned from a visit to South Africa – from where the Bishop had been expelled. In consequence, a good part of the conversation related to the future of the apartheid state.

Lord Denning was known to be loved and feared in equal measure for his uncompromising stance against injustice. At the time, support for a boycott was the only way in which the world could put pressure on the apartheid state to change its policies. For this reason, I kept my ears open for any reference the judge might make to obligations if any in that regard, resting on Great Britain – given its historical responsibility for the creation of the apartheid system. It didn't come and therefore clouded somewhat for me the thrill of having been a guest at the great house.

On the way back to The Monastery I asked the Bishop about his bidding the worshippers clap their hands at the service that morning. I had been sitting in a front pew when he made his entry from the sacristy, resplendent in bishopric attire – to arrest mid-verse the singing of the first hymn.

'Didn't you notice their resistance to me?' he asked.

As bishops of the Church in foreign lands had no status at home, they were dependent on parish priests, as he had been that day, for invitations to lead Sunday services. I assumed that he was referring to his reputation, as an engaged cleric – almost a latterday John Wesley – having preceded him to the genteel village parish. I had noticed no tension waiting for the service to begin. But stealing a glance at the worshippers in the pews behind me, I had seen smiles breaking out on staid faces when he told them that in Africa, his parishioners used to clap their hands for sheer joy to be worshipping the Lord.

At The Monastery later that day I overheard the Bishop and a colleague discussing the suitability for the priesthood of a candidate. When reference was made to the applicant's spirituality, I thought I knew what was meant.

My next encounter at The Monastery was with Leonard Nangoloh Auala, the Lutheran Bishop of Ovamboland, who was on a visit to Bishop Winter while on a European tour. Winter had drafted a famous letter that had been sent over Auala's signature to the South African Prime Minister, John Vorster. In Lusaka, my mother had asked Peter Nuunguluh what he thought of requesting Bishop Auala to arbitrate between the factions in SWAPO. Peter enthusiastically endorsed the idea and expressed his desire that the Bishop be called to Lusaka.

Winter arranged for Auala to meet with me in private. During a quiet walk in the verdant English countryside I conveyed Peter Nuunguluh's prayer to the Lutheran bishop and briefed him about my own observations. He thanked me but didn't indicate what course he would follow.

A DESPERATE CRY FOR HELP

In London the next day I called Fred Bridgeland for a chat. Since our last meeting in town he had parted ways with Reuters and moved to Edinburgh with his family. Fred invited me come up and visit him, whereupon I boarded a night train to Edinburgh, where he met me at the station. After breakfast served by his wife Sally, he sprang a surprise on me. He showed me a letter that had been posted several weeks before to his address in Lusaka. There it had awaited his successor's arrival before it got sent on to him. He had received it only a couple of days earlier.

The letter was written on behalf of 'over one thousand' guerrillas interned near the town of Kabwe some one hundred kilometres north of Lusaka. Three of the camp's inmates had been killed and thirteen wounded during an assault by the Zambian soldiers guarding the camp. The prisoners had been starved in an effort to have them drop their demands against the SWAPO junta.

It would take a long time before I would hear the full story about a letter that couldn't have had a more poignant origin. Among those interned at the concentration camp in Mboroma were two women, Julia and Sally, who eventually were granted asylum in Norway. Sally was among those wounded; she had a long scar on her arm to prove it. Julia was not hurt that day, but her baby had died of undernourishment. Ironically, the Zambians were sticklers for proper procedure when deaths occurred. The little corpse had to be transported to the mortuary in Kabwe for a post mortem. As the locals wouldn't handle the Namibian dead, Julia and her friend Sally had to be accompanied by one of the Namibian men. Hidden in the cloth, in which the small body was swathed, they took with them three copies of the letter.

After delivering their precious burden to the mortuary, the Namibian invited the two Zambian guards for a beer at a bar, and then stole away to drop the letters into a nearby post-box. One copy went to South Africa, and was broadcast on radio; the other went to the US and was never heard of again; the third was addressed to Fred, Reuters' correspondent in Lusaka.

My first thought after reading the letter was to alert Bishop Auala about its contents. During our talk, the Bishop had informed me that he would soon be meeting SWAPO representatives Katjavivi, Amathila and Muyongo at the Lutheran World Federation's headquarters in Geneva. The meeting was hosted by the Namibian pastor, Albertus Maasdorp. At the SWAPO office the day before, I had asked Peter Katjavivi what they would be discussing. His answer was that the question of a government-in-exile would come up, together with relations with the churches.

'He [Peter Katjavivi] already fancies moving to more secure offices, preferably in London's diplomatic quarters,' I had written to Edel. 'The way I understand it Lars Gunnar Eriksen's IUEF (i.e. Norway and Sweden) would be doing the financing. Just think of it!'

In Edinburgh, with the guerrillas' letter in hand, the full force of what Peter had said struck me. The church would be invited to give its blessing to the status the SWAPO junta enjoyed at the UN as 'the sole and authentic representative of the Namibian people.' This would seal the fate of the Namibians in the camps. With Fred's permission, I immediately called Maasdorp's office at the LWF.

A couple of weeks earlier in Oslo I had heard that Maasdorp, a pastor from my hometown Rehoboth, would be attending a church conference in the Swedish city of Uppsala. I reasoned that with a Namibian at the Lutherans' headquarters, what moral authority they commanded could be brought to bear on the SWAPO junta to bring about reconciliation with the people that they had wronged. I had to call several times, leaving messages for Maasdorp without getting a response – until late one evening I was finally put through to him. 'Listen here', Maasdorp interrupted me when he heard what I wanted to talk to him about, 'A new constellation has come into power in SWAPO, and the best we can do is to come to terms with it.' With that, and mentioning the late hour and the fact that he had to get up early the next morning, the Lutheran pastor terminated the call.

When I now got through to Maasdorp in Geneva, he pretended not to know who I was and refused to let me speak to the Bishop. As a last resort, I left with him Bridgeland's phone number with the request that he ask the Bishop to call me. I waited the whole day for a call that never came.

Having had his doubts about the authenticity of the letter dispelled, Fred Bridgeland published the story about the massacre at Mboroma in *The Scotsman*. On my return to London I called Tony Hodges, a journalist who wrote for the *New Statesman*, and went to see him at his home. After I showed him the letter, Hodges also wrote about Mboroma.

The day after his article appeared, I dropped by the SWAPO office. There I found only Jane, visibly upset. Producing the *New Statesman* for me to see Hodges' article, she informed me that it was based on three months-old information that the *Sunday Times* had refused to print after another journalist, unlike Hodges, had called Peter Katjavivi to check the facts. Tony Hodges was a no-good journalist, she stated vehemently.

Without realising it, the lovable Jane had thus informed me that Peter Katjavivi had done his best to prevent the desperate cries for help of his countrymen from being heard. I sat down to re-read the article before handing it back to Jane, wordlessly shaking my head.

A third journalist of my acquaintance happened by the office. The last time I had seen Anders Johansson of *Dagens Nyheter*, the Stockholm daily, we were aboard the same train in Zambia, returning to Lusaka from Livingstone where Kenneth Kaunda and John Vorster had cut a deal that left SWAPO guerrillas in Zambia disarmed. From Zambia, Anders had next gone to Angola. He now informed me that he knew Andreas Shipanga from as far back as 1967, when his paper had sent him to Cairo to cover the war between Egypt and Israel. Andreas had provided him with contacts in the Egyptian capital.

Anders was concerned about the fate of his old friend, but mentioned that Katjavivi had assured him several times that the 'rebels who had played into the enemy's hands', would not come to any harm. This made me realise that Peter could not have known he was speaking to a newshound with intimate insight into the circumstances that had unleashed the crisis in SWAPO.

Asked whether he would consider writing a piece about Mboroma for his paper, Anders suggested that I do it, promising to translate it. The result of this collaboration appeared as a full page story in *Dagens Nyheter*, under the name of *Pekka Ovambo* – a Finnish Ovambo.

APPEAL TO NORWEGIAN GOVERNMENT

Back in London from Edinburgh, I stopped by the Norwegian Embassy, where I expected to find an old acquaintance from whom I had bought a ciné camera before our departure for Zambia. The first person I met as I entered the building happened to be the Embassy's second in command, an acquaintance from my student days. On hearing what I had to tell, he immediately suggested that I take the story to the Norwegian Foreign Minister, who would play host to his Zambian counterpart the following week.

This totally unexpected prospect changed my day. The thought of putting the matter of the imprisoned Namibian youth into the hands of the Norwegian Foreign Minister was more than I had even thought of. When, at his suggestion, I called him the next morning, the diplomat informed me that the Foreign Minister, Knut Frydenlund, would be ready to meet with me two days later.

That same evening I boarded a plane to Oslo, with my mind preoccupied with what I ought to say at the Foreign Office. Reasoning that my imprisoned countrymen had no other spokesperson than me at that moment, I decided to use the same straightforward language that I had adopted in my letter to President Kenneth Kaunda.

As I was shown into his office, Foreign Minister Frydenlund rose from behind his desk to offer me a chair at a tea table where he joined me. With his personal secretary Leonard Larsen – together with whom I had attended a course at university – as well as another person in attendance, the gravity of the occasion bore down on me. Instead of speaking, I handed the Minister the note I had prepared.

Frydenlund read the paper in silence and then looked up to ask what I wanted him to do. I replied that the imprisonment and ill-treatment of so-called dissidents cast a long shadow over Namibia's future, and that because of all the support that the 'liberation movement' had received from Oslo, Norway was well placed to exert friendly pressure that could not be ignored – to help bring about the release of the imprisoned Namibians in Zambia and Tanzania.

The Foreign Minister made no reply, but came with an unexpected query. He wanted to know what I could tell him about the new Zambian Foreign Minister. I had forgotten that Kaunda had fired Rupiah Banda from the post and had paid no notice to the man who replaced him. I could therefore not think of anything to say, though I ventured that the new minister was a member of the Zambian elite. I was glad that Frydenlund didn't pursue the matter.

A few days later, the Norwegian media carried a denial by the Zambian politician of the charge that any Namibians were held prisoner in his country. Some journalists pointed out that this contradicted an admission of the facts by Ben Amathila shortly before. According to Ben only two hundred persons were held in prison and would be there only while investigations were underway. SWAPO was trying to find out whether any one of them could be held accountable for a South African attack against a SWAPO guerrilla base in Zambia. (The attack referred to happened a fortnight after the guerrillas had been imprisoned.)

OBSERVATION POST LONDON

A week or two later I looked up Emil Appolus, who was residing in London at the time. That day he was with Kozonguizi and Charles Kauraisa. The conversation with them proved as interesting as that with Jane XXX – for the information they unwittingly imparted. That evening I wrote a letter to Edel:

'They would seem to be embittered about Sam Nujoma, and it seems they are not satisfied with me and with Martha [Ford, my sister] either. I learnt that Martha is responsible for the support SWAPO enjoys amongst the Rehoboth Volksparty as well as among the Nama groups in the South. When I heard that, I decided to defend my membership in the party – with the arguments you know well. They laughed at me for having been expelled. Charles tried to dismiss my arguments by saying that he had heard them before – presumably from Swedes – and that they were not original. To this I answered that good arguments need not be original at all. He blamed me for not launching a public attack against the SWAPO folks to try to free the prisoners. I dismissed such a procedure, saying that I didn't know who our enemies were besides the Zambians and the Tanzanians. It seemed to me that they would be glad for anything that could weaken SWAPO. To them, SWAPO equaled Sam.

'Something that pleased me: Charles complained that they didn't know details about the arrests, etc. I said, 'But I have heard about an article that had appeared in *Dagens Nyheter*?' 'Oh yes', he said, 'it had been very well written and had put Ben Amathila in a squeeze'. Ben had sent a response and complained that DN [*Dagens Nyheter*] refused to print it. From a journalist he had, however, heard that Ben didn't have anything new to say, all he wanted was to know who the writer was so as to be able to attack the person. This was something the paper could not go along with. But, he said, the article had provided an opening, while I was in possession of the facts. He didn't seem to have the faintest suspicion that I had been responsible for the article.

But it was nice to know that it had done some good. The DN editor's response to Ben might be one of the things that warn Peter and Co about the direction the wind is blowing.'

Around that time I also had a meeting with Bishop Richard Wood, Colin Winter's successor as Bishop of Damaraland. We had become acquainted when I arrived in Lusaka the year before. Again I cite from a letter I sent Edel:

'To him I said it would be better for the Church (this time the Anglican) to speak out in a manner that could hurt the party, rather than sitting quietly while time flies and innocent people remain interned and exposed to whatever. It would strengthen the Church's moral standing among ordinary people. If the Church was unwilling to go that far, it ought at least to tell SWAPO that the Church would definitely be willing to go public – unless the SWAPO leadership did the right thing. I added that to keep people barred in until their will is broken is, if possible, even worse than merely keeping them imprisoned. In response to my arguments, Bishop Wood agreed that an eventual letter would have to be written by Winter and that he (Bishop Wood) would take it up with him.'

Relations between Peter and me were not as strained as to bar occasional conversations. In the letter to Edel that I quote above, I further wrote:

'My meeting with him [Peter] hadn't been very fruitful. He kept going on about the UN until I asked him: What about our people in Zambia? "Yes", he said, "I see references" – with a meaningful look at me – "about more than a thousand people. But I believe that is wrong. Haven't most of them been sent to Angola? I haven't heard anything for a while" he added.

'I said that as far as I knew there were a thousand people, and that the situation became worse the longer they sat there. He then asked what could be done – possibly thinking that I didn't have any proposal.

'I replied that it could be an idea to send Auala as peace dove. But of course only after the people in Lusaka had admitted that they had made a mistake – or have they become so high and mighty that questions as to right and wrong no longer exist as far as they are concerned? He visibly reacted to that, but collected himself and said, "If we wish to get anywhere, that is not the way to go about it."

'Later he said that the idea of sending Auala as go-between could not come from him. I don't know whether he thinks that someone else is to take it up. One with whom he is to get in touch. Besides that, I don't know what they, the party members and the church people, had talked about in Geneva.

'He did in a manner confirm the information I had received from Siegfried Tjijorokisa, a member of SWANU I'd met in town, that the church people had been invited to take part on SWAPO's side in an eventual conference with the South Africans about the future of Namibia. That is probably the way they have compelled the men of the church to keep their peace. And, for me at any rate, they have managed it with Winter and of course with Maasdorp. That is the reason he showed so little interest in taking up the case of the prisoners.

'PK [Peter] made a show about how well he is informed about my efforts, showed me a memorandum by [Danish theologian] Jørgen Leistner to his colleagues in the LWF, and mentioned that I had had contacts with diplomats[40] from two countries in Stockholm. Asked if I had been in Stockholm, whereto I said no (!), whereupon he said that the contact had been with diplomats from Tanzania and Nigeria. To which I didn't say anything.

'As to Leistner, I today tried to contact him, called Geneva, and left a message for him to call me – without anything hitherto having happened. I

---

[40] In Stockholm one of the diplomats I had called on the phone to request a meeting with, was the Sudanese Ambassador. On hearing what it was about, he expressed his support of Nujoma and peremptorily told me off. So much for African *diplomatists*, I thought to myself. On a later occasion I had an opportunity to see Ghana's Foreign Minister, Roger Joseph Felli, on a visit to Oslo. He listened carefully to what I had to tell him and undertook to take up the matter on his return home – but was soon afterwards dismissed from office in the *coup d'état* that brought Flight Lieutenant Jerry Rawlings to power in that West African country.

don't believe there will be any assistance from his side for my planned flight to New York.'

I concluded my letter to Edel with the following summary:

'I expect the newspaper articles to build up pressure that cannot be ignored. Fred Bridgeland has also in the meantime got his article placed in the Windhoek Advertiser. (From a special correspondent in Lusaka). Saw a copy of it at the office yesterday. This is important as people at home are not willing to believe anything negative about the chaps outside. They like to believe that the articles are enemy inspired. Tony Hodges says a longer article will also be printed in Africa Development (a mining company financed publication, too bad) in January.

'Beside that Fred has probably got an article with information from Andreas' letter in Africa Confidential – the gossip number for the initiated that The Economist publishes. Costs £40 or thereabouts for an annual subscription for two weekly numbers marked 'confidential'. Peter's office gets it as well. It puts pressure on him personally as all these articles must have some effect on the credibility he has built up in the media and amongst others.'

A couple of weeks later I had reason to write Salatiel Ailonga, the only other 'dissident' who had escaped imprisonment in Zambia. Dated 15 November 1976 from London, it is as close to a verbatim account of a conversation I had on the phone with Leistner. At our introduction by a mutual acquaintance in Oslo some time before, he had been interested in my account about the situation in Zambia; it had encouraged me to put a request to the LWF through him for assistance to travel to New York.

I cite the letter *in extenso* as it provides insight into the LWF's response to the SWAPO conflict. The men of God showed themselves allergic to information that challenged the opportunistic standpoint they had adopted – with a striking lack of compassion for Christians pining away in an African concentration camp and prisons.

THE LETTER TO SALATIEL AILONGA

LONDON, MONDAY 15 November 1976

Dear Brother Ailonga,

Thank you and Anita for the copy of Mifima's letter as well as for the earlier copies. After several futile attempts I finally made contact with Jørgen Leistner at the LWF today. I wanted to inquire from him about the approach that I had made a month or so ago and about which I had informed you as well. It was the most distressing conversation and it took me the better part of the afternoon to get over the effects of it. I shall here summarise it because it tended to confirm my suspicion that tactical considerations, rather than Christian principles and compassion, dictate the reaction of the LWF to recent developments concerning us.

During the conversation lasting probably a quarter of an hour and where there were the most frank exchanges, it developed that they were unwilling to extend support that could sustain activities that have now become indistinguishable, so far as I was concerned, from those of the South African Government and BOSS, and which could only lead to an exacerbation of the split in SWAPO. Andreas Shipanga and his colleagues, including you, had been engaged in activities most unfavourable.

I wanted to know what sort of evidence the LWF had heard and seen and from whom?

Leistner said evidence from independent sources in addition to party sources, but he wouldn't identify these any closer, nor elaborate the nature of the evidence. However, it seems to have been so strong that even Maasdorp, who said he was a friend of Shipanga's, was satisfied with it.

I said 'Maasdorp, yes', and mentioned to him the fact that Peter Katjavivi had shown me a copy of Leistner's internal memo to his colleagues about the conversation I had had with Leistner – as evidence that SWAPO was keeping track of my movements and doings. Could it have been Maasdorp who had sent Katjavivi that copy? And could the silence of the church organisation be due to the fact that SWAPO spokesmen had promised them representation on a SWAPO delegation at an eventual conference with the South Africans?

Leistner didn't think it was Maasdorp, but somebody else that he had in mind could have been responsible. He seemed also to be fearful of Katjavivi's reaction to the memo. His own colleagues had reacted very negatively to it.

Earlier in the conversation Leistner didn't have a positive reply when I pointedly asked whether the LWF had in fact made protests to the SWAPO leadership about the people, whom he called dissidents, held in jail and detention. I supposed they had not done so. I therefore reassured him that his memo had been very wisely drawn up, no fault could be charged, and that he had in fact done the LWF honour by having written it – to which he responded by suggesting that if it is regarded by Katjavivi as an expression of concern by the LWF, then perhaps it had done its service.

He however said that my activities could only serve the interests of BOSS and South Africa, who must know about it, to the detriment of the liberation struggle. He mentioned the instance of my speaking to various people, including himself.

I told him that I had approached him personally on the advice of a Norwegian friend who has known me since 1959 and is a friend of long standing of our liberation struggle. I had also not spoken to [anyone] other than friends and occasional churchmen, such as bishops Winter and Wood.

Leistner became very interested in what Bishop Winter's response was, trying to press significance out of my hesitant 'but ...' – as if Winter's failure to make public remonstrance satisfied him that the (un)published charges against the 'dissidents', were true.

I then repeated that with my approaches to friends I had hoped for nothing but that they would make their concern and dissatisfaction known to the SWAPO leadership in straightforward if very private terms. Even though adverse publicity is the only sanction against arbitrary action on the part of those in power, I would have hoped that such approaches from undoubted friends would succeed. I reiterated my belief in very strong terms that it was their Christian and ethical obligation to be forthcoming with such criticism, even though it might be regarded as damaging to 'our cause'.

He thought that while that might be true in the case of states, it was a different matter in the case of a liberation movement still struggling towards its goal.

As I suppose this is a position for which there can be adduced a convincing theological argument, I leave it to you!

I must add, however, that he also said that the best way to deal with the problem is to leave it to Nujoma and SWAPO to sort it out themselves. To which I responded wholeheartedly, but added that the interference of Kaunda and Nyerere had made that very difficult indeed.

Leistner mentioned that the figure of a thousand detainees had been rejected by his informants from Zambia (identities unknown). It was impossible. I then told him that I had heard from a journalist that *The Observer* in London a month ago had decided to print that story about the people held in detention in Zambia only after the Minister of Foreign Affairs of that country had confided to an *Observer* journalist that there were in fact 500 persons in detention. Making allowance for the Minister's natural disinclination to own up to the detention of such a large number as a thousand, the figure doesn't seem fanciful.

In addition, Ben Amathila had told a journalist in Scandinavia that a thousand was an exaggerated figure. Only about two hundred people were being kept in detention while their responsibility for a South African attack on a SWAPO camp was being investigated. However, when the same Foreign Minister was interviewed by the press in Oslo two weeks ago, he stated flatly that no SWAPO guerrillas were being kept in detention. Only a few members of the party had been jailed for a short time after a split early this year, he said.

Leistner to this said, what is one to believe then? He also mentioned that I had spoken to newspapers in a censorious way.

To this I asked him: 'You tell me what I am to do when the Zambian Government kicks my wife and myself out of Zambia in disgrace and states that we are agents of the South Africans and when Sam Nujoma mentions my name together with that of Ailonga and others as individuals to be tried by military tribunal and executed by firing squad?'

Such things are duly taken up by the press in Norway and elsewhere; my chances of obtaining funds to do research are hurt, my reputation is dented, it becomes impossible to land a job. Must I shut my mouth and discount the risks to those of my countrymen who are being abused in detention? I related to him the account of Andreas Nuukwao being subjected to a thirty-day course of torture (in Tanzania – solitary confinement and denial of food and physical comforts) for writing letters abroad.

To the suggestion that I am running the errands of BOSS, I informed Leistner that I had in fact advised people in Rehoboth, as I have other Namibians, to join SWAPO. The decision of the Rehoboth Volksparty to join SWAPO had let loose a landslide in favour of the party in the southern part of the country. Even though I had been expelled by Lusaka I therefore regarded myself as a member in good standing.

To conclude, where the name of the game is play safe, people seem willing to grab at any chance to escape from having to adopt a position. Let us hope that this does not mean that our brothers and sisters will have to sit another six months at the pleasure of Sam Nujoma, Kenneth Kaunda and Julius Nyerere.

Yours,

Hans Beukes

POST SCRIPT

The Norwegian Lutheran Bishop, Gunnar Staalsett, represented his Church at the LWF headquarters while the concentration camp prisoners were crying for help from the 'international community'. In 2011, a year before his death, Andreas Shipanga related to me the comment with which, during a visit to the country, the Norwegian man of God had dismissed a suggestion by Namibian churchmen that he meet with Shipanga. The Bishop of Oslo's response was that he didn't speak to Quislings.[41]

---

[41] Vidkun Quisling was the leader of a political party that grabbed the reigns of government in 1940 when Nazi Germany invaded Norway and the legally elected government fled the country. His collaboration with the occupying power rendered his name eponymous for a traitor.

MY MOTHER'S OBSERVATIONS

When my mother returned home from her visit to Lusaka in May 1976, she took with her letters that, being the son of a shoemaker, I had hidden in the heels of her shoes. In a letter I received back from her months later, she illuminated the responses inside the country to the coup by which a SWAPO junta had grabbed absolute power over the lives of their countrymen. She wrote:

'These things we cannot send through the post; therefore I'm sending you this letter with a Lutheran Sister who's on her way to Germany. On my return home, I told them everything and handed over the papers, but SWAPO's [domestic] leaders are extremely cautious. They say they hear so many diverging things from different people who arrive back in the country after visits abroad. Therefore they cannot do anything. They ask why Johnnie Otto and the like are on Sam Nujoma's side. But they also fear internal splits. They ask why Peter Katjavivi doesn't give a clear message about what is going on. They say the Basters always want to be know-alls, while they can think for themselves. Such snide remarks are not spoken openly, as they could hardly claim that it is because you are involved that we act in the way we have done. Further, SWAPO would have received much more support, but the majority of people say, how can one join an organisation that kills its own people. *This is the reason why many now refuse to join the party. It is also why many Namibians now join the Army.* (My emphasis.)

Kehat has made them aware of the dirty role that Kaunda plays in the struggle for Africa's liberation, and has said they ought to demand that he set the people free so they can go to Angola. This drew support. I should also mention that the Basters who had joined SWAPO are now working hard to collect money. It would have been very good to have had a car. The majority of people who have joined are very poor. Something else: [the Ovambo priest] Father Naholo from Walvis Bay told us that he knows Peter Nanyemba well and that he cannot stand him.

My personal impression is that SWAPO locally fear that the struggle will suffer if they were to depose Sam Nujoma. But what they possibly do not think of is that once he arrives with his military forces, nobody would be allowed to say or do anything. I am thinking of my grandchildren and us – when I see all the refugees [from the war in Angola]. Yes, SWAPO here also say that they have heard many things that do not speak in favour of Andreas Shipanga. For that reason they do not want to intervene between Andreas and Sam. Sam Nujoma also sets in circulation many rumours that cause doubts in people's minds. Anita Shimbuli's mother is very worried about her and angry at Sam. Can't you write and tell where she is and how it goes with her? The family is doing fine.'

I had of course no idea what had become of the hapless young men and women who constantly dropped by our place, anxious to relate to Edel (interestingly, not to me) what they knew about the unfolding drama in Lusaka.

BROTHER HEWAT'S ACCOUNT

From my younger brother Hewat I received two letters that provided some insight into what passed for political organisation 'at home' – on which the guerrilla organisation SWAPO was awarded UN status as 'sole authentic representatives of the Namibian people'. Hewat was educated in Cape Town and had evidently been influenced by 'The Mother City's' uncompromising radicalism. His first missive was dated 10 June 1977:

'I would firstly like to give you my interpretation of our political situation. From the outset I've deplored the expectations that we may be independent in one or two years time. This type of prediction and the consequent atmosphere of expectation in 1974 [after the coup in Portugal] have triggered off power struggles and polarisation within the country. I even think that this irrational expectation was felt outside. What we seemed to forget was that we could not draw parallels between the South African situation and the Portuguese colonial situation. Nor could we equate the easy "independences" of British colonies to that of the Portuguese and the South African colonies. In the case of British colonies they, the British, were the main investors (exploiters) of these countries and they could easily settle for a neo-colonialist solution and still maintain their control!

'Independence for Angola and Mozambique came quickly because the broad mass of the Portuguese people did not benefit by a colonialism [that was] rather to their detriment. In our case, Namibia and Zimbabwe are not only economically linked to SA but politically, socially. The struggle within Namibia and Zimbabwe is threatening the very foundations of Boer Nationalism. It is this that makes the type of neo-colonialist "solution", that the West favours, very, very difficult. Vorster was a puppet of the West but could afford to be that only up to a certain point. He is at present 'fighting for the existence of the Afrikaner Volk' ...

'To return to our situation inside. The South Africans are, with blinding speed, creating countless channels for building a vast middle class and a well-above-the-breadline worker. Multinational corporations are involved, charity (under the guise of self-reliance and literacy) organisations are involved.

Matriculated youth are offered sponsored training (university and other) with job securities. Contract labourers are allowed to bring their wives south and not allowed to take property north (a resettling process). The churches – I've seen notes on their discussions – want western involvement, but very subtly. They are hanging onto the liberation struggle with all their might. By 'They' I mean the leaders. The lower church officials are normally the most reactionary (apolitical). The Christian Centre (the director is a SWAPO Exco member), which has close links with the Anglican and Lutheran churches, is one of the channels through which these self-reliance projects are launched. So they are even succeeding in getting an unsuspecting SWAPO leadership involved in their dangerous schemes. Another of their trump cards: The press has been very receptive to SWAPO. Some leaders (of which Martha is one of the most important) are invited frequently to wine and dine at the West German Consulate and meet with German government officials.'

On 7 November, Hewat had another chance to smuggle out a letter to me, this time with an account of the organisational work in which he and his wife Erika were engaged. They appeared to have formed as critical an opinion of the domestic SWAPO's senior executives as the SWAPO Youth League had done of the Nujoma regime abroad. In contrast to the situation in South Africa, where the ANC and the PAC were banned, SWAPO's internal wing was allowed to operate seemingly freely.

'Our situation inside the country,' wrote Hewat, 'is not a very encouraging one, but we are trying our best to define our struggle. Our National Executive [the Ovambo region] consists mostly of elitist elements and they are, in fact, trying to stifle revolutionary work and activity. Whether they will succeed remains to be seen. We are trying to build a revolutionary youth and here I think we are successful. When they started to implement the draft constitution of the Central Committee I warned against the "extension of elitism". A centralised leadership issuing orders to regional and then to the lower levels does not necessarily establish a people's leadership, especially as the structures set out in that constitution are based on bureaucracy. The so-called extension of the leadership is a sham. As far as I interpreted it, only the top leadership shall have any power whatsoever and they shall also be their own electorate. We made sure, however, at the last National Conference, that it went through as a draft still to be discussed.

'Rehoboth now serves as an outstanding example of political work. Those from other places, when coming in contact with this region, wish to transplant the example to their places. Attie Beukes [not related to us], a 24 year old man, originally from Mariental, is leading the movement there. He is highly sensitive to the people's needs and although of very small stature, he has got all the guts in the world. The police ripped his placard off a shop window. He then drove to the police station in great fury and climbed into them. They first tried roughneck stunts but were so mesmerised that they apologised. He of course did not accept.

'During the homeland elections we held a meeting ... surrounded by the SA Army. Thereafter, we staged a march and the procession was five hundred metres long. In fact, the work in Rehoboth is a shining token of the sham of tribal generalisation because they have successfully integrated all tribal groups politically and socially. My wife has started mobilisation in Khomasdal (Coloured township in Windhoek) but because we could not remain there the elites are at present taking over. 'However, in a series of training programmes which I am planning through our region, I hope to consolidate our line.

'As far as Zambia is concerned we went to the south to speak to the people there. I had some quarrels with the National Exco, but, because of lack of standpoint and clear future aspirations, we made no headway. Of course, the dissatisfaction inside is rife but they are all scared of rifts, etc.

'Others have the type of apologetic tribal attitude and shall probably never play any role other than as appendixes. Attie, myself and others refuse to be part of liberal tribalism disguised under the cloak of nationalism. If we are dissatisfied we are dissatisfied as co-leaders of SWAPO, and as such we have brought much more light, especially to the youth. I am working entirely outside my own tribal area as the organiser of the Western Region. At present there are two regions (unofficially three): The southern and western regions (the central region, consisting of Windhoek, Rehoboth and Okahandja is still to be formalised). I am planning training courses for our cadres from 10 to 18 December in Swakopmund, and then during January in Omaruru. I am at present busy on research and reading. We are not very much liked by the elite.

'Our greatest drawback is finance. In order to travel around I have spent most of my salary of £237.[42] I am in financial difficulties at the moment. We would also like to work faster but the National Exco is not very helpful – except when engaged in their sham activities. We have made many loans to buy a car which became a necessity.'

---

42 Hewat worked as a teacher at a school 70km north-west of Omaruru, in a small tribal settlement called Okambahe. The school complex is 7km out of Okambahe itself, and housed 150 students.

JUDGE STEYN, PLEASE DO NOT PRAY FOR ME

Given such activism, it was not surprising that the Security Police went for Hewat. They stopped his car midway between Omaruru and Okambahe and commandeered him into their vehicle, leaving Erica with their small children on the deserted dirt road. This led to a famous confrontation between my father and the South African Administrator-General, Marthinus T. Steyn.

Assuming that the shoemaker had come to plead for the release of his son, who was imprisoned under solitary confinement in the distant town of Gobabis, the judge adopted a patronising tone. He opened with a stern warning about the danger from communists that the country was facing.

Not one to be spoken down to, Father expressed his deeply felt desire that communists would in fact come to power in Namibia. He had heard, he explained, that communists summarily executed their opponents, in contrast to the regime that the judge represented. Their way of dealing with opposition was to show cruelty, citing the instance of his daughter-in-law who couldn't drive, having been left stranded without food or water on a lonely road with two small children. If the judge wanted to challenge the low opinion he held of both his own government and their German predecessors, he invited him to visit islands off the coast where the bones of Hereros, left there to die by the Germans, were said to be still visible in the sand.

Advocate Anton Lubovski, who would be assassinated during the transition period, had accompanied my father as his lawyer to the interview. He wasn't given a chance to say anything while his client had a field day with the apartheid regime's representative.[43] The confrontation between judge and shoemaker had started with an exchange of letters to the editor of the *Windhoek Advertiser*. Responding to a spirited attack against his administration from my father, the judge had replied that he prayed for the likes of Hermanus Beukes. In a response headed, 'Judge Steyn, please do not pray for me', the would-be beneficiary of the judge's intercession with the Almighty, cited an arcane text from Scripture. It was to remind the judge that it displeased the Lord to have His authority brought into a fray to decide its outcome. He went on: 'Arrest without charge is a denial and rejection of any form of justice, democracy and any civilised mind-set.'

This exchange, incidentally, bespeaks a discourse about public affairs that Namibians availed themselves of at a time when the South African media filtered out the expression of political opinion by Blacks. Credit for this, as far as I could determine, was due in large part to Hannes Smith, the editor of the

---

43 Father used to unwind with a blow-by-blow account to the family after such altercations with representatives of the regime.

Windhoek Advertiser and subsequently of the *Windhoek Observer*. Smith and his colleagues in the Namibian media presented the opinion of their Black readers, including SWAPO's spokespersons, on an equal footing with that of their White readers.

DANIEL TJONGARERO – A CAPTIVE OF HIS OWN CONSCIENCE

Although the circumstances under which it had been written were questionable, a document came into my hands that nevertheless reveals the parlous state of the 'organisation' that had been certified by the UN as 'sole legitimate representatives of the Namibian people'.

Dated 4 December 1977, the handwritten document was authored by Dan Tjongarero, the domestic SWAPO's deputy chairman and information secretary. Dan's signature is witnessed by one Lieutenant-colonel W F Schoon – presumably a member of the Security Police. It appears to have been drawn up after Dan and other activists, including my sister Martha, had been apprehended by Security Police while on a trip to Ovamboland, and confronted with the testimony of ex-SWAPO guerrillas and documentation of atrocities that had allegedly been committed by SWAPO.

Instead of sleeping that night, Dan appears to have wanted to state clearly where he stood as a Christian committed to the brotherhood of man, and to disassociate himself from the violence SWAPO abroad had been responsible for in the country.

The information that Dan provides about himself, bespeaks a well-educated and widely-travelled man. Having read political philosophy in Germany and studied ancient Greek thought in South Africa, he associated with church leaders both at home and in South Africa. He had read the contemporary Afrikaans authors of protest literature known as the *Sestigers* (of the sixties), discussed politics with Steve Biko (the prophet of the Black Consciousness Movement in SA) and his associates, and delivered a paper on 'recognition' at a seminar organised by the BCM. There he had argued against the taking up of arms to gain recognition, and made a case for a revolutionary movement to seek recognition at home rather than abroad. Dan had also been invited to address audiences at several universities in South Africa, where he had explained 'SWAPO's thinking', basing himself on a document entitled *A Discussion Paper on the Constitution for an Independent Namibia*.

(This happened to be a document that I was acquainted with. In 1975, Peter Katjavivi had proudly handed me a copy of it. Assuming that it was the work of one of his lawyer friends in London, I had advised him to prefix it with the words 'a discussion paper' – so as to avoid the charge that SWAPO had arrogated unto itself the right to dictate the country's constitution.)

With reference to his disquiet about the charges that SWAPO had become a terrorist organisation, Dan pleaded to having become 'a captive of his own conscience'. His statement read:

'My motivation for joining SWAPO, was to make a peaceful contribution towards a settlement in my country. I can never claim to have had ambitions of becoming a leader. I wanted to serve the country with my education. I saw in SWAPO's 'Proposals for a constitution for Namibia' my guideline, and associated myself with these principles, which I regarded as best for the country. My own personal outlook was: that I cannot tolerate racism, be it White or Black, and that I cannot demand human rights for myself only to deny [others] the same human rights after I have got mine. Numerous people who have now left, prodded me to leave the country, and although I was bitter because of constant refusals to my passport applications for study, I was and am for peace and not for violence, which in fact is manifested in my whole outlook towards life: If somebody disagrees with you don't beat the wits out of him. Have an open mind and convince him with your arguments and faith. If he has better arguments, you must give in to reason.

'I am aware of Russian imperialism, and that's what I don't wish for my country. I have become aware of the senseless murders committed by SWAPO, by mouth of an ex-guerrilla, and I don't want to be party to this. If this is the liberation that we are fighting for, I have serious doubts about it. I didn't join SWAPO for this and thus I am tendering my resignation immediately. I am not a protagonist of violence in any of its forms. However, there is one dilemma. Without the support of the Executive I would not be able to do anything other than putting my neck on a block. It must be clear, however, that I condemn SWAPO's involvement in terrorist activities – especially if I can recall the senseless killing of an 81 year old man and the raping of a mother of a small baby, and numerous other things. This is not fighting for liberation but a manifestation of the animalistic instincts of barbarism. On numerous occasions I have phoned Lusaka and London for information on atrocities. The blame was squarely put on the SADF – even by labourers who went to work in the south. They said: 'It's the Boers' or 'we know our enemy'. For me, sitting in Windhoek is difficult. Yet I do not want to justify my ignorance. I wanted to remain safe by not confronting others with my wavering interest in SWAPO. But on the basis of evidence put before me, especially seeing that my information was one-sided, I was through my own conscience forced to re-consider my position.

'I am guilty of the atrocities because I contributed to giving false information unknowingly. I allowed myself to be misled by slogans to which conscience will ultimately dictate what I am going to do. I have up to now only known SWAPO's one side, most probably only a tenth of what SWAPO is, but that's enough. Humanity can do without senseless killings.'

Dan lamented the extent to which the domestic SWAPO had turned itself into a loudspeaker for the external organisation and how he himself had been used as its mouthpiece:

'With my joining SWAPO there was talk of two SWAPO's, the external and the internal wings. But the re-election [by the internal wing's Congress in 1975] of office-bearers outside the country shattered this illusion. There were a few office-bearers in the country who objected to the methods used to achieve liberation, but the fear of being labelled traitors resulted in such violence neither being condoned nor condemned. There were only references to freedom fighters, but these references were always heroic and subjective.'

The SWAPO Congress had elected Dan as Publicity and Information Secretary. But, according to his statement, his colleagues told him what to write and how. They nevertheless soon found him to be wanting, while he felt frustrated with slogans that to him sounded 'outdated, hollow and without meaning'. His job as Publicity and Information Secretary, and later as Deputy Chairman, was to remain in constant contact by telephone with John Otto in Lusaka, Theo-Ben in New York and Peter Katjavivi in London. They were to give him: 'Information on the progress of the struggle in the diplomatic missions, as well as to clarify to the Executive allegations against SWAPO in the local press: for example, the Shipanga issue, and the expulsion of SWANU students from the Namibian Institute in Lusaka ...'

On hearing about the Western initiative to engage with SWAPO, Dan's disillusionment was complete:

'My last hope for the idea that we were headquarters and could dictate with the outside arm was shattered. We issued a statement demanding that the West see the whole SWAPO, but our leaders outside went to see them alone. This showed that we were merely here as functionaries. We were not indispensable.'

For me, Dan's and Hewat's letters merely reinforced the impression of an organisation that existed in name only, one nevertheless endowed with a most invidious status by the UN.

UN COMMISSIONER SEAN MACBRIDE

With the election of Sean MacBride as UN Commissioner for Namibia in 1973, the Namibia lobby at the UN acquired as champion one of the more colourful figures in Irish politics, a man who had followed in his father's footsteps in the Irish fight for independence from British imperialism. Major John MacBride had organised a brigade to fight on the side of the Boers against the British in the War of 1899-1902, and finally had been executed for leading an Irish uprising in 1916. Sean MacBride had taken part in the Irish War of Independence; and he opposed the 1921 Anglo-Irish Treaty that put an end to that war. MacBride's mother was Maud Gonne, a woman to whom the Irish poet William Butler Yeats had lost his heart.

Sean MacBride's association with SWAPO began in 1966, with the imprisonment of Andimba Toivo ya Toivo in Namibia. Travelling from Cairo, where he was stationed at the time, Andreas Shipanga had sought MacBride's assistance, as co-founder of Amnesty International, to secure lawyers for the defence of his old comrade and co-founder of SWAPO. Thanks to MacBride, George Bizos, one of South Africa's premier defence lawyers, and a colleague were retained for Toivo's defence.

It was a move, Shipanga informed me the last time the two of us met, that Sam Nujoma, clearly fearing displacement by the senior and respected Toivo, had angrily opposed.

Within a year of his appointment as UN Commissioner for Namibia, MacBride issued a decree that nationalised Namibia's natural resources. Even though the power to enforce the decree was illusory, it should have laid the cornerstone of a prosperous society if it had been wisely built upon by the government of an independent Namibia.

The first time I met MacBride was in mid-1974, when I visited the SWAPO office in London on the same day as he happened by. It turned out that the man who would be awarded the Nobel Peace Prize later that year had a special message for SWAPO. It was to intensify its guerrilla activity so as to underline the seriousness of the situation posed by the refusal of South Africa to abide by UN resolutions about Namibia – before the resumption of the annual debates at the UN.

This would have been music to the ears of Nujoma and his coterie. Elevated to the stature of the 'only authentic representatives of the Namibian people', they were already engaged in sending young men across the Namibian borders on armed 'missions'.

For me, the question raised by MacBride's encouragement of a confrontation with the South African Defense Force, was whether by temperament the hero of the Irish War of Independence was the right man to head Namibia's quest for liberation.

One of the first things Mburumba Kerina and I had discussed when I arrived in New York in mid-September 1959, had been how our people could possibly rid themselves of the apartheid regime at home. The thought of taking up arms against the military might of the SADF was so preposterous it didn't even merit discussion. Two generations after the genocide visited upon them by the Germans, the people of central and southern South West Africa, imprisoned in reservations, were still in dire need of rehabilitation. The northerners were subdivided into tribes under each its chief, or king, about their allegiance to the rest of the country we could make no assumptions. The division of the country into two parts by a 'red line', drawn from east to west, barred northerners, excepting males on contract, from entering and interacting with the people of the central and southern regions. A discourse, among the native peoples, about 'national' issues, had never taken place since their subjugation by the colonial powers. It was recognition that such a discourse could not take place without political organisation that had led Kozonguizi to form SWANU and Kerina to seek to outdo him by calling on the numerically superior Ovambos to form SWAPO.

Little had changed in the intervening fifteen years, except that the status accorded to SWAPO by the UN had effectively relieved the guerrilla group of having to seek a basis of understanding with either SWANU, which opposed a military option, or pay heed to other activists at home.

In a letter dated 9 February 1959, Mburumba Kerina wrote to Toivo Ya Toivo, 'Together we shall smash those Whites out of the Government without using force but our brains.'[44]

But how to go about it, that was the question. We were in 1959 very aware of our privileged status as 'wards of the international community'. This had endowed us with the right – that we were in fact exercising – to demand of the member states of the UN that they honour their obligations under international law to protect our people. We also knew very well that governments do not act unless pressured by public opinion. Therefore we had, as I had been advised by Allard Lowenstein in Cape Town, to challenge the information monopoly enjoyed by the apartheid regime on the world stage.

Improbable as this assignment sounded, we were in fact already engaged in it – and in a world torn by a Cold War between the major powers. To me, the 1963 South West Africa campaign in Norway had shown the potential of a strategy that reaffirmed respect for the human rights of friend and foe alike.

---

44   ICJ source cited p.39.

The appeal was to people's sense of fairness and decency, not their thirst for blood. As a result, the campaign drew support from left to right across the political spectrum – as did similar campaigns in other countries – and Oslo became a bastion of the anti-apartheid movement.

The National Archives in Namibia can now provide access to unique documentation about the extent to which something similar had played itself out even in the US. In 1998, I spent a week in New York to assist Mrs Elizabeth Landis, well advanced in years, in an act of dedication to a cause on which she had lavished the better years of her life. In a self-recruited work of love she cleared out, all by herself, the office of a departed member of the Congregational Church, Bill Johnston. He had left a priceless record of books, newspaper cuttings, memorabilia, offprints, student papers, and so on, that showed four decades of campaigns nationwide against apartheid.

The swell of opinion that had been raised compelled universities, and eventually even the US banks, to reconsider their investments in the apartheid state. The resulting loss of credit-worthiness was what dramatically undermined faith in the staying power of the apartheid state – gaining it the image of a lost cause even among its hardiest supporters in the West.

That UN Commissioner Sean MacBride and his sharp-shodded staff of top diplomats could have overlooked all this, speaks volumes about how militarism seems to dictate reflexes even at UN headquarters – notwithstanding the UN's Charter *outlawing* war in its paragraph 2.4.

MY NEXT encounter with the UN Commissioner was at a senate meeting of MacBride's creation, the UN Institute for Namibia in Lusaka. I was summoned quite unexpectedly at noon that day to present myself for an interview for a job as teacher at the institute. Unprepared as I was, the interview did not go well.

The last time I saw the Commissioner was at his hotel in London late that same year. Since the UN's *de jure* authority over Namibia was vested in him, I thought he ought to be informed about the pleas of the interned guerrillas at Mboroma. MacBride made no comment about the copy of the letter that I handed him. After a question about my future plans, the audience came to an end. He said: 'It was good to have met you.' I closed the door of his suite behind me, uncertain as to what significance to attach to those parting words.

In his valediction to the people of Namibia early in the New Year, Sean MacBride warned that '*the setting up of an interim government in South West Africa could provoke a Black civil war. (It) could lead to another Angola because*

SWAPO was likely to call for outside assistance from Black neighbouring states and Cuba'.[45] (My emphasis.)

The notion that an organisation, accorded observer status at the UN, could legitimately call on member states to launch military attacks on another member of the organisation, beggars belief. The suggestion that any one or all of South Africa's Black neighbour states could pose a credible threat to the SADF, equally misrepresented reality. The decade-long confrontation with Cuba, that would exact a disproportionate cost in terms of lives and means from the distant island state, for the loss of a fraction of that number on the SADF side, had just commenced.

Tragically, by thus seeking to lend credence to SWAPO's illusory diplomatic powers and military capabilities, the UN Commissioner for Namibia and Nobel Peace Prize laureate made his exit on the same bugle call as had been sounded at his entry onto the scene.

A TRUST BETRAYED

Late in 1976, the Herero Chieftain, Clemens Kapuuo, arrived in London on an errand. My meeting with him was fleeting, but the pain of it will be with me forever. I had gone to Chatham House to listen to a talk I'd heard he would be delivering. On the way out of the building, Kapuuo noticed me sitting alongside the isle and, stopping for a moment to give expression to his surprise at finding me there, said: 'So, Hans, are you also one of those who want to kill me?' With that he left, ignoring my stuttering efforts at denial.

The first time we had seen each other was late one evening in June 1959. He had sent me off with a special mandate: 'Hans, it is up to you and Kozo to get us the help we need to free ourselves.' I had felt elated by the inclusiveness of that statement. As I had driven home to Rehoboth that evening my heart had swelled with pride – for being thus embraced.

Kapuuo had been in London as the representative of the National Convention, formed at Rehoboth on the initiative of my father. At home the local representatives of SWAPO had taken part in the first ever *indaba* about their common future by the Territory's people. In London, Peter Katjavivi had rejected his outstretched hand by referring to the special status that the UN had accorded to SWAPO. Then, at the Commonwealth gathering in Jamaica he had succeeded in portraying Kapuuo as a puppet of the regime. Under the circumstances, no one could blame the Herero chieftain for taking a hard look at where he stood, to persuade himself that he had been checkmated and

---

[45] Reported in *The Windhoek Advertiser* on Tuesday 25 January 1977.

that participation in the Turnhalle Constitutional Conference, even though sponsored by the occupation regime, might open new possibilities.

The challenge Kapuuo faced was that the South African regime evidently had no intention of giving up the interests it had acquired in Namibia. Confirmation of this I obtained quite by chance. En route to London through Germany, I made the acquaintance of Wolfgang Thomas, a Namibian-born economist of German ancestry. He had been on the advisory panel of 'experts' at the Turnhalle Conference. I asked Thomas why they had not advised the participants at the Turnhalle to put some challenging questions on the table, questions relating to Namibia's relations with the Republic: reasonable demands that would have needed to be raised by true defenders of the national interest. If such questions had been put, the credibility of the Turnhalle Alliance that was formed would have been enhanced. There was no shortage of issues that could have fit the bill: the status of Walvis Bay – which South Africa regarded as its territory; the monopolisation of the Namibian market by South African producers to the detriment of local production; the benefits to South Africa of having Namibia's foreign exchange earnings supporting the Rand, and so on.

A visibly embarrassed Thomas replied: 'To say it like it was, the attitude of my South African colleagues was, *laat ons die kaffers verneuk* (let us fool the *kaffirs*)!'

GERMAN ADVICE

On my way back from London to Norway late 1976 in Hamburgh, I dropped by two old acquaintances from the 1960's, Freimut Duve and Helmut Bley. An historian with a special interest in Namibia, Bley had become an adviser to the German foreign aid agency. This evidently provided him access to the reports of the Federal Intelligence Service, the *Bundesnachrichtendienst*. Though I didn't ask, Bley now informed me that a pro-Soviet group had taken over control of SWAPO. I understood this to mean that I could not expect my German friends to be of much assistance to my imprisoned countrymen.

Duve was in the publishing business and influential in Social Democratic politics. As a journalist he had closely followed the Algerian war of independence, and its political aftermath. This had provided him with a jaundiced view on the dynamics of liberation movements. At a conference about the ways and means of bringing the apartheid regime to account in which we both participated at Oxford in 1964, he had cautioned me against 'staying in the game'.

While having to admit the realism of these two ideological workhorses, it had brought me no relief from thinking about my imprisoned countrymen, whose fate had become my own.

A NORDIC SAFARI

In Lusaka I had become aware of the extent to which the Swedish government supported SWAPO with supplies for consumption and heavy duty vehicles. In Stockholm, Ben Amathila had been provided with office space in a building situated a stone's throw away from the Foreign Office. And Anders Bjuner had given me reasons why the Swedish Government wouldn't be moved by the imprisonment of Namibians by SWAPO's leaders to cut its support to the guerrilla movement. Yet, with acquaintances dating back to 1960 in governmental positions, I thought it worthwhile to submit a personal plea for them to do something about my imprisoned countrymen.

In addition to Ola Ullsten and Hans Blix – with whom I had become acquainted at the Waffelry (WFLRY) Conference – at the head of the Foreign Office, there was David Wirmark of the World Assembly of Youth, and Oluf Poluha, with whom I had attended a student conference in the Outer Mongolian capital of Ulan Bator in 1967.

It was on Poluha's door that I knocked first, to be escorted to Wirmark's office. Just then a call came in from Hans Blix who happened to be in Geneva right then. Alerted to an 'old friend' that was visiting them, a short three-way conversation ensued. Afterwards Wirmark leaned back in his chair to ask about my errand. He listened without comment and then suggested that I apply for re-admittance to SWAPO's good graces.

Recognising that my errand in Stockholm evidently had come to nought, I rose to leave. In response to his advice, I reminded Wirmark of Nujoma's death threat against me.[46] The wordless glance in the Swede's eyes confirmed that I had knocked at his door in vain.

HELSINKI

After Stockholm, I boarded a ferryboat to Helsinki in order to meet with Salatiel Ailonga and his wife Anita, the only other SWAPO 'dissidents' to escape Kenneth Kaunda's concentration camps and Julius Nyerere's prisons.

---

[46]   A newspaper report from Dar es Salaam in early August 1976 quoted Nujoma as naming the Reverend Salatiel Ailonga and myself as South African agents that would be court-martialled and shot. In Oslo, *Dagbladet* editorially decried 'the absurdity of calling Hans Beukes a South African agent' and lamented the tragedy of Nujoma's statement. I had dismissed Nujoma's statement as an unwise outburst from a man whose ambition was to become a leader of Namibia's people at a time when independence was yet a distant prospect.

The devout couple struck me as deeply affected by what had come to pass in the movement. On top of that, I learned that they had been frozen out by the church community that had sent Anita to Namibia as a missionary.

During a walk through the city, Salatiel and I ran into the diplomat Kari Karanko, who had been called home to a lower post in the Foreign Office. In Lusaka he and I had been on easy terms, having availed ourselves on afternoons of a football field around the circumference of which to jog – he much more energetically than I. Now he appeared uncharacteristically subdued. Anita assumed that his demotion was a reprisal for providing asylum to Jimmy Ampala while the latter was on the run for his life.

On the day of my departure, Salatiel and Anita joined me on the train to the harbour city of Åbo where they took me to the home of a missionary colleague. This was a man named Ihamäki, who turned out to be a man of God blessed with a sense of humour. His worldly anecdotes visibly lifted the spirits of his ex-colleagues. With his generous support, drawn from a pension with which he had to support wife and children, we could send some financial succour to our friends in Tanzania's jails – with a prayer that it would reach them. I then boarded the ferry back to Stockholm.

MORAL SUPPORT

My Nordic round trip had not been entirely futile. On the train to Stockholm from Oslo, I had shared a compartment for part of the way with Professor Torkel Opsahl of the Law Faculty in Oslo. As I knew of his work with human rights issues, I informed him about the reason for my trip to Stockholm. Back from Finland, I sent him copies of the pleas I had received from the SWAPO prisoners.

On 2 November, I received a letter from Opsahl to inform me that he had taken up the issue with an official at the Foreign Office, suggesting that 'Norway, for humanitarian reasons, ought to take up the matter of the internees during negotiations for increased support to SWAPO.' He had added that, 'In this manner, Tanzania and Zambia would be made aware that the fate of these prisoners is a matter of concern in Norway.' Opsahl listed other strategies that we might employ later, such as addressing questions to the Foreign Minister in Parliament. The University, he pointed out, wouldn't be very useful, since he was obliged to keep in mind that he had recently become a member of the UN's Human Rights Committee.

This was the most uplifting declaration of support that I had received from anyone throughout this period.

THE SOLIDARITY MOVEMENT SHOWS ITS TRUE COLOURS

In general, 'solidarity movements' operated through a symbiotic relationship with 'liberation movements'. This symbiosis connected people from host countries, mainly youths, to individuals from the global south. The connection enabled the visitors to make their cases known to the public of the host countries in a manner few would have been able to manage on their own. Their hosts gained political insights garnered from privileged contact with persons that they might not otherwise have come into contact. The Norwegian Youth Council for Southern Africa, in particular, became a launching pad for a career in public affairs for many of those serving on it.

Through encounters I now had with representatives of the Norwegian 'solidarity movement', I would experience to what extent the SWAPO spin concerning 'enemy agents' had fallen on good soil. One of my erstwhile colleagues on the Youth Council, who in the meantime had become a researcher at a prestigious institute, showed me the door for contesting his understanding of the events in Lusaka. Next, students at a teacher training school who had invited me to deliver a talk about the apartheid state, were told by the new man in charge at the *Fellesrådet* that they had made a mistake. The person in question would build himself a reputation as an 'expert' on South African affairs and acquire tenure at another of the country's research institutions.

Deciding to investigate the matter in person, I made my way to the offices of the *Fellesrådet*. There I found the young director sitting cowered over his desk – as if he feared a physical assault. He had no answer to give when I demanded to know why I was being blacklisted by the likes of him. Getting no answer, I turned my back on the figure on the chair, and on an organisation that I now had difficulty relating to. But it was with dismay that in subsequent years I would observe the heroic welcomes extended by officials of *Fellesrådet* – with their feet already on the first rungs of careers in the media and public life – to SWAPO officials on visits to Oslo. I once had an opportunity to charge both SWAPO and their claqueurs in the Norwegian Youth Council with the fratricide they were covering up. The Council's secretary, a cub journalist, entered a gathering with Moses Garoeb on her arm, the latter uttering a sotto voce smirk 'what are these people doing here' – with reference to myself and three of the recently released SWAPO youth leaguers. And I was at a loss for words.

From friends of long standing, I heard that even persons in the Lutheran Church, with whom I was hardly acquainted, had for some reason felt the need to put distance between themselves and me. The first instance concerned a trained theologian who got the good people of the town of Elverum to sponsor a Namibia Association with the aim of supporting SWAPO. The Association acquired a stately old timber cottage as its headquarters where visitors were received. The SWAPO junta, with Nujoma in the lead, were invited to be feted there as heroes. No clearer message could have been sent to the slayers of their brethren that they need fear no opprobrium from the Norwegian 'solidarity movement'.

Then I heard about having been 'rejected' – *slått hånda av*, was the Norwegian expression – by an official of the church who had been entrusted with disbursing government funds to the liberation movements. This was news to me, as I had been unaware of being the beneficiary of either the man's prayers or of any other favours that it was in his power to bestow on the needy.

THE SWISS SOLIDARITY MOVEMENT

Esmé Shipanga sent me a copy of a letter she had received from Geneva. It was dated 20 December 1976 and signed by Paul Rutishauser and Conrad Gerber, respectively president and vice-president of the Swiss Anti-Apartheid Movement. It was addressed to Sam Nujoma and the Central Committee of SWAPO – to protest the treatment of SWAPO members and in particular of Andreas Shipanga. This was the only similar protest from any so-called solidarity movement that I have seen. They wrote:

'We do not know all those who were arrested. However, Andreas Shipanga was very well known to us because of the information work he carried out for many years, especially in Europe. In Switzerland, contact with him was very useful to us in order to publicise the struggle of the Namibian people and the role of SWAPO. In all that he did, Andreas Shipanga showed remarkable determination and political aptitude, proofs of a total commitment to his people. It therefore appears utterly impossible to us that the accusation of 'high' treason is founded.

'No new inquiry can take place in the absence of the main accused. Accordingly, we ask you to rescind your decision and authorise the return [from Tanzania] of Andreas Shipanga and the other accused.

'Should a trial take place, we would request you to allow us to send an observer. In effect, as a movement in solidarity with the Namibian people, it is important for us to be able to testify to the exercise of perfect democracy within SWAPO at a moment when many people in Europe are beginning to question us. The fact that the trial would be held by a military court and that information relating to the efforts by the South African police to infiltrate within SWAPO could be revealed, should not prohibit the presence of a foreign observer, since this observer would be closely associated to a movement that has been engaged alongside the Namibian people for many years.

'As we suggested at the beginning of our letter, the opening of a new inquiry would probably permit the question to be resolved in favour of the unity of SWAPO. This would also help all the friends of the Namibian people to enlarge their solidarity at a moment when the South African government's manoeuvres, enforced by imperialism, are becoming more and more insidious.

For the independence of Namibia!

For the unity of the Namibian people.'

THANK YOU AND GOODBYE

The Swapo response to this letter was dated 10 January 1977. It reads in part:

'In the first place, I wish to make it very clear to your group that the leadership of SWAPO takes very strong exception to both the content and tone of your letter. We consider it an effront to our integrity for your group to tell us how well you "know Shipanga" his "determination and total commitment to his people," and that it is "utterly impossible" for your group to believe that he could commit high treason. You have, furthermore, considered it proper to tell us that it was only "a situation of confusion" which led to the leadership of SWAPO to make "unbelievable accusation" against the man whose "total commitment to his people" you know so well.

'In our view, these are chauvinistic demands set out to dictate to us how SWAPO should be run. They are reprehensive demands whose paternalism cannot be mitigated by any past support or assistance your group might have given to SWAPO.

'For your group, the plot which Shipanga and his co-conspirators organised within our movement is probably a matter of academic concern. Your academic and legalistic concern in the matter is made clear by your other demand for the opening of a new inquiry to which you should be invited in order to "testify to the exercise of perfect democracy within SWAPO". This too, is a reprehensive demand, asking us to divert our attention from the urgent and burning problems of the liberation struggle of our people in order to indulge in legalistic arguments so as to prove to your group the "exercise of perfect democracy within SWAPO".'

Over the signature of Sam Nujoma, (Moses Garoeb) nevertheless felt it necessary to set out allegations about Shipanga, with the assertion that 'there is, in fact, no problem of disunity within SWAPO. The overwhelming majority of our cadres are carrying on with the liberation activity. A small clique of counter-revolutionaries is naturally being contained so that the liberation activity is not interfered with unnecessarily.'

STILL NEW YORK, BUT A DIFFERENT UN

To persuade me to take a heroic jump into the unknown in 1959, Al Lowenstein had claimed that the apartheid regime would remain in power through its monopoly on opinion about South Africa. What I found abroad was a host of people who had made up their minds that apartheid had to be fought for the suffering it caused their fellow human beings. Everywhere they stood ready to lend refugees from the oppressive regime support in furthering their cause. An informal alliance – a worldwide Anti-Apartheid Movement – arose between refugees and these resident peoples.

One of the more engaging supporters of our case with whom I had become acquainted in the early seventies was the Welshman Peter Jones. During a visit he paid Edel and me in Ski, he regaled us with an enthusiastic account of the flowering of nationalist movements in Scotland and Wales. He was particularly proud of the regeneration of the Welsh language. Like most political activists he had a vast network of contacts, so it didn't surprise me to receive a letter from Peter dated 1 October 1976 that had been posted in the New Zealand city of Auckland. He had heard from Jörgen Leistner that I was safe in Norway, but had been confused by the imprisonment of party members:

'So you could perhaps put forward suggestions about how we could support you in persuading SWAPO's leadership to cut out the hard-handed treatment of those who disagree with the current party line, etc. I accept that it is an internal SWAPO matter, but feel unwell at the way one of the parties treat the opposition. That doesn't bode well for a Namibia of the future under SWAPO's leadership. I should also have liked to know where bishops Winter and Wood stand in the matter. I got hold of a press communiqué from SWAPO in which it is stated that the dissidents were supported by South Africa, etc. This I thought was a good example of George Orwell's 'Newspeak' – after I got to know that you, Andreas and priest Ailonga were among the dissidents.'

This letter inspired me to travel to New York to confront Theo-Ben Gurirab with the consequences of the coup that he had orchestrated in Lusaka, and to protest the inactivity of the UN diplomats who were rewarded with money and status for exercising the international community's authority in regard to the people of Namibia. In a letter to Esmé Shipanga, I explained my motives and asked for financial support.

'As I mentioned to you, I have ordered an air-ticket to New York for 21 November. My intention is to take up the matter concerning the arrest and continued detention of Andreas Shipanga, Solomon Mifima and the around 1 000 SWAPO members at the different UN institutions. In my view, Namibia is a UN-territory wherefore Namibians ought to be able to count on the UN for the protection of their right to a decent life and other rights – such as individuals can normally count on from their national authorities.

I do this in consultation with Ailonga, who is in Finland with a passport that had expired and who cannot therefore travel anywhere. I have asked for support for the flight from all sorts of agencies in Norway and abroad (including the Lutheran World Federation). But it seems that the matter is of such a kind that no one wants to provide any support. The name of the game is 'play safe'.

As you know, I have had to travel forwards and backwards to Oslo where my family lives. This comes in addition to having to finance my sojourn here in London, which has drained most of the resources Edel and I command. The flight to New York with a week's sojourn there comes to about £350.

Any support you might be able to get from good friends would be of great help. It would, however, have to be given under the full understanding that the left hand doesn't know what the right hand does.'

A COUPLE of days before I was to board the flight to New York, I came across a copy of *Counter Spy*, an American publication specializing in the nefarious activities of the CIA. The issue of 31 October 1976 published details of a 'confidential UN-memorandum' that had 'unmasked a covert American action against Namibia'.

The article claimed that the CIA, in cahoots with their South African counterpart BOSS, was involved in a campaign to strengthen the apartheid regime's grip on Namibia. The campaign aimed at weakening SWAPO's leadership, Angolan support for SWAPO, SWAPO in Zambia, the UN Commissioner for Namibia and SWAPO's internal wing in Namibia and to build support for a Kapuuo-Mudge transitional government.

It was obvious to me that the article was intended to portray the SWAPO junta as victim by violating reality: neither South Africa nor the US had put forward demands for Zambia and Tanzania to release the imprisoned Namibians. In my view, this would have been the only way in which the junta could be weakened. Further, the Soviet Union and Cuba would have been better placed than the American CIA or the South African BOSS to exert any influence on Angola.

The notion that SWAPO in Zambia could be further weakened was meaningless. That had already been done the year before when Zambia's Kenneth Kaunda met with South Africa's John Vorster. What remained of interest in the *Counter Spy* article was the claim that Sean MacBride was being targetted for a rough ride. But even the suggestion concerning a weakening of the UN Commissioner for Namibia lacked veracity. In a letter dated 27 October from Helsinki, Anita Ailonga had written me to say that a well-informed Finn had told her: '*It is now confirmed that MacBride will step down and the name of Finland's ambassador in Tanzania, Martti Ahtisaari, is being put forward.*' '*This is good*', was her comment, '*since he knows the truth. And we will continue to inform him when he arrives here.*' (My emphasis.)

Although the article's claims were totally without foundation, that it was circulated made it clear to me what sort of reception I could expect if I were to knock on some of the doors I had in mind. I nevertheless decided to carry on, so as to form a personal opinion about the situation in New York. Besides that, I wanted to confront Theo-Ben Gurirab.

THEO-BEN GURIRAB

I have afterwards had some difficulty recollecting what I had actually believed I could achieve by confronting Theo-Ben, the man who had orchestrated the coup that would prove so catastrophic for our people.

Memories streamed through me as I was on my way to the skyscraper situated at the corner of New York's 3rd Street and 42nd Avenue, where the SWAPO offices were located. It was in this same building I had been welcomed seventeen years earlier by Mozambique's Eduardo Mondlane and the clergymen George Houser and Homer Jack of the American Committee on Africa.

In an office where one wall was fully covered by a detailed ordnance map of Namibia, and another taken up by a window, I greeted the man who watched me warily from where he sat behind his desk with his hands in his lap. Offering me a seat, Theo-Ben indicated the straight-backed office chair across the desk from him.

To lighten the mood I expressed my admiration of the map, asking whether he had already picked out a farm he wanted for himself. Noticing a half-smile on his face, I reminded him of our last meeting at the home of Andreas Shipanga in Lusaka, where I had briefed him on the situation I had encountered there. And then I expressed my dismay at what had happened to Gottlieb Nakaamboh.

Only now did Theo-Ben react. He dismissed my concern for a father of four who had been forced to dig his own grave before being hacked to death. In a phrase made famous by the disgraced US Vice-President, Spiro Agnew, he said, 'You are lily-livered, Hans. If we had not done what we had, I would not be sitting here and our president wouldn't be Sam Nujoma any longer.'

He went on to inform me that I hadn't actually been guilty of anything. My mistake was to have been associated with the wrong people.

Just then my nose started to bleed. This interruption gave me time to remind myself that I didn't want to antagonise the man, I wanted him to talk. With my nose still in my handkerchief I briefly mentioned the worries that had brought me to him, and asked what he would advise me to do.

Theo-Ben now gave me an account of what he had experienced during his visit to Lusaka: the party was facing the greatest threat to its existence. The Zambian government was complaining that the guerrillas had become a threat to their own security. He had participated in a meeting between the government and SWAPO. It was after that meeting that the party had requested the Zambians to arrest the 'troublemakers'. He had himself written the request. It was signed by Mishake Muyongo, who acted with full authority in Sam's absence. The expanded Executive Committee later reiterated the appeal to the government. He himself was convinced that if they hadn't acted Shipanga, and not Sam Nujoma, would be president and he, Theo-Ben, wouldn't be sitting where he was sitting. In this vein he came to the conclusion that none of the internees could be released, and that Shipanga would never trust him again.

His advice to me, Theo-Ben Gurirab informed me with overbearing mien, was to write a letter to SWAPO to ask for forgiveness so as to be reinstated as a member.

I was fairly stunned by this bland mixture of moralism and mendacity. Theo-Ben Gurirab's mention of Muyongo as the Caprivian's 'full authority', seemed to invest in him (Muyongo) the powers of life and death over the members of the political party he represented. His 'expanded Executive Committee' was a fiction in as much as the triumvirate wielding power had never before allowed the properly constituted Executive Committee, of which Solomon Mifima and Andreas Shipanga had been elected members, to function.

As both Theo-Ben and I knew, what his 'troublemakers' had been demanding was precisely the convening of a party congress so as to legitimise the exercise of power. To top it all: revealing self-pity, Theo-Ben appeared to be feeling a tinge of remorse at the damage his base act of betrayal had done to Andreas Shipanga's opinion of him. Otherwise he appeared to be quite pleased with himself. I let Theo-Ben enjoy the moment.

NAHAS ANGULA'S EXPLANATION

From the SWAPO office, I crossed over to the UN headquarters to look up Nahas Angula, who had been appointed to Sean MacBride's staff. It proved much easier to talk to Nahas than to Theo-Ben. But then he was occupying a diminutive hideaway behind a standard-sized UN desk in the tall building.

I reminded Nahas that when we had last seen each other, it had been under altogether different circumstances. He was running the party's educational programme for refugees in the bush outside Lusaka. Now he stood with his feet on the first rung of the steps leading upwards in the mighty bureaucracy. This brought a smile to his face and the reply that the salary could have been better.

I now expressed my sadness at the consequences of what they had done in Zambia. To my surprise, Nahas came out with the second admission of guilt I would hear within an hour that day. He said, 'We were facing a mutiny, and had to do something to prevent things from getting altogether out of control.'

Quite unconsciously Nahas Angula thus revealed the class formation that had taken root among Namibians abroad: a cabal of hand-picked executors of their masters' will, lording it over foot soldiers, whose task was not to question why but to do or die.

Astounding as was the insight I acquired that afternoon into the mentality of the men who had assumed charge of the party I had joined, I couldn't quite take them seriously. That was also the reason why I failed to fully grasp the implied threat to the lives of the concentration camp prisoners when Theo-Ben Gurirab had said that none of them could be released.

ANNE-MARIE STOKES

New York is a city one doesn't leave without indelible memories. While I was walking along a quiet street behind Grand Central Station one morning, I caught sight of a familiar figure, that of Mrs Anne-Marie Stokes. She was walking with a little more difficulty than she had seventeen years earlier, when she often dropped by the UN office for NGO's. Laden down with groceries, she didn't protest when I proffered a helping hand, and invited me to join her for tea in her penthouse situated on a nearby hotel's top floor. A French noblewoman, Anne-Marie Stokes had been married to an American but remained French, as far as I could judge.

When I asked if she had visited France in the intervening years, she got up and rummaged through a drawer to find a postcard that she handed to me.

It showed a stately building in France to which she had been entitled. A couple of American advocates had intervened on her brother's behalf, she explained, to deprive her of her inheritance. And then she turned away from that subject to ask what had brought me to New York.

Anne-Marie Stokes had been an engaged witness to the many years of Michael Scott's pleading the case of South West Africa before the UN. Then she became concerned about the treatment of Puerto Rican immigrants in New York. Now she listened with great patience to the story that I had to tell. When I finished she said, with a smile, 'You know, Hans, a French philosopher has said: we own the world, but our desires dispossess us'.

The comment stunned me. I became uncertain as to what she was conveying to me: was it an expression of sympathy, or an admonition – that I needed to examine my own motives? It didn't occur to me that in her countryman's wisdom, Mrs Stokes might have found comfort for the pain that she herself had suffered at the hands of her brother – who had been supported by lawyer 'friends' from New York.

NORWEGIAN GOVERNMENT 'SUPPORTS SWAPO'

My visit to New York had persuaded me that there was no more I could do to bring about the release of my countrymen in Tanzania and Zambia. What had made it possible for me to pursue the thankless task was Edel's income and the exhaustion of our meagre savings. I now got down to searching for a job, sending out applications by the dozen for months on end – to no avail. To keep some contact with the outside world, I sought and was granted permission to occupy office space at the Institute of Peace Research with which I had been associated some years before.

During this time the person who seemed to sense my needs was Dr Milton Leitenberg, with whom I had become acquainted during my earlier association with the institute. Now resident in Stockholm, where he was associated with SIPRI, the Swedish Institute of Peace Research, Milton kept sending me most valuable documentation for keeping abreast of developments in southern Africa. Even after returning to the University of Maryland, he generously kept this up.

Acquaintance with Milton, and with Dr Marek Thee, an ex-Polish diplomat and himself a refugee who was also associated with PRIO, provided that moral support without which refugees – whose ranks I could no longer deny having joined – are wont to sink into despondency. Marek Thee untiringly edited a *Bulletin of Peace Proposals*, that was published by PRIO.

A LITTLE more than a year went by before I finally received a call from a school in need of a teacher. It was the Tønsberg Handelsgymnasium – Business High School – and located on the opposite side of the Oslo fjord. Most considerately they reduced my attendance to four days, which allowed me to spend three days at home each week.

During this time the BBC's shortwave news bulletins were our daily source of information about events on the African continent. As Edel and I sat down at our kitchen table on the morning of 1 May 1978, it broadcast an item that made us lose interest in breakfast. With the voice of an Australian correspondent, the BBC reported the arrival in Nairobi of four Namibians who had escaped the concentration camp at Mboroma in Zambia. They told the press of comrades who had been killed, about others who had died of hunger and of the dangers they had to overcome to reach Nairobi to call for help. Even as I shrunk inwardly at having failed to plead their cause more aggressively, I decided to follow up on my reminder to the Norwegian Government that the young people in the prison camps were entitled to international protection.

The Foreign Minister was out of the country, but his deputy, Thorvald Stoltenberg, would be attending a Workers' Day ball at *Folkets Hus* (The People's House) that evening. I had first met Stoltenberg some years earlier, while showing a SWAPO representative the way to the headquarters of the Norwegian Federation of Labour Organisations, where he headed the office for international cooperation. I had been impressed by his apparent grasp of the situation in southern Africa.

When I arrived at *Folkets Hus* at 8 pm that evening, the Deputy Foreign Minister was swinging a partner in a lively dance on the floor. When the dance ended I observed the couple finding a seat for a rest on a bench running alongside a wall. Equality being a cornerstone of Norwegian society, I felt no hesitation about approaching them and settling down next to him. I told Mr Stoltenberg that I had something urgent I wanted to talk to him about – at his office. Without questioning what it might be about, he replied that he would be available the next morning at ten, if I could make it. With that I left and took the next train back home.

Two other persons were present at my meeting with the Deputy Foreign Minister, his own secretary, and Leonard Larsen, Foreign Minister Frydenlund's personal secretary. I knew Larsen: we had taken a course together at the university. Mr Stoltenberg listened with friendly interest to the anxiety I expressed about the threat to Namibia's future should the issue of the so-called dissidents remain unresolved. He even seemed to agree with me. Yet, as I left the office, I began to feel doubt that anything would come of my urgent plea.

As the two secretaries accompanied me towards the entrance I turned and addressed Leonard Larsen. 'Leo', I said, 'why do I have the feeling that what I'm telling you is not being taken seriously? Have I ever made any statement about the situation in my part of the world that was not truthful?'

Looking me straight in the eye, Leo replied that they had no reason to doubt what I had told them. But, he declared, 'We support SWAPO!'

I was not quite prepared for the implication of such a message, from which I inferred that I had become an irritant in the Norwegian government's relations with the Nujoma junta. Leo's pointed rebuff reminded me that whatever they were, Norway's national interests were what counted – regardless of the cost to Namibians. This left me wondering what sort of investments in Namibia's future the Norwegians had made, with the SWAPO junta as the recipients of whatever *quid pro quo* was thought fitting.

With anger consuming me I boarded the train back to Ski – and to the nadir of my sojourn in the country that had offered me asylum.

MBOROMA EMBARRASSMENT FOR ZAMBIA

As expected, the BBC report on May Day had embarrassed the government of Zambia. From Øystein Opdal, an old acquaintance from my student days in Oslo who had served as the UNHCR's representative in Lusaka, I would eventually hear what had transpired that day. Within hours of the broadcast, the Zambian Justice Minister, Aaron Milner, knocked at Opdal's door with a request for money to buy a supply of food for the Namibian prisoners. Until that moment, the Zambians had denied their existence. Opdal replied that he would be pleased to write out a cheque, if Milner would only, in keeping with routine, send him the request in writing. He waited in vain for such a letter to arrive that day.

On 2 May, Opdal left Lusaka for a tour of the Copperbelt. Halfway between Lusaka and Kabwe, he stopped for a long column of trucks loaded with people that was headed in the opposite direction. It turned out to be ex-Mboroma prisoners who, he was informed, had decided 'to return to SWAPO'. They were being transported to Nyango, the organisation's refugee camp in West Zambia. This was the camp that I had visited in company with Shipanga and Ailonga. It was out of bounds to international refugee agencies.

Opdal also learned that two hundred other prisoners had spurned the invitation to return to the fold of the organisation that had ordered their imprisonment. Instead, they had chosen refugee status, which made them the concern of the UNHCR.

SWAPO-D

When, for lack of any credible evidence against them, the Supreme Court of Zambia finally came around to ordering the release of Andreas Shipanga and his companions, Kenneth Kaunda lost a chance to defend the Rule of Law in the country over whose affairs, and reputation, he was presiding. Collaborating with Tanzania's Julius Nyerere, that other icon of the 'liberation struggle', Kaunda let the prisoners be flown to Tanzania. There they were informed by the country's Home Affairs Minister that they would be imprisoned for a breach of the public order under Tanzania's Anti-riot Act.

To prevent concerted strikes by the prisoners they were then spread to prisons throughout the country, to begin a daily struggle for survival under conditions that took the lives of less hardy locals. However, as expected, the BBC's Labour Day report about the fate of the prisoners held in a Zambian concentration camp had its effect even in Dar-es-Salaam. In late May I received an unexpected call from the Norwegian Refugee Council with the news that three Nordic countries – Norway, Sweden and Finland – had offered asylum to the prisoners newly released in Tanzania. They requested that Edel and I house Ndeshimona Uyumba, the only woman among the group of eleven.

I immediately called Otillie Abrahams in Stockholm where she and her husband had been granted asylum after fleeing from Namibia in 1963. In Cape Town the couple had been active in establishing SWAPO, but had become involved in conflict with the Nujoma phalanx on their arrival in Dar-es-Salaam from Botswana. I was now hoping that they would extend a helping hand to the prisoners who would be arriving in Stockholm. Until that moment I was not aware that they still nurtured a proprietary interest in the party that they had supported in its infancy. With the impending release of their old comrade, Andreas Shipanga, Otillie made no secret of the fact that they saw a chance of making a reappearance on the liberation-struggle stage. The very next day she called again, this time to inform me that I had become a member of a new party.

'New party?'

'Yes,' she replied. 'It is called SWAPO-D. D for democrats,' she warbled excitedly. *D for disaster*, I thought, and decided that SWAPO-D was one bus I wasn't going to take. Otillie now also in passing informed me that her sister Norah, also a political activist, was living in Tanzania. From this I gathered that SWAPO-D must have been conceived in discussions with Shipanga while he was still sitting in jail, or immediately after his release while still in Dar es Salaam.

To find out what was afoot, I told Otillie that I thought the plan for a

SWAPO-D sounded exciting, but that I needed to see the constitution, etc. of the party that I had become a member of. The papers would be sent to me, she answered, adding that they were planning on holding a press conference at Stockholm's Airport when the plane with the prisoners aboard landed.

With my heart sinking deeper at the prospect, I asked Otillie what the press conference would be for. It would be to give the prisoners a chance to tell the world what they had suffered at SWAPO's hands, she replied.

As I could see no good coming out of an emotional outburst that was not informed by a clear objective, particularly where so much was at stake for all of us, this information worried me. Hoping that the Swedes would do something to prevent the refugees from being exposed to a welcoming committee, I wrote Andreas Shipanga a letter, care of Esmé in London, in which I expressed my fears. I suggested that what needed to be done was first to bring the Nujoma junta to account, and 'to find the basis for reconciliation between the rank and file and leadership'.

With the US Secretary of State Henry Kissinger's manoeuvres in mind, I expressed the opinion that his, Shipanga's, arrest and detention had been 'the result of a CIA-inspired coup in the party, executed by Theo-Ben Gurirab, Hage Geingob, Hidipo Hamutenya and others. The intention had been to eliminate the 'radicals, the hawks, the Marxists' etc. before delivering Namibia, like Zimbabwe, to the 'moderate Blacks'. But the Soviet Union had seen through the scheme and decided to strengthen rather than weaken Sam Nujoma. The price for the Soviet support was that more pro-Soviet cadres were to be given top jobs in the leadership. I pointed out that the days were gone when one could speak of SWAPO as an independent party or political force. 'At the top there are men who depend for their survival on the commitment to their persons of either the CIA or the KGB.'

I questioned the Abrahams' plan for a SWAPO-D joining up with a group called the NNF to form a so-called third force in Namibian politics – on the reasoning that SWAPO would poll 40 per cent at an election, the Democratic Turnhalle Alliance another 40, which would enable the NNF to decide the colour of the new Government in Namibia with its expected 20 per cent of the vote.

The evening after the prisoners landed in Stockholm, Otillie called me again. This time it was to voice her anger and frustration at what had happened at Arlanda. The moment the plane came to a stop outside the terminal building a mini-van had rolled up, whereupon Keeshipelao Nathanael and Martin Taneni, the two Namibians aboard, were transferred to it. The welcoming committee hadn't even had a chance to say hello to them before they were whisked away to the reception centre for refugees in mid-Sweden.

Inwardly I thanked the Swedes for having saved the day for us. To Otillie I expressed sympathy about what they had experienced.

There was no such drama when the plane carrying Andreas Nuukwao, Ndeshi Uyumba and Sheeli Shangula landed at Fornebu Airport in Oslo. What was surprising was the presence of two other prisoners that had been released along with them: a man from Zimbabwe and Philemon Nangoloh, known by his *nom de guerre* of 'Castro'. In due time I would learn that he had been the sole survivor among the first group of SWAPO guerrillas sent into Namibia from Zambia, and that he had been imprisoned in Tanzania at the request of Sam Nujoma, on charges of treason, which he disputed. In turn, he wanted to know why Sam, their 'supreme commander', who had gone to Windhoek at the time when they were crossing the border, had been returned to Lusaka without being charged.

Andreas Shipanga was flown to London, where Esmé was waiting to welcome him. The other prominent prisoners, Solomon Mifima, Jimmy Ampala, Emmanuel Engombe and Philip-Haukonjo, were sent to a refugee camp in Greece.

A week or so after the arrival of the three Namibians in Oslo, the Abrahamses summoned us all to a meeting at their home in Stockholm for what would be the launching of SWAPO-D. I had already informed the others of my misgivings, but I welcomed the opportunity this meeting would provide for a discussion of where we stood. With the others' concurrence, the four of us set off for Stockholm in my little Saab. En route we stopped at the refugee centre in the village of Fläm, to pick up Keshii. There we found the ex-president of the SWAPO Youth League seething with anger at an encounter he had had with Kenny Abrahams. We heard that the good doctor had come to look them up with a ready-made proposal for a break-away party. I understood that Kenny had evidently overlooked the fact that he had come to see a wounded political animal, one in great need of clarification and self-assertion, and one not to be taken for granted. Keshii declined the invitation to join us on the way to Stockholm.

At the Abrahams residence, I was surprised to find Jariretundu Kozonguizi, who had come all the way from Windhoek, in addition to Andreas Shipanga, who had flown in from London. But far from being welcomed, the reception I received could not have been colder. Otillie accused me of having tried to turn the 'youth' against them; Andreas held nothing back in speaking of his displeasure at finding me there. As this was so uncharacteristic of the man I knew, I felt an immense pity for him. Here was a man who had dedicated his life to the cause of our liberation. With his deep voice, his wisdom and hearty laughter he had won us friends wherever he went; resisting the temptation to avail himself of funds destined for his people he had, nonetheless, defended his colleagues for the good of the party. Yet, bent on destroying him, they had blocked his path with a vengeance when he was about to secure an appointment in Geneva that would have enabled him to withdraw from the fray without doing damage to the party.

However, thus challenged, I simply expressed the opinion that the conflict with the Nujoma crowd called for an entirely different approach than simply trying to steal the name of SWAPO. To my passengers I stated that when their deliberations were done, they had a number in Stockholm where they could call me. Thereupon I left the meeting to spend the evening at the flat of an acquaintance in the city. On the way out, Kozo, with whom I had looked forward to chat, called me aside to let me know that there was reason to be concerned about the situation of my sister Martha Ford in Angola.

The three 'youth leaguers' Ndeshimona Uyumba, Sheeli Shangula and Andreas Nuukwao, called sooner than I had expected, with the request that I come to pick them up. I learned that they had not been happy with the way things were being handled at the meeting. The drive back to Oslo took place largely in silence.

A day or two later I received a call from Charles Kauraisa, a Windhoeker with a doctorate in political science from the University of Stockholm and friend of the Abrahamses. I could hardly remember ever being called by Charles, and his willingness to communicate surprised me greatly. What he had to tell made me realise that the SWAPO-D project had been much more advanced than I had been informed by Otillie Abrahams. Kozo had arrived in company with a Windhoek banker by the name of Fitzgerald. This suggested that SWAPO-D would be bankrolled once it had been registered. Charles had cautioned Otillie about sidelining me, whom he regarded as a 'favourite son' in Rehoboth. This had met with her derision. I had of course no way of knowing whether Otillie was dismissive about my potential merits as a tribal politician, or whether she still harboured the hard feelings she had vented about my father in a letter to me from Botswana years earlier. What I didn't tell Charles was that to me, regardless for what reason, Otillie had a point. SWAPO-D was a bus on which I had no intention of travelling.

Soon afterwards there arrived a letter from the group in Greece to inquire about asylum in Norway, and to authorise me to represent them in meetings with Shipanga and the others. In response I informed them of the break that I had been compelled to make with Andreas Shipanga, 'who had launched himself as the president of an organisation called SWAPO-D, while Otillie Abrahams had tried to make out that I was a SWAPO agent.'

I heard from Solomon Mifima only once again. It was to express his group's disappointment at the frustration of their 'hopes for a start-off towards something that, for the past two years, has been craving in our minds that may tangibly contribute in putting the wheel again in motion towards a genuine independence for Namibia.'

Together with his companions, except Jimmy Ampala, Mifima returned home to Namibia as a member of SWAPO-D, where he soon afterwards died. Andreas Shipanga joined the Turnhalle Alliance and was appointed its government's Minister of Environmental Affairs.

CHAPTER TWELVE

Countdown to regime change

NAMIBIA – A PAWN ON A BIG POWER CHESS BOARD

Exiled and estranged from the movement of which I had been a part, I became a distant observer – often with a time lag and through others' eyes and ears – of the tug-of-war about Namibia's future. Contacts made through the years nevertheless from time to time supplied me with documentation about what had become the 'passing show', or, rather, a charade where what could be presented as 'a relatively straightforward question of self-government (became) overlaid with an incredibly complex array of false solutions' – as it was characterised by Mrs Elizabeth S Landis. In a report 'designed to penetrate the tangle' she analysed five-and-a-half years of 'delicate negotiations managed by South Africa's five Western allies.' They were negotiations that dealt in proposals for 'so-called solutions that (became) part of the problem.'[47]

The fears behind those manoeuvres became manifest when the US Secretary of State, Henry Kissinger, in 1976 began an unprecedented series of diplomatic forays into Africa – to build up an alliance of so-called moderate states, i.e. states headed by declared anti-communist, ipso facto pro-Western, leaders. This meant that regimes and political movements matching the description, or merely declaring intent, need not fear too close a scrutiny of their track records – for their palms to be greased. For 'anti-communist' Kenneth Kaunda to accede to the request from Theo-Ben Gurirab, fresh from New York, to imprison 'troublemaking and radical' Namibians, was as clear a declaration of intent as could be desired.

What had clearly set off the alarm bells in Western capitals was the coup, staged by a group of revolutionary Portuguese military officers on 25 April 1974. By all accounts it heralded the break-up of the Portuguese colonial empire in Africa – enabling Guinea-Bissau, Mozambique, Cape Verde Islands, Sao Tome and Principe, and Angola to shrug off 500 years of subjugation.

With its role as a colonial power in Africa having become impossible to maintain, the enfeebled Portuguese regime – NATO's guardian of its southern

---

47 Namibian Liberation – Self-determination, Law and Politics. Episcopal Churchmen for South Africa. New York, 1982.

flank in the Cold War – set a date in November 1975 for relinquishing its control of Angola. This in turn meant that South Africa – and with it 'the White man's' control of most of the continent's natural resources – would lose its buffers and become directly exposed to uncontrolled 'winds of change'. This made it imperative to find collaborators among the 'liberation movements' contending for supremacy in the soon to become independent colonies. In Angola there were three: UNITA, led by Jonas Savimbi, the FNLA, led by Roberto Holden and the MPLA, with Aghostino Neto at its helm. In Mozambique Eduardo Mondlane's FRELIMO, now headed by Samora Machel, appeared to be unchallenged in its race to displace its colonist administration.

Fred Bridgeland, the first journalist to reveal the presence of South African military officers at Savimbi's headquarters, told me how the resourceful leader of his people became bounden to an alliance with the SADF. 'If you cannot swim,' Savimbi had responded when Bridgeland mentioned the political risks he was taking by accepting the support of the South Africans, 'and you fall into a raging river, you don't ask whose hand it is that grabs yours to pull you out.' With the MPLA receiving weapons and military advisors from the Soviet Union, the offer of help from Pretoria and, covertly, from the American CIA, clearly persuaded Savimbi that he could trump his adversaries in the struggle for control of Angola.

To forestall independent Mozambique from providing a safe haven for Zimbabweans seeking to overthrow his government Ian Smith, the Prime Minister of the rebel Crown Colony of Rhodesia and a redoubtable player in the field, backed a contending organisation named RENAMO. The resulting civil war would lay waste to large parts of the country.

For South Africa's policy-makers, the loss of its buffers and with the Soviet Union gaining influence in exchange for supplying weapons to the guerrilla movements, meant that the bogey of 'a total Marxist onslaught' against the apartheid regime had become a marketable argument. This meant that notwithstanding its international status – affirmed and reaffirmed by the UN in a slew of resolutions, and fixed in law by the ICJ, in a reversal of its notorious decision of 1966[48] – South West Africa/Namibia was to be pressed into serving as the replacement buffer state for Angola.

---

[48] Mrs Landis points out that the Court's Advisory Opinion of 1971 about the Legal Consequences of the Continued Presence of South Africa in Namibia (South West Africa) notwithstanding Security Council Resolution 276 (1970), contained two propositions new to international law: (i) that Article 25 of the UN Charter made the Security Council resolutions on Namibia binding on UN members even though they were not taken under Chapter VII; and (ii) that apartheid was, on the public record and without considering any other evidence, a flagrant violation of the purposes and principles of the Charter – this latter argument in effect adopting the position taken by Ethiopia and Liberia in the South West Africa Cases a decade before. (Landis, op.cit. p4)

Given its *de facto* replacement of Portugal as NATO's southern flank in the Cold War, it was a course that South Africa could pursue with impunity. Thus, as Mrs Landis continues:

'After establishing the constituent assembly (Turnhalle) in early 1979, South Africa was suddenly ready to negotiate again, but it began to insist on the representation of the new assembly in the process – a direct challenge to, inter alia, General Assembly resolution 2145, the World Court Opinion of 1971 and Security Council resolution 439.

'From that time forward, the course of negotiations was up and down like a roller coaster path: The negotiations flourished whenever the General Assembly or the Security Council was about to meet on Namibia – leading the Contact Group to try to suppress the discussion completely or at least to tone it down, so that nothing would interfere with the "delicate negotiations" just getting under way.

'Then they would collapse when that danger to South Africa passed, only to rise once more when the subject came before another international forum. Every time that an accommodation was reached on one issue – usually at SWAPOs expense – a new South African objection appeared.'[49]

Regarding the 'roadblock' – the presence of Cuban troops in Angola – that would stall for a decade progress towards independence for Namibia, Mrs Landis states, '(T)he evidence is strong that the South Africans took up this demand from the US government, which suffers from an irremediable Cubaphobia.' And she adds, 'Ridding Angola of Cubans is an ideological imperative as well as a necessity in the American overall world strategy. The Administration seems convinced that Cuban withdrawal would result in the creation of a stable, moderate southern Africa, a desideratum of present and past administrations.'

In 1976 the UN General Assembly – 'dismayed at the three Western Permanent Members of the Security Council's veto of an arms embargo against South Africa, to try to compel it to leave Namibia' – '*voted to endorse the Namibians' armed struggle to free their country, for whose administration the Assembly was responsible.*'[50] (My emphasis.)

Thus did the representatives of the 'international community', assembled in New York, mock Woodrow Wilson's motivation for the mandates system and disregard the very *raison d'être* of the UN itself – *to save succeeding generations from the scourge of war.* (My emphasis.) Their votes justified tribesmen from the most isolated parts of the giant Territory to be thrown against the most redoubtable military

---

[49] Landis, op cit. P8-9.
[50] Landis, citing A/RES/31/146, para 3 (1976)).

force on the African continent, one that, in addition, could draw on the resources of a modern industrial state. Adding insult to injury they recognised SWAPO as 'the sole and authentic representatives of the Namibian people' and granted them observer status at the UN (A/Res/31/152). This imbued the less than half a dozen self-elected individuals, representing no one else but themselves, with the powers of a government-in-exile in all but name – of a territory housing the most diverse population groups.

UNSC RESOLUTION 435

I was present in the chamber when the Security Council passed Resolution 435 – with reference to the guerrilla organisation's preparedness to abide by its terms. What depressed me was the implication that a militarised SWAPO appeared to be considered as standing any chance in Namibia.

The explanation was nevertheless clear. Following up on Henry Kissinger's efforts to undo the foothold that the Soviet Union and Cuba had established in Angola, the 'Western big five' had evidently begun what could only be termed a courting, if humouring were not a more fitting term, of the SWAPO junta.

Fragments of a document that came my way some time after the events threw light on the 'negotiations' between five Western powers and SWAPO that preceded the adoption of Resolution 435. Dated February 1978 and marked confidential, the document contained proposals submitted to the Nujoma junta.

The proposals cited SCR 385 (1976) that called on South Africa to permit all Namibians abroad to return to participate fully and freely in elections without risk of being arrested, hindered or intimidated. Significantly, no mention was made of the prisoners held by SWAPO in camps in Zambia and in prisons in Tanzania.

Nevertheless, in a response dated 10 February 1978, the SWAPO junta expressed willingness to consider, as '*a demonstration of goodwill*', the release of the eleven '*contra-revolutionaries and enemy agents who had committed criminal acts against the Namibian liberation struggle*'. (My emphasis.) About the thousand plus in concentration camps in Zambia they made no mention.

Yet they demanded the release of all Namibian political prisoners held in South Africa's custody.

A WAR OF ATTRITION JOINED

On 25 April 1978 South Africa signed the Western proposals that required both SWAPO and the Republic to cooperate with the UN Secretary General in the implementation. The apartheid regime thus appeared to finally have accepted the right of the diverse peoples of the mandated territory, whose fates had been merged by colonialism, to deliberate about their common future. However, seen in the light of its moves almost immediately afterwards, it appeared South Africa was merely paying lip service to a principle that it clearly calculated on twisting to its own advantage – in collusion with the USA. Thus on 4 May 1978, a mere nine days after South Africa had signed acceptance of Resolution 435 (25 April) the SADF launched a most destructive attack on two SWAPO bases in Angola. And when a so-called contact group, representing the top foreign affairs officials of the five Western powers arrived to discuss procedures for the transition of power in Namibia, Pretoria demanded that implementation of Resolution 435 be made conditional upon the withdrawal of Cuban forces from Angola.

General Magnus Malan was the officer in charge of the Namibia section of the SADF from the early sixties onwards, subsequently head of the armed forces and eventually Minister of Defence. Making no mention of what there is reason to assume had been a ploy inspired by the US, he gives a self-congratulatory account of how the South African negotiators, comprising Foreign Minister Roelof (Pik) Botha, the Secretary (Senior Civil Servant) of Foreign Affairs and himself, had exploited the self-importance and lack of coordination of their adversaries to gain acceptance for the demand that compliance with Resolution 435 be made conditional upon the departure of Cuban forces from Angola.

This being acceded to by the Western powers, the Angolan-Namibian border region became the theatre for a war of attrition that would last another decade. And in Windhoek the government formed by the Democratic Turnhalle Alliance, the outcome of the Turnhalle Constitutional Conference, was secured tenure that lasted from its inception in 1977 to 1989.

In his autobiography, *My Lewe met die SA Weermag* (My life with the South African Defence Force), General Malan provides insight into the regime's *military* responses to the perceived threats. It is a triumphant account of the damage the SADF under his command had visited upon its adversaries – at a claimed fraction of the cost in terms of manpower and material. With reference to SWAPO's guerrillas, it catalogues their systematic and almost complete annihilation.

His step-up of the 'border war' began with Operation Savannah, the code name for the invasion of Angola in support of UNITA. Malan represents it as a military success that was aborted short of reaching the goal only when the US Congress pulled the rug from underneath the CIA's covert involvement. This should have left South Africa with the equivalent of a Vietnam on its hands as an occupying power. Moreover, despite the military prowess demonstrated, the operation had revealed the inferiority of South Africa's armoury to that of the modern weapons supplied by the Soviet Union to its clients in Angola. 'With our weaponry, a later encounter would most likely have meant the demise of the Defence Force', writes the general.[51] The subsequent failure of the combined Cuban and FAPLA (MPLA) force to pursue the SADF across the border into Namibia he ascribes to lack of intelligence about the parlous state of their opponent's true strength combined with fear of the fighting ability it had demonstrated in Operation Savannah. While keeping its enemies at bay for the next dozen years, the SADF modernised its armoury with domestically manufactured armaments, including the production of nuclear weapons.

MAGNUS MALAN – SOUTH AFRICA'S STRATEGIST

General Malan graduated from the US Command and General Staff College at Fort Leavenworth in Kansas – the premier US college for generals – presumably sent there to join the fraternity of the Western World's leading military men. In anticipation of the kind of threats that the liberation movements were likely to pose, he introduced Mao Zedong's theory of revolutionary warfare as an obligatory course of instruction for his officers; for hunting down foot-bound guerrillas in the sparsely vegetated Namibian veld he progressed from horses and helicopters to drones. '*Anticipating SWAPO's behaviour*', he wrote, '*we could prepare ourselves even before the shoe began to chafe*.' (My emphasis.)

One of the measures General Malan takes credit for – presumably having been inspired by the US Army's practice during World War II – was that, within the constraints set by legislation, under his command the SADF did what it could to ignore apartheid within its ranks. As reward, he states that servicemen recruited from all ethnic groups developed an *esprit de corps* where depending on and caring for one another on the battle field became the norm.

In contrast, for political reasons SWAPO's guerrilla army was recruited from mainly one ethnic group, and it spread fear even among the people it claimed to represent. As happened when in March and April 1977 Toivo Shiyagaya, the Minister of Health in the Ovambo Administration, and

---

[51] Page 143. My translation.

Chief Clemens Kapuuo of the Hereros, were assassinated. In Windhoek, in retaliation, Herero tribesmen set upon and killed Ovambos. Without giving absolute numbers, General Malan states that 95 per cent of the SWAPO fighters killed in action or taken prisoner, were Ovambos.

An incident involving Sam Nujoma would appear to suggest that the SADF regarded a military confrontation with SWAPO as not only inevitable, but desirable.

In 1966 Nujoma had himself and Lukas Pohamba flown to Windhoek from Lusaka on an errand that led to speculation about his purpose. Instead of being imprisoned, they were sent back to Lusaka. According to Malan, who was in charge of the SWA segment of the SADF at the time, it was established that Nujoma had hoped to 'embarrass the Administration and at the same time to encourage protest marches, civil commotion and violence against the authorities in South West Africa so as to draw the attention of the international community to SWAPO as a liberation movement'.

The plan was thwarted when the plane landed earlier than announced and Sam's 'welcoming committee' turned out to be Malan himself alongside the chief of the Territorial Police. The question as to what to do with the guerrilla leader was answered after four or five days of deliberation. Deciding the issue had been an 'evaluation by Military Intelligence of enemy targets, of which Nujoma was one'. According to Malan, '*One of the main reasons for (returning him on the same plane as he had arrived) was that intelligence sources were of the opinion that Nujoma would be more valuable to us if he remained with his own forces than if he were to be in our hands*'. (My emphasis.)

Given the circumstances it would appear that Nujoma had been 'evaluated' as incapable of appreciating what it would cost to take on an adversary with the resources at its command of the SADF, but, having demonstrated bravado, one likely to stay the course he had chosen, even if it meant the annihilation of the people under his command – which was clearly the SADF's intention.

BUTCHERS ACCOUNT

The list of occasions on which SWAPO bases in Angola were destroyed, killing a number of SWAPO warrior running into the thousands and maiming many more, starts with the assault of 4 May 1978 code-named Operation Reindeer. The targets were the bases known as *Cassinga* and *Chetequera*.

According to official Angolan statistics, the attack on the Cassinga base left 624 dead of which 167 were women and 298 children. One hundred and fifty Cuban soldiers, who were in the vicinity, also lost their lives. Malan, whose figures and comments I cite, mentions the loss of only one serviceman in a parachute accident. On the same day an attack on the base at Chetequera left 1 000 SWAPO combatants dead and 200 taken prisoner. Large amounts of weapons were taken as loot.

Operation Safraan – in response to a SWAPO attack launched from Zambian territory that had killed 10 servicemen and wounded another ten – is said to have practically eliminated insurgency in the Caprivi. No mention is made of the number of killed and maimed SWAPOs, but the toll must have been considerable.

Operation Sceptic, launched in June 1980, destroyed a SWAPO base in Angola. 'A very great quantity of enemy weapons, equipment, supplies and vehicles' was taken as booty. An estimated 400 SWAPOs killed – for the loss of 17 SADF 'heroes'.

Then followed a number of operations (Carnation, July 1981; Protea, August 1981; Daisy, October-November 1981; Super, May 1982; Meebos, July 1982; Phoenix, February 1983 and Askari, December 1983-January 1984) during which, 'without exception the Defence Force gave SWAPO's military wing, PLAN, a good hiding'

During Operation Carnation around 200 'terrorists' lost their lives. Operation Protea was aimed at destroying 'a great amount of heavy weapons and war material that had been amassed within a stone's throw of the border'. 'More than 1 000 SWAPO insurgents were killed and 3 000 – 4 000 tons of the most modern Soviet war material, including tanks, taken as booty.' A Soviet officer was one of the casualties and another was taken prisoner.

In Operation Phoenix the SADF in combination with the South West Africa Territorial Force encountered a PLAN force of 1 700 that had crossed the border. In the ensuing battle 309 SWAPOs lost their lives for 27 lost on the SADF side.

In addition to these large-scale operations, South African forces clandestinely stationed in Southern Angola are said to have hunted down and killed an unknown number of guerrillas.

General Malan refers to a South African initiative '*to bring the regional conflict to an end so as to ensure an internationally recognised independence for Namibia*'. (My emphasis.) This initiative led to intensive discussions in February 1984 with the participation of South Africa, the MPLA and the USA. The so-called Lusaka Agreement that was the outcome spawned a Joint Monitoring Commission between Angola and South Africa. Its task was to oversee the concurrent withdrawal of South African troops from certain areas held in

Angola, and the prevention of Cuban and SWAPO forces from moving in.

The initiative foundered on SWAPO's disregard of its terms. The Cubans and the Soviet Union bore the cost. General Malan puts the blame on SWAPO: 'On account of the greater involvement of Cubans and Russians in the border conflicts annually more Cubans died and the USSR lost increasing quantities of weapons. Every year the Soviet Union thus had to bring in more weaponry and the Cubans more troops. These replenishments were indispensable to keeping in check the growing UNITA attacks and the destructive actions of the Defence Force.'

The turning point in the decade-long war of attrition along the border was reached in 1988. A combined force of 50 000 – 60 000 Angolans, Cubans and East Germans, all under the command of Soviet generals, began a march towards the town of Jamba in south-east Angola, where South Africa's ally, UNITA's Jonas Savimbi, had his headquarters. The attacking force was armed with a vast array of the Soviet Union's most modern tanks, fighter and bomber aircraft, helicopters, radar and guns. Opposing them was a combined force of 3 000 South African servicemen and 8 000 UNITA troops.

The encounter lasted from six to eight months with the last battle fought on March 23 1988. Malan describes the campaign that culminated at the Lomba River as the most ferocious land battle on the African continent since El Alamein of the Second World War. While the casualties on the SADF side are said to have numbered only 31 – together with an unstated number of UNITA fighters – the loss to their enemies is estimated at between 7 000 and 10 000 casualties and a further many thousands of wounded.

General Malan ascribes the resounding victory to superior intelligence on the ground combined with superior military prowess. There is little reason to question his conclusion, especially when considering the subsequent political developments, not only in the region but globally:

'This remarkable success played a decisive role in the international change-of-course that took place in Africa. It also contributed to the fall of international communism in 1989,' Malan wrote.

What this came down to was that there no longer existed any state or groups of states on the African continent south of the equator, capable of, or likely to pose, a credible military threat to the apartheid regime. The mortal threat it continued to face was represented by the youth of its own country – who it had robbed of hope for a better future.

A DIPLOMATIC COUP DE GRÂCE

On 22 December 1988, at a sitting of the UN Security Council, the South African Foreign Minister, Roelof Botha, signed the so-called Tripartite Agreement between Angola, Cuba and South Africa. It committed his country to withdraw from Namibia – on the condition that Cuba withdrew its troops from Angola.[52]

The agreement was the outcome of an olive branch that Botha had held out to his Cuban counterpart, Jorge Risquet, during a break in negotiations chaired by the American Deputy Secretary of State, Chester Crocker, in Cairo on 24 June earlier that year. It followed upon an aggressive exchange that could have aborted the conference when Risquet threatened to send ten thousand fresh Cuban fighters to Angola, to which Botha reposted that he would then have to send another thousand South Africans.

Crocker called a hasty adjournment to prevent the negotiations from breaking down. During the interval, Botha conceded to Risquet that it would be unacceptable for President Fidel Castro to withdraw from Angola without an honourable exit, and suggesteded that the war could be brought to an end by allowing Castro to take credit for having brought about Namibia's independence. In turn he, Botha, could reassure South Africans that the feared Cubans had departed from Angola.

A Soviet diplomat, who had overheard the exchange in the venue's bar, persuaded the Cubans to go along with Botha's proposal.[53] The pugnacious Risquet was replaced with a more seasoned diplomat and Botha's proposal formed the basis for what would become the Tripartite Agreement.

In terms of the Agreement, Angola was to oversee the withdrawal from its border with Namibia of both Cuban and SWAPO forces. The UN was to send in the UNTAG – transition assistance group – that had been made provision for by SCR 385 in 1976.

Yet, true to the opinion Malan's Military Intelligence appeared to have formed of Sam Nujoma's character, he gave orders for SWAPO's guerrillas to breach the Agreement's strictures. On 1 April 1989, 1 629 PLAN fighters crossed the border in what was clearly calculated to establish the myth that Namibia had been liberated 'through the barrel of a gun'. The SADF having begun its withdrawal in compliance with the Agreement, the Namibian Police, who were left in charge of public order, suffered a number of casualties. In the inevitable re-engagement with the SADF that followed, many hundreds of the guerrillas were made to pay with their lives for the folly of their leaders.

---

[52] See http://lcweb2.loc.gov/frd/cs/angola/ao_appnb.html.
[53] Leopold Scholtz writing in the South African newspaper, *Rapport*, 4 November 2012.

In the ultimate of ironies, the men who had sent them and thousands of their brothers and sisters to die unnecessary deaths could nevertheless count on the unquestioning votes of a tribal majority to descend on Windhoek as the rulers of an independent Namibia. And, in testimony to the new fear for the future they had engendered among the remainder of Namibia's people, those were the only votes they would get.

A NOBEL PEACE PRIZE

As a resident of Oslo I have always enjoyed attending the annual announcement at the Nobel Institute of winners of the Nobel Peace Prize. The prize involves a sum of money to be paid out from the proceeds of investments made by one of the world's wealthiest men of his time more than a century ago. In his will, Alfred Nobel stipulated that a prize be awarded to 'fredsförfäktare' – champions of peace – and annually to 'those who shall have done the most or the best work for brotherhood between nations, for the abolition or reduction of standing armies ...'

In October 2008, Professor of Medicine Ole Danbolt Mjøs, the chairman of the Norwegian Nobel Committee, announced that the prize was to be awarded to Martii Ahtisaari, ex-UN Commissioner for Namibia for his efforts to secure the peaceful transition to independence of Namibia.

Back home, I called Mburumba Kerina in Windhoek, the man who had scripted the moves to be made by his countrymen to gain their independence by peaceful means – 'using our brains'. Mburumba was as dumbfounded as I was about what Ahtisaari could possibly have done to be so honoured.

I next looked up the name Ahtisaari in General Magnus Malan's autobiography – on the expectation that as head of the SADF and Minister of Defence, he should have had some dealings with a 'champion of peace' at the UN. I found one reference. On page 301, Malan identifies the UN Commissioner in a picture taken on 22 December 1988 in the chamber of the UN Security Council. Ahtisaari was sitting in the row behind the South African Foreign Minister, Roelof Botha, on the occasion of the signing of the Tripartite Agreement – the crowning achievement of Botha's skill as a diplomat.

Even more germane to the issue was that after the SADF had defeated the Soviet Union's and Cuba's purposes in the region, there no longer existed a combination of forces on the African continent that could possibly pose a military threat to South Africa. Having thus laid to rest the fear – real or convenient – of a 'total communist onslaught' the apartheid regime itself became amenable to finding ways of ending its international isolation and the growing threat of the country becoming 'ungovernable'.

This was the threat that was heralded on 16 June 1976 when Black school pupils walked straight into police fire – as if to say, 'so far, and no further'.[54] But then there was the surprise expressed in 1991 by Francis Wilson, one of my classmates at UCT, who in the intervening years had become a professor of Economics there. The release of Nelson Mandela had come as a bolt out of the blue sky, Francis told me when I paid him a visit on the UCT campus. Yet he didn't expect any great changes to happen. The apartheid system stood 'as cast in concrete', was the opinion of one of the country's leading academics.

Thus, paradoxically, everything was set to change, and did do so, while in essentials nothing changed. Still, by such political sleight-of-hand the people of South Africa bought themselves apparent peace. This being the case, the question as to what contribution the Finnish diplomat could possibly have made to bringing about the incidental, antecedent 'peaceful' transition to the independence of Namibia, remains a mystery to me.

What still bleeds is the fact that the UN Commissioners MacBride and Ahtisaari had knowingly failed to do anything to protect the lives of Namibians for whom they had legal responsibility: young men and women who had 'left the comfort of their homes to fight the apartheid regime on the world stage – where it enjoyed a monopoly of opinion' – in Allard Lowenstein's words.

---

[54] In *Pale Native* 2003, journalist Max du Preez gave an account of his eye-witness observations of the student uprising, when the police opened fire on demonstrating youth – who continued to defy them: 'For the first time in my life I fully understood that there was something fundamentally wrong in my society, and that it would have to change drastically and soon.' p 68.

CHAPTER THIRTEEN

From South West Africa to Namibia

A HOMECOMING

During the early years of exile, I thought I would be on a flight home within twenty-four hours of the apartheid regime declaring an end to its occupation of South West Africa. That fantasy began to fade on the day in 1976 when I had to flee the African continent for a second time. My experience in Zambia had also made me aware that immigration authorities never forget. I was also mindful of the warning that had been addressed to me by the South African President, P W Botha, at the time Deputy Minister of Internal Affairs, when in 1959 he said that I'd regret it if I were ever to return to South Africa.

And I could still hear Gottlieb Nakaamboh's advice on the tactics of survival, spoken in Lusaka one evening many years before, 'No, no, no! Straight ahead ... now you can turn left ... now right ... they must never be able to guess where you are going.' After having had to flee from Zambia I was told that SWAPO's henchmen had transported Gottlieb into the bush outside Lusaka where they told him to dig a hole – whereupon they hacked him to death.

In consequence the question, from where the shot might come, or whence the knife, or where the road 'accident' might occur, became an obsession as I contemplated a three-week visit to the Territory that was to become Namibia.

Despite such misgivings, soon after the UNTAG had been deployed in Namibia, I took a flight 'home'. After three decades of absence I was consumed by a longing to embrace, if I could, the country of my birth. Borrowing a Toyota Corolla of indeterminate vintage – but known in South Africa as *Kanniedood* (Can't Die) – from my brother Kehat, I drove from north to south, and twice crossed the Namib to visit the coastal towns of Lüderitz and Walvis Bay. As I put my boots down on the ground I thought to myself, 'this is where I belong; here nobody dare ask me where I come from and how long I intend to stay'.

However, such emotional highs were soon dampened by the anxiety which practically everybody I met gave expression to. Far from elation at the imminent independence of the country, there was unease about the junta that would be succeeding the departing apartheid regime. The unease was expressed in two words, dissidents and dungeons. A dissident was anyone who for any reason had displeased Nujoma or any of his minions. Dungeons were holes dug in Angola to which dissidents were confined as punishment.

SWAPO'S ANGOLAN DUNGEONS

The existence of dungeons in Angola became known in 1984 when Lusaka was the venue for another meeting about Namibia's future. SWAPO had invited a number of people from Namibia: prominent businessmen, church leaders, party sympathisers and activists, including Attie Beukes, whose reputation as a fearless opponent of the apartheid regime distinguished him.

If the purpose of the conference was to establish the credentials of a movement primed to bring about beneficial changes to a much abused society, the impression Attie formed was dismal. The words of sweet reason from the junta's leaders belied the suspicion and fear that Attie encountered even among his old 'comrades'. One of those was Priscilla, the youngest daughter of my Aunt Sara and Uncle Charles van Wyk. In Rehoboth, Priscilla had been an avid distributor of SWAPO's propaganda material. The arrival of the Security Police on her parents' farm, to interrogate her mother and Aunt Martha about their support for SWAPO, put Priscilla in a state of panic. Fearing imminent arrest and imprisonment, she joined a group of Ovambo party members and fled to Angola. However, no sooner had they arrived at the SWAPO base of Cassinga than it was destroyed by the South Africans. Taapopi, the leader of the youth league of which she had been a member, was one of the casualties.

A nervous tick in Priscilla's face told Attie that all was not well with her. To be able to see her privately, he told the SWAPO guards, who insolently demanded to know what he wanted to speak to her about, that Priscilla had borne him a child. He then learned that after Taapopi's death, Priscilla was reduced to a position of handmaiden for Pendukeni Iivula-Ithana, a woman on the way to becoming one of the dominant members of the junta and an eventual candidate for the presidency of the country. Priscilla's fear was related to what she had seen and heard about the physical punishment meted out to other of her comrades, including their confinement in dungeons where they lived in fear of snakes and other vermin. On Attie's advice, Priscilla applied to either the US or the Canadian embassy for asylum; when she eventually arrived in the US, she was broken in health and spirit.

Attie's inquiries about the whereabouts of Walter Joseph Thiro, the brother of my sister-in-law Erika, returned conflicting replies. Born in 1954, Walter had qualified as a motor mechanic, but grew tired of racist harassment at the hands of his German employers. Eventually he also jumped the border, 'to join the fight for his country's liberation', as others had done before him. In Lusaka he made contact with SWAPO and was admitted to the UN Institute for Namibia – and nothing has been heard from him since. When Attie was finally able to corner an old 'comrade' with a query about the whereabouts of Walter, a wordless gesture suggested that Walter had been thrown into a hole in the ground. Subsequently Erika heard that her brother had been sent to Angola where 'dissidents' landed in dungeons – 'some for no reason other than being who they were: members of Namibia's non-Ovambo minorities from the south and unable to speak Ovambo'.

Even Ovambos, born and raised in Central and Southern Namibia where Afrikaans is the lingua franca, experienced the wrath of the UN-certified 'sole authentic representatives of the Namibian people'. In 1985 Erika Beukes formed a 'Committee of Parents' to compel SWAPO to account for the whereabouts of a large number of refugees who were said to have been imprisoned. For her pains she was dismissed from her job at the Namibian Council of Churches – on the advice of a Norwegian donor of aid to the internal SWAPO. The Council's director was the Reverend Abisai Shejavali, a Lutheran priest who is on record as having justified the measures taken against 'dissidents' by SWAPO abroad. The Committee of Parents has received no response from either the UN agency charged by the international community with responsibility for Namibia, or from the perpetrators themselves.

The brutality to which the junta's victims were exposed became visible to me when Henry Boonzaaier, one of those fortunate to return home alive, took off his shirt to show the scar tissue where his skin appeared to have been ripped off.

And at my brother Hewat's place I became acquainted with two very accomplished young Ovambo women, Ndamona and Panduleni Kali. They had survived as if by miracle five years of incarceration in dungeons in Angola. There they were subject to unspeakable ill treatment at the hands of SWAPO operatives who had evidently received instruction in 'revolutionary methodology' as practiced in the Soviet Union and by the East German *Stasi*.

My sister Martha was the person, among the living, who I missed most of all. On being tipped off that her days of freedom were counted, she had fled across the border into Angola, taking along her youngest daughter and only son. With her reputation as a SWAPO activist, PLAN guerrillas respectfully conducted them to SWAPO's headquarters. For the same reason, she was sent abroad on party missions to front the junta's alleged feminist image.

But Martha soon lost the illusions she had formed about the organisation to which she had dedicated herself. She sought protection from the MPLA women's section, and a life of isolation in Luanda – resisting all calls for her to return home. She even ignored pleas for information about her situation. Unable to obtain a visa to Luanda, I had to depend on accounts from occasional visitors who had met her. Thus we learned that her eleven year old son had died under mysterious circumstances in the SWAPO camp where he had been held. With a father from Cape Town and an equally outspoken mother, the boy was said to have offended the camp commanders with his fearless speech – a case of cultural conflict of which the innocent child had become the victim. It would take many years before Martha's daughters in Windhoek, Mildred and Libet, could eventually persuade her to return home. She did so shortly before her death, physically and spiritually a shadow of herself.

NANYEMBA AND KALENGA

Although the internal dynamics of the SWAPO junta had ceased to be of personal concern to me, I was not unmoved on hearing of Peter Nanyemba's death. In charge of SWAPO's guerrillas Nanyemba had formed one leg of the triumvirate at SWAPO's core; the other leg – alongside Sam Nujoma – being Peter Mueshihange who was said to be in charge of foreign affairs. Having run the guerrilla operation for ten years – from 1966 to 1976 – Nanyemba might have revealed doubt about where it was leading when he upbraided the young fire-brands at the Old Farm near Lusaka on Namibia Day in 1975. Their parents would mourn their deaths, he bluntly warned them, if they were to get their way. Given the rumour Edel had picked up in Lusaka, namely that 'in Moscow Nanyemba was regarded as Savimbi's man', it did not surprise me to hear that he had found his death under mysterious circumstances. He is said to have been warned one day of an imminent threat to his life, whereupon he hastily fled – only to have the vehicle in which he was traveling rammed by a truck that had come from 'out of nowhere'. In Lusaka one evening in 1975, he paid me the compliment of admitting that my youthful act of protest leaving the country, had inspired him to follow suit.

I had noticed doubts about the guerrilla war even in Peter Mueshihange's mind. Slight of build and retiring of attitude but with a prominent gold tooth-filling, I had difficulty forming an opinion about the third leg of the SWAPO triumvirate. During a visit to Oslo in 1966, when he slept at our place in Ski, the questions he put to me suggested that he had reservations about the destruction of buildings, businesses and infrastructure that would be the inevitable outcome of the guerrilla war that they had decided upon – capital, he pointed out, that was required for the country's economic development.

I never heard under what circumstances Linekela Kalenga had died. We had become acquainted when in 1966 a sizable number of students in exile had gathered in Uppsala to found the South West Africa Students Association – where I was elected to serve as 'secretary-general' with him as my deputy. When ten years later our paths crossed again, this time in the Zambian bush, he told me, 'We are not fighting for an ideology, Hans; we are fighting for a country'. To me, this comment explains what has been playing itself out in post-independent Namibia, where the self-defined liberators of the country have assumed an ethnically based monopoly over the exercise of power at every level of government throughout Namibia.

NAMIBIA GETS BORN – WITH A HORDE OF FOREIGN EXPERTS IN ATTENDANCE

In contrast to the brutality to which 'the authentic representatives of the Namibian people' had descended abroad, I was struck by a new civility that appeared to have taken hold in interpersonal relations among the country's inhabitants. Perhaps it had always been there, but now it was recognised in speech. My brother Kehat cautioned me when I addressed a petrol jockey as *jong* (young man), it could be misunderstood. 'We are all "Sirs" now,' he explained.

Kehat could now also attend to White patients – something he was barred from doing previously – in the State Hospital where he had been chief surgeon for some years. It was a position he had claimed as of right when the Administration, in window-dressing exercises during the Turnhalle process, made token changes to some discriminatory laws. On a round of his wards one Sunday noon, only the good-natured barbs that he exchanged with his White colleagues betrayed their more rancorous past.

At this time, Kehat had been upset by hints of changes to be made in the medical services when the SWAPO regime took charge. One of the foreign 'experts', a Norwegian at that, who had descended on the country had told him that the Namibian health services were to be reorganized on the Botswana model. 'They don't ask us how we think public health could be improved,'

Kehat said. 'They don't ask us what we think of the Botswana model, when people from western Botswana and southern Angola have for years been flocking to Windhoek for specialist treatment.'

He went on to describe a health care service that appeared to me to be as rationally organised as it could possibly be. It took into account the country's geography and available resources: qualified nurses manning village clinics diagnosed and medicated straightforward cases and got on the phone to Windhoek for advice if required. An effective ambulance service brought patients in need of specialist care to regional hospitals. Cases that could not be operated on in Windhoek were flown to Cape Town, where two hours later some of South Africa's foremost medical expertise could attend to them at the Tygerberg University Hospital. The nurses' qualifications were constantly upgraded by doctors who routinely visited the district clinics. 'The situation could be compared,' Kehat explained, 'to you sailing a ship that cost 20 million, and here somebody comes around to give you a million you hadn't asked for, and then expects you to hand over command of the vessel.'

My brother's outburst made me curious about what his White senior had to say about the 'foreign experts'. This doctor's response, no less vehement than Kehat's, now kindled my interest in the role of foreign experts in the country's post-apartheid process.

For my next 'informant' I chose the head of the National Housing Corporation, a businessman who had considered leaving South Africa for his ancestral home in England before a visit to Namibia had persuaded him to settle in the desert Territory. 'The Americans are the worst,' he exploded when I brought up the question of foreign 'experts'. 'They said they would provide us with five experts who would tell us how to solve our problems.'

How had he tackled the situation? 'I advised them to please keep their experts at home. I told them that that would be the best possible help they could give us.' Who wouldn't be pleased to have a man like that by one's side?

After this meeting with the administrator, I had a quiet conversation with a professor of Education, an elderly Afrikaans-speaking academic with a much gentler temperament. He too had sought wider freedom in Namibia than South Africa, under apartheid, would let its citizens enjoy. He spoke with great erudition about the changes that needed to be introduced to the curricula that were in force. By availing themselves of the capacity of such a man, I reflected, independent Namibia would be well served.

It wasn't to be. Taking advice from foreign 'educational experts' brought in tow by the SWAPO regime, changes were made to the educational system that, I have been told, would have put even the Verwoerdian curse – *of what use would it be to instruct Blacks in Mathematics, when they wouldn't require it in the occupations open to them* – to shame.

At the base of the new educational policy, as in much else, is the concept of 'previously disadvantaged' – a partial truth that is as obnoxious in effect as the 'red line' that in the service of apartheid divided 'Ovamboland' from the rest of the country.

To have poorly instructed pupils acquire school certificates, both the curricula and the standards were watered down: currently an A grade corresponds to 65 per cent performance on a scale of 0 to 100, I was informed by the principal of the high school that I had once attended.

The 'reforms' are said to have rendered a generation of Namibians not only incapable of acquiring higher education, but even of gainful employment. From a spare parts dealer I heard, during a recent visit to the country, that he employs kids who hadn't gone to school in preference to school leavers. He finds the former easier to instruct than the latter – even in the use of computers, which are indispensable to his business.

FARMER JAN ENGELBRECHT, AND NAMIBIA'S FOOD SUPPLY

A local expert I had much joy becoming acquainted with was the cattle and maize farmer, Jan Engelbrecht. For an impression about how Windhoek was shaping up for its impending status as the capital city of an independent state, I paid a visit to the city administration, where I was well received. The conversation turned to the issues of water and food supply and I learnt that 90 per cent of the territory's food was imported from South Africa. At this point one of the officers urged me to speak to a farmer for whom the issue of the country's food supply had become the criterion for its independence from South Africa.

Even though I had only three days left before my departure from the country, I called the farmer with a request to interview him. He would see me, he agreed, if I could make it to his place at eight the next morning. With only two or three hours of sunshine left, I filled up Kehat's ancient Toyota Corolla and started out on the 500 kilometre drive to the north.

On arrival at the farm early the next morning, I encountered a farm worker outside the farmhouse gate, cutting lucerne for feeding horses. His ready answers to my queries revealed that his employer was respected and well liked. While we were talking, Mr Engelbrecht himself emerged from the farmhouse. He was on the way to his regular morning meeting with all of the farm's employees. Noticing me, he turned around and invited me for breakfast.

'I'm sorry about it, Hans', he said, as we sat down at the kitchen table, 'but 90 per cent of what we are about to eat, is imported from South Africa'. He then launched into the theme with which he had inspired the man at the City Hall in Windhoek.

The opportunity to become acquainted with a gracious couple, and a man with a deep understanding of his people's needs, proved to be only one of the rewards of my visit to Hoba[55] that day. The ambience – the smells, the sounds, the voices with the occasional shouts – awoke in me memories of my childhood.

The poster at the farm gate informed visitors that Jan was responsible for the farm's business, while Minnie kept a flock of sheep. I learned that the sheep represented Minnie Engelbrecht's claim to independence. 'You know how it is with us,' she confided to me with a small smile, speaking on behalf of all of the country's women. 'It is an advantage to secure your own income.'

With Jan having returned to his meeting with the workers, she took me on a tour of the farm's community hall to show me where she instructed the workers' children of the earliest school-going ages. The sight of a neatly clad flock of Black farm children meeting us was a welcome novelty.

Jan Engelbrecht's interaction with his farm workers showed the mutual respect that I had sensed when speaking to the workers that morning. He spoke to both men and their wives with unaffected courtesy and they responded without the customary 'baas' that still signalled the relationship between White employers and Black workers elsewhere. There was a measure of pride in his voice when, during the interview, he told me about the readiness of all to lend a hand at harvest time when the maize had to be shipped out. My hour with him developed into a wide-ranging and instructive exposition of the problems farmers had to face throughout the country.

The next stop that day was the cattle market where an auction was in process. The auctioneer put on a show that alone would have been worth the visit. Listening to his completely unintelligible torrent of words about an animal on sale, one of the farmers would raise his hand whereupon a sale would appear to have been made.

Turning the Corolla's nose southward that afternoon I felt a rush of emotions. I had been warmly welcomed by people who had experienced the tensions and fears of war and were now looking to the future with hope, though they couldn't hide a sense of anxiety with which their hope was tinged.

During my next visit to Hoba, Jan Engelbrecht, then the Chairman of

---

[55] Hoba had been made famous by a 60-ton meteorite which fell to earth around 80 000 years ago, and has never been moved from its original site in the Otjozondjupa Region of Namibia.

the Namibian beef cattle association, asked me to find an importer for their beef in Norway. I had to throw cold water on his expectations with the remark that with regard to agricultural policy, the farmers were the tail that wagged the Norwegian dog. Jan's spontaneous retort: 'And what's wrong with that?'

THE SWAPO ELITE – LORDS OF THE LAND IN WAITING

One acquaintance from my SWAPO days that I happened to meet by chance was Hidipo Hamutenya. This happened when a winding bank queue unexpectedly brought us standing abreast of each other. 'Fancy seeing you here', I blurted out. He, equally surprised, asked about my family and how long I had been in the country. I felt myself warming towards him and asked how things were going. 'Oh, so so', he replied, adding, 'It could be better'. Then he seemed to recall under what circumstances we had last seen each other. The queue, moving forward two steps, brought the conversation to an end.

I interpreted Hidipo's spontaneous lament as revealing the insecurity that the members of the junta must have been feeling. Their efforts to prevent the public from getting to know the full horror of what they had been responsible for in Zambia and in Angola – confining hundreds of their countrymen to concentration camps and dungeons – had failed. Excepting for the votes of the demographic majority of the northern regions, they could therefore not expect much support in the forthcoming elections for a constituent assembly. In the meantime, ironically, they were dependent for their security on the South African trained security forces observing the terms of the agreements.

On an impulse I decided to look up Moses Garoeb at SWAPO's head office. After waiting some twenty minutes, I was finally admitted to the second floor office complex occupied by the general-secretary, with its impressive view of Windhoek's government complex.

Moses Garoeb stood at a corner of his desk as if on his way somewhere, with sheaves of papers in his hands. As an afterthought he freed his right hand for a limp shake as I approached the desk. His stance was not to be misunderstood: he was merely showing me the courtesy of listening to what I had in mind. He had, after all, sent me a telegram some thirteen years earlier to let me know that my membership of SWAPO had been terminated. Having taken in all of this, I realised that we in fact had nothing to say to one another. For form's sake I therefore merely asked Moses about the negotiations concerning the transfer of power in which he was engaged. He responded with a brief but factual report, the gist of which I had read in a paper that morning.

With that I took leave of the man who had been Sam Nujoma's brain for some twenty years. On the way out of the office complex I recalled the pleasant conversations I had had with Moses in Lusaka in 1970, and reflected about what power does to a human being. While I had been pessimistic about the prospects for the liberation of our country, he had expressed the improbable belief that independence, if not imminent, was due by 1974. In 1976, six years later, I could recognise in him the wear and tear on moral fibre that the years of 'struggle' caused. It did not surprise me to hear that he, alongside Muyongo, was said to have given orders for the Zambian soldiers to fire on the prisoners at Mboroma.

I next kept an appointment with Peter Katjavivi. In a postcard home I wrote to Edel: 'It seems he has been engaged as leader of SWAPO's department for electoral research. He also expects to fly to Oslo to take part in PRIO's project concerning 'ethnic conflicts in Namibia.' Fancy that. When they could have been of use they showed no interest – but now the time is ripe for the 'experts'. Peter clearly does not feel too happy – in view of the daily reports about the atrocities that people from central and southern Namibia, particularly the well-educated ones, had had to endure at SWAPO's hands. There is talk of some 1 400 persons about whom nothing had yet been heard.'

THOSE WHO HAD BECOME 'IRRELEVANT TO THE STRUGGLE'

In Lusaka I had been told of the 'dissidents' having been rendered 'irrelevant to the struggle'. During my short sojourn in Namibia I also met a number of the other old boys, Kozonguizi, Shipanga and Ngavirue who, like me, answered to that description. They had become involved in the so-called Turnhalle Alliance of which Shipanga had become Minister of Environmental Affairs. With the self-deprecation that was his most winning trait, Shipanga recounted a speech about nature conservation that he had delivered in Ovamboland. Afterwards, one of the tribal elders had risen to address him with, 'My son, you are now trying to teach us something that we have been practising from before you were born. That is why you will still find lions around here, and elephants.'

Through the years, I had thought that redistributing the land, which had been alienated from its rightful owners within living memory, would be a priority for the government of an independent Namibia. When I asked Kozo about this at a gathering one evening, his response surprised me: a redistribution of land was not an issue his group would take up in the current negotiations. It was a stance that I should have been prepared for. Ten years earlier I had written a letter to Solomon Mifima who was stranded in a Greek refugee centre after his release from prison:

'The next step after the formation of SWAPO-D is intended to be the joining up with a new grouping at home called the Namibian National Front, where SWANU is the major party. The NNF has a policy item which would forbid the nationalisation of the country's natural resources and of the land. My view of this is simply that it is traitorous: Namibia's claims to right of control of its resources and to claims against the foreign countries exploiting them illegally since 1966, is established by resolutions of the UN and in particular of the Security Council. To join such a policy platform would put us in the class of those Africans who are prepared to make a present of their people's property to foreigners, so as to gain personally.'

As the Ovambos had lost no land, it was clear to me that no pressure on that score could be expected from the SWAPO junta. Indeed, Sam Nujoma himself has acquired himself a farm in lands belonging to the Bondelswarts in the Karasburg district. To get there he lets his courtege of 'bodyguards' in half a dozen vehicles occupy both lanes of the trunk road – forcing oncoming traffic on to the shoulder or off the road entirely. In 2011, Edel and I were travelling from Keetmanshoop to Mariental when we encountered this grandiose procession – and narrowly escaped becoming a statistic one other-wise peaceful Sunday around noon.

NEW PREMONITIONS

As to myself, even though the hopes that I had once entertained about being of service to my people had been dimmed, I could not quite divest myself of the sense of obligation that had motivated my youthful rebellion against my country's foreign occupants. During that first visit home, however, my mind became exercised by two further issues.

First, on a trip to the coastal towns of Walvis Bay and Swakopmund, I observed a giant pipeline running parallel to the road from the coast to the Røssing uranium mine some seventy kilometres inland. It meant that the desert country had been turned into the exporter of water in the form of uranium oxide. A giant aquifer near Walvis Bay was being drained for the purpose. As fossil water is non-renewable, extraction must necessarily cause a change of the water table in its region. It made me suspect this as cause of the dead evergreen trees that I had observed driving around the Rehoboth district – a couple of hundred kilometres inland. A local farmer told me that when I left the country thirty years earlier, they could find water at a depth of thirty six metres, while they now had to bore to a depth of more than three hundred metres. In short, to satisfy the demands for a life-threatening energy resource elsewhere, the semi-desert country appeared to be doomed to irreversible desertification.

Second, for a country that could rightly claim to have no enemies, the maintenance of a military force struck me as something bizarre. Military forces form a parasitic drain on economic resources that could be used to do away with the poverty suffered by the majority of people. And then there is the inclination of military men – their nations' watchdogs – to conclude that they are predestined to run the affairs of their countries. This motivated me to place an article in two newspapers to point out the benefits of doing without a military establishment. I did it merely for the record. A cabal that had come to power on the myth that they had done so by military means, could not be expected to let go of the warrior image. I subsequently read that, off his own bat, Sam Nujoma sent a detachment of the Namibian army to protect diamond-mining properties he had acquired in the Democratic Republic of Congo.

REGISTRATION AS A CITIZEN

Before departing from Rehoboth I wanted to enter my name on the voters' roll for the upcoming constitutional elections. This had to be documented from an entry into the police records of births and deaths in the district.

I was alarmed to find my name missing on the list of births registered in the year of my birth. Without such registration I couldn't document that I was born in South West Africa, or indeed anywhere. My father explained that it was due to my Grandfather's obstinacy. Johannes Timotheus Beukes could never reconcile himself to the termination of Rehoboth's self-government when South Africa took charge of the Territory's administration. Even while the status of outlaw, to which he had been condemned was lifted many years before my birth, he still found it offensive to bow to the impositions of an administration that he regarded as illegitimate. He therefore made no mention of my birth when a police patrol arrived on the farm shortly after the event. For him it sufficed that my name be entered into the register of the Methodist Church that had recently been established in Rehoboth – a move for which he had been one of the initiators – in a breakaway for political reasons from the Lutheran Mission Church.

DOCUMENTS PERTAINING TO THE 'BEUKES CASE'

A GOVERNMENT ENSNARES ITSELF

Throughout my school years the South African media frequently reported, and the files in the National Archives in Pretoria now detail, cases of passports being denied or confiscated – stories about hopes and aspirations dashed that would soon be forgotten by all excepting the victims. One such case that filled me with revulsion concerned a Black Johannesburg schoolboy – I think his name was Stephen – who was deprived of a chance to take up an offer of tuition at a high school in New York – on funds collected by the school's pupils. If it had been a White student …

The voluminous documentation – memoranda, newspaper clippings, etc. – that fills the file on the 'Beukes case', suggests that the ramifications had been much more extensive than even I could have hoped for at the time. Most significantly, all talk about the integration into the Union of the British Protectorates of Bechuanaland, Basutoland and Swaziland – the political nightmare of successive Botswanan chieftains – reiterated in Parliament by the South African premier in Parliament as late as on 24 June that year, finally died down. A string of memoranda, also styled *aides memoir or aides memoires*, faithfully record the failure of all attempts to enforce Pretoria's will beyond the country's borders. There ensued a series of most acrimonious exchanges between Union and British officials, with culmination in New York where the Minister of External Affairs roundly *lectured* his British counterpart about the British having 'aided and abetted a person who had left without a passport or exit permit in order to attack South Africa at the United Nations'.

But I did find reason to revise the opinion I had formed about P W Botha, the Deputy Minister of the Interior who moved on to become South Africa's President. While still trying to come to terms with the prospect of indefinite exile in Bechuanaland, I had received a letter from an old classmate in Cape Town with assurances from Botha that I need fear no reprisals on returning to UCT. It was an invitation that I had scorned. The documents in the file under my name show that on three occasions, not least one within minutes of the departure of my flight from Salisbury, Mr Botha had blocked moves to have me extradited from the Central African Federation, or failing that from Nairobi in Kenya, where the plane from Johannesburg to London was due to land next. While referring to the likely damage to South Africa in the event of the attempts failing, it seems reasonable to assume that he had been mindful of the promise he had made his constituent in Cape Town that no harm should befall me.

The selection of documents from the 'Beukes case' that follows outlines the progression of the passport debacle – from its sordid start to its elevation into an issue of international politics that would, but for the fact that it was thrashed out in secrecy, have been most damaging to the apartheid regime.

An early departmental memorandum, dated 9 June 1959 and signed by 'AB' (Burger), Under Secretary at the Department of External Affairs, refers to queries that had been raised about 'the Coloured from South West Africa' who had been awarded a Norwegian bursary and had submitted an application for a passport. Fearing 'that the bursary award might be directed against our Apartheid policy', 'Interior' had wanted External Affairs to find out from the Norwegian Consul whether 'their National Union (of students)' was 'a bona fide organisation'.

'AB' observes that even if the Norwegians were to regard their Students Union as 'bona fide', that was 'certainly (not) necessarily the case as far as we are concerned'. As to the applicant in question, he notes that the Police had had nothing unfavourable about him, 'excepting that once in South West Africa he had been fined for being in possession of 15 .22 cartridges'. He also notes that I had requested a response to my application by 11 June .

The story about the possession of small-calibre ammunition was one I remember very well. I had boarded a train in the coastal town of Swakopmund bound for home in Rehoboth, unsuspecting that the pigeons I had been shooting on my grandfather's farm months earlier would induct me into the Mandated Territory's annals of crime. As the train pulled out of the station a Policeman accosted me and, as if he knew what he'd find, zipped open the chest pocket of the leather jacket I was wearing – to fish out the incriminating evidence. In Windhoek a magistrate offered me the choice of 21 days in jail or a fine of three pounds. The lawyer who had advised me to plead guilty charged me a further three *guineas* for his fee. It was more money than I could afford just days before departing for the Cape to enrol at UCT – to read law. My appearance before the Magistrate had taken less than ninety seconds by my watch, no longer than the time it took for each of the twenty or so of my co-prisoners, arraigned for various offences under the Pass Laws, to be sentenced to three months in jail that morning.

The next entry filed under the 'Beukes Case' is dated 10 June 1959 and addressed by the Secretary of External Affairs, GPJ.(Jooste) to the Assistant Secretary (AB) about 'Norwegian bursary – Hans Beukes'. Jooste records his discussion of the matter with 'the Minister', presumably of External Affairs, Eric H. Louw. The latter is said to have felt that *'whatever might be Beukes' mindset at the moment, there could be little doubt about what his attitude would be after he had been indoctrinated in Norway'.*

The Minister had also recalled a protest that had emanated from the National Union of Norwegian Students against the Union Government about separate university facilities. 'Under the circumstances', GPJ records, the Minister had declared himself 'not ready to support the application'.

GPJ concludes his memo with a query as to whether the Assistant Secretary 'had been able to determine whether this person is related to the Beukes that had addressed a petition to the United Nations Organisation'.[56]

Some time the next day AB scribbles a reply at the bottom of GPJ's typed note. It records that he had given a copy of the text to Boise of Interior Affairs who had informed him that in their reply, the South West Africa Administration had stated that they had no objection (to a passport being issued) if the Police didn't have any. The Administration hadn't said anything though about whether Beukes was related to the petitioner, a query to which Interior had specifically requested an answer, AB notes. He concludes his memo with the additional observation that Japie Basson (MP for Namib district in South West Africa of a party allied to the Nationalists) 'was believed to be supporting the application strongly'.

It would seem then that what the Department of the Interior had to weigh were the relaxed attitude of the South West Africa Administration, with the strong support of a renegade Member of Parliament thrown in *against* the Minister of External Affairs' presumption of my guilt by association, or in anticipation.

In the event Interior would seem to have been predisposed to let the student enjoy the benefit of the doubt. In possession of my first ever passport, I next agreed to a suggestion by my classmate, Adrian Leftwich, that his sister, a journalist at the Cape Times, conduct an interview with me.

The third entry into the Beukes file suggests that it had been unwise to spread the news about the good fortune that had befallen a 'Non-White', as Miss Leftwich's story was headed. The Minister of External Affairs, Eric H. Louw, had evidently either seen or been alerted by others about the report and realised that his reservations had been ignored. Dated 23 June 1959, he scribbles a note on a sheet of paper to which a cutting of the Cape Times article of 19 June 1959 had been pasted. He addresses it to the Secretary with the message that information had been received from 'a dependable source, according to which Beukes intended to proceed to the USA. It is assumed that possibly he would there join up with Getzen and Konguiziki' (sic). Louw adds that he

---

[56] Petition addressed earlier that year by Jacobus Samuel Beukes that had resulted in the Prime Minister, Dr Verwoerd, setting out his Government's policy about its stand on South West Africa and the UN.

had 'brought the information to the attention of the Prime Minister' (Dr H.F. Verwoerd), and that 'it is believed he will call (illegible, presumably Naudé, Minister of the Interior) if necessary'.[57]

Addressing Eric Louw's note to another Under Secretary late on 24 June, AB adds the following scribble, 'The Minister this afternoon informed me at the train station that the passport had been retracted yesterday. Please notify Secretary, in case I do not succeed.'

I must relate that on returning to the NUSAS office in Cape Town from Port Elizabeth, I had picked up a rumour that the Secret Police had interviewed other passengers with whom I had shared the train ride back from Rehoboth after my visit home. While I could remember that there had been two men from Cape Town in the carriage with me, I had been struck by the suggestion that the Security Police were feeding their government with the fanciful talk of passengers aboard the country's trains. But I had also felt chastised by the realisation that in talking to the two Capetonians, I had forgotten Clemens Kapuuo's advice about exercising discretion at all times.

If the men at the helm of South Africa's affairs were set to forget all about the 'potential threat' to their regime they had disposed of, a telegram that ticked into the 'Office' at Union Buildings at 9:50 on the morning of 25 July 1959 should have set off the alarm. Addressed to the Secretary for External Affairs, it was sent from South Africa's Permanent Delegation at the United Nations with the following text:

No.26. SECRET (EAS)
1. 'Committee on SWA decided yesterday grant oral hearings Kozonguizi and Hans J. Beukes.
2. Request for Beukes made by Michael Scott in telegram asking that United States authorities be requested grant visa and that Scott be advised of outcome.
3. Scott also forwarded letter from Beukes written from Cape Town 29 June 1959.
4. Press report today, Beukes now in Bechuanaland. However, Secretariat has no knowledge of this.
5. Copy of Beukes' letter being airmailed today'.

From that moment onwards what had become the 'Beukes Case' would seem to have occupied the minds of the South African Government for an

---

[57] Getzen was the name by which Mburumba Kerina had left Namibia; Jariretundu Kozonguizi left South West Africa in early 1959 to represent the Herero at the UN.

extraordinary amount of time. The story of how the passport had soured relations with South Africa's closest allies, Great Britain, The Rhodesian Federation, and to some extent the United States, is minuted in a succession of aides-memoires dutifully penned by the senior civil servants at the departments of External Affairs and of the Interior. Tempers would flare and language harden, as all efforts to prevent my passage beyond their reach would prove to no avail.

Confronted with an intractable 'case' of their own making, Pretoria's anger resembled that of a King Lear, 'I will do such things. What they are, yet I know not; but they shall be The Terrors of the earth'. The assessments made of the situation probably proved fatal for some later would-be fugitives from the apartheid state.

The same day (25 July) as the telegram from New York was received, a handwritten note initialled AB, records that the Secretary (Jooste) had recommended that the Police be instructed to keep a watch on Beukes' movements so as to prevent him from leaving the country and, 'like Kozonguizi', find his way to the UN.

The next day an 'immediate cipher telegram' was sent out to all South Africa's six diplomatic stations on the African continent and at the UN, to inform them that Beukes had left Serowe for an undisclosed destination; that he was not in possession of a valid passport, that his departure from the Union was therefore illegal, and that if he should approach them for passport facilities, they were to impound any travel document in his possession which was 'most likely falsified and report immediately for further instructions'. The possibility of Beukes travelling under an assumed name was not to be overlooked.

In a letter dated 28 July, a follow-up to his telegram of the 25th, the Permanent Representative at the UN sounded a new theme: Beukes in the context of the Cold War 'struggle' for the minds of the post-colonial world. Wrote the Permanent Representative:

'I am sorry that I was not aware of Beukes' telegram (of 15 July from Serowe) when I sent my cable No. 26'. Whereupon he relates the context into which a representative of the Third World had pitched the passport issue:

'According to a UN press release, Mr Carpio of the Philippines, in supporting the request for the oral hearing for Beukes, suggested that the Committee might want to go further and send a cable to the Union Government interceding on his behalf. He is reported as saying that the Beukes case appeared to him 'one of the most eloquent examples of how dependent peoples are subjected to the most onerous conditions of suppression so as to prevent them from acquiring the necessary knowledge and insight that would enable them to have an equal chance with the rest of the world at enjoying all our modern civilisation offers'.

Mr. Carpio went on: 'the colonial powers are repressing voiceless millions of dependent peoples'; and he added that it was time for the Committee to 'show a little bit more than mere interest'.

The Permanent Representative added the further observation, that '(o)ther members of the Committee, it appears, took the position that the Committee should not prejudge the case and should await Mr. Beukes' hearing.'

Secretary of External Affairs Jooste promptly summoned the American Ambassador to South Africa for a meeting at which he lamented the prospect of the USA granting me a visa. The ambassador (Crowe) asked that a note be addressed to him in order to enable him to report the matter to his Government:

The memorandum transmitted to the American Embassy the next day reads as follows:

CONFIDENTIAL

AIDE-MEMOIRE

HANS JOHANNES BEUKES OF the Rehoboth Community of South West Africa was a student of the University of Cape Town. He was awarded a scholarship by the National Union of Norwegian Students for three years study at Oslo University.

A passport was granted to him on the 15th of June of this year to enable him to take up the scholarship, but just before his intended departure the passport was withdrawn by the Minister of the Interior as a result of information which in the meantime had come into the possession of the Government indicating that Beukes had been associated with political activities deemed inimical to the interests of the State. The Government had good reason to believe that he would continue such activities outside the Union.

On the 24th of July the South African Permanent Delegation in New York reported that the United Nations Committee on South West Africa had on the previous day agreed to grant an oral hearing to Beukes. A request for a hearing was made on behalf of Beukes by the Rev. Michael Scott.

Beukes then disappeared without trace and subsequent press reports claimed that he had left Serowe in the Bechuanaland Protectorate for an undisclosed destination but presumably the United Nations Headquarters in New York. There is of course no passport control between the Union and the

Bechuanaland Protectorate.

Since Beukes is not in possession of a valid South African passport or other travel document, his departure from the Union would be illegal.

These facts are brought to the notice of the United States Embassy in the event of Beukes approaching United States Diplomatic or Consular representatives anywhere for facilities to enter the United States en route to the United Nations Headquarters.

In the light of the Union Government's well-known attitude towards the granting of oral hearings by the United Nations on South West Africa, and on the basis of the friendly relations existing between the United States and the Union, the Union Government desires to express the most earnest hope that the United States authorities would not facilitate Beukes' access to the United Nations Headquarters, as was done in the case of F J Kozonguizi.
WCN (Secretary for External Affairs W.C.Naudé)
PRETORIA
29 July 1959

A NEWS item in the *Rand Daily Mail* for 30 July might have brought some gratification. Under the headline BEUKES MAY NOT APPEAR, it reported doubts expressed by UN officials about whether the 23-year-old student from the University of Cape Town would be able to make it to New York. It quoted a UN spokesman as saying, 'so far as we are aware, he is not in New York.' Further gratification would seem to have been drawn, in view of the use made of it, of newspaper reports emanating from my hometown on 2 and 3 August. Journalists who had descended on the sleepy town to look at the background of the young man who had become a *cause célèbre*, reported back that both my father and grandfather had denied that I had been authorised to speak on behalf of the Rehoboth Community at the United Nations.

A new telegram from New York dropped into the 'Office' at Union Buildings at 8:20 on 3 August. Sent off at 5:06 pm on 31 July, it read in part: 'Understand Committee has agreed postponement of hearing and has cabled Beukes through Scott that United States prepared to issue visa to him for purpose of hearing.'

Bearing the initials of several officials, a note scribbled over an illegible signature suggests the concern with which that bit of intelligence was regarded. It reads: 'Mr. Jones, I think I have already passed on the Secy's wish that we should write to Am. Embassy – urgently.'

It is unclear, in view of the ambivalent proviso 'at this stage', whether much comfort could have been drawn from a report of 3 August from B.G.

Fourie, South Africa's representative at the United Nations. He wrote that as far as he could determine,

'the Norwegians were not busy making things difficult for us at this stage. On the contrary, it is possible that they were afraid of themselves becoming embarrassed by the way things were developing in the Committee on South West Africa.'

A Norwegian diplomat was nevertheless said to have intimated to the South West Africa Committee that 'it would be extremely difficult, if not impossible, for Norway to issue Beukes with a visa, unless he were in possession of a valid travel document'.

This raises the question whether the Norwegian diplomats at the UN had become apprehensive at the context into which Mr Carpio had thrown the passport issue. At the time, the Norwegians could not be said to have come anywhere near enunciating a clear policy with regard to the apartheid state. Their diplomats, with commendable exceptions, appeared to share the prejudices of the colonial powers.

In a report that would seem to belie the belief, widely held at the time, that the South African Government had eyes and ears everywhere, my whereabouts in Serowe appears to have been unknown in Pretoria. 'It was still not known with certainty where Beukes was or what his plans were when newspapers on 14 and 15 August broke the story that he had been refused entry into Southern Rhodesia … and been sent back to Serowe because he had no valid travel document,' wrote an unidentified official on an undated document.

It seems curious that nobody appears to have made the suggestion that the fugitive be apprehended and returned to South Africa – a lapse that could perhaps be ascribed to the secrecy in which the deliberations were being conducted.

A fortnight later, on 1 September, the 'Beukes Case' took its most serious turn when the British High Commissioner requests to see Secretary Jooste 'on a matter of urgency'. Jooste's aide-memoire, drawn up the next day, details the extraordinary context of international politics into which a passport denied had landed one forlorn South West African native. The High Commissioner's démarche also revealed in unmistakable terms the imperial disregard with which the British Government would set aside a South African complaint when it decided that its own interests were at stake.

CONFIDENTIAL

AIDE-MEMOIRE

'At 5 pm on 1 September 1959, I received the British High Commissioner, at his request, on a matter of urgency.

Sir John Maud informed me that he had been instructed by his Government to discuss with us the matter of Beukes' passage abroad through British territory.

The purpose of Sir John Maud's discussion was to inform us that the whole question of Beukes' passage through British territory had been reconsidered by the United Kingdom authorities who had weighed the advantages of preventing Beukes from proceeding abroad against the disadvantages of being accused of obstructing Beukes from appearing before a committee of the United Nations, which had invited him to give oral evidence.

In this connection the United Kingdom Government of course agreed with the Union Government that oral hearings could not constitutionally be granted by the United Nations to inhabitants of South West Africa. Indeed, the United Kingdom delegations had consistently supported the Union in this matter at the United Nations, and continued to regard invitations from the South West Africa Committee to the inhabitants of South West to give oral evidence as *ultra vires* the Charter.

On the other hand the UK authorities believed that to prevent Beukes from proceeding through British territory to the United Nations could be construed as 'obstruction', which could militate against the interests of all concerned (both the UK and the Union) in the Organisation. The following considerations were given special attention:

1. The UK was a member of the Good Offices Committee and it was most desirable that the UK should therefore not fall foul of the Organisation in a manner which would detract from the status of the Good Offices Committee. Here Sir John also referred to recurring talk in the United Nations of taking legal action against the Union in regard to South West Africa.

2. There was a real danger of Nyasaland being discussed in the United Nations, and it was essential that the United Kingdom's position should not be weakened in the Organisation in regard to matters affecting dependent territories.

3. There was a similar danger of 'our friends', the Portuguese, en-countering trouble in the United Nations in connection with their

African territories. Here again the UK's position in the Organisation was of importance.

4. Lastly there were the current efforts of the United Kingdom to ensure South Africa's election as a vice-president. In all the circumstances, the UK authorities had come to the conclusion that as Beukes could in fact add little to what had already been stated in the past by other persons who had been granted oral hearings on South Africa, the disadvantages of 'obstructing' outweighed the advantages of refusing to allow Beukes to proceed from any British territory on his journey abroad.

The High Commissioner then reminded me of the fact that in view of the Federation's present constitutional status, the United Kingdom Government was responsible for the Federation's affairs at the United Nations. In the circumstances the UK Government had informed the Salisbury Government of their views in this matter. If, therefore, the Federation authorities permitted Beukes to proceed abroad it would no doubt be as a result of the views expressed by the British Government.

The following is the gist of my reply:

1. The attitude of the UK Government would, I believed, be viewed in a serious light by the Union Government. Beukes was a Union National who had left the Union illegally. The UK authorities were aware of this fact. His presence in Bechuanaland was not illegal because of the conventional open frontier, but if the Protectorate authorities permitted his onward passage, in the full knowledge of the real purpose of his journey, they would in fact be abetting him. This must of necessity be viewed in a serious light.

2. Similarly if Beukes were to be 'assisted' by the Federation authorities to proceed abroad (to the UN) their act would undoubtedly be seen in an unfriendly light. Having regard to our present relations this would be 'most unfortunate'. In any case I could not ignore the information the High Commissioner had given me and would therefore have to contact Salisbury in the matter.

3. As regards the British view that their decision was also in the interests of the Union, I suggested that this was a matter which the Union Government should be permitted to judge for itself. We would always value the advice of our friends, but the ultimate decision as to what was in our best interests rested with our own Government. Similarly, the UK would judge for itself what was in

its own interests, and, therefore, if the British view was that, having regard to the UK's position in the UN, it would not be in their interests to prevent Beukes from proceeding abroad, they would be acting within their rights – however much we might disagree with them as to the legitimacy of their views, and however much we might deprecate their actions.

On the question of 'obstruction' I expressed the view that there was a vast difference between refusing Beukes the right of passage through British territories in the event of his possessing a valid Union travel document, and action which amounted to assisting him in what was clearly an illegal act. I was quite satisfied that if our positions were reversed, the Union Government would not permit Beukes to pass through Union territory.

A long argument followed, in the course of which Sir John intimated that it would be unreasonable on our part to ignore the validity of the considerations on which the British decision was based – especially as they were not party to the decision to withhold a passport from Beukes, and had, in fact, not been consulted in the matter. In reply to this I pointed out that the granting of a passport to a Union National was a matter which fell within the exclusive jurisdiction of the Union Government – a matter in which we would not dream of consulting any external authority. This, surely, was the position in all sovereign countries.

I explained, further, that the Union Government had taken the decision to withhold the passport 'with its eyes open' as to the possible reactions abroad, and that I could not see how the considerations governing the British attitude could be interpreted as being also in the interests of the Union. To this the High Commissioner reacted by asking; 'Do you mean to tell me that you regard the UK's position in the UN as of no importance to the Union?' I replied that such a question was hardly fair, and drew his attention to South Africa's attitude in the United Nations on the question of Cyprus, which had cost us the friendship of Greece. True enough, our attitude was based upon Article 2(7) of the Charter, but the manner in which we supported the United Kingdom rested also on a relationship of friendship. I assured him that the position of the United Kingdom in the UN, as well as that of any other friendly Western state, was of great importance to the Union. I did not, however, think that the Union could be expected to abdicate its authority over its own National in order to prove this.

In conclusion I informed Sir John that I viewed this matter in so serious a light that I would have to report it to the Prime Minister, who was, at the

moment, also the Acting Minister of External Affairs. I intimated that it might be necessary to suggest that he call on the Prime Minister in regard to this matter.
(initialled) GPJ
PRETORIA

The meeting with the British High Commissioner would seem to have steeled GPJ's resolve. Perhaps, as he was about to dictate the above aide-memoire, he charged his Under Secretary to phone South Africa's High Commissioner (ambassador) in the Central African Federation with the following instructions: 'that the High Commissioner immediately make representations to the Federal authorities to point out that Beukes had left the Union illegally, and to apply for the man to be returned to the Union.'

By 8:45 am, the Under Secretary puts his initials (AN) – Naudé – to his own aide-memoire, detailing almost verbatim the manner in which he had carried out his assignment, and recording the intelligence he had gathered *en passant*.

Nearly two hours later, the High Commissioner calls back with his own detailed report, which AN duly records. The spokesman for the Federal Department of the Interior, 'had heard' that Beukes was on his way to Salisbury and that the US authorities had authorised the extension of a visa to him. The case had 'international complications', the spokesman had added, but had promised to look into the matter.

The South African High Commissioner in Salisbury had next called the American Consul, a Mr Mulcahy, a man of Irish origins who proved most unhelpful – and appeared to be enjoying it. He was in fact expecting Beukes to call on him, he told the High Commissioner, explaining that no travelling document was required for people with business at the UN. The visa was issued as a separate piece of paper and did not have to be attached to a passport. He made it clear that with reference to the site agreement between the US and the UN, it would be 'extremely difficult' for the US to withhold visas. To emphasise the point he mentioned the circumstances when 'they could confine people to parts of Manhattan', i.e. 'in the case of known communists', adding that 'they could be stricter if the person concerned planned to overthrow the United States Government'.

To a request by the South African to tarry a while ('n bietjie te sloer') before issuing the visa, the Consul had replied that that was something he couldn't promise.

Thirty-five minutes later, AN records, his correspondent had called again to report that in the meantime he had been in contact with the Federal Department of External Affairs to be briefed in detail about the circumstances (British pressure) that had compelled them to facilitate Beukes' passage through the Federation …

Within minutes, at 11:15, the South African envoy in Salisbury calls for a third time to add something that he 'had forgotten'. It was that during his second conversation with the Acting Secretary of External Affairs, the latter had 'acknowledged' that the Federal authorities had already admitted Beukes to the Federation and that he hadn't been in possession of a travel document.

With his subordinate's reports in hand Jooste (GPJ) now drafts a confidential note addressed to the Prime-cum-Foreign Minister, Dr Verwoerd, to draw his attention to the following points: a) that Beukes was in Salisbury and that the Federation authorities had decided not to hinder him from travelling to New York, and b) that the USA had decided to supply Beukes with a document to enable him to reach the UN.

As to the first point, Jooste notes that the British Government had clearly put pressure on the Federation. Considering that the situation created (for South Africa) was an 'especially difficult' one, he nevertheless advises that the 'High Commissioner of the Federation be summoned and that the implications of his Government's action be explained to him'. GPJ evidently wanted authorisation to put the Rhodesians under such pressure as to obtain 'repatriation' – which Dr Verwoerd seems to have given him.

As to point b, Jooste refers to two unidentified items 'flagged A and B on the ledger' and suggests that copies of all the relevant items be sent to the Minister of External Affairs who was then on a visit abroad, so as to enable him to discuss America's actions in the 'Beukes Case' with the Americans themselves, either in New York or in Washington.

GPJ concludes his memo with an observation that would soon become an ominous refrain: '*Our difficulties are of course to be ascribed to the fact that there is free access to the High Commission territories and that our border with the Federation is relatively open*'. (My emphasis.)

Appearing to reflect the tensions that were clearly felt in the corridors of the Union Building, Under Secretary AN on 3 September sends his secretary the pasted cutting of a one-sentence notice that had appeared in that day's edition of the Afrikaans-language daily, *Die Transvaler* under the heading 'Beukes Swyg' (holds his tongue) – about the latest complications in the 'Beukes Case'.

On the basis of inquiries AN had made about the 'story's' source, he concludes that Beukes had still been in Serowe on 29 August , when the report was despatched by the local postmistress (doubling as agent for the South

African Press Association).

At 9:30 am the following morning (4 September), the South African envoy in Salisbury calls AN to let him know that he had just received a phone call from the US Consul with the information that Beukes had called on him the previous afternoon. He had been accompanied by the Quaker representative in Salisbury, a Mr George Loft, who appeared to be 'an unwilling companion and not at all happy about being involved'. Mr Loft had, however, 'arranged accommodation at one of the hostels'.

The American Consul had also said that while 'everything was found to be in order', Beukes did not have the necessary certificate of 'inoculation' but that he 'had been booked provisionally by the Federal Immigration authorities on Flight 116 of BOAC that was due to leave Salisbury on Sunday'. Beukes had plus-minus £86 in his possession but was expecting $600 to be forwarded to him by Seretse Khama. It was money that had been sent him by 'a Mr Lowenstein … apparently a student whom (he) had met while … studying in the Union'.

With AN's latest memorandum in hand, Secretary Jooste typed a message to the Prime Minister to inform him that his order to inquire into the possibility of having Beukes extradited had been assigned to Interior Affairs and that the Police were taking urgent steps towards that end. Minister Naudé had 'naturally been consulted and had concurred'. Interior Affairs had pointed out that a Press commotion could be expected and had asked whether an application ought not also to be lodged with the British for the extradition of Kozonguizi, who was thought to be in the UK.

In a clear instance of a government official having given advice that had led to an untenable situation, and now seeking to cover his tracks by letting Dr Verwoerd take the blame, Jooste points out that relations with the Federation could suffer, if the latter were to refuse extradition, and that the possibility of hostile reactions at the UN ought not to be lost sight of either.

Since it was imperative that there ought to be no leak about the planned action, he was not, he wrote, '(repeat not)' going to discuss the matter with either the British or Federal high commissioners – before extradition had been applied for.

The plan would seem to have been that in Salisbury both the British and Federal authorities would be presented with a *fait accompli* – an application for extradition submitted to a judicial authority, bypassing the political authorities that ordinarily would have been acceded to. It would appear that the Federation authorities themselves were apprehensive about Pretoria making precisely such a move.

A scribble in the margin records that Jooste's note had been read at 3:30 pm to the secretary of the Prime Minister, who happened to be in Pietermaritzburg that day, and that he would be calling the Secretary of the Interior at home that evening (4 September).

While waiting for word back from the Prime Minister, AN minutes a call that he had placed at 3 pm to the Secretary of the Interior, Mr du Preez. As instructed by his Secretary (Jooste) AN wrote that it was 'to explain that the whole question concerning the extradition of Beukes now rested with the Department of the Interior'. External Affairs had nevertheless wanted to emphasise 'one little point', namely that to avoid falling foul of the Federal authorities, the steps taken (by the Union) had to be 'legally 100% correct'.

Revealing anxiety about crossing Dr Verwoerd's path, AN informed du Preez that the Prime Minister, who was being briefed as they were speaking, was expected to take a decision in the matter. In consequence it was up to Interior to decide whether to take action immediately, at the risk of pre-empting a decision by the PM, or to delay action, at the risk of Beukes making a getaway in the meantime.

There was also, he added, the State Prosecutor's indication that he might want to initiate action off his own bat.

Perhaps not unreasonably, du Preez protested that a great onus was being placed on his Department. But, he said, he would call 'colonel' Wessels to ask what that officer would regard as a 'deadline' for action. In the meantime, AN was to find out whether the Prime Minister had received the message.

An uninitialled aide-memoire (presumably by AN) of later that afternoon recounted an interdepartmental meeting that was called after word had arrived that the Prime Minister had finally decided that a bid for extradition be looked into. In attendance were both the Minister and Deputy Minister of the Interior (respectively Naudé and Botha). Among the 'cardinal facts' of the case mentioned by the Secretary (of External Affairs) there was the breach of Act No 34 of 1955 for the Regulation of Departure from the Union. A direct telephone call from the meeting to the Prosecutor General, Mackenzie, had him point out that the matter rested with the chief prosecutor of the Cape Province as Beukes had left the Union through Bechuanaland. In the meantime, he advised that the Police are alerted, whereupon a 'brigadier' Wessels was brought into the picture. The meeting ended with a decision to make a go for extradition. Following a statement to be made by a senior official at Interior, the Police were to ask the Federal Police in Salisbury to arrest and detain Beukes until such time as he could be apprehended by a Police officer from the Union.

ACCORDING TO the flimsy carbon copies deposited in 'the Beukes file', Saturday 5 September would appear to have been a day when the minds of two governments (even with the Federation's being distracted by a struggle concerning its own very existence) were seized with a single issue, the imminent departure from Salisbury airport of a passport-less fugitive. None more so than the mind of Secretary Jooste, for whom the day appears to have been spent dictating aides-memoires and executing démarches late into the evening.

Early that morning he had met with the High Commissioner of the Federation to discuss the matter with him. Afterwards he wrote a 'Personal and Confidential' memo to his Prime Minister, doubling as Minister of External Affairs in the latter's absence, to report that in keeping with the Prime Minister's order, he had conveyed to the High Commissioner the Prime Minister's request that Beukes be sent back. The Rhodesian had undertaken to call his government 'immediately'.

A little later Jooste addressed a further, secret message to the Prime Minister where he incidentally reveals his reliance on the erroneous impression, created by Mulcahy, that their quarry was scheduled to depart from Salisbury only the next day, Sunday, and not later that very afternoon. Jooste also reported that after the Police had looked further into the matter, they had begun to doubt whether an application for repatriation would succeed. Given the short time left (a day and a half), it was thought impossible to clarify all the issues.

In terms that reveal the dimensions that his quarry had begun to assume in his mind, Jooste pointed out that should the Federation go against repatriation Beukes would be able 'to launch heavy attacks against the Union, in case he was to reach the UN.'

And then, in an observation that would further reveal why from the start he had considered it imperative to prevent my going abroad, he adds the comment: 'In this connection it ought to be kept in mind that he is an inhabitant of South West Africa.'

This was an implicit reference to the conflict in which the Union was engaged with the United Nations about the Territory's mandated status, in terms of which I could claim what protection international law extended to natives of South West Africa under the mandate. The belief that I enjoyed such protection was in fact precisely what had sustained me all along.

Jooste further informed Verwoerd about a discussion which had taken place that morning between himself and the two ministers at Interior, Naudé and his deputy P W Botha, where the latter had expressed reservations about proceeding with extradition, in view of the doubts expressed as to whether they would succeed. Botha had cited endorsement of his opinion by the Minister (of Justice) Swart.[58] At that meeting, Jooste wrote, it was decided to call off the attempts to have Beukes extradited.

Jooste added that he was scheduled to discuss the matter with the Federation's High Commissioner that morning, and with the British on the latter's return from Johannesburg (to Pretoria) later than afternoon. His aide-memoire tells how he had handled the two ambassadors, and the conclusions he had drawn from the encounters with them.

AIDE-MEMOIRE

GEHEIM/SECRET

In view of the decision not to proceed with the proposal to request the extradition of Beukes (in view of doubts expressed by the Police as to whether such action would succeed) I immediately requested the Federation High Commissioner to call on me. This he did at 10:15 am.

I apprised the High Commissioner of all the facts concerning the refusal to grant Beukes a passport and referred to the failure of the representations made in Salisbury by our High Commissioner. The Prime Minister, who had been informed of the whole position, I then stated, had instructed me to explain the implications of the action of the Federation authorities in deliberately permitting Beukes to enter their territory without a valid Union travel document. I particularly emphasised the Prime Minister's great concern because of the effect which the Federation's actions could have on the traditional relations between our two countries – pointing out that the Union Government could not possibly countenance a situation which enabled its citizens to flour (sic) its authority – especially with what in fact amounted to the assistance of neighbouring territories. The Union Government would have to give serious consideration to measures which would enable it to enforce the Union's laws in the public interest.

In this connection I referred, on my own initiative, to the possibility of refusing to permit offenders falling within the present category to return to the Union. If no such powers existed, the Union Government would perhaps have to take such powers. In any case, Beukes, and those falling within the same category, would be aware of the punishment which would await them

---

[58] Swart was appointed the Republic of South Africa's first president after the country had left the Commonwealth in 1961.

on their return, and might well decide not to return. There was therefore a possibility that those people would have to seek domicile elsewhere. Would the Federation, I enquired, be prepared to be a sanctuary for them?

I repeatedly drew the High Commissioner's attention to the fact that Beukes was guilty of an offence and that his Government must all along have been aware that he was an offender whom they had deliberately permitted to enter their territory – knowing also that it was his intention to proceed to the United Nations in order to attack and vilify the Union.

After a full discussion of all the implications, I added that I had been instructed by the Prime Minister to request that the Federation authorities force Beukes to return to the Union in view of the fact that he had <u>entered their territory illegally</u>.

Mr Fitt clearly indicated that he fully appreciated the position and undertook to convey the Union Government's protest and the request for the return of Beukes telephonically to his Government.

(Of importance is the fact that in the course of the discussion, Mr Fitt stated that it was not an offence in the Federation to leave their territory without a passport or a permit from the competent authorities – which of course, according to our Police, is a *sine qua non* to obtain extradition.)

Some time later, approximately midday, Mr Fitt phoned me and stated that he had been in telephonic touch with his Department who were greatly concerned because of the turn of events and who had assured him that their action was due entirely to the instructions of the British Government. In this connection it was again pointed out that, constitutionally, the UK Government had the requisite authority and, in any case, was responsible for the Federation's affairs in the United Nations.

Mr Fitt added <u>in strict confidence</u> that had it not been for British interference the authorities in the Federation would have followed a different course and Beukes would not have been allowed to enter their territory. In the event of his having succeeded in doing so in a clandestine manner, the Federation authorities would have put him back across the border.

(Initialled) GPJ

PRETORIA

5.9.1959

Even though the decision to drop extradition had been taken, Jooste evidently still hoped that frank talk with the Federation's representative would make them reconsider. His next 'aide-memoire' testifies to the vacillation of the region's most powerful men as they were trying to come to terms with an Imperial fiat.

SECRET/GEHEIM

AIDE-MEMOIRE

At approximately 1:45 pm Mr Taswell phoned me and stated that Mr Parry, Federal Secretary for External Affairs, had contacted him and asked whether the Union had considered the possibility of asking for extradition. In reply to an enquiry from me (I gave no indication that this course had been considered) Mr Taswell explained that Mr Parry had in fact indicated that they were not at all certain whether we would succeed in a request for extradition.

At 2:15 pm I informed Mr du Preez, Acting Secretary for the Interior, of my discussion with Mr Taswell.

Shortly afterwards Mr du Preez informed me that he had discussed the matter with his Deputy Minister (P W Botha) who had stated that in view of the uncertainty which subsisted as to whether an application for extradition would succeed, we should adhere to the decision taken not to proceed in the matter.ta

At 2:40 Mr Taswell once more phoned through and stated that Mr Parry (Secretary for External Affairs) had again phoned him and informed him of a meeting which had just taken place at Ministerial level, where the view was expressed that after a further study of the position it appeared that the Union could have succeeded in obtaining extradition. Mr Taswell added, however, that Beukes was due to leave Salisbury 'in about 10 minutes' time'.

Mr Taswell concluded by intimating that Beukes was not in possession of a yellow fever certificate and that it was possible that he might have to remain over in Nairobi. It was also possible that he would not be able to proceed from the United Kingdom unless this international requirement (yellow fever inoculation) had been complied with.

I immediately phoned this information through to Mr du Preez who in turn again contacted his Deputy Minister. Mr Botha, however, maintained that as there was no certainty that the Union would succeed in securing extradition from Kenya – and no doubt the UK – the original decision should stand. (Mr Taswell had also mentioned, in the course of his last telephonic communication, that according to Mr Parry the authorities in the Bechuanaland Protectorate had requested the Federation authorities to facilitate Beukes' passage. He had also pointed out to him after the Ministerial meeting in Salisbury that they could not assume responsibility in view of the British instruction and that the British had undertaken to explain the position to the Union and to make it quite clear that they – the UK Government – accepted full responsibility). I requested Mr Taswell to

furnish me, as soon as possible, with a full report.
(initialled) GPJ
5.9.1959

There can be little doubt but that the civil servant in charge of South Africa's Foreign Affairs had felt thoroughly upset on the afternoon of Saturday 5 September 1959. On a day when most White males would either be on a rugby pitch or shouting themselves hoarse from the stands in support of their favourite teams, he had been constrained to keep counting the goals scored against his government, the one more damaging than the other. That evening he vented his wrath upon the United Kingdom's representative in the Union.

GEHEIM/SECRET

AIDE-MEMOIRE

Sir John Maud, UK High Commissioner, called on me at my request at 5 pm on 5.9.1959.

I informed him that I had reported fully to the Prime Minister (Acting Minister of External Affairs) on our discussion of 2.9.1959 in connection with Beukes, and that Dr Verwoerd had asked me to convey to him (the High Commissioner) his concern because of the British attitude and the actions of both the United Kingdom Government and the Government of the Federation.

I then stated that the Prime Minister had taken exception to the view expressed by Sir John that the British decision was also regarded by the UK Government as being in the interests of the Union. I made it quite clear that the Union Government would always appreciate any advice tendered to it by friendly Governments on matters of international concern but could not accept the right of any external authority to decide for us as to what was in our interests, especially when in the light of such a decision that external authority saw fit to take action without any prior consultation with us. Viewed against this background the British action, and especially Sir John's statement, could not but be regarded as trespassing on Union sovereignty. The UK Government was of course always at liberty to take whatever action it regarded as being in its own interests. Such action should however not be related also to Union interests, as in the present case.

I then informed Sir John that the Prime Minister was at a loss to understand how it could have been expected by the UK authorities that they should have been consulted in the matter of the withdrawal of Beukes' passport. This was a matter falling entirely within the domestic jurisdiction of the Union. Moreover, in matters of this kind consultation was unprecedented.

The High Commissioner regretted the impression he had given that his Government had sought to determine what was in the best interest of the Union – thereby 'trespassing on the Union's sovereignty'. He explained that the action taken by his Government was motivated by a desire to prevent a situation in the United Nations which could be harmful to British interests in the Organisation. He added that what he had in mind at the time of our first discussion was the conviction of his Government that the situation they wished to avoid could also be harmful to the Union.

Turning to the second point (consultation re passport) he assured me that it was never in his mind to suggest that the matter was one which did not fall within the domestic jurisdiction of the Union, and that the Union Government was under no obligation to consult any outside authority in a matter of this kind. He added, however, that the situation which had developed in consequence of the withdrawal of the passport had involved his Government in its relations with the UN. He did not wish to pursue this point, or even to stress it, as he was most anxious not to give offence to the Union authorities.

I replied that the UK and Federation authorities had become involved in the matter only because of British action which enabled Beukes to pass into Federal territory contrary to the laws of the Union. Had Beukes been refused admission in conformity with past practice neither the United Kingdom nor any one else, apart from the Union, could possibly have become involved in the matter. It was clear to me that Sir John found it difficult to accept my reasoning on this point.

In the course of a very long discussion, lasting well over two hours, I gave the High Commissioner a full explanation of the implications of the British decision – of how the authority of the State was being undermined, how subversive action in the Union could be promoted by assisting agitators, communists and fugitive offenders to escape 'the authority of the Union Government' and to find their way to the United Nations, which was gradually becoming a refuge for such persons. I dealt fully, also, with the possible effects of this affair on the Union's relations with the UN, the United Kingdom and with the Federation, and stated that as the Union Government could not countenance such a state of affairs it would have to give serious consideration as to what action it would have to take in future in order to ensure the enforcement of its laws and to remedy the present situation. It was essential, therefore, that the Prime Minister should be informed whether the action taken by the UK and Federation authorities in the present case should be regarded as a precedent, and whether Bechuanaland would in future serve as an 'escape route' for Union Nationals who sought to leave the Union contrary to the decision of the State.

In this connection I pointed out, *inter alia*, that people such as Beukes, who proceeded abroad in violation of the Union's laws, could expect punishment in the event of their return. This fact would of course be realised by them, and it was possible that they would therefore not seek to re-enter South Africa, in which case they would have to seek domicile elsewhere. Moreover, the Union Government might well have to take action which could serve as an effective deterrent – such as depriving the persons concerned of their Union nationality. As far as I knew, our present laws did not permit of this but it was conceivable that such a course would have to be considered. In this connection I referred to American legislation on this matter.

Sir John Maud appreciated the seriousness of the position and asked whether the questions to which the Prime Minister desired replies could be properly formulated and transmitted to him. I undertook to do this.

The High Commissioner also referred, in passing, to the possibility of extradition under the Fugitive Offenders Act. I showed interest and enquired whether an application for extradition would have been successful – pointing out that, according to our information, Beukes had already left the Federation. The High Commissioner could not give any assurance in this matter.

In the course of the discussion I also mentioned information which we have received that the Federation had been requested by 'authorities' or 'persons of standing' in Bechuanaland to facilitate Beukes' passage. In this connection I mentioned Seretse Khama. The High Commissioner replied that while the Federation had acted in accordance with the views expressed to them by the UK Government, the Bechuanaland 'authorities' had made no such request. On this point he gave me an unqualified assurance.

(Initialled) GPJ

PRETORIA

8.9.1959

The Prime Minister gave his assent for the following letter to be sent to His Excellency Sir John Maud, G.C.B., C.B.E., High Commissioner for the United Kingdom, Pretoria, on 26 September 1959.

SECRET

My dear Maud,

On 5th September, when we discussed the matter of the departure of Beukes from the Union, I told you that I had reported our previous conversation to the Prime Minister, and that he had remained unconvinced by the reasoning advanced by the United Kingdom Government to justify its intervention in the case. He was perturbed to note that, as a result of certain steps taken by or at the direction of the United Kingdom authorities, it had been made possible for Beukes to travel freely from the Bechuanaland Protectorate to the Federation of Rhodesia and Nyasaland and from there onwards, in spite of his not being in possession of a valid travel document. There were certain possible consequences to this action, on which the Prime Minister had posed questions which I undertook to put to you in writing.

The question at issue is really this: are we to regard the action taken on this occasion by the United Kingdom Authorities (so far as Bechuanaland is concerned) and by the authorities in the Federation (at the behest of the United Kingdom) as a precedent for the future? In other words, must we envisage that from now on, any person who is not in possession of a valid passport or other document enabling him to leave the Union legally, and who may be seeking an 'escape route' to the United Nations, will be permitted to pass freely through Bechuanaland and the Federation?

At present, as you know, there is free access from the Union into Bechuanaland, but until now, any South African attempting to cross into the Federation, either from the Union itself or from Bechuanaland, without a proper travel document, was turned back by the Federation authorities – as Beukes himself was turned back when he first sought entry into the Federation. The Prime Minister has pointed out that, if this position no longer obtains, the Union Government will have to consider what steps it should take in order to ensure that its law relating to departure from the Union cannot be so easily evaded.

I am sure it will be realised that the Union Government cannot but view these developments with grave concern.

Yours sincerely,

G P Jooste.

As if these hard words were not sufficient, in a memorandum dated 18 September 1959, South Africa's Minister of External Affairs recounts his own confrontation with the British Foreign Minister, Selwyn Lloyd. It caps the increasingly acrimonious exchanges that had taken place between South Africa and its closest ally with reference to the passport.

In what appears to have been a remonstrance delivered verbatim on meeting his counterpart in New York, Eric Louw charged the British with having committed 'an unfriendly act in the international sense of the term'.

MEMORANDUM

I yesterday by appointment called on Mr. Selwyn Lloyd, the United Kingdom's Secretary of State for Foreign Affairs, in order to discuss with him the action of the United Kingdom Government in exerting pressure upon the Government of the Federation of Rhodesia and Nyasaland in order to induce them to permit a South West African student to enter the Federation in spite of the fact that he was not in possession of a passport or of an exit permit, required by the law of the Government of the Union of South Africa. Furthermore it appears that the Government of the Federation facilitated his departure from the Federation in order to proceed to New York for the purpose of giving evidence against South Africa when the South-West African question is discussed by the Fourth Committee of the United Nations.

The gist of my statement to Mr Selwyn Lloyd was as follows:

'I regret to have to see you about a somewhat unpleasant matter and would add that I am doing so on the instructions or our Prime Minister, who regards the matter in a serious light'.

(After giving information regarding the circumstances which led to the cancellation of Beukes' passport, and after quoting from a SAPA dispatch regarding the visit of foreign correspondents to the Rehoboth reserve, from which it appeared that both the father and grandfather of Beukes strongly disapproved of his intention to give evidence for the Fourth Committee and also repudiated his right to speak on behalf of the Rehoboth people, I then proceeded with my statement).

'The Union Government regards the action of the UK Government in a serious light in that –

    (a)   it is an unfriendly act in the international sense of the term;[59]

    (b)   it impugns the sovereignty of the Union;

    (c)   it constitutes an interference in our domestic affairs.

---

[59]   This was explained to me as referring to espionage.

The issue of a passport, and of an exit permit is a matter wholly within the sovereign power or the Union Government, and the action taken by the UK Government has, therefore, come as a shock to the Union Government, the effect of which cannot but impair co-operation and good relations between the two Governments.

Before my departure from the Union I asked the British High Commissioner to see me, and informed him that the Union Government was disturbed by the fact that on more than one occasion, certain persons had used the Bechuanaland Protectorate as an escape route. I told Sir John Maud that if the British authorities allowed this to continue, the Union Government would have to consider placing restrictions on movements between the Union and the Bechuanaland Protectorate. Such restrictions might even have to be extended to the Basutoland enclave.

The position is thus that the UK Government, through its High Commissioner in the Union, was aware of the Union Government's attitude in regard to Beukes' 'escape' to the Protectorate, which makes even more serious the action later taken by the UK Government.

The position is further aggravated by the fact that at no time was the Union Government consulted by the British authorities, or informed beforehand of their intended request to the Government of the Federation to permit Beukes' entry and to facilitate his departure. The High Commissioner was also aware that leaving the Union territory without an exit permit, is an offense in terms of the South African laws.

When Beukes first tried to cross into Rhodesia, he was refused entry by the Federation's authorities. Thereafter he returned to Serowe where it appears that he had discussions with Seretse Khama.

Apparently he also got into touch with Michael Scott and his other friends of 'Christian Action' in the UK. Shortly afterwards Beukes again travelled to the Rhodesian border and on this occasion was admitted. Funds were sent to him care of Seretse Khama.

When Mr Taswell our High Commissioner in Salisbury became aware of Beukes' presence in the Federation, he immediately contacted the Federation Government, and was then informed that Beukes had been admitted at the request of the UK Government. Mr Taswell also ascertained that the United States Consulate at Salisbury was fully informed about Beukes' movements, and had already been instructed to furnish him with a travel document and also a visa permitting him to travel to the United States. Beukes subsequently left by BOAC plane without an inoculation or yellow fever certificate. It can safely be assumed that the BOAC authorities permitted this on instructions either from the Federation or UK Governments.

If there were any doubt as to the fact that the UK Government exerted pressure upon the Government of the Federation, such doubts are settled by admissions made to the Secretary of External Affairs in Pretoria, by the United Kingdom's High Commissioner.

(I here quoted several extracts from the report received from the Secretary of External Affairs.)

From the extracts, as quoted, it is clear that the Federation acted on instructions from London, but more serious is the fact that the motives for these instructions appear clearly from Sir John Maud's statement, namely that the UK Government took this action for the purpose of protecting its own interests at the United Nations, particularly with a view to probable criticism of measures taken in connection with the Nyasaland uprising. This was frankly admitted by the UK High Commissioner. He also referred to the fact that Sir Charles Arden-Clark was the British representative on the Good Offices Committee. It is also clear that the UK Government did not wish to antagonise the American Government in view of the fact that the American Consul in Salisbury had been instructed to grant Beukes a travel document and visa. My personal opinion is that a possible other motive for the UK action was the approaching general election in Britain.

What would the attitude of the British Government have been if, for instance, Dr Hastings Banda had crossed the border into Mozambique before his arrest, and had been admitted by the Portuguese authorities without a passport, and if they had thereafter furnished him with a travel document and visa in order to enable him to give evidence against the UK at the United Nations?

Before concluding, I would once again stress the fact that in this matter the UK authorities did not consult with the Union Government in spite of the fact that I had before my departure from the Union fully informed Sir John Maud as to the Government's attitude regarding Beukes' flight to Bechuanaland.

What in effect happened, was that the UK Government aided and abetted a person who had left without a passport or exit permit in order to attack South Africa at the United Nations. Moreover, this assistance was given to a person who is of no standing whatever, and who cannot purport to speak on behalf of the Rehoboth people. This fact was published in the press, and must have been known to the British High Commissioner.

The damage has now been done, and I can therefore do no more than to convey the strong protest of my Government against the action of the UK

Government. I do not know which United Kingdom authority instructed the Government of the Federation to admit Beukes and to facilitate his departure to New York – whether it was the CRO or the Foreign Office.

This unpleasant incident emphasises the point which I made in discussions last year with Commander Noble, viz, that in regard to strictly foreign affairs, the Governments of Commonwealth countries should communicate directly with the United Kingdom Secretary for Foreign Affairs, and not with the Secretary for Commonwealth Relations (CRO), who, in such matters, acts only as a sort of post office.

This unprecedented action of the UK Government of impugning the sovereignty of a Commonwealth country and interfering in its domestic affairs, cannot but have the effect of seriously disturbing relations between South Africa and the United Kingdom. It would also have had the serious effect of disturbing the traditionally friendly relations between the Union and the Federation, were it not for the fact that the Federation authorities admitted to our High Commissioner in Salisbury that they had acted on pressure from the UK Government.

(Signed) EH Louw
NEW YORK
18 September 1959

South Africa's representative at the United Nations, B.G. Fourie, sent a copy of the memorandum about 'the discussions' his foreign minister had had with his British counterpart, to the Prime Minister, Dr Verwoerd. The comment the latter penned on the covering letter seems to have been what prompted Secretary Jooste to put his *Geheim/Secret* stamp not once only, but three times on the sheet of paper. Dr Verwoerd commented: 'It is rather a memo of Minister Louw's protest, and not one about a discussion as averred above, it lacks Selwyn Lloyd's reaction. We should very much have liked to know what he had had to say. H.F.V. 30/9/59.'

ANNEX 2

NORWAY'S DIPLOMATIC REPRESENTATION IN SOUTH AFRICA.

In 1959 Norway was represented in South Africa by consulates in Cape Town and Johannesburg, manned respectively by Fredrik Colban and Fredrik Holtung.

As mentioned above (page 137), in January 1960, Holtung publicly declared his support of apartheid.

In view of the ramifications the confiscation of the passport would have on public opinion in Scandinavia, a couple of memoranda about the communications that had taken place between the South African Government's advisers and the Norwegian consular representative in Cape Town half a year earlier, acquire some interest.

In a memo to his Departmental Secretary (Jooste), dated 29 June 1959, his Under-Secretary (Burger), had wondered whether the Norwegian Student Association was '*bona fide*', and suggested various approaches he could adopt to finesse the Norwegian Consul-General (Fredrik Colban), who had been instructed by his Government in Oslo to inquire about reasons for the retraction of the passport. Burger had invited Colban to his office – so as to avoid, he noted, having to use the telephone.

In a memo dated the next day, Jooste instructs Burger to follow the strategy alternative he himself had outlined under the heading of point b in his memo of 29 June. After keeping his appointment with Colban, who seemed to have followed him willingly down the garden path, Burger submits a self-congratulatory blow-by-blow account of the session:

Colban: 'We do not propose to issue a press communiqué, but when approached by the press what may we tell them?'

Answer: 'I cannot say, not having handled the Norwegian press before. The Press Section of the Norwegian Foreign Office would have wide experience in this regard and would best know how to handle the matter. But perhaps they could merely reply that they had been in touch with the Union Government, that the matter is of course one of purely domestic concern to the Union Government, but that they are satisfied that the withdrawal of the passport was for reasons which the Union Government consider adequate and which the Union Government does not wish to disclose as a matter of policy. Alternatively, they could allow the matter to die a natural death.'

Colban: 'But the Norwegian press will not allow it to die so easily.'

Answer: 'Perhaps they could dispose of the whole issue by suggesting to the press to forget it since it is a matter of domestic concern to a friendly Government. I cannot see in any case why the Norwegian Government should allow itself to be put under pressure since the bursary after all is not one awarded by the Norwegian Government.'

Colban: 'But the Communists and the Left Liberals will not play.'

Answer: 'In that case why not talk the friendly press out of it in the manner suggested and brush off the others with the statement that it is a matter of domestic concern to a friendly Government on which the Norwegian

Government is not competent to comment.'

Colban: 'The *Cape Times* knows about the call on the Department. How would I react to a question from the *Cape Times*?'

Answer: 'My reaction will be, "no comment", in line with the attitude expressed above.'

Mr Colban then cordially thanked me for receiving him and for my courtesy in explaining our attitude to him: He fully understood the position and would so inform his Government. It would seem, I am pleased to say, that my attitude had the desired effect as this morning's edition of the 'Cape Times' did not carry any report whatsoever on the Beukes case.'

(Signed) A Burger

CAPE TOWN

30 June 1959

INDEX OF NAMES

Made in the USA
San Bernardino, CA
03 May 2016